THE GREAT WAR
IN AMERICA

ALSO BY GARRETT PECK

The Prohibition Hangover: Alcohol in America from Demon Rum to Cult Cabernet

Prohibition in Washington, D.C.: How Dry We Weren't

The Potomac River: A History and Guide

The Smithsonian Castle and the Seneca Quarry

Capital Beer: A Heady History of Brewing in Washington, D.C.

Walt Whitman in Washington, D.C.: The Civil War and America's Great Poet

THE
GREAT WAR
IN
AMERICA

*World War I
and Its Aftermath*

GARRETT PECK

PEGASUS BOOKS
NEW YORK LONDON

THE GREAT WAR IN AMERICA

Pegasus Books, Ltd.
148 W 37th Street, 13th Floor
New York, NY 10018

Copyright © 2018 Garrett Peck

First Pegasus Books cloth edition December 2018

Interior design by Maria Fernandez

ISBN: 978-1-68177-878-5

10 9 8 7 6 5 4 3 2 1

Printed in the United States of America

Distributed by W. W. Norton & Company, Inc.

To my parents with love.

Contents

Introduction

Mere anarchy is loosed upon the world,
The blood-dimmed tide is loosed, and everywhere
The ceremony of innocence is drowned

—from "The Second Coming,"
William Butler Yeats

The Great War of 1914 to 1918 was the most important war of the 20th century. It was the first continent-wide conflagration in a century, and it drew much of the world into its fire. By the end of the conflict, four global empires and their royal houses had fallen, shattering the balance of power in Europe. The British and French broke up the fading Ottoman Empire, setting the artificial boundaries of the modern Middle East and building resentment that lingers to this day. The war catapulted Bolshevism onto the world, setting the stage for the Cold War that would last until the Soviet Union imploded in 1991. The punitive nature of the Treaty of Versailles, which forced Germany to assume blame for the Great War and pay the victors for it, undermined Germany's fragile democracy, and sowed the seeds for the 20th century's most brutal dictator, Adolf Hitler. An estimated seventeen million people died, making the Great War the most costly and destructive war in human history, surpassed only by World War II.

The combatant nations in the Great War developed destructive weaponry that could kill vastly more people. Airstrikes, chemical weapons, and flamethrowers were first used, and submarines were unleashed to sever enemy supply routes. Heavy artillery, such as the French and Germans employed at the war's most symbolic battle, Verdun, inflicted massive casualties and obliterated the landscape, leaving behind muddy craters, broken barbed wire, toxic soil, and body parts. Machine guns made massed infantry attacks futile, yet generals still employed these assaults, only to see their men mowed down. The Great War was one everlasting siege, and bunkers and trenches came to symbolize the static nature of this war, the two sides separated not by a moat, but by a muddy wasteland called no-man's-land. Thousands of men could be killed over a few hundred yards while the front line barely budged. Total warfare unleashed war not just against a country's army, but against its citizens, as each side attempted to undermine the other economically, militarily, and morally.

War leaves a scar on a nation's psyche, one that never fully heals. I have been to Ypres (officially Ieper), Belgium and witnessed the nightly Last Post ceremony at Menin Gate commemorating the loss of so many people who fought for the British Empire in the Great War. It is a moving ceremony, and the British express genuine mourning for so many who died for so little. I have walked the battlefield at Verdun and seen the Hall of the Dead, an enormous ossuary holding the remains of 130,000 people, the intermixed bleached bones of many nationalities. Arlington, Virginia, is my home, and every Memorial Day it witnesses tens of thousands of Vietnam War veterans who descend on the nation's capital in the motorcycle cavalcade known as Rolling Thunder. The veterans seek an answer to unanswerable questions: What good is war, and is the sacrifice ever worth it?

To which I might add with the Great War in mind: Can war solve the world's problems? Can war bring peace? Or does war just create new grievances and new conflicts? The Second World War proved the bloody sequel, refighting unresolved issues and injuries to national pride.

This book focuses on America during the Great War. It was a remarkable time, one in which President Woodrow Wilson struggled to keep the country out of the war during his first term in office, then declared war on Germany at the start of his second term. Wilson became a wartime president, marshaling the country's industrial might, its railroads and navy, and millions of soldiers to fight and win.

The Great War was an enormously contentious issue in the United States. The country debated for more than two and a half years whether to intervene. A third of the American population was first- or second-generation American, the highest ratio of foreign-born citizens in the country's history, and there were major divisions in American society over the question of the war. German- and Irish-Americans detested the Allies, hawkish Anglophiles hated the Germans, while a sizable contingent of pacifists and socialists supported neither side. The country did little to prepare for the war except strengthen its navy. "The World War found us absorbed in the pursuit of peace and quite unconscious of probable threat to our security," wrote General John Pershing, the commander who would lead American troops to victory. "We would listen to no warnings of danger. We had made small preparation for defense and none for aggression."[1]

The U.S. was late to enter the conflict when President Wilson ultimately decided Germany's belligerence demanded a military response. The United States declared war in April 1917 to protect itself from the threat of German submarines, but in his War Address President Wilson framed it as a high moral cause, saying, "The world must be made safe for democracy." The Great War was the most idealistic war the United States ever fought.

The Wilson administration mobilized the economy on a scale not seen since the Civil War five decades earlier. Most everyone contributed toward the war effort, and millions of young men were drafted into the armed forces. Pershing wrote after the war, "America's part in the contest could be successful only by the combined efforts of the armies and the people. The man with the rifle was merely the privileged representative of a thousand others who were as deeply concerned in the result as he was." [2]

More than 4.7 million Americans served in the Great War—and more than two million fought in Europe. The U.S. suffered 116,516 dead and 204,002 wounded, most of them in the last six months of the conflict when the American Expeditionary Forces got into the fight. American involvement tipped the balance against the German-led Central Powers and helped win the war. It earned the United States a negotiating seat at the Paris Peace Conference in 1919.

The United States' involvement in the Great War was shorter than in the bloody sequel, World War II (nineteen months versus forty-four months). Both wars witnessed tremendous mobilization of the American economy and manpower, and in both cases the country achieved a decisive victory. Yet World War II became the last "good war," in part because the good guys were good, the bad guys were evil, and the United States achieved an elusive goal: national unity after Pearl Harbor. The Great War was more consequential but far more divisive in its outcome. National unity proved elusive. After the decisive victory over the vaunted German army, the U.S. returned to its partisan squabbles. Many Americans opposed President Wilson's efforts to win the peace.

The Great War was a coming of age for America. The young republic stretched its limbs and discovered it was a world power. For the first time in American history, millions of young men were sent overseas to fight a war. Unlike the Allies, the United States had no territorial ambitions. Instead, its cause was establishing a peaceful new order to stop the aggression of tyrants. But having helped win the war, the country then retreated from the world stage, not liking what it saw beyond its continent and its two protecting oceans. The country was still young and naïve, believing it could live without foreign entanglements.

The war brought enormous and often unexpected political and social changes to the United States. The worst race riots the country had ever seen rocked the country in 1919, and many feared a race war between blacks and whites. American panic at the Bolshevik takeover of Russia led to the first Red Scare, an episode repeated in the 1950s. Women finally won the right to vote, prompted by their sacrifices for the war effort. Prohibition became the law of the land, all because the dry crusade framed its message as a way to defeat the Kaiser. After the failure to win a just peace, the U.S. withdrew into isolation and "normalcy," as Wilson's successor Warren Harding called it.

This is not a biography of Woodrow Wilson. Many fine biographies have already been published about the nation's twenty-eighth president. Rather, this is a history of America at war. It is a story about a nation that was rapidly growing up—and yet not mature enough to accept its global responsibilities. For the United States, the outcome from the Great War was to retreat from the world's stage. It would take another vicious war for the country to accept that it was a global superpower. One must wonder how the course of events might have differed had the U.S. remained engaged throughout the 1920s and 1930s, when the rise of fascism in Germany, Italy, and Japan challenged the world order.

Wilson was that rare president who had a transcendent vision: he imagined the world at peace. He sought to build an international framework to mediate conflicts before they erupted into war. He came up short, but his ideas were prophetic and would influence how the United States responded to the Second World War, the Cold War, and afterward. He failed to convince the United States to join the League of Nations in 1919, but his ideas lived on with the United Nations, founded in 1945. Wilson embraced America's role as a global power, an internationalism known as Wilsonianism. Wilsonian diplomacy promoted democracy worldwide, even via interventionist policies. It became a dominant theme of American diplomacy.

President Wilson was a proponent of peace, even during the war, and supported the armistice that ended the fighting, some would argue prematurely. He was a deeply principled man, yet there were times when his rigid commitment to principle got in the way. He made crucial missteps. How different might things have been had Wilson delegated the Paris peace negotiations, rather than leading them himself, or if he had focused on toning down the Allies' desire for revenge against Germany to prevent a draconian peace. What if Wilson had shown flexibility in splitting the Treaty of Versailles from the League of Nations—the thing that he fought for more than anything else? Many of his advisers cautioned that he should do exactly that. Instead, he insisted that the two issues be considered as one. That was ultimately a costly mistake.

In pursuing the war effort, Wilson's administration committed major, even astonishing civil liberties violations against African-Americans, German-Americans, pacifists, radicals, and socialists, as well as engaged in censorship against dissenters. After the war, his attorney general Mitchell Palmer rounded up thousands of leftists and deported many with little due process out of fear they were anarchists or Bolsheviks. From a common purpose to win the war came a trampling of basic civil liberties.

The Great War marked the twilight of America's Progressive Era, an era that harnessed the government's power to improve society. Capital investment, electrification, and industry had transformed the country. In the second decade of the 20th century, the balance between rural and urban America shifted in favor of cities, as immigrants flocked to manufacturing and mining jobs, mechanization of farm work freed up millions, and poor African-Americans left the Deep South to work in northern factories and to escape Jim Crow laws.

One of the challenges in researching and writing about Woodrow Wilson is how the president is viewed through a 21st-century lens. He was probably the most famous person alive in his day, and many historians consider him one of our better presidents. But among the public today, he is widely dismissed. His many accomplishments as a progressive reformer and his quest for world peace are forgotten; what people remember most was his allowing the segregation of the federal workforce and dismissing African-American managers. After I had initiated a discussion about the president on Facebook, one friend chimed in dismissively: "Wilson was a bigot and a racist." Playing the race card tends to shut down the conversation over Wilson's legacy. Truly, Wilson's stance on the race question was questionable. How could he ignore African-Americans at home while championing the rights of ethnic minorities worldwide? This is a sensitive question, but it is something that we have to address honestly. Dismissing Wilson on the race question tends to be one-sided. More importantly, it lacks the nuance of examining the many sides of a person and the context of his time in history. Weighed by these scales, Wilson's accomplishments were considerable and did far more good than bad.

Wilson is considered the architect of 20th-century American liberalism. Without him there would be no New Deal from Franklin Delano Roosevelt, nor a Great Society under Lyndon Baines Johnson. He championed the rights of workers to unionize and challenged the trusts that threatened to monopolize parts of the American economy. He addressed the growing income inequality with progressive income taxes and reduced tariffs to make American goods more competitive in global markets while cutting costs for consumers. He established the Federal Reserve to modernize the country's financial system and wrest control of the country's finances from the bankers, the so-called "money trust."

When the United States declared war on Germany on April 6, 1917, Wilson had less than seven years left to live. He would be incapacitated for more than half of that time after suffering a major stroke in October 1919, which came at a crucial time as he tried to convince the country to join the League of Nations. The president remained debilitated for the rest of his term, and the U.S. Senate rejected the Treaty of Versailles and the League. Wilson's presidency became a Greek tragedy.

The last surviving American veteran from the Great War, Frank Buckles, died in 2011 at the age of 110. Every person who fought in the war has been lost to us—but they have not been lost to history. They were a generation that experienced the deadliest conflict in world history up to then. Do we learn from their experience, or are we destined to repeat it? Whether we take to heart the high cost of war, whether we fight for justice and peace, whether we decide that the human race is one global community, and that conflict is best resolved through diplomacy and engagement rather than taking up arms, is entirely up to us. The alternative is to forget the lessons of history, and doom each passing generation to the never-ending cycle of violence and war.

A final note. No one from the war era referred to the conflict as World War I; that term would not be applied until the 1940s as World War II raged. The catastrophe of 1914 to 1918 was simply called the Great War or the World War. And it is how I will refer to the war throughout this book.

ONE

The Great War

The Great War began with a wrong turn in the Bosnian capital of Sarajevo. On June 28, 1914, the driver for the unpopular Archduke Franz Ferdinand, heir to the throne of the Austro-Hungarian Empire, got lost and was forced to turn around. Austria had annexed Bosnia-Herzegovina five years earlier, a former province of the Ottoman Empire. This riled up Slavic nationalists in neighboring Serbia. The Serbs secretly supported terrorist groups such as the Black Hand Gang to resist Austrian rule. One gang member, an eighteen-year-old student named Gavrilo Princip was eating lunch when he saw the archduke's automobile turning around. He jumped onto the open car, drew a pistol, and fired point blank at the archduke and his wife, killing them both.

The *New York Times* covered the assassination on the front page, but the news was hardly earth-shattering for most Americans.[1] Europeans were enjoying the fine summer weather, blissfully unaware that a crisis was about to unfold. Many assumed war was impossible, as many European monarchs were cousins. Most were interconnected thanks to Queen Victoria of England, who had raised a large brood of children who were then married into other royal families. Germany's ruler, Kaiser Wilhelm II, was a grandson to Victoria. Czar Nicholas II of Russia was his first cousin. King George V of England was cousin to both emperors.

That war was on the horizon was not a total surprise. The continent had long been tense as Balkan states declared their independence from the declining Ottoman Empire, resulting in a series of little wars. Russia stepped up its support of Slavic nationalism in the Balkans and allied with France in 1892, which in turn led Kaiser Wilhelm to believe that Germany was encircled by enemies, a challenge he met by building up his army and fostering a national military obsession known as Prussianism. Future president Herbert Hoover called the Germans the "Spartans of Europe."[2]

Germany had only been united as a country since 1871, but it had quickly become the leading economic and political power of Europe. Still, Kaiser Wilhelm felt inherently insecure. "She was menaced on every side," the Kaiser said. "The bayonets of Europe were directed at her." The Kaiser was not content just to dominate Europe's landmass and its economy; he wanted control of the seas as well, and built up a powerful navy at great expense to challenge the Royal Navy. This drew the ire of the British, who had long been a German ally. Europe divided into two armed camps: The French-Russian alliance would become the Triple Entente (more commonly known as the Allies) once England joined; and the Central Powers, composed of Austria-Hungary, Germany, and Italy.[3]

In spring 1914, American president Woodrow Wilson's special envoy, Edward House, sailed to Europe on his first private mission to negotiate détente between England and Germany. He was stunned at how militaristic the Germans had become, as he wrote the president from the German capital, Berlin: "The situation is extraordinary. It is militarism run stark mad. Unless some one acting for you can bring about a different understanding there is some day to be an awful cataclysm." Just two months later, the cataclysm began.[4]

Austria wanted revenge for the assassination of Archduke Franz Ferdinand. Within three weeks, it delivered an ultimatum to Serbia demanding accountability for the assassination—or there would be war. Rather than counsel Austria to hold back, Kaiser Wilhelm gave his ally a "blank check" to proceed against Serbia. Serbia had its own alliance with Russia, and Russia could not stand by idly while its fellow Slavs were punished. Rejecting the Serbian concessions, Austria declared war on July 28, exactly one month after the archduke's assassination. Czar Nicholas of Russia ordered his army to mobilize.

In a matter of days, much of Europe found itself at war, falling into the conflict like dominoes. Kaiser Wilhelm asked his cousin Nicholas to cancel the mobilization; when the czar refused, Germany and Russia declared war on each other on August 1. Two days later, France and Germany went to war. On August 3, Germany declared war on Belgium in order to invade France from the north; England in turn declared war against Germany to protect Belgium. Within weeks, the war turned global as Japan declared war against Germany and swiftly seized its Chinese and Pacific colonies. The flailing Ottoman Empire entered the war on the side of the Germans in late October.

◆

As the European powers tripped into war in early August, President Wilson and his family gathered in the White House at the bedside of his wife Ellen. The First Lady was terminally ill with Bright's Disease, a kidney ailment. She died on August 6, sending Wilson into a deep, inconsolable depression. He was heartbroken. Wilson was a solitary figure with few intimates, but Ellen was one of the few exceptions. She had served as his lifelong confidante. She worked behind the scenes, advising him on key policies, and helped direct his energies toward advancing his career. Ellen eschewed the limelight, spending her time raising their three daughters and attending to private matters.

The death of Ellen put Woodrow in the deepest despair. He had lost his closest adviser and his life partner. But for the crisis unfolding in Europe, Wilson may have shut down completely. It took the friendship of an unusual man to help pull the president back from despair, a man who observed the president's double burden of a world war and the loss of his wife, "His burdens are heavier than any President's since Lincoln." The friend was Edward Mandell House.[5]

House and Wilson first met in 1911 as House sized up Wilson, then the Democratic governor of New Jersey. House was impressed by the governor's clean record of reform and his outsider status. They soon found themselves as fast friends, and House worked quietly behind the scenes to ensure Wilson got the presidential nomination in 1912, rather than three-time failure William Jennings Bryan. After Wilson's election win, House helped vet Wilson's cabinet appointments. Wilson hoped to appoint House to the cabinet, but House declined, preferring to remain a private citizen and presidential adviser, a unique role he carved out for himself and singular in American history.

Like President Wilson, House was a child during the Civil War. Growing up in Houston, Texas, he witnessed the deprivation and destruction from the war. He remembered soldiers returning home and the lawlessness that ensued—the threats of violence, murder, crime, and robbery. It left a lasting impression on House about the evils of war. He was as close to being a pacifist as one could be without actually being a pacifist.[6]

Edward House had inherited land and was successful in his investments, giving him a solid income and the leisure time to pursue his hobby: politics. He became a progressive political rainmaker in Texas. House had never served in the military, but a governor whom House had backed in a crucial election began calling him "Colonel." The moniker stuck, and henceforward Edward House was known as Colonel House.

House spoke quietly, with a soft Texas drawl, and people had to lean in to hear him, like he was speaking in confidence. He was trim, rather frail, but always nattily attired. He obscured his narrow face and small chin with a large white mustache. In photos, he usually appears with a hat covering his balding head. Journalist George Creel had perhaps the best single description of House: "Soft-spoken, selfless, unassertive, but an epitome of alertness, the colonel was a high-class sponge, with the added beauty of being easy to squeeze."[7] He was an excellent source of information, as he could win people's trust, consult with insiders, sift through facts, and provide shrewd analysis. Humorist Will Rogers cracked a joke about House that was both astute and true: "Lot of men have *fought* their way into fame and *talked* their way into fame but Colonel House is the only man that ever just listened himself in."[8]

The Texas summer was far too hot for House. He maintained a home in Austin and rented a seaside house in New England during the summers. House spent much of the year in New York City, where he kept a small apartment, and frequently traveled to Washington to meet with Wilson, especially when the president needed advice on the wording of a major speech. Wilson was an idealist, while House was a realist who had a far firmer grasp of international affairs than the president. "Mr. House is my second personality," Wilson remarked. "He is my independent self. His thoughts and mine are one." House became known as the "silent partner" for being the man behind the scenes, the private citizen who had the president's ear.[9]

Wilson and House had a mutual belief in peace, and it was the president who sent House to Europe in spring 1914 as his back-channel diplomat to defuse tensions on the continent. The mission proved unsuccessful, and House sailed back to the U.S. on July 21, shortly before the war broke out. This was the first of House's numerous peace missions to Europe. He conducted diplomacy on a personal level, often person-to-person.

Newton Baker was the mayor of Cleveland, an industrial city whose population was three-quarters foreign born. When the war began, he warned the chief of police to step up efforts to patrol the multiethnic city, lest ethnic groups engage in a miniature war that reflected the war in Europe. The chief of police knew better: "Most of these people came from Europe to escape the very thing now going on there and their chief emotion will be thankfulness that they have escaped it and are not involved," he told Baker.[10]

Assistant Secretary of the Navy Franklin Roosevelt, attending the opening of the Cape Cod Canal and a keen observer of international events, wrote his wife Eleanor—"Babs," as he called her, on August

1, the day that the Germans and Russians declared war. "A complete smash up is inevitable," he wrote prophetically. "These are history-making days. It will be the greatest war in the world's history." [11]

The New York Stock Exchange plummeted with the war outbreak, and its directors agreed to temporarily close the exchange. This was designed to keep the Allies from repatriating their capital investments in the American economy to fund their war effort. The stock exchange would ultimately remain closed until December 1914. [12]

Frank Cobb, the editor of the liberal *New York World*, took no sides in the exploding conflict, but framed the war as a fight between autocracy and democracy in one of his best-known editorials, published on August 4. "What was begun hastily as a war of autocracy is not unlikely to end as a war of revolution, with thrones crumbling and dynasties in exile," he wrote presciently. "This is the twilight of the gods." [13]

◆

Germany under Kaiser Wilhelm maintained a philosophical belief in destiny, that their hour had arrived to dominate Europe and the world. The empire would either expand to dominance, or it would fall. To the Kaiser's mind, he was fighting a defensive war: Germany was encircled, and he would rush to attack before the country's enemies could defeat the fatherland. When the war broke out, the Germans quickly took the offense, invading Belgium, Luxembourg, and France.

Germany developed a two-front war strategy that would allow it to defeat both France and Russia. It would have to strike quickly against France on the Western Front, geographically closer than Russia on the Eastern Front. The German general staff developed the Schlieffen Plan, a right-hook to invade France and knock the country out of the war within six weeks. German armies invaded neutral Belgium—a small country whose sovereignty and territory the European powers had agreed to uphold in the 1839 Treaty of London—to attack France's exposed left flank. When the British challenged the Germans for violating Belgian neutrality, German chancellor Theobald von Bethmann-Hollweg asked the British ambassador undiplomatically, "Why should you make war upon us for a scrap of paper?" That scrap of paper brought England into the war against Germany.[14]

The Schlieffen Plan was predicated on the Russians mobilizing slowly. In fact, the Russian army moved more swiftly than expected, invading Prussia and upsetting the German invasion timetable in France. The Germans shifted thousands of troops to the Eastern Front to fight the Russians; they surrounded and destroyed the Russian 2nd Army in late August in the Battle of Tannenberg, then demolished the Russian 1st Army in the Battle of Masurian Lakes. The officer who won the victory was a general hastily called back from retirement: Paul von Hindenburg, aided by his chief of staff Erich Ludendorff. These two would become the face of the German war effort.

Meanwhile the German army faced unexpected opposition as it marched across Belgium. The small Belgian army held up the Germans at Liège, upsetting the timetable to invade France. From the German invasion of Belgium came lurid stories of atrocities, such as troops cutting off the hands of Belgian children, most of which were not true, as the German army was disciplined and well behaved. However, the Germans did take hostages and execute civilians when they believed they had been fired on, and burned down many villages in reprisal. At Dinant on August 23, the Germans executed some 674 Belgian civilians. Two days later, the Germans destroyed much of the university town of Louvain and its Renaissance architecture and historic library. They also bombarded Belgium's main port of Antwerp before capturing it.

The American public watched the war unfold from the sidelines, largely reading about it in newspapers. Many viewed German actions in Belgium as barbaric, and though public opinion was largely neutral, opinion shifted toward the Allies. Journalists were often split over which side to support. William Randolph Hearst, the newspaper magnate, did little to disguise his pro-German views. He refused to run British propaganda in his newspapers and would not print stories of German atrocities in Belgium. Likewise, the British often censored Hearst publications, and his journalists had to find other ways to route their stories from Europe to the U.S. Richard Harding Davis, a famed war correspondent, covered the early part of the war and was incensed at the German destruction of Louvain. "When a mad dog runs amuck in a village it is the duty of every farmer to get his gun and destroy it," he wrote, clearly siding with the Allies while criticizing American neutrality.[15]

Toward the end of the war, American painter George Bellows created a series of gruesome paintings that highlighted alleged German atrocities, including one called *The Germans Arrive* showing a soldier restraining a terrified, ghostly white Belgian youth who has just had his hands cut off, while the hulking perpetrator looks down at the bloody sword. Bellows never traveled to the war zone; he created the paintings based on what he had heard. Herbert Hoover, who spent much of the war overseeing the Commission for Relief in Belgium, knew that the atrocities were overstated. "There exists a vast literature upon German atrocities in Belgium and France," he wrote. "It is mostly the literature of propaganda," much of it created by the British to influence public opinion.[16]

Yet many Americans clung to the belief that Germans were barbarians. The German ambassador in Washington, Count Johann Heinrich von Bernstorff, noted the aspect of American culture that dismissed facts in favor of myth: "It is quite incredible what the American public will swallow in the way of lies if they are only repeated often enough and properly served up," he complained shortly after the war. "It all turns on which side gets the news in first; for the first impression sticks."[17]

Having finally pushed the small Belgian army aside and beaten back a strong French counterattack, the Germans marched south into France, headed directly toward Paris in early September. The further south they marched, the more the Germans exceeded their supply lines, and their soldiers were exhausted. Just as the German army approached the gates of Paris, French General Joseph Joffre counterattacked with the support of the British Expeditionary Force, driving the Germans back in the First Battle of the Marne. The battle saved France from defeat.

The Germans turned their attention to outflanking Paris to the west and capturing the English Channel ports, which was the lifeline for the British army in France. Despite a fierce German offensive, known as the Race to the Sea, the Belgians and British held onto a small corner of southwest Belgium at Ypres. Over the course of the war, the Germans would launch three major offensives against the Ypres salient, including the first use of chlorine gas, but they would never capture the town. This tiny corner of Belgium, known as *La Libre Belgique*, or Free Belgium, remained free from German occupation. King Albert and Queen Elisabeth of Belgium remained in the salient to give heart to their countrymen. Elisabeth was Bavarian, but her loyalty was to her husband and to Belgium. Albert was educated at Oxford University and had worked on the American railroads as a young man to gain practical experience.

Thousands of American businessmen and tourists were trapped in Europe when the war unexpectedly broke out. They would quickly run out of cash, as banks closed their doors and hoarded cash. President Wilson requested an emergency appropriation from Congress, and on August 6, the cruiser *Tennessee* sailed for Europe with $8 million in gold.[18]

Christian Heurich, who owned Washington, D.C.'s largest brewery, was aboard ship en route to take the cure in Carlsbad, the notable spa resort in what is now the Czech Republic, when news arrived about Archduke Franz Ferdinand's assassination. He thought little of it and continued with the vacation. After several weeks, however, his wife Amelia (the worrier in the family) became concerned. As the countdown to war began, she penned in her diary, "Great excitement prevailed here. I wanted Christian to pack up right away and leave Carlsbad—but no he wants to finish his cure."[19] They finally departed on August 2 for Nuremberg—the day after Germany declared war on Russia. They found the city crowded with Americans, all urgently trying to make it home. The Heurichs spent three weeks there, trying to secure passage on a ship. They helped arrange a special train from Munich to Amsterdam, a difficult task, given that trains were prioritized for transporting German soldiers to the front. But when they got to Rotterdam, the Heurichs discovered that their ship was greatly overbooked.

The Heurichs had to wait two more weeks for another ocean liner, the SS *New Amsterdam*, which they boarded on September 12 and sailed for New York City. However, the wealthy family was assigned to an "evil smelling little cabin." They slept in the passageway, rather than endure the odor. British warships stopped the liner at sea several times, and Royal Navy officers boarded to question the passengers. "I came in for their particular attention as my passport showed plainly that though an American citizen in good standing I was nevertheless a native of the country with which their country was at war," Heurich recalled. They finally arrived in the U.S. on September 21. Heurich would one day be subjected to the same kind of intense scrutiny at home because he was born in Germany. [20]

A self-made American mining engineer, Herbert Hoover was living in London when the war began. His thriving private practice came to a crashing halt and he turned to public service in these uncontrollable circumstances. He helped lead relief efforts for Americans trapped in England. When British businesses stopped taking dollars, Hoover's engineering firm lent its petty cash to help those without resources weather the crisis. He then organized the American Committee to help people get by while they awaited ships back to the states. Hoover was far from charismatic. He was dour, humorless, and pessimistic. He was not personable, yet he was quite capable. The future president was a committed Republican who became one of the accomplished technocrats of the Wilson administration.

A humanitarian crisis soon developed in Belgium with the German occupation, as the country was dependent on food imports. The Germans refused to allow English or French food to be shipped to Belgium, and the Belgians risked starvation. Hoover organized the Commission for Relief in Belgium in September 1914 and leapt into action: "I called a broker and gave an order to buy 10,000 bushels of Chicago wheat futures, as that price was bound to rise rapidly with the war and with any announcement of Belgian buying." [21] Hoover thought leading the CRB would be short term, as he assumed the conflict would be short—as did everyone. But no, the war would last more than four years, and the need for food relief would become enormous. Over the course of the war, the CRB supplied five million tons of food to Belgium and northern France, saving nine million people from starvation, at a cost of $928 million.[22] The food was routed through Rotterdam in clearly marked ships. Hoover set up an office in Brussels and crossed the English Channel many times to work out diplomatic and supply kinks. The CRB employed a staff of three hundred Americans—all volunteers who worked without pay. The Belgians used the cotton bags that had carried American flour to produce clothing, which was then sold abroad for additional food relief.[23]

Hoover traveled to the United States in 1915 when Senator Henry Cabot Lodge attacked Hoover in the press. Lodge insisted that Hoover's relief efforts were involving the U.S. in a foreign war. President Wilson met with Hoover and warmly supported him, announcing the formation of an advisory committee that would assist Hoover's efforts. Hoover then paid a visit to Lodge to confront him directly. Though Hoover's humanitarian efforts were universally acclaimed, and he had the sanction of the president and the ambassadors, the senator insisted that Hoover's actions would land him in jail for violating American law. Former president Theodore Roosevelt then called Hoover to Oyster Bay for lunch. Roosevelt was a friend of Lodge's and howled with laughter upon hearing Lodge's accusations. He reassured Hoover that the senator would no longer be a problem. "I will hold his hand," Roosevelt promised. Lodge made no more problems for Hoover. This was but a foreshadowing of the trouble that the conservative Lodge would make.[24]

For his relief efforts in Belgium, King Albert and the Belgian parliament later named Herbert Hoover a Friend of Belgium and Honorary Citizen. The titles even came with a passport—and an invitation to stop by the Belgian embassy in Washington anytime for a drink, which Hoover did frequently during Prohibition in the 1920s.[25]

Another prominent American, wealthy novelist Edith Wharton, lived in Paris when the war broke out. Rather than flee the war zone, she remained and engaged in relief work, often bringing relief supplies to frontline hospitals. She supported indigent women, raised funds, and founded hostels for refugees. Wharton published *The Book of the Homeless* in 1916, a compilation of articles and art from leading notables, including an introduction by Theodore Roosevelt, to raise funds for her charitable endeavors. An ardent Francophile, Wharton was appalled by Prussianism. She wrote frequently about the war and the need for America to intervene, claiming that the conflict was a war against civilization.[26]

Having failed to knock France quickly out of the war, the Germans now had to defend the territory they had captured while fighting a two-front war. A stalemate developed in northern France and Belgium. Both sides dug enormous trench lines to bolster their defenses as the war devolved into a siege. The Western Front stretched more than four hundred miles from the Swiss border to the English Channel. Artillery fire obliterated the landscape for several miles on either side of the front, while machine gun nests dotted the terrain. One machine gun could mercilessly kill hundreds of infantrymen who might attempt a suicidal frontal attack. Both sides settled into a war of attrition.

In December 1914, a *New York Times* reporter interviewed President Woodrow Wilson, who hoped the deadlock in the war "will show to them the futility of employing force in the attempt to resolve their differences." Wilson recognized this was a war of attrition, and that it was probably best if no country won, but rather settled their differences "according to the principles of right and justice." Already one sees how Wilson's idealism would seek to build a framework for peace.[27]

Mr. Wilson Goes to Washington

The United States in 1914 numbered about one hundred million people, putting it on par with Europe's largest countries. The country had grown rapidly since the Civil War five decades before. Once it had fulfilled its Manifest Destiny to settle the continent between the Atlantic and the Pacific oceans, it stretched beyond its borders and shattered Spain in a brief war in 1898, acquiring in the process a small global empire that included the Philippines and Puerto Rico. It opened the Panama Canal in 1914, a strategic asset to support the country's two-ocean navy. The United States had arrived as a global power, yet few Americans had a global worldview. They were still bound to their parochial regional interests, and still believed that the two vast oceans would protect them, come what may.

The Industrial Revolution had transformed the country in the 19th century, and the decades after the Civil War saw the rise of great business trusts and concentration of wealth among tycoons. The Gilded Age was gilded for a select few. The rich commanded the nation's wealth, while farmers and the working class struggled to barely get by. It was this widening inequality that in turn led to the Progressive Era (1900–1920), two decades that harnessed the federal government to improve American society.

In Europe, rapid industrialization had witnessed the political rise of socialism. Inspired by the writings of Karl Marx, socialists opposed capitalism and believed that the community or state should control the means of production. It turned the working class into heroes. The Socialist Party of America was cofounded in 1901 by Eugene Debs and Victor Berger, though it remained a political niche in the U.S. The country seemed committed to capitalism, as most industrial workers opted for unionization rather than socialism. That is, they joined forces to collectively negotiate for better wages and working conditions, rather than advocate for state control of industry. Unions had a strong supporter in President Woodrow Wilson.

Wilson was the final president of the Progressive Era. He would serve two distinctly different terms. His first (1913–1917) focused on domestic affairs and produced notable reforms. His second term (1917–1921) focused on foreign policy and leading American forces to victory in the Great War, as the United States could no longer rely on the safety of the oceans for protection. He produced notable reforms that would strengthen America's hand in the coming war.

With Democratic control of Congress, Wilson took action against the "money trust," as Congressman Charles Lindbergh (father of the aviator) called it. Bankers like J. P. Morgan had much control over the economy. Likewise, the federal government had had no central bank to oversee financial markets and interest rates since 1833, when Andrew

Jackson disbanded the Second Bank of the United States. Southerners in particular were distrustful of a powerful central bank, believing it yielded too much power to the federal government.[28]

President Wilson successfully defied his Southern base by supporting the Federal Reserve Act in 1913. It created not one central bank but twelve regional banks, along with a governing board. The Federal Reserve's task was to handle the country's money supply, keeping currency circulating, rather than having it sit idle in safes. The Federal Reserve set the country's financial system on a sounder footing. It brought the country many advantages, including establishing the U.S. as a global financial power. The timing for this reform was advantageous, given that it was on the eve of the Great War. The dollar soon became the currency of global trade as the U.S. went from a net importer to a net exporter of goods.[29]

Wilson also reduced tariffs, which had been a prime source of federal revenue, while also raising income taxes. Historian Steven Weisman called the income tax "one of the most important progressive achievements in the making of modern America."[30] These fiscal measures served to open global markets, stimulate exports, and lower the cost of consumer goods, all while creating a new source of revenue. This rebuffed generations of Republican protectionist orthodoxy. Progressives also sought the income tax to replace alcohol excise taxes, as prohibitionists wanted to ban drinking.

The Department of Labor was created in 1913, and the president appointed William Wilson, a former coal miner and union leader, as the first secretary of labor. For the first time, labor had a voice in the cabinet. The president fought to reduce the working day to eight hours for railroad workers—an accomplishment that would replicate across the economy and in every industry. He also established the National Park Service to administer the growing number of national monuments and parks.

Wilson's two terms in office saw the ratification of three constitutional amendments: the Seventeenth (giving voters the right to elect U.S. senators, rather than state legislatures); the Eighteenth (banning the manufacture, sale, and transportation of alcohol, better known as

Prohibition); and the Nineteenth (granting women the right to vote). These were reform amendments. The Seventeenth, ratified during his first term, ensured that no plutocrat could buy their way into the Senate by bribing a state legislature.

An unusual aspect of Wilson's presidency was the frequency with which he kept Congress informed. He frequently dropped by to deliver a speech or read a statement. He directly lobbied committees for specific bills. He was no stranger in the halls of Congress, a place where he himself had never served—but had studied for years while an academic. He spoke before Congress more than any president before or since. He reinvented the State of the Union Address, discarded over a century earlier by Thomas Jefferson. Wilson did not employ a speechwriter but wrote his own speeches by hand then finalized the draft on his typewriter.

Wilson was an exceptional orator who could address large crowds without microphones or electronic megaphones, as neither existed yet. Mass media like radio had not yet become influential, and political campaigns were about reaching constituents personally, often delivering barnstorming speeches to hundreds of audiences. Wilson could be professorial in his speeches, reasoning with the audience as he influenced them on a course of action; he could also move people to tears, such as his great Memorial Day speech at the Suresnes military cemetery, and on his 1919 barnstorming campaign to ratify the Treaty of Versailles.

Wilson was bookish, literary, and an intellectual. Though he had a doctorate in political science, Wilson actually had little actual political experience beyond the tussle of academia at Princeton University. He had never served as a kingmaker, rainmaker, or ward boss. He was first elected as governor of New Jersey in 1910. Wilson promptly turned on the Democratic political machine that got him elected so he could position himself as a reformer and an outsider. Two years later he ran for the presidency on a domestic reform platform known as the New Freedom. It seemed a long shot. Between the Civil War and 1912, only one Democrat had been elected to the presidency, albeit twice: Grover Cleveland.

In 1912, Wilson had emerged as the winner in a four-way presidential election: he beat Republican president William Howard Taft and former president Theodore Roosevelt, who ran on the populist Progressive Party (better known as the Bull Moose Party) platform, as the Republican party had split between the conservative Taft and the progressive Roosevelt. Another contender, Socialist Eugene Debs, took a distant fourth place. Wilson won by plurality, capturing less than forty-two percent of the popular vote.

Wilson was a serious, scholarly man, at least in public. He had the reputation of a dour Presbyterian. It was to a certain extent a persona. Among biographers' most frequently used words to describe the man was "dogmatic." The public never saw his keen sense of humor, or the silly limericks that he enjoyed reciting, or the comical impressions he only shared with very close friends, his wife, and three daughters. After daylight saving time was first introduced in March 1918, a cook was told to have dinner ready for the Wilsons by 7:00 P.M. "By what time—Wilson's time or Christ's time?" the cook answered with some irritation, but it made everyone laugh. Wilson overheard the comment. "That is irreverent," he said. It never bothered him to be the butt of a joke.[31]

Count Johann Heinrich von Bernstorff, German ambassador from 1908 to 1917, was keenly observant of the president. "Mr. Wilson could only tolerate subordinates, and not men with opinions of their own." This was not exactly true—he had a high regard for a number of men in his cabinet, such as William Jennings Bryan and Josephus Daniels, who maintained strong opinions. Yet his closest adviser was practically a Wilson doppelganger, Edward House, a man devoted to the ideals of peace, but who too often parroted the president. Bernstorff also noted the president's introverted habits and thoughtful demeanor: "President Wilson, who by inclination and habit is a recluse and a lonely worker, does not like company." Bernstorff overstated his case about Wilson—the president was privately very warm to his close associates and far from reclusive or lonely, but he was right that the president's decision-making process involved lengthy time alone to ruminate on a crisis at hand.[32]

Wilson would mull over problems for a long time, often retreating to a private room so he could think. "While he would on occasion make momentous decisions quickly and decisively, the habitual character of his mind was deliberative," wrote Joe Tumulty, the president's private secretary. "He wanted all the facts and so far as possible the contingencies." Wilson would also bounce ideas off cabinet members for their opinion. His cabinet was a collaborative team, where there was often much freewheeling debate, not unlike an academic setting. His personality encouraged this sort of push-and-pull. Wilson seldom tried to control the conversation, but let people speak their minds. [33]

Though a splendid public speaker, the president did not relish crowds or parties. He preferred the company of his family and close friends—and his own company. Two of his three daughters would have White House weddings, including Eleanor (better known as Nell), who married Treasury Secretary William McAdoo. McAdoo was twice her age and was a widower with six children. Mac and Nell would have two of their own children.

Despite his reputation as an aloof intellectual, Wilson was not a cold person, but neither was he a bossy extrovert like Theodore Roosevelt. "In his daily intercourse with individuals he showed uniform consideration, at times deep tenderness, though he did not have in his possession the little bag of tricks which some politicians use so effectively," recalled Joe Tumulty. "He did not clap men on their backs, call them by their first names, and profess to each individual he met that of all the men in the world this was the man whom he most yearned to see." [34] This was likewise the assessment of David Houston, Wilson's secretary of agriculture. "He was weak in the technique of managing and manipulating men, and he had no desire to gain strength in this art," he wrote. "He relied on the strength of the cause in which he was interested." Houston added, "Wilson belonged to the aristocracy of brains." [35]

Woodrow Wilson was born in Staunton, Virginia in 1856 and witnessed the Civil War as a child. By the time the Great War began, there were still many living Americans who remembered the war's terrible cost of more than 600,000 dead. Numerous members of Congress had fought in the war, such as Senator Henry du Pont of Delaware, who won a Congressional Medal of Honor at the Battle of Cedar Creek; Wyoming's Senator Francis Warren, the father-in-law of General John Pershing; and Senator Ben "Pitchfork" Tillman, a Confederate veteran and devout segregationist. The Senate majority leader, Thomas Martin, had been a teenaged Virginia Military Institute cadet who had fought at the Battle of New Market opposite Senator du Pont. On the U.S. Supreme Court sat Chief Justice Edward White, a Confederate veteran, as well as Union Army veteran Oliver Wendell Holmes, who was known as the "great dissenter." Representative Charles Stedman of North Carolina was the last remaining Civil War veteran to serve in Congress. He died in 1930. One thing was clearly absent from Congress in 1914: there was not a single black congressman or senator, though there were twelve million African-Americans in the country. Blacks were largely disenfranchised, thanks to Jim Crow laws in the South. The highest-ranking black federal official was Emmett Scott, the assistant secretary of war. His boss, former Cleveland mayor Newton Baker, was not a Southerner.

Slavery was America's original sin. Even after the institution was stamped out in 1865, the country spent considerable effort pretending the problem no longer existed. Northern whites did not want to compete against black labor and accepted the idea that blacks were racially inferior. President Wilson's views on race were in line with those of white Northerners, one of not so benign neglect. Southern whites, on the other hand, practiced a more hard-core racism. They carried out violence to intimidate and control African-Americans. They maintained a mythology that the U.S. was a white country, and that blacks needed to remain at the bottom of the ladder, chained to sharecropping and low-wage service jobs. This system ensured that blacks remained slaves in all but name—and that Southern whites still controlled their fate. Commentator H. L. Mencken wrote scathingly of the South: "The southerner, whatever his graces otherwise, is almost destitute of the faculty of sober reflection. He is a sentimentalist, a romanticist, a weeper and arm-waver, and as full of superstitions as the Zulu at his gates."[36]

Woodrow Wilson's cabinet was crowded with Southern Democrats, who formed the basis for the party. They were mostly so-called Bourbons: conservatives who represented the South's commercial interests, though there was a sprinkling of progressives as well. The Democratic coalition also included working-class Northeasterners, especially the Irish, as well as Midwestern farmers.

Thomas Marshall of Indiana served as Wilson's running mate in the 1912 election. His ability to garner midwestern Democratic votes for Wilson earned him a place on the ticket as vice president. But he would never be one of Wilson's confidants or trusted advisers. Instead, he spent most of his time presiding over the Senate, where he could only vote in the event of a tie. Marshall had a talent for puns and storytelling. When a senator was reciting a lengthy catalog of the country's needs, Marshall famously quipped, "What this country needs is a good five-cent cigar." Marshall liked to tell a joke about two brothers: "One ran away to sea, the other was elected vice president, and nothing was ever heard of either of them again."

William Jennings Bryan was the best-known figure in the cabinet. The Nebraskan had run for the presidency three times and was always defeated—the last time in 1908. Bryan ran on the financial platform of "free silver," a widely disparaged ideology that promoted expanding the money supply based on silver in order to benefit farmers against Wall Street interests. His nickname was the Great Commoner for his fiery populism. He was a committed pacifist—and he was completely unelectable. One historian called him an "inept moralist."[37]

A less well-known cabinet member was an unlikely choice for secretary of the navy. Publishing magnate and political kingmaker Josephus Daniels was head of the Democratic National Committee and had convinced Bryan not to run for the presidency in 1912, clearing the field for Woodrow Wilson. It earned Daniels a cabinet position. In fact, Bryan threw his political weight behind Wilson, likewise earning himself the prestigious position as secretary of state.[38]

Daniels had no military experience, but he turned out to be an effective naval secretary, reforming its antiquated structure and preparing it for the war to come. He quickly scaled up the navy's capabilities and allowed women to enlist. Daniels oversaw Wilson's gunboat diplomacy, intervening in Mexico in 1914 and 1916, Haiti in 1915, the Dominican Republic in 1916, and Cuba in 1917. He also had to administer Nicaragua. Daniels would be the rare cabinet secretary who served for Wilson's two complete terms. His cabinet diaries of Wilson's presidency provide a rare inside view of the discussions and debates, as well as Wilson's sense of humor among intimates.

As a Methodist teetotaler, Daniels was perhaps best known for drying up the navy. On June 1, 1914, he issued General Order 99, which banned officers from serving alcohol aboard ship. The navy was now officially dry. Instead of liquor cupboards, ships were to be outfitted with coffee mugs. It was a wildly unpopular move at the time. Sailors began to call a cup of coffee "a cup of Josephus," which was shortened to today's "cup of Joe."[39]

Like Wilson, Daniels was born shortly before the Civil War. He became emblematic of the New South—a man who made his fortune running newspapers, rather than in agriculture. He was a leading Progressive whose views were borderline socialist, yet an avowed supporter of Jim Crow laws that segregated blacks from whites. He had engineered the Democratic Party sweep of North Carolina in 1898—and with it the wholesale disenfranchisement of African-Americans. To Southern Democrats, the Progressive movement viewed Jim Crow as part of their agenda, as blacks voted Republican.[40]

Daniels chose a young Franklin Delano Roosevelt as his assistant secretary. Roosevelt was an ambitious, urbane New Yorker and cousin to the former president Theodore. Daniels had a knack for identifying men with a political future. He had served as rainmaker for Woodrow Wilson, and now he would mentor Roosevelt, who would one day occupy the Oval Office. Franklin was tall, bespectacled, patrician, and good-looking. Like his cousin Theodore, he always had a toothy smile on his face. He had a habit of lifting his chin when he spoke, giving the impression that he looked down his nose at others. Franklin was an eternal optimist who seldom allowed anyone to see his darker moods, let alone hear him complain.

FDR's hero was his fifth cousin Theodore Roosevelt, and he would model his own career after Teddy—including serving as governor of New York, assistant secretary of the navy, and eventually becoming president. Both men fathered six children and had notable wives. And while Theodore offered a "square deal" to voters to rid politics of corruption and ensure the working man had a chance, Franklin would offer a New Deal to help the country recover from the Great Depression.

Theodore Roosevelt was a larger-than-life character, an enthusiastic and energetic force of nature who enjoyed the presidency possibly more than any other president. He had bowed out too early from politics in 1909 and desperately wanted back in the game. He was far too young, ambitious, and restless to retire—and he simply loved being at the center of everything. Americans loved Roosevelt for his manliness, his barrel chest, mustache and pince-nez that adorned his face, and that enormous toothy grin. Roosevelt originated the term "lunatic fringe" to describe fanatics. He was a demagogue whose loud voice could outtalk, outshout, and outbully just about anyone. Roosevelt was fond of playing backseat president, and he hoped to occupy the office again one day.[41]

Save for perhaps President James Polk, who had seized vast western territories from Mexico in the 1840s, Roosevelt was the leading expansionist in American history. He often publicly called for war, believing it was healthy for the country to test its manhood. He foresaw that the United States would replace Great Britain as the leading global power and would need a two-ocean navy to project that power. Roosevelt was Woodrow Wilson's greatest political rival and constantly sniped at him. Wilson wisely ignored TR.

One vocal person who had a particular dislike of Woodrow Wilson was the literary critic Henry Louis Mencken, or H. L. Mencken, as he was known. Then again, Mencken seemed to dislike every politician. "Wilson was a typical Puritan—of the better sort, perhaps, for he at least toyed with the ambition to appear as a gentleman, but nevertheless a true Puritan," Mencken wrote, noting that he had a lifelong dislike of Puritans.[42]

Mencken was a journalist for the *Baltimore Sunpapers*, but also the editor of a monthly literary magazine known *The Smart Set*. He was an outlier in his time, a first-rate crank, a freethinker, and a committed atheist. He saw the temperance movement for what it was: a Protestant crusade to cement its moral agenda. Mencken had scathing disregard for religious fundamentalists, attending the John Scopes trial in Tennessee in 1925 and famously dubbing it the "Monkey Trial." He parted his hair in the middle and pomaded it back, a popular look in the day. He often chomped on a cigar as he punched the keys on his typewriter or held court. As a journalist, Mencken was a staunch defender of freedom of speech, and he described himself as an "extreme libertarian."[43] A second-generation German-American, Mencken was squarely on the side of Germany in the Great War and loudly said so. H. L. Mencken wrote many anti-English articles and editorials for the *Baltimore Sun* in the first year of the war. This would come back to haunt him in 1917.

The War in 1915

The brief war that everyone expected continued into its second year. Both sides raised the stakes in order to gain an advantage over their enemies. New soldiers were conscripted and flung at enemy lines, even as the stalemate on the Western Front continued. A brief, impromptu cease-fire took hold on Christmas, but then the fighting continued.

With one of the most advanced industrial sectors in the world, Germany deployed unprecedented technology to turn the tide in their favor in spring 1915: dirigibles known as zeppelins for indiscriminate bombing campaigns by air; poison gas to suffocate Allied soldiers, first used at Ypres; and diesel *U-boats* to wage unrestricted submarine warfare on England. It was the U-boats that would nearly drag the United States into the war.[44]

Both sides sought to use another recent invention to tip the scales in their favor: the airplane, which the Wright Brothers had invented in 1903. Flying technology advanced considerably during the war. Armies first used airplanes for reconnaissance, then developed fighters to shoot down enemy planes, often resulting in exciting plane-to-plane dogfights. Both sides developed bombers to attack the enemy on the front lines, as well as railroads and other military targets. The image of the intrepid scarf-wearing aviator was one of the few romantic notions that emerged from the war. Pilots were knights of the sky.

Germany stood strong against the Allies and captured much of Poland from Russia, but its own allies were weakening. Austria-Hungary was consumed by domestic affairs and growing nationalism within its multiethnic state, which threatened to rip the empire apart, as each group demanded its independence. Germany's other major ally, the Ottoman Empire, was widely derided as the "sick man of Europe" for its corruption and obvious decline.

Germany provided significant military assistance to help the Ottoman Empire resist the Allies. As the Western Front reached stalemate, the British planned an enormous amphibious landing to capture the Dardanelles—the narrow straits that protected Istanbul—and that would open a supply line to Russia. The Allies had plans for the Ottoman Empire: they wanted to divide most of its territories among themselves and hand Istanbul to the Russians. In April 1915, forces from Australia, Britain, and New Zealand landed on the Gallipoli peninsula and immediately met resistance from the German-supported Turkish army. The Turks occupied the hills above the landing zone and entrenched their lines. When the British forces attacked in frontal assaults, the slaughter was similar to that seen on the Western Front. The British dug in for the stalemate, then finally acknowledged defeat when they evacuated the peninsula in January 1916. First Lord of the Admiralty Winston Churchill, who had championed the offensive, was forced to resign, and it nearly ended his political career. The Ottomans won the Battle of Gallipoli, but it was nearly the last gasp of their empire.

Worried that the Christian Armenian minority within the Ottoman Empire would side with the Russians, the Ottomans massacred nearly 1.5 million Armenians in 1915. It was the first genocide of the 20th century. Though the Turks denied the massacres, Theodore Roosevelt countered that, "The Armenian horror is an accomplished fact"—one that he laid at the feet of American pacifism for its unwillingness to get involved. [45] President Wilson encouraged relief efforts for Armenian refugees. In November 1917, the Armenian-American community presented Wilson with a painting by Hovsep Pushinan. In it a beautiful dark-haired Armenian girl (the artist's niece) dressed in a bright green costume holds a white flower. He called the painting *L'Esperance*, or Hope.

Italy switched sides and joined the Allies in 1915, as it had claims on Austrian territory that would give it control of the Adriatic Sea. The Germans retaliated by bringing Bulgaria into the war that fall. The consequences were disastrous to Serbia, as a combined Austro-Hungarian, Bulgarian, and German campaign swept through the country and inflicted massive casualties on the Serbian army. Much of the population fled to the Adriatic coast. The Allies attempted to rescue the Serbs by landing a force at Salonika (officially Thessaloniki) in Greece, but it came too late to help. Germany now had a direct rail link from Berlin to Baghdad through Istanbul. The Germans' decisive victory in the Balkans led them to believe that they were winning the war and that victory was at hand in 1916.

American Neutrality and the Freedom of the Seas

President George Washington's Farewell Address in 1796 warned Americans against foreign entanglements, and many held this as gospel, not just policy. At the beginning of the World War, President Wilson pledged that the United States would remain strictly neutral. "We must be impartial in thought as well as in action, must put a curb upon our sentiments as well as upon every transaction that might be construed as a preference of one party to the struggle before another," he appealed to the citizenry. He understood that much of the American population came from the various countries that were now at war, and that the temptation to cheer on one alliance over another would violate America's impartiality. Instead, the president offered his services to mediate, though this fell on deaf ears.[46]

Theodore Roosevelt, Wilson's most significant political rival, echoed these sentiments. "It is certainly eminently desirable that we should remain entirely neutral and nothing but urgent need would warrant breaking our neutrality and taking sides one way or the other," he declared in *Outlook*.[47] He wrote an English friend shortly after the outbreak: "In this country the feeling is overwhelmingly anti-German. It is emphatically in favor of England, France, and Belgium." TR was off base in his assessment; many Americans were in fact anti-British. He went on to privately lambast Wilson for his efforts to arbitrate the conflict: "In international affairs Wilson is almost as much of a prize jackass as Bryan."[48]

Watching the events unfold from across the Atlantic, President Wilson naively clung to his belief that America could mediate this conflict. He spoke to the Associated Press in New York on April 20, 1915, an address that became known as the America First speech. "I am not speaking in a selfish spirit when I saw that our whole duty, for the present, at any rate, is summed up in this motto: 'America first.' Let us think of America before we think of Europe, in order that we may be Europe's friend when the day of tested friendship comes." For the next two years, this would be Wilson's line as he offered mediation between the combatants.[49]

Wilson was not prepared to give up on peace. He sent his private envoy, Edward House, back to Europe in January 1915. House sailed on the RMS *Lusitania* to commence the peace mediation effort. He shuttled between capitals that winter and spring, traveling between London, Paris, and Berlin, to reduce the tension. If Great Britain could lower its blockade to allow food to reach Germany, perhaps Germany could call off its submarine campaign, declared that winter. There was much bitter feeling in Germany at the U.S. for selling arms to the Allies. House returned without much success.

German ambassador Bernstorff was born in London in 1862, the son of the ambassador to the Court of St. James. English was his first language. Despite his aristocratic lineage, Bernstorff had strong democratic views and a love for politics. He had a keen understanding of American culture and a shrewd eye for shifting public opinion in a liberal democracy. His was a challenging job, having to protect German interests while representing an expanding empire. Bernstorff had to negotiate repeatedly to defuse conflicts. Despite the bombast from American imperialists like Theodore Roosevelt, Bernstorff recognized the undercurrent of pacifism in American society. Americans tended to be sentimental and willing to overlook facts when their emotions were activated.[50]

Vice President Thomas Marshall noted with some comic exaggeration how unpopular Bernstorff was in the nation's capital, a city that sympathized with the Allies. Everyone attended soirees given by the French ambassador Jean Jules Jusserand, whom Marshall called the "dean of the diplomatic corps." However, it was difficult to find guests for the German ambassador. "When it came to the dinner to Count von Bernstorff I never knew, until the influenza struck the town, such an epidemic of illness. There were forty-seven prominent persons who were too ill to attend, and it took two weeks to get twenty people who were willing to dine with von Bernstorff."[51]

Edward House frequently met with Bernstorff, as the president asked House to intermediate with the Germans. The two came to know each other quite well and corresponded often. House summed up his impression of the ambassador, "I think better of Bernstorff than most people who know him, and if he is not sincere, he is the most consummate actor I have ever met."[52]

Bernstorff also understood that English cultural influence was stronger in America than German culture, and this meant an inherent bias. Despite Wilson's avowed neutrality, the president was "very much under the sway of English thought and ideals," Bernstorff noted.[53] Indeed, the U.S. had much in common with England: a democratic system of government, language, and trade. The British seized a major advantage in August 1914 when they cut German transatlantic cables, severing direct communication between Germany and the U.S. This meant that news from Europe would likely come from British sources. The Germans had to rely on coded letters and radio transmissions to communicate with their embassies—both of which were susceptible to deciphering. They had two wireless stations in the United States to send long-distance telegrams—one in Sayville, New York, the other in Tuckerton, New Jersey—but these were poor substitutes for undersea cables. Communications with Germany became exceptionally slow, and it could take days or even weeks for a message to get through to Berlin.[54]

Another reason why American neutrality was skewed toward England was because of the country's dependence upon British trade and investment. England owned fully half of the world's merchant marine, while the United States had a paltry two percent. There were few alternatives to carry American goods overseas. This also left the U.S. vulnerable to British authorities arbitrarily deciding what goods could be shipped on their vessels, or to which country they could be sent.[55]

But there was also serious hostility directed toward England, particularly after the Royal Navy declared a general blockade of the North Sea—the vast ocean between Norway and Scotland—to cut off German commerce from the world in November 1914. Americans demanded "freedom of the seas" to trade with whomever they wanted, while the Royal Navy acted as an oceanic traffic policeman, sometimes putting up roadblocks to commerce. England could effectively determine whom the U.S. could trade with. This key question had dogged Anglo-American relations since the War of 1812.

By international law, a blockade had to physically close off an enemy's coastline and block ships from entering or leaving territorial waters, generally considered three miles from the shoreline. Britain was playing with a new rulebook. It insisted on the right to stop, search, and detain any neutral vessel in the quarantined area for carrying German contraband. The U.S. made a feeble protest, which the British ignored. Historian Barbara Tuchman called it a "shadow duel."[56]

Britain greatly expanded what was considered "contraband." The traditional list included anything that could support the enemy's military, including arms and munitions. The British counted anything that could support the German economy, including clothing, food, and raw materials like cotton. This would de facto halt all trade with Germany. On February 9, 1915, the British seized the American steamer SS *Wilhelmina*, which was bound for Hamburg with its hull full of grain.[57]

At the beginning of the war, German merchant ships and ocean liners at sea feared capture by the British, and so many of them sought refuge in American waters. Soon ninety-one German ships were docked in American and Philippine harbors, while a squadron of Royal Navy cruisers patrolled just outside American waters to keep the German ships bottled up. The vessels included the enormous 54,000-ton transatlantic liner *Vaterland*, as well as the SS *George Washington*.[58]

The Royal Navy had effectively closed off the North Sea, and the German high command decided that its High Seas Fleet was not strong enough to challenge the British blockade. The fleet remained bottled up in its main anchorage at Heligoland Island. The Germans also had a number of battle cruisers stationed with its global colonies, and when the war broke out these raided Allied shipping. Most of these commerce raiders were sunk by the end of 1914, so the German navy turned to a much more disruptive weapon: the submarine, or *Unterseeboot*—better known as the U-boat.

The point of a submarine was not to take the enemy's ship as a prize or to capture its cargo, as privateers had done in the past, but rather to send it to the bottom of the ocean. It was intended to cut the enemy off from its lifelines. Great Britain was especially vulnerable, as it depended on imports for much of its energy, food, and raw materials.

The Germans responded to the Royal Navy blockade by declaring the waters surrounding the British Isles as a war zone in February 1915. Anything sailing in these waters was liable to be torpedoed and sunk, whether from a belligerent or neutral nation. They called it unrestricted submarine warfare. The German submarine campaign violated international customs, known as the "cruiser rules," which required ships first to be halted and searched for contraband before being sunk. Raiders were required to ensure the safety of the crew and passengers, but the small U-boats simply did not have room for either. German submarines were given permission to sink on sight. They left thousands of civilians and sailors stranded in the water for the Royal Navy to rescue.[59]

It would be a mighty struggle for Americans to remain impartial in the Great War, given that the country's trading partners were at war. As President Wilson remarked to Joe Tumulty in August 1914, "We cannot remain isolated in this war, for soon the contagion of it will spread until it reaches our own shores." The United States had two massive oceans protecting its shores, and it had long maintained a sense of impregnability. German U-boats would challenge the assumption that America was safe from attack.[60]

Both England and Germany threatened the freedom of the seas. British actions did not cost American lives—only commerce, and much or even more was made up by the brisk trade with the Allies during the war. Germany's submarine warfare, on the other hand, could cost many lives and destroy property. Americans were likely willing to go to war over the German submarines, but not over the British blockade. It was a hypocritical stance, but Ambassador Bernstorff recognized that the U.S. would never confront England over it except at the peace table.[61]

Shortly after the Germans announced unrestricted submarine warfare, President Wilson sent them a diplomatic note, warning that there would be consequences from their submarine campaign but stated it in suitably vague terms. He feared that neutral ships might be sunk and citizens from neutral nations might lose their lives. If this happened, the American government would hold the Germans to a "strict accountability." No one knew what this meant or how the U.S. would respond.[62]

On March 28, a German U-boat torpedoed the British steamer RMS *Falaba* with the loss of one American life. On May 1, another submarine attacked the American ship *Gulflight*, killing two Americans. This was but a foreshadowing of what was to come with unrestricted submarine warfare. German submarines could indiscriminately murder American citizens sailing on the high seas.

The Lusitania Sinking

The Germans correctly suspected that the British were transporting munitions from the United States in ocean liners, despite the civilian nature of these vessels. Kaiser Wilhelm authorized his navy to sink Allied shipping in British waters, not just warships. Every type of ship was a target—and if they were carrying passengers from neutral countries (such as the United States), well, that was a risk. The Imperial German Embassy in Washington took out advertisements in major newspapers, warning American citizens of the risk in crossing the Atlantic in British-flagged ocean liners, as they were fair targets for Germany's submarine campaign. The warning in the *New York Times* appeared on May 1, the same day that the Cunard Line's ocean liner RMS *Lusitania* sailed from New York for Liverpool.[63]

On May 7, 1915, the *Lusitania* was steaming unescorted off the southern coast of Ireland when it encountered the submarine *U-20*. Without warning, the sub fired a single torpedo into the liner's hull, but soon a second explosion ripped through the ship and it sank in eighteen minutes. The British publicly claimed that two torpedoes had struck the liner, when in fact they knew there had only been one: the civilian ship was indeed carrying munitions, some four million rounds of small arms ammunition, shrapnel artillery shells, and percussion fuses. Fearing that detonating artillery shells had caused the second explosion, they developed a cover story of a second torpedo (investigations later revealed that it had been steam pipes exploding). Two-thirds of the crew and passengers died. Among the 1,198 lives lost were 128 Americans. The *Lusitania*'s sinking came just three years after the sinking of the RMS *Titanic*, a precedent that did not go unnoticed.[64]

There was enormous international outrage over the sinking of the *Lusitania*. In the U.S., the attack made the front page of most newspapers, many of which provided considerable coverage, since there were so many Americans aboard the doomed liner. The *New York Times* denounced Germany's policy as "war by assassination," that the country had gone insane, and was "at war with the whole civilized world."[65] The *Baltimore Sun* was more evenhanded, the editors noting, "We refrain from expressing any opinion in such a serious hour as this as to the effect which the sinking of the *Lusitania* will have on our relations with Germany." It noted that the event could only play into the hands of the British, and that Germany's actions would only build animosity with neutral countries like the United States.[66]

The Europeans had been at war for nearly a year and had experienced catastrophic casualties. Though the number of deaths from the

Lusitania sinking was high, that number of people might be killed in just minutes on the Western Front. Yet Americans were not involved in the war, and the sudden death of 128 citizens was shocking. Public opinion swung feverishly against the Germans. Ambassador Bernstorff was in New York on business and found himself mobbed by reporters at the Ritz-Carlton Hotel. He escaped out a side door, but reporters followed him to the train station. He refused to make a statement. Back in Washington, he stayed out of sight until the anger ebbed.[67]

"I have spent many sleepless hours thinking about this tragedy," President Wilson told Joe Tumulty. "It has hung over me like a terrible nightmare. In God's name, how could any nation calling itself civilized purpose so horrible a thing?"[68] The *Lusitania* sinking ended Edward House's European peace effort. He wrote the president: "America has come to the parting of the ways, when she must determine whether she stands for civilized or uncivilized warfare. We can no longer remain neutral spectators." House accepted that American entry into the World War was inevitable.[69]

Three days after the *Lusitania* catastrophe, Wilson spoke to a group of newly naturalized citizens in Philadelphia. The president was still bewildered by the sinking, but he did not see America's role as having changed. Rather, the U.S. must set the example for peace. "There is such a thing as a man being too proud to fight," he stated. "There is such a thing as a nation being so right that it does not need to convince others by force that it is right." That tone-deaf argument—"too proud to fight"—would haunt Wilson for the rest of his presidency. It seemed to invite other nations to bully the United States, while Wilson would only turn the cheek.[70]

Wilson's Philadelphia statement did not go over well. His political nemesis, Theodore Roosevelt, was livid. He penned an article called "Murder on the High Seas" in which he called the Germans guilty of murder and piracy, and pointed out alleged German atrocities in Belgium, while the U.S. stood by. "In the teeth of these things, we earn as a nation measureless scorn and contempt if we follow the lead of those who exalt peace above righteousness," Roosevelt wrote in a calculated dig at the president, "if we heed the voices of those feeble folk who bleat to high Heaven that there is peace when there is no peace." He went on to describe American neutrality as something "which would have excited the emulous admiration of Pontius Pilate—the archetypal neutral of all time." Although Roosevelt did not call for war, he did call for a cessation of all commerce with Germany while increasing arms shipments to the Allies.[71] A group of peaceniks wrote Roosevelt, offering to buy him a gun and send him alone to Europe to fight for the Allies or for the Germans, his choice. Since he was so eager to get into the war, let him do all of the fighting.[72]

The *Lusitania* sinking was a public relations disaster for Germany. The *New York Times* opined four weeks after the sinking, "Germany never in the world's time can erase the stain of the *Lusitania*."[73] Ambassador Bernstorff understood that submarine warfare would likely bring America in on the side of the Allies, and he pleaded with Berlin to end the campaign. Though American neutrality favored England and France, a neutral America was far better than a belligerent America, where it would likely tip the scales against Germany. Bernstorff became a strong defender of Wilson's policies to keep the U.S. out of the war and to negotiate peace.

On May 13, Wilson communicated that he would hold the Germans to the promised "strict accountability" for waging unrestricted submarine warfare. Rather than sign the diplomatic note that he believed would lead to war, Secretary of State William Jennings Bryan resigned from the Wilson administration. It was a mistake on the pacifist Bryan's part, as he would no longer be the insider who could counsel the president against war. Bryan had been the dove in the cabinet; the last major antiwar cabinet member remaining was Secretary of the Navy Josephus Daniels.

Robert Lansing replaced Bryan, and he shared neither Bryan's nor the president's commitment to peace, and he would never have the president's ear. Lansing was an interventionist, believing from the beginning that America would have to go to war on the side of the Allies. Wilson and House would do the real work of American diplomacy going forward.

Lansing was relegated to the role of role of adviser for diplomatic notes and international law. Treasury Secretary William McAdoo concluded, that both figuratively and literally, "Lansing was a silent member of the Cabinet." [74] Secretary of Agriculture David Houston likewise had a low opinion of Lansing: "He will not be of much assistance than he would have been as an expert in the Department" of State. [75]

In addition to having little trust in his secretary of state, Wilson was not well served by two important ambassadors, Democratic political appointees who had supported the president's campaign but who had little experience at diplomacy. The American ambassador to England, Walter Hines Page, was an unabashed anglophile and interventionist. Page was such a strong British proponent that he seemed to forget which country he represented. Wilson tuned out his hysterical, long-winded letters. The ambassador to Germany, James Gerard, was no better. He was a New York attorney with close connections to Tammany Hall. Like Page, Wilson ignored Gerard's recommendations. Instead, he put his faith in Edward House, the prince of back-channel diplomacy. [76]

A series of diplomatic notes over unrestricted submarine warfare passed between Wilson and the German government. Then on August 19, a German submarine torpedoed and sank the SS *Arabic*, a passenger vessel, killing more Americans and setting off a new crisis. The German high command quietly ordered its U-boats to stop targeting passenger ships. In September, Germany publicly yielded, apologizing for the *Arabic* incident and offering an indemnity.

The German submarine campaign put Ambassador Bernstorff in a difficult position to justify his government's policy that he personally opposed. Had Germany wiped the slate clean after the *Lusitania* tragedy, apologized, and canceled unrestricted submarine warfare, the U.S. and Germany might have jointly addressed the British blockade and the international right to the freedom of the seas. [77]

In the wake of the *Lusitania* sinking, a group of more than one hundred notable American internationalists gathered at Philadelphia's Independence Hall on June 17. They elected former president William

Howard Taft as their leader and named the organization the League to Enforce Peace. They supported a vision of the United States taking a global role in helping mediate conflicts through an international organization of peace. President Wilson paid close attention. Many of the conceptual ideas for Taft's league would become fact with the League of Nations after the Great War closed. [78]

TWO

Preparedness

reshly back in the United States after his failed 1915 European peace mission, Edward House counseled President Wilson that the country should prepare to fight as a means to avert war: "If war comes with Germany, it will be because of our unpreparedness and her belief that we are more or less impotent to do her harm." House suggested what would become known as the "Preparedness" campaign to beef up the country's armed forces.[1]

The American public was split over the war. Pundits such as former president Theodore Roosevelt vowed that the U.S. should assist the Allies against the Germans. He and his friend General Leonard Wood even advocated conscription. The interventionists were challenged by isolationists, pacifists, radicals, socialists, Midwesterners and Southerners, the Germans, and the Irish, all of whom opposed getting involved in the war. Much of public opinion was against intervening in what many viewed as a European conflict. And many were upset at the British blockade that interfered with American global commerce.

Secretary of State Robert Lansing observed, "Many more Americans were directly affected by these British practices than were affected by the activities of the German submarines." Isolationism remained a powerful force in both Democratic and Republican parties. [2]

The most popular song in the U.S. in 1915 became "I Didn't Raise My Boy to Be a Soldier." It strongly expressed the pacifism that many Americans embraced. The Woman's Peace Party, led by Jane Addams, attended the International Congress of Women in April 1915 in The Hague to press for peace. Addams would meet with President Wilson numerous times upon her return and pushed for peace negotiations.

Another leading pacifist was automobile manufacturer Henry Ford, who sailed to Kristiania (now Oslo), Norway with a small peace delegation on December 4 aboard the SS *Oscar II*, what became known as the "peace ship." Inspired by the impromptu Christmas cease-fire of 1914, Ford hoped that the soldiers in the trenches would strike against the war and refuse to fight. [3] The actual peace mission went nowhere, and Ford returned to the U.S. Edward House dismissed Ford's peace effort as a stunt, calling it "crude and unimportant." [4]

President Wilson understood the strong undercurrent of isolationism and pacifism in American society. That said, he also agreed with Edward House's advice that the country was unprepared for an armed conflict and fairly helpless in the face of adversaries, whether British or German. After the *Lusitania* sinking, the United States got serious about Preparedness. It was a contentious program, and it took a significant effort for the president to convince Congress to upgrade the nation's defenses. Preparedness began on December 7 when Wilson spoke before Congress and called for a major increase in military spending. [5]

Once Wilson signaled his support for Preparedness, his fiercest opponents were his fellow Democrats. The party had a strong contingent of pacifists, largely followers of William Jennings Bryan, who publicly fought Wilson on the question of military readiness. The pacifists "organized he largest, most diverse, and most sophisticated peace coalition to that point in U.S. history," according to historian Michael Kazin. In Congress, the leading peace activists were Democratic House

Majority Leader Claude Kitchin from North Carolina, and Republican Senator Robert La Follette of Wisconsin.[6]

Shortly after President Wilson commenced his Preparedness drive, Edward House returned to Europe at the end of December 1915. He visited first London, then Berlin. The goal for the trip was to discuss a future peace conference and terms that would bring combatants to the table. House quickly learned that the Germans were not in the mood for peace, as they believed they were winning the war. His diplomatic mission did not bring the sides closer to the peace table, but it did help mend the rift with Germany for a time. House quietly let the Allies know that the Wilson administration was essentially coming around to their side, as the president saw German militarism as a threat to the world. If it appeared that the Germans might prevail, the U.S. would be more likely to intervene to prevent such an outcome. But just how Americans would intervene was another question, given their scant army and navy.[7]

American Volunteers

There were some Americans whose ideals would not wait for a declaration of war. While many Americans disliked England, and others disliked Germany, everyone loved France. France was America's first ally in the War of Independence, and hundreds of young men volunteered to fight for the land of Lafayette. Many of them serving in the French Foreign Legion, the Ambulance Corps, and the Medical Corps. An American poet, Alan Seeger, fought with the French Foreign Legion. He wrote the poem "I Have a Rendezvous with Death," and in fact was killed at the Somme in 1916.

A number of soldiers in the Foreign Legion eventually transferred to French aviation forces, and lobbied for the creation of an American squadron, an escadrille. The *Escadrille américaine* was formed in April 1916 as a pursuit squadron, its plane fuselages decorated with an Indian head. The squadron first saw action at Verdun. Many of the squadron's first volunteers were the college-educated sons of well-to-do families who could afford expensive flying lessons. One of the more prominent leaders was Norman Prince, who helped organize the squadron. Prince died on October 15, 1916, three days after being thrown from a crash that shattered his body. He was awarded the French Legion of Honor. Pilots had a high casualty rate: combat was deadly, aircraft were built of wood and fabric, and if a plane was shot down, there was no parachute for the pilot.

The Germans protested that neutral Americans were fighting for France, so the squadron was renamed the Lafayette Escadrille in November 1916, named after the Marquis de Lafayette, the Revolutionary War hero. Once the U.S. entered the war, the squadron was incorporated into the United States Army Air Corps as the 103rd Pursuit Squadron in February 1918.

The Left Bank of Paris had long been the destination for artists, but it was in the war zone now, and crossing the Atlantic was too dangerous. American artists who might have gone to Paris found another destination much closer: Provincetown, a fishing town at the very tip of Cape Cod that hosted four competing art schools, the most notable under Charles Hawthorne. Socialist and activist writer Mary Heaton Vorse lived in Provincetown and convinced like-minded bohemians from Greenwich Village to flock there in the summer of 1916, prompting the *Boston Globe* to declare it the "biggest art colony in the world." Artists like painter Marsden Hartley, poet Harry Kemp, wealthy arts patron and columnist Mabel Dodge, painter and sculptor Maurice Sterne, poet and journalist John Reed, playwright Eugene O'Neill, and poet William Carlos Williams were all found in Provincetown that fateful summer. Eugene O'Neill staged his first play, *Bound East for Cardiff,* for the Provincetown Players on July 28 in a fish wharf owned by Mary Heaton Vorse. Mabel Dodge, who intensely disliked Vorse, started a brief, doomed affair with John Reed, then ended up marrying Maurice Sterne that year. Reed moved on to the beautiful journalist Louise Bryant. The two moved to Russia in 1917 and witnessed the Bolshevik coup.[8]

Not all of the American idealists went to France. A young American journalist, Wilbur Durborough, with his photographer Irving Ries, visited Germany for seven months in 1915 and took extensive movie footage of the German army. When they returned, they screened a nearly two-hour documentary called *On the Firing Line with the Germans*, which sympathetically showed the soldiers as well-behaved young men, contrary to Allied propaganda. The film ran in many cities until the threat of war silenced German propaganda. Shot in the days of combustible nitrate film, it is now in the Library of Congress.[9]

Edith and Woodrow

President Wilson remained cool during the trial of 1915, when the American public was outraged at the sinking of the *Lusitania* and some called for intervention in the war. It may have helped that he had fallen in love with a handsome widow, and she proved more than a passing distraction. Wilson was a man who needed a wife. He was lonely without female companionship.

Rear Admiral Cary Grayson was the president's personal physician. A man with keen listening skills, he became one of the president's few close personal associates. Grayson had cared for Ellen Wilson on her deathbed, and so he would with Woodrow in his final years. He was deeply devoted to Wilson, and yet remained acutely apolitical, something that the president appreciated. It meant that the two men could play golf together and not talk shop. Grayson's presence was a welcome relief from the constant correspondence and cabinet secretaries who sought presidential advice. In turn, the president listened to Grayson's advice regarding his health. Wilson had led a largely sedentary life and was not "naturally vigorous." He had asthma, stomach ailments, and was partly blind in one eye. He had long suffered from hypertension. Dr. Grayson got the president to take up golf as a form of exercise, and the two men played most Saturday mornings across the Potomac River in Virginia.[10]

It was Dr. Grayson who inadvertently introduced Wilson to Edith Bolling Galt. Edith was a forty-three-year-old widow with no children. She had married into the Galt family, which owned a long-running jewelry store in Washington, and the business provided her a decent income after her husband died six years earlier. Edith was worldly and had the expectations of the upper middle class. She was tall and attractive with her jet-black hair, being a proud descendant of Pocahontas, with a fine Virginia lilt to her voice. She was charming, funny, and opinionated. Edith came from a slaveholding family, and though she got along with African-Americans, she always viewed them as subordinate. She was not particularly well educated or well read. She relished fine clothes and the social scene—and valued her independence. She drove her own electric car and was more than capable of taking care of herself. Edith was comfortably single with no intention to get remarried.

Edith was friends with Dr. Grayson and had connections to the White House. One March day she was walking with a friend and dropped by the president's home. It was a muddy day, and their shoes were covered in mud. And there they bumped into President Wilson, who was just back from playing golf with Dr. Grayson, and who was equally muddy. Edith immediately tut-tutted the president's clothes. "They were *not* smart," she recalled. [11]

Wilson was impressed with Edith's beauty, which his friends quickly picked up on. They decided to make a more formal introduction. Edith reluctantly agreed to go on a double date with the president, who was sixteen years her senior. He was immediately smitten. The months of loneliness and purposelessness since Ellen's death had suddenly found resolution. Wilson needed a new companion.

The president wasted little time. He began writing Edith daily. In early May 1915, he told Edith that he loved her. She was taken aback and thought it far too soon, given that his wife had died only ten months earlier. But Edith gradually came around over the subsequent months, and in September the president proposed—and Edith accepted. The two began to be seen in public together. They attended vaudeville shows at Keith's Theatre on Saturday nights, went to baseball games together, and often took automobile rides through the city. They made excursions on the presidential yacht, the USS *Mayflower*. Wilson nicknamed Edith his "little girl."

Wilson married Edith Galt on December 18, 1915 in her home in Dupont Circle, rather than in a church or the White House. They honeymooned at the Homestead Resort in Hot Springs, Virginia, which they cut short when they returned on January 4 to take up the Preparedness campaign in earnest.

With Woodrow's marriage to Edith, the president's attention was drawn to his new wife, and no longer to his friend Edward House. Along with Joe Tumulty, House had opposed Wilson remarrying so early after the death of his first wife. He declined to attend the wedding. Edith initially disliked the Texan, finding him slippery and sycophantic. She told her husband, "It seems to me that it is impossible for two persons *always* to think alike, and while I like Colonel House immensely, I find him absolutely colorless and a 'yes, yes' man." She later called him a "jellyfish."[12]

Edith lacked Ellen Wilson's political instincts, or her depth in understanding issues. She was there to support her husband—and his agenda was her agenda. Edith also disliked the president's private secretary Joe Tumulty, whom she found brash and garrulous, a coarse Irish Yankee, not at all cultivated and refined. (Unlike House, Tumulty attended the wedding, and kept a piece of the wedding cake as a family heirloom; his grandson donated it to the Woodrow Wilson House in 2013.) Edith quickly sensed that Treasury Secretary William McAdoo would be a problem. The man married to her stepdaughter Nell was ambitious, and rumor had it that he wanted the presidency. Edith eventually came to appreciate Edward House, though she may have been jealous of his friendship with her husband. She came to regard House as a close friend until the Paris Peace Conference. After Wilson's stroke, she shut House out—but then again, she shut almost everyone out.[13]

The Preparedness Push

In 1914, the U.S. Army had only 92,482 soldiers on active duty, mostly stationed along the former frontier to guard against a Native American threat that had long passed, or in coastal defenses to protect the country from an invading fleet. Significant detachments were in China, Hawaii, guarding the Panama Canal Zone, and in the Philippines, which the U.S. had captured from Spain in 1898. In addition, the National Guard—a state-run militia—had just over 127,000 citizen-soldiers to call upon. These were minuscule numbers that simply would not suffice in the muddy trenches of the Western Front, where countries massed millions of soldiers to fight a war of attrition.[14]

Shortly after Woodrow and Edith Wilson returned to Washington from their honeymoon, they set out on a six-day whistle-stop tour of the Midwest on January 29, 1916 to sell the idea of Preparedness. The public was only willing to accept so much. When Secretary of War Lindley Garrison proposed universal military service, increasing the active duty army to a 400,000-man Continental Army, it met much noisy protest from the populist left. Wilson did not fully support this sizable increase, which undercut Garrison, who resigned on February 10.[15]

Wilson nominated Newton Baker, the mayor of Cleveland, to replace Garrison. Baker was both young—just forty-four years old—and diminutive in stature, but he proved a quick study as secretary of war. He would become one of the most capable men to serve in the cabinet, an irony given that he was a pacifist. Baker would oversee the Preparedness campaign.

The Liberty Bell was trundled out of Philadelphia and sent on a four-month nationwide tour aboard a train known as the Liberty Bell Special in support of Preparedness. Witnessing the public shift toward patriotism, H. L. Mencken penned a snarky letter to novelist Theodore Dreiser in February 1916: "I believe that both of us will be killed by patriots within six months." Both men were of German descent and opposed the saber rattling. Neither would in fact be killed in the next six months.[16]

Meanwhile, the interventionists were hardly standing still. General Leonard Wood established a series of military training camps to train civilians: first at Gettysburg, Pennsylvania, and Monterey, California in 1913, then Plattsburgh, New York two years later. Plattsburgh had been the site of an army and navy victory against British forces invading from Canada in 1814. Plattsburgh trained the sons of the elite families—often from Harvard and Yale—in soldiering. Participants paid $100 to attend the thirty-five-day training course. Theodore Roosevelt sent three of his sons to Plattsburgh. It would become the model for the army's basic training. [17]

In May 1916, a year after the *Lusitania* sinking, and after much debate, Congress finally passed legislation expanding the army. It would gradually double the size of the active force by 1921 to nearly a half million soldiers—larger than Garrison's aborted 400,000-man army plan—while federalizing the National Guard to protect the border with Mexico. Congress formally endorsed the Plattsburgh model for soldier basic training and created the Reserve Officers' Training Corps, or ROTC. Wilson signed the law on June 3. The army bill was contentious, as there was strong distrust against having such a large standing army in peacetime. [18]

Advocates for a stronger national defense held Preparedness parades around the country. A huge Citizens' Preparedness Parade was held in New York City on May 13 with 150,000 people marching. It lasted all day. [19] A month later, 60,000 people marched in a Flag Day parade in the nation's capital. President Wilson declared a holiday so that federal workers could participate, and he led the parade down Pennsylvania Avenue, marching just behind the Marine Band, attired in a dapper blue blazer and white duck pants, and carrying an American flag. Once he reached the White House, he peeled off to the reviewing stand, where Edith and he watched the rest of the Preparedness parade. One thing conspicuously absent were soldiers in uniform: this was a civilian parade. Thousands of women, including many suffragists, dressed in white. It was a sea of straw hats and waving flags. [20]

While much of the country came around to support Preparedness, militant anarchists were prepared to throw bombs in protest. On July 22, more than 50,000 people marched for Preparedness in San Francisco. At 2:06 P.M., just a half hour after the parade started, a time bomb inside a suitcase exploded on Steuart Street near the Ferry Building. The explosion ripped through the dense crowd of paraders and watchers, killing ten people and injuring scores. Authorities had in fact been warned of the bombing: anarchists had explicitly warned in a published letter that they would target the parade. Eight days later, another act of terrorism occurred when German saboteurs blew up the Black Tom arsenal in New Jersey.[21]

Wilson proposed to strengthen the army over three years to 670,836 soldiers, a nearly sixfold increase while leaving the National Guard at roughly the same size. The cost was significant: an estimated $182 million annually, in addition to $104 million for equipment over four years to upgrade the army's capabilities. Meanwhile, the Naval Appropriations Bill of 1916, passed in September, was a major victory for the big navy movement. It funded $315 million to build an entirely new fleet, including ten battleships, sixteen cruisers, fifty destroyers and torpedo boats, as well as numerous submarines and support vessels.[22] To pay for Preparedness, Congress doubled income tax rates from seven to fifteen percent, raised corporate taxes, and added an estate tax and a war profits tax in September.[23]

Little was done to improve the country's nascent aviation industry. American aviators trained in an unreliable biplane, the Curtiss JN-4 "Jenny," that was not suitable for combat. The plane, however, made its way into postage stamp lore in 1918 when one hundred stamps were issued with the plane accidentally printed upside down, the so-called "inverted Jenny" stamp issue. This was the status of American military aviation.

Comedian Will Rogers poked fun at American Preparedness in his vaudeville stand-up routines. "There is some talk of getting a machine gun, if we can borrow one. The one we have now they are using to train our army with in Plattsburgh. If we go to war, we will just about have to go to the trouble of getting another gun."[24] Rogers was not far off the mark. When the war started, the army's inventory was 285,000 Springfield rifles, 400 light artillery pieces, and 150 heavy guns. The army owned 1,500 machine guns, but of four different models, as the War Department could not decide which to procure.[25]

William Jennings Bryan had thrown himself into lobbying Congress for the pacifist cause, attempting to thwart the Preparedness plan. He did not succeed. In winning a major increase to the defense budget and tax increases to pay for them, Wilson proved that he was the leader of the Democratic Party, not Bryan.

Submarines and Diplomacy

The diplomatic crisis over Germany's unrestricted submarine warfare campaign lingered on, with diplomatic note after note sent to Germany, followed by counter-notes. An Austrian submarine sank the Italian ocean liner SS *Ancona* with Americans aboard, six months after the *Lusitania* sinking. The Germans finally backed off targeting passenger ships in February 1916.

Just as relations with Germany improved, a U-boat torpedoed the passenger ferry SS *Sussex* in the English Channel on March 24, killing a number of Americans. The Germans had a "genius for always doing the wrong thing in the wrong way and at the wrong time," complained Secretary of State Robert Lansing.[26] The torpedoing of the *Sussex* violated the Kaiser's February promise not to target passenger vessels. Much of the cabinet, led by Lansing, wanted to take action—yet the president remained hesitant. Edward House wrote critically in his diary about Wilson's response to the *Sussex* crisis: "He does not seem to realize that one of the main points of criticism against him is that he talks boldly, but acts weakly." Wilson issued an ultimatum threatening to sever diplomatic relations and hinted at war. That got the Germans' attention.[27]

Working behind the scenes, Ambassador Bernstorff helped strengthen German Chancellor Bethmann-Hollweg's position against the militarists who wanted to resume unrestricted submarine warfare, a campaign that would end badly for Germany if the U.S. entered the war against them. The chancellor convinced Kaiser Wilhelm of this wisdom. On May 4, the Kaiser ordered his U-boats to halt attacks on merchant and passenger ships without warning. The Germans returned to the old cruiser rules. It was the end of unrestricted submarine warfare—for now. The Germans reserved the right to resume submarine attacks if the freedom of the seas was not restored. A full year after the attack on the *Lusitania*, Wilson had a major diplomatic victory without resorting to war. The crisis had been averted, and American-German relations greatly improved.

Edward House, whom Wilson had sent to Europe in December 1915, returned to the States in March. He reported to the president about this trip. Wilson approved, and sent an appeal on March 7 for a peace conference. Neither side particularly welcomed Wilson's mediation offer as long as they believed they could win the war. This was just as the springtime fighting commenced in 1916, a year that would witness cataclysmic but inconsequential battles like Verdun and the Somme, and horrendous casualties on both sides.[28]

Wilson began to support the idea of a League of Nations in 1916. He and Edward House had long discussed the concept and how to make it work. It was not Wilson's idea—the league proposal had long fermented with the British and even Theodore Roosevelt, though he later walked away from the idea. William Howard Taft had organized the League to Enforce Peace in 1915 to champion conflict mediation.

With improved German-American relations, President Wilson put forward publicly his ideas for a League of Nations. On May 27, he delivered a major foreign policy address before two thousand members of the League to Enforce Peace at Washington's New Willard Hotel. He laid out three basic tenets: that all peoples should be able to choose their form of government, that small countries should have equal respect and status as large countries and empires, and that the world had a right for peace and to be free of aggression. The United States stood ready to help mediate a peaceful resolution to the Great War.[29]

As a goodwill gesture and to demonstrate to Americans that Germany was serious about the freedom of the seas, the Germans dispatched an unusual boat—an unarmed merchant submarine known as the *Deutschland*—to the United States. It arrived in Baltimore in July 1916 loaded with 750 tons of dyes worth $1 million, in a period when the submarine crisis had been averted and better relations were restored with Germany. The Germans promised more such merchant subs would follow, though none did.[30]

This was followed by a surprise visit of the *U-53* to Newport, Rhode Island, on October 7. After a courtesy meeting with local commanding naval officers, the German submarine cruised into the shipping channel off Nantucket and sank six England-bound vessels the next day. The German captain explicitly followed the cruiser rules, stopping each vessel, inspecting their papers and cargo for contraband that would aid England's war effort, allowing the crews and passengers to abandon ship, then torpedoing the vessels. By the end of the day the *U-53* was out of torpedoes and returning to Germany. No one could complain that the submarine had violated international law. The Germans made it explicit that they were following the rules. They had also sent a strong warning that U-boats could easily operate in American waters.[31]

Just as relations improved with the Germans, things got much worse with the British. A diplomatic crisis brewed over the Royal Navy's strict blockade of the North Atlantic. The British seized cargo and vessels it suspected were destined for Germany, even if its stated destination was a neutral country like the Netherlands, Spain, or in Scandinavia. Ships were not just stopped and searched, as the cruiser rules recognized; instead, they were directed to a nearby British port for adjudication. Once the ship had docked, British wartime censorship rules now applied, which allowed officials to open mail pouches, read letters, and open packages to ensure no German communications could get through. And British merchantmen flew neutral flags, including the American flag, as a ruse, which was a clear violation of international law.

In July 1916, British authorities blacklisted more than eighty-two American companies and individuals for having done business with Germany. This placed a major strain on Anglo-American relations. It was an unnecessary action, one that needlessly antagonized its key source of finance and munitions. Americans expected to trade with whomever they wanted. As most American cargo was carried in British ships, Democrats in Congress responded by legislating the United States Shipping Board, a law that Wilson signed on September 7, 1916. The U.S. created a state-owned merchant marine to counter

British dominance of shipping, and appropriated $50 million dollars to build ships.[32]

Even as the European powers bled each other's armies, the year 1916 provided a pronounced opportunity to mediate peace before the disastrous war turned into a fight to the finish. England was stubbornly committed to the blockade and command of the sea. Germany had plans to bleed France dry at Verdun, while the Allies goaded Romania into entering the war. Wilson was ready to offer mediation; however, this was a presidential election year in the U.S. Wilson understood that his peace effort would have to wait until after the November election.

Allied Arms Purchases—and German Espionage

J. P. Morgan Jr.—known as Jack—had taken over his father's banking empire after the elder Morgan died in 1913, the same year that the Federal Reserve was created. Morgan was an unapologetic Anglophile, spending half of the year in England. He sided with the Allies once the war began. Not all bankers did, however; many Jewish bankers were of German descent, and they sided with the Germans (an irony probably lost on most as the Second World War approached).

It was not illegal under international law for a neutral power to sell arms to combatants. Combatants would have to buy the arms, take possession of them, and carry them home. Nor was it illegal for an opposing combatant to declare such arms as contraband and destroy them on the open seas under internationally recognized cruiser rules. American neutrality allowed anyone who could reach American shores to trade for arms. That obviously excluded the Germans, whose ships were prevented from crossing the Atlantic, and in this way American neutrality greatly favored England. German Americans demanded an embargo on selling munitions to the Allies, a policy that the Wilson administration would never follow.

The U.S. would not make financial loans to either side. Prodded by Jack Morgan, however, Assistant Secretary of State Robert Lansing lobbied President Wilson to allow banks to extend credit to the Allies in the early days of the war. American farmers and industries needed to sell their surplus products, and if credit had not been extended to European borrowers, American businesses would have faced stiff losses and the economy might have entered a steep recession. These credits were technically not loans, though in fact they allowed the British, French, and Russians to buy vast quantities of armaments and supplies from American companies.

In September 1915, Jack Morgan underwrote an Anglo-French credit for $500 million, one that came with generous underwriting fees. Over the course of the war, J.P. Morgan & Co. alone extended credits of $1.5 billion to the Allies and made considerable profits. In return, the British exempted the House of Morgan from wartime censorship. The Germans received no such credits, and in any case had no way to ship goods to their harbors, given the British blockade. [33]

When the war began, the United States was a net debtor, but that reversed as the Allies made billions in purchases to supply their armies. The credits proved a tonic to the American economy, fueling a rapid war boom as industrial production ramped up and crop prices rose. The United States was a giant supplier for the Allies: clothing, food, horses, locomotives, mules, munitions, steel, and more were transported to harbors, where Allied ships eagerly loaded the supplies for their war effort. The American economy effectively reached full employment. Prices rose rapidly in this inflationary environment, and there was much labor unrest as workers demanded greater pay to combat the rising cost of living.

Since the end of Reconstruction in the 1870s, the South had instituted a caste system, with blacks on the bottom row just beneath poor whites. Sharecropping had replaced slavery, leaving blacks in a state of poverty and servitude. Southern whites subjected the black population to terrorism to keep them in check through lynching and Ku Klux Klan intimidation. With Jim Crow laws, whites stripped away black civil rights, in essence depriving blacks of their citizenship and human dignity.

Then came the Great War. Northern industries struggled to find laborers for their factories. They realized a large, inexpensive labor force existed in the country in the millions of poor African-Americans who lived in the South. Industrialists began sending labor agents to recruit black workers for the munitions factories, shipyards, and steel mills. During the decade of the Great War, about 550,000 blacks left the South to work in northern factories. (By 1970, some six million blacks had abandoned the South.) It became known as the Great Migration. Historian Isabel Wilkerson called it a "leaderless revolution," as people just picked up and moved. These were largely poor, rural blacks who helped tip the balance toward the cities as the country rapidly urbanized. Blacks left the South in waves, a stream of humanity fleeing inhumanity.[34] They transplanted jazz from New Orleans to northern cities, turning the musical style into a national movement in a matter of months.

With the start of the war, the Germans realized they had almost no intelligence assets in the United States and quickly had to set them up. Ambassador Bernstorff undoubtedly knew of spying operations and possibly even had his hand in them, but he was careful to leave no documentary trace that could implicate him in violating American neutrality. Instead, two naval officers ran the spy operations: Captain Karl Boy-Ed and Captain Franz von Papen. They were stationed in New York City with its large German population and dozens of German ships and crews interned there. The bored, listless sailors made excellent recruits for espionage missions.[35]

German saboteurs found ways to strike back against the massive flow of matériel that benefited the Allies. They created time-delayed pipe bombs the size of cigars. These were manufactured on an interned ship in New York harbor, SMS *Friedrich der Grosse*, then smuggled aboard Allied munitions-carrying ships with the help of Irish stevedores. The explosives detonated when the ships were at sea, crippling the freighters and in some cases even sinking them. The first victim was the SS *Phoebus*, which mysteriously caught fire at sea.[36] Between March and September 1915, there were thirteen explosions on ships at sea that had originated in American ports.[37]

Kaiser Wilhelm threatened the American ambassador in Berlin, James Gerard, that "he would attend to America when this war was over," as the supposed neutral Americans were helping the Allies but not the Germans. Gerard did not take the threat too seriously, although it did give President Wilson pause to the threat that German militarism posed to the world.[38]

On Saturday, July 2, 1915, an explosion rocked the U.S. Capitol. Three sticks of dynamite had blown up in the Senate reception room around midnight. The blast destroyed the adjacent phone booths and shattered a chandelier and mirror, but otherwise caused no extensive damage. No one was injured, though a watchman on the floor below "said he was blown from his chair by the explosion," according to the *New York Times*.[39]

President Wilson and Washington's four major newspapers received letters signed by an "R. Pearce," who took responsibility for the bombing. The bomber stressed that his intentions were peaceful, and that he simply wanted the United States to stop selling explosives to Europe. "By the way, don't put this on the Germans or [William Jennings] Bryan," he noted. "I am an old fashioned American with a conscience." The letter was postmarked two hours before the bombing occurred.[40]

The next morning, an intruder named Frank Holt carrying two revolvers and sticks of dynamite entered the Long Island estate of Jack Morgan, who was having breakfast with the British ambassador, Sir Cecil Spring-Rice. Holding Morgan at gunpoint, Holt demanded that Morgan stop financing Allied purchases of American munitions. Morgan lunged at Holt, who shot the financier twice, though the wounds were not fatal. Morgan's wife and servants subdued Holt until the police arrived to arrest him.[41]

The police quickly connected the dynamite to the bombing at the Capitol the night before. And soon they discovered something equally interesting: Frank Holt was an alias for a fugitive, a German-born man named Erich Muenter who had served as a professor at Harvard University. Muenter fled in 1906 after being indicted for murdering his wife. He then worked as a stenographer at a Mexican mine, taught at Polytechnic College in Fort Worth, Texas, remarried in 1910, and finally taught German at Cornell University—all under the alias Frank Holt.

As witnesses from the 1906 murder case were coming to identify him, Muenter leaped to his death in his prison cell in Mineola, New York the night of July 5.[42] The Secret Service investigated if Muenter had accomplices or foreign help, and the crews of two ocean liners bound for Liverpool searched their ships after Muenter's last letter to his wife insinuated that there were bombs aboard. No bombs were found aboard those ships, though an explosion tore through the munitions ship SS *Minnehaha* bound for France on July 7.[43]

Whether Muenter was connected to German intelligence was unknown, and his suicide would leave that question unanswered. But German espionage was certainly active—and its activities were publicly disclosed even while the public still simmered over the *Lusitania* sinking. In a tremendous lapse, the German commercial attaché Dr. Heinrich Albert absentmindedly left his briefcase on a New York subway, which an American intelligence officer tailing him immediately picked up. It detailed many German spy operations. Treasury Secretary William McAdoo, who oversaw the Secret Service, described the briefcase as being full of "documentary dynamite." The Secret Service eventually uncovered that Dr. Albert had received more than $27 million for clandestine operations.[44]

With President Wilson's approval, Lansing and McAdoo leaked the German espionage papers to the *New York World*, a newspaper friendly to the Wilson administration, which published them on August 15. The papers documented German attempts to foment labor unrest, acquire newspapers for propaganda purposes, and buy munitions plants. There was more outrage and more bad press for the Germans. Many Americans now wondered if their German neighbors were spies. It threw German-Americans on the defense. Later that year, British intelligence intercepted more papers documenting German espionage in the U.S. and published them. This worked both to embarrass the Germans and to provoke the Americans. New York City police soon rolled up the German cell that placed bombs on ships. The Wilson administration sent captains Boy-Ed and von Papen back to Germany.[45]

Yet the sabotage continued. German intelligence staged what was so far the largest act of sabotage on American soil. In the early hours of July 30, 1916, they blew up the enormous munitions depot known as Black Tom Island in Jersey City, New Jersey. The explosion was felt several states away. Windows were shattered in Brooklyn and

Manhattan, and the Statue of Liberty was damaged (her upper arm holding the torch was subsequently closed to the public). Some $20 million in munitions destined for British and French armies was destroyed and hundreds of people injured.[46]

Repairs were made to the famous statue that stands guard over New York harbor, which France had given the country in 1886. On December 2, some four months after Black Tom, the Statue of Liberty was lit up with electric lights. President Wilson attended the ceremony from the presidential yacht, the *Mayflower*. He was given a carpet that showed historic sites from each of the then forty-eight states. Years later, while recovering from his 1919 stroke, Wilson slowly walked across the carpet in his library and remarked to his physician, Cary Grayson: "Doctor, that is not a bad stunt for a lame fellow, to walk over Niagara Falls this morning."[47]

Trouble in Mexico

While Europe was consumed with the World War, the United States faced trouble with its neighbor to the south, Mexico, albeit on a far smaller scale. Mexico was an unstable but strategically important country. It owned a quarter of the world's then-known oil reserves and was the principal source of petroleum for the Royal Navy. The Americans needed to keep the country out of unfriendly hands, as the two countries shared a long border.

Mexico was in turmoil. The trouble began in 1911 when Francisco Madero overthrew the country's dictator, Porfirio Díaz. Madero gathered the support of the military but learned in February 1913—a month before President Wilson was sworn in—that he could not command them. A power-hungry Mexican general, Victoriano Huerta, overthrew Madero and had him shot. Huerta declared himself president.

Civil war broke out as constitutionalists, led by Venustiano Carranza, Francisco "Pancho" Villa, and Emiliano Zapata, rose up to oppose Huerta. In April 1914, upon learning that the Germans were sending a ship loaded with arms for the Huerta administration,

American forces violently seized Veracruz, the main Mexican port. President Wilson and Secretary of the Navy Daniels were concerned that Germany would violate the Monroe Doctrine by establishing a naval base in Mexico. Cut off from the outside world and with his regime teetering, Huerta resigned from the presidency in July. Carranza rode into Mexico City to lead the country. The U.S. recognized Carranza's regime; however, the trouble was far from over.[48]

Huerta eventually made his way to the United States, where he conspired with German intelligence to resume the Mexican conflict. American officials arrested him on charges of sedition, and he died in an El Paso, Texas, prison in January 1916, eighteen months after fleeing Mexico.

Carranza's deputy was Pancho Villa. Now that Carranza was the Mexican president, Villa revolted against the new regime. He lacked the resources to take on the Mexican government, and his rebellion remained largely in the northern part of the country. Villa was upset at American support for Carranza. In January 1916, his forces stopped a train in Chihuahua and executed seventeen American mining engineers who were aboard.

To draw more attention to his crumbling cause, Pancho Villa took an extraordinary and extreme step: he crossed the border to raid Columbus, New Mexico with nearly five hundred men on March 9, killing eighteen Americans. His ragtag force engaged in a firefight with American soldiers stationed at Camp Furlong, and Villa's force got the worse end of it, withdrawing to Mexico but earning Villa much desired publicity as a folk hero who fought the Yanquis.[49]

The American response to Villa's raid was immediate: American soil had been invaded and blood spilled. Villa's raid on Columbus was coincidentally the first day on the job for Newton Baker, the new secretary of war. The president authorized an incursion into Mexico—without permission from the Mexican government—to apprehend Villa. Baker appointed Major General John Pershing to lead a 4,000-man Punitive Expedition into Mexico on March 15.

The expedition, which peaked at 12,000 men, was wracked by sickness. It skirmished more with the Mexican army than with the

Villistas. Lieutenant George Patton, who was a cavalry officer and a 1909 West Point graduate on Pershing's staff, led raids not on horseback but in automobiles, presaging his future role as a mechanized armor commander. Wilson called up the National Guard to protect the nation's borders on June 8. By the end of the month, 108,000 guardsmen were patrolling the Mexican border.[50] Former president Theodore Roosevelt offered to raise a division of volunteers to serve in Mexico under his command.[51]

The American incursion into Mexico played into Germany's hands, which hoped the U.S. would remain tied down. It gave them ideas on how to keep the Americans from providing substantial help in the European war. Historian Barbara Tuchman called the American incursion into Mexico "a prolonged and famous fumble." Pershing never caught Pancho Villa. The U.S. withdrew from Mexico in February 1917, just in time for a new threat from another direction.[52]

The War in 1916

Europe entered its third year of war in stalemate. Both sides would attempt to break out of the deadlock, but neither were powerful enough to knock the opponent out of the war. Just as it had tested new lethal weaponry in 1915, the Germans would test the boundaries of civilized warfare in order to win.

The Irish had chafed at British rule for centuries. With German encouragement and support, Irish nationalists planned what was called Easter Rising to liberate their country, and the Germans brought Roger Casement to the Emerald Isle in a U-boat, where he was promptly captured. The British executed Casement for treason and published his diaries, full of stories of homosexual liaisons, to discredit the Irish revolutionary movement. Still, the bloody Easter Rising began in April 1916, diverting England's attention and beginning a six-year civil war that would lead to Ireland's independence. Irish-Americans were incensed at British brutality, and England's crackdown did little to help the Allied cause in America.

With the U-boats temporarily in check, Kaiser Wilhelm decided to use his large surface fleet to challenge the British blockade of the North Sea. The Battle of Jutland took place off the coast of Denmark on May 31, 1916. The naval battle was a draw, but the German High Seas Fleet returned to port and never ventured beyond the Baltic again until after the Armistice. German strategists began rethinking how effective the initial U-boat campaign had been, and shipyards doubled their efforts to build a new generation of U-boats that could greatly expand a renewed submarine campaign in early 1917.

Of the many battles of the Great War, no battle was more powerfully symbolic as the Battle of Verdun in 1916. When the Germans attacked France in 1914, they had pivoted around Verdun to the west, but never took the city. It remained a salient protruding into German lines. Verdun was symbolically important: in 843 C.E., Charlemagne had divided his empire into three parts at Verdun. The chief of the German General Staff, Field Marshal Erich von Falkenhayn, knew the French would do anything to defend the city. He devised a strategy to lure the French army into the cauldron, then pummel it with artillery and inflict mass casualties.

The Germans attacked Verdun in February 1916, capturing a number of the forts on its outskirts, then prepared for the French counterattack. The French took the bait as planned. Large numbers of French divisions were pulled from quieter fronts and fed through the meat grinder of German artillery. By the end of the battle, most of the French army had seen the devil's grounds. The French gradually pushed the Germans back and inflicted unexpectedly high casualties. All told, some 750,000 men were casualties with no decisive outcome for either side. Falkenhayn was relieved of his command, replaced by the men who were considered the face of the German war effort, Paul von Hindenburg and his quartermaster general Erich Ludendorff.

To relieve the pressure on Verdun, the English and French opened an offensive on the Somme River, 170 miles to the northwest on July 1. For seven days, English artillery pounded the German lines, though a high percentage of shells were duds. The bombardment had little impact on the deeply entrenched German bunkers. When British officers blew their whistles and the infantry waves rose out of their trenches to attack, the German machine guns went to work, mowing down the young men. On the first day of the Somme, nearly 20,000 English were killed and more than 38,000 wounded. The Battle of the Somme ended in November, and the English suffered more than 131,000 dead, eclipsing the American casualty list for the entire Great War. For the massive casualties, the Allies had only pushed the Germans back a few miles. Little remains today of the Somme battlefield but for a three-hundred-foot hole known as the Lochnagar Crater; however, the Somme left a national scar on England that left generations questioning the wisdom of war.

The battles of Verdun and the Somme failed to break the stalemate. Neither side was able to break through enemy lines. The only outcome was the massive casualties of young men in the muddy trenches. The landscape of battlefields was virtually obliterated, covered in craters from thousands of artillery shell explosions that left hardly a tree standing. Soldiers remained in the trenches sometimes for weeks before they were relieved. Bunkers became their homes, and sanitation was limited. Rats fed on the corpses and multiplied, while lice infested the men. There was the inescapable stench of putrid, decaying bodies. The stalemate continued on the Western Front in the seesaw war of attrition.

In June, the Russians launched the Brusilov Offensive against the Austro-Hungarians in Galicia, now part of Ukraine. The Austrians had concentrated much of their forces against Italy, leaving their eastern flank weakened. Russian General Aleksei Brusilov attacked along a broad, three-hundred-mile front, using short artillery bombardment and specially trained shock troops to assault Austrian weak points. The offensive was one of the most decisive battles of the Great War, capturing hundreds of thousands of prisoners and forcing the Germans to end the Verdun campaign and transfer numerous divisions east to prevent Austria from collapsing.

With this decisive victory in hand, the Allies goaded Romania into the war in August, promising it could annex Transylvania, home to a large Romanian minority. The hope was that the pressure from the

Romanians might knock Austria-Hungary out of the war. It turned out to be a disastrous decision for the Romanians. A combined Austrian-German force under Falkenhayn made quick work of the country, knocking it out of the war in five months and occupying Bucharest. The Germans demanded steep reparations and large quantities of food for their war machine.

Despite the success of the Brusilov Offensive, things had not gone well for Russia. The German army bested it in nearly every battle, casualties were high, and the Russian economy was nearing collapse with food and fuel shortages, rampant inflation, and worker rebellions. The autocratic Czar Nicholas had taken personal command of the army, and with its defeats his popularity plummeted. His wife Alexandra was under the influence of the mystic Rasputin, whom aristocrats assassinated in December 1916. The situation was rapidly unraveling for the ruling Romanov dynasty.

The first of two Russian revolutions occurred in March 1917. Hungry munitions workers staged a massive strike in Petrograd, the Russian capital, and they were soon joined by the army. Czar Nicholas was forced to abdicate, and a left-leaning Provisional Government under Alexander Kerensky took charge. The Russians desperately wanted to remove themselves from the war, but the Allies would only deliver urgently needed assistance if Russia continued to fight. Recognizing that Russia teetered on collapse, the Germans gave it a push in April by allowing communist revolutionaries living in Switzerland, such as Vladimir Lenin, to cross German territory in a special train. Lenin made his way through Sweden and Finland, and was soon in Petrograd. Russia remained in the war for another year, with the disastrous consequence of yet another political coup in November that would unexpectedly reshape world history for much of the 20th century.

Americans misread the March revolution in Russia, believing it a victory for liberal democracy, when Russia was rife with internal conflict between the fragile new government and the Bolsheviks, who were infecting the army with propaganda and soldier committees known as soviets. The Bolsheviks were something entirely new: neither liberal, nor democratic; they were radical Marxists who like Christian missionaries wanted to convert the world to their revolutionary cause. Under Lenin they were absolutely ruthless. Russia went from an autocratic government to a totalitarian state.[53]

The 1916 Election

The year 1916 was a banner year for Woodrow Wilson. He got labor laws passed, including one that limited child labor. He pushed through an income tax increase to fund the country's Preparedness campaign, and successfully established the estate tax system to prevent massive amounts of money transferring from one wealthy generation to another, which would have worsened economic inequality. Wilson appointed Louis Brandeis to the U.S. Supreme Court, the first Jew to serve on the highest court. It was a lengthy confirmation battle, taking more than four months. Brandeis was famous for his support of the working class and for criticizing the money trust, which made him unpopular among bankers. "We must make our choice," Brandeis once remarked. "We may have democracy, or we may have wealth concentrated in the hands of a few, but we can't have both."[54]

Wilson sought a second term as president. He was popular, but his liberalism was controversial and the Republican opposition was strong. The question of the Great War lingered over the country, one that split along ethnic rather than partisan lines. Interventionists like Theodore Roosevelt demanded that America enter the war, but they remained a minority. Pacifism was still a pervasive stance, and most Americans wanted to stay out of Europe's war. Wilson's opponent was Charles Evans Hughes, a conservative and Supreme Court associate justice who stepped down from the court for the campaign.

The 1916 presidential campaign was considered the first modern election, and Wilson ran an operation that tapped into new forms of mass media, opposition research, and targeted advertising, including short ads in movie theaters. Many of Wilson's proxies used the slogan: "He kept us out of war," a powerful message that echoed strongly with the public, though Wilson's campaign did not actually use it, knowing that war was a possibility. Vice President Thomas Marshall went so far as to say, "Nobody is able to trace to him any statement of that kind." Wilson's campaign kept his opponent Hughes on edge over the question of entering the war, a question that Hughes was eager to dodge. [55]

Edith Wilson thought that her husband's defeat was likely in 1916 and began making postelection plans. "What a delightful pessimist you are!" Woodrow told her. "One must never court defeat. If it comes, accept it like a soldier; but don't anticipate it, for that destroys your fighting spirit." [56] On Election Day, the couple traveled to New Jersey, Wilson's home state, to vote. Suffrage was not yet legal in the Garden State, so she remained in the car while her husband voted in his Princeton precinct. Once the Nineteenth Amendment passed, she was able to vote just one time in a presidential election: 1920. She and her husband mailed in their ballots that year as New Jersey residents. She never got to vote in a presidential election again, as she became a resident of Washington, D.C. again once they left the White House. [57]

Woodrow Wilson won the 1916 presidential election by a narrow margin. He narrowly took the popular vote, and the Electoral College vote was 277 to 254. Wilson won the South, West, and crucially, Ohio. But Wilson had also won an actual majority of the vote, unlike in 1912, when he won on a plurality. Democrats lost some seats in the House of Representatives, though they maintained a twelve-seat majority in the Senate. Wilson was the first Democratic president to win consecutive terms since Andrew Jackson. He had a narrow mandate to continue as president.

Wilson had in fact kept the country out of the deadly World War that had raged for more than two years. With his reelection, the president could now turn his attention to mediating peace between the combatants, whom he believed surely realized that this war was not winnable.

Mediating Peace

President Wilson had long signaled that he would lead a new peace initiative to end the Great War. He sought to be the mediator who would bring the world back from the brink of disaster. But mediation, peace, and war were a complicated dance involving multiple partners and competing agendas. Wilson planned for the peace campaign to begin in December, shortly after the presidential election, but then caught a terrible cold, further delaying his initiative.

The Germans finally grew tired of waiting for Wilson. With the recent victory over Romania in hand, they were in a stronger position than the Allies and believed they were winning the war. The Germans preempted Wilson's expected mediation effort with a peace offer of their own on December 12, 1916. Germany undermined Wilson's peace effort by offering a disingenuous olive branch with an arrogant list of demands. The Allies rejected it out of hand.[58]

On December 18, Wilson began his long-awaited diplomatic initiative, offering to mediate peace with the belligerents. Each side was to declare its war aims, and the U.S. would then help them negotiate a middle course that would be acceptable to all. Wilson fixated on the belligerents' war aims but without understanding why they were fighting. The note was received coolly.

Secretary of State Robert Lansing irreparably damaged Wilson's mediation effort by issuing a statement explaining Wilson's peace initiative in the context that both sides were stepping on American rights. "I mean by that that we are drawing nearer the verge of war ourselves," an assertion that many interpreted as meaning that the U.S. would enter the war if this diplomatic initiative failed. The stock market immediately plunged, though soon recovered. The secretary backpedaled later the same day by saying that the U.S. intended to remain neutral.[59]

Lansing was a hawk who viewed the German government as autocratic and believed that the U.S. would eventually enter the war on the side of the Allies. He later called the president's peace efforts a "useless waste of time."[60] The Central Powers refused to state their war aims as Wilson requested, believing that it would weaken them at the negotiating table. Meanwhile the Allies submitted their war aims in January 1917, demanding that Germany accept blame for the war, pay reparations, and restitute Alsace-Lorraine to France. The Germans considered this a nonstarter.[61]

The president was frustrated but undaunted. He consulted with Edward House, his private adviser, who was equally displeased as Lansing with Wilson's botched peace initiative. House warned that war might be inevitable and that it would be wise to make prepara-tions. "There will be no war," the president countered. "This country does not intend to become involved in this war. We are the only one of the great white nations that is free from war today, and it would be a crime against civilization for us to go in."[62]

Wilson renewed his peace overture in January 1917, this time without Lansing's help, and in fact, very much kept secret from him. Wilson never fully trusted Lansing's counsel and excluded Lansing for obvious reasons. Instead, the president enlisted his wife Edith and Edward House for their advice. House asked Wilson if he would show the draft peace proposal to the secretary of state. No, he responded, but he would before releasing it. "He thought Lansing was not in sympathy with his purpose to keep out of war," House recorded in his diary.[63]

On January 22, Wilson addressed the Senate to commence his new peace plan, giving a speech that was one of the most memorable of his presidency. He restated his position, one that he had advocated since the beginning of the war: The United States was prepared to help mediate a reasonable and just peace, one that would ensure no one side could win over another. It was to be a "peace without victory." He went on to explain how "Victory would mean peace forced upon the loser, a victor's terms imposed upon the vanquished," one that would leave "a sting, a resentment, a bitter memory upon which terms of peace would rest, not permanently, but only as upon quicksand. Only a peace between equals can last." These were prophetic words. Wilson laid out concrete aims: an independent Poland, freedom of the seas, limited naval armaments, and an end to military alliances. The U.S. would help resolve conflicts through a League of Peace.[64]

Republicans widely criticized Wilson's peace plan. His perennial political opponent, Theodore Roosevelt, called the president's words "the idlest and most empty of all empty words." His searing response went on to refute Wilson's plan point-by-point.[65] A week later, after Wilson stated that he was against conscription, Roosevelt took up the charge again. "Peace without victory is the natural ideal of the man who is too proud to fight," he wrote, cleverly rehashing Wilson's 1915 statement after the *Lusitania* sinking."[66] The *New York Times* took to Wilson's defense, calling Roosevelt the "Regressive of Oyster Bay."[67]

Both the Allies and Central Powers were desperate for Wilson's peace plan, but neither could admit it. They had gone too far. Neither side would back down and were committed to fighting the total war to the end, an end that was nowhere in sight. Wilson's "peace without victory" speech was all for naught. The Allies wanted nothing but victory and wondered how they could get the Americans to join them, rather than to arbitrate a peace settlement. Meanwhile the Germans were preparing to escalate the conflict to knock England out of the war by renewing unrestricted submarine warfare. They did this knowing full well that the United States would likely enter the war on the Allies' side.

THREE

The Decision

After Robert Lansing's public acknowledgement in December 1916 that the U.S. might enter the Great War, the German high command concluded that American involvement in the war was inevitable. Germany did not worry about America's puny army, untrained for modern warfare, but feared its industrial might and bountiful food supplies. Great Britain was especially dependent on American provisions, so the Germans determined to knock Britain out of the war before the U.S. could marshal its forces. The high command estimated that a concentrated submarine campaign would take six months to force Britain into submission. Unrestricted submarine warfare would recommence on February 1, 1917. It was a calculated risk, one that ultimately failed.

Perhaps war with the United States was inevitable. The German high command assumed it was. Lansing certainly thought so—and in fact his words had ensured that the Germans would not come to the peace table. Only Wilson was committed to exhausting every peace opportunity before time ran out. He hoped to play a role in mediating an end to the conflict.

German Ambassador Johann von Bernstorff received notice of the submarine campaign's renewal on January 19 via coded telegram; he was to inform the U.S. government of the campaign on February 1. In the intervening period, he pleaded with Berlin to reconsider. Wilson was ramping up his next peace initiative, making his "peace without victory" speech on January 22. Bernstorff knew that the submarine campaign would mean war with the United States.[1]

The German response to Wilson's peace initiative—unrestricted submarine warfare against England, and by proxy, against the United States—showed contempt for Wilson and made an enemy out of the one person who could have helped stop the war, and just as the Germans were beginning to prevail against the Allies. Ultimately it was the Germans who blundered, alienating the United States and earning a new enemy they could ill afford. They lost their best chance for a negotiated peace. And had the U.S. remained neutral, they may well have won the war.

On the eve before unrestricted submarine warfare resumed, Chancellor Bethmann-Hollweg secretly sent Ambassador Bernstorff the list of Germany's war aims, a condition that the U.S. had requested for future peace negotiations. Bernstorff shared them with Edward House in the hopes of forestalling a war. But the chancellor noted it was too late to halt the submarine campaign. His own political power was nearly irrelevant by early 1917.[2]

Likewise, Kaiser Wilhelm's authority was waning. He was erratic, impulsive, and proved an inadequate wartime leader. The German high command had usurped much of his authority. The Kaiser watched impassively as Ludendorff—known as the "silent dictator"—took charge of the economy and war policy. The politicians knew that resuming unrestricted submarine warfare was reckless, but the military saw it only through their need to defeat England.

On Sunday, January 31, Ambassador Bernstorff handed over the message to Secretary of State Robert Lansing that unrestricted submarine warfare would resume the next day. Lansing was probably quietly pleased, as it significantly strengthened the hand of the interventionists. But before Bernstorff dropped by Lansing's office, he sent a coded message to the captains of German ships interned in American harbors. It was the signal to destroy their engines. Bernstorff knew war was imminent and that the Americans would seize the vessels.

The American press erupted in denunciation at the German submarine declaration. "This is but a proclamation of a new career of crime, more dreadful, more extended, more ruthless, and even more callously lawless than that other in which her naval commanders took such a huge toll of innocent human lives," avowed the *New York Times*.[3] Many commented that Germany had de facto declared war on the United States. The country's leading pacifist, William Jennings Bryan, meanwhile praised Wilson's peace efforts before the American Neutral Conference: "I have faith, not only in the President's desire to keep us out of war, but in his ability to do so." Bryan acknowledged that war was now a possibility, but he was willfully ignorant of the shift in public opinion against the Germans.[4]

Edward House jumped on a train in New York bound for Washington on February 1 at the president's request. The two men met with Lansing to discuss their options. They quickly agreed that severing diplomatic relations with Germany was the proper decision. Lansing ordered his staff to prepare Bernstorff's passport. Wilson was deeply saddened. "The President said he felt as if the world had suddenly reversed itself; that after going from east to west, it had begun to go from west to east, and that he could not get his balance," House wrote. The submarine warfare renewal came as quite a shock, though his advisers had been telling him that it was a likely outcome.[5]

The State Department was expecting a renewal of unrestricted submarine warfare, but Wilson was truly surprised by the German announcement. He was fully expecting to launch a serious peace initiative, only to see the Germans take an aggressive posture that threatened the United States. Wilson still hoped for neutrality, and still wishing to avoid war, the logical next step was to arm American merchant ships so they could protect themselves from German U-boats.

The cabinet met on February 2, as Wilson wanted their input on the next steps. "Shall I break off diplomatic relations with Germany?" he asked. David Houston, the secretary of agriculture, recorded that Wilson made a rather surprising statement that getting involved in the war would weaken the white race, in particular against the "yellow race" like the Japanese.[6] After allaying Wilson's concerns about the Japanese gaining strength in Asia, Houston gave his recommendation for how to deal with Germany: "Immediately sever diplomatic relations and let come what will. Tell Congress what you have done."[7]

Wilson followed this advice. The next day, he spoke before a joint session of Congress, announcing that he was severing diplomatic relations with Germany. "I refuse to believe that it is the intention of the German authorities to do in fact what they have warned us they will feel at liberty to do," Wilson declared. "Only actual overt acts on their part can make me believe it even now," yet he still had hope for peace. It was not a war declaration. With the phrase "overt acts," Wilson left it in the hands of the Germans to decide if they wanted a war with the United States. Congress was nearly unanimous in its support of Wilson's actions. Much of the country still supported peace, though the pacifists were weakening.[8]

The Secret Service immediately assumed control of the Imperial German Embassy in Washington while Ambassador Bernstorff and his staff packed their bags. They sailed for Denmark on February 14. If the German government wished to communicate with the Americans, it would have to do so through the Swiss government.

In addition, Wilson ordered the seizure of a number of German vessels interned in American ports. These included two auxiliary cruisers in Philadelphia, the SS *Kronprinz Wilhelm* and SS *Prinz Eitel Friedrich*, the ocean liner SS *Kronprinzessin Cecilie* in Boston, and the liner SS *Appam* in Newport News. Other ships were detained in Panama, and guards were placed on ships in New Orleans. American officials were concerned that the Germans would attempt to sink these ships in American harbors; however, when officials boarded the vessels, they soon discovered that the Germans had sabotaged the engines so that they were dead in the water.

Wilson confirmed two days later that the U.S. would continue to protect and respect German property.[9]

The National German-American Alliance (NGAA) issued a statement in support of the president after he severed diplomatic relations. Charles Hexamer, the organization's president, urged its members to remain loyal to the United States. The NGAA endorsed Wilson's move against Germany. The organization was collecting money for the German Red Cross, but the board voted to give the money to the American Red Cross instead in a gesture of patriotism.[10]

The *Washington Post*, an anti-Wilson newspaper, denounced Germany's military actions as violating the Monroe Doctrine. "The attempt by Germany to deny the use of the high seas to neutral nations is essentially an act of war," the paper declared, though it hoped the country would not have to resort to conflict, nor depend on complicating alliances. "The prime duty of the United States is to protect democracy throughout the New World," the editorial concluded, falling short of President Wilson's vision to protect democracy throughout the entire world.[11]

Theodore Roosevelt stood at the sidelines, stunned as to why Wilson had not acted more decisively. "He is yellow all through in the presence of danger, either physically or morally, and will accept any insult or injury from the hands of a fighting man," the former president wrote his close friend Senator Henry Cabot Lodge. Roosevelt clearly believed that war was not only imminent, it was preferable. He called the leading pacifist in Congress, Republican Senator Robert La Follette "an unhung traitor, and if the war should come, he ought to be hung."[12]

On February 3—the same day that Wilson severed relations with Germany—unrestricted submarine warfare claimed its first American victim ship: the SS *Housatonic*. The submarine *U-53* maintained the cruiser rules, stopping the ship to warn it, evacuating the crew, then sinking it. On February 12, the schooner *Lyman M. Law* was sunk under similar conditions near Sardinia. The German submarine campaign quickly ramped up. In the first month, the Germans sank 252,621 tons of shipping. This more than doubled to 564,497 tons in March. They sank a staggering 860,334 tons in April, far more than the Allies could replace.[13]

Even with severed diplomatic relations, the U.S. and Germany were not at war. American shippers responded to the submarine campaign by ordering their ships to stay in harbor, reducing the risk of being torpedoed. Wilson's response was "armed neutrality," a policy to arm merchantmen so they could fight back against an attacking submarine. It was an unsound policy, as submarines could remain submerged, and once a ship fired on a U-boat, the sub could then legitimately sink the ship. Wilson was reluctant to act without Congress's backing, so the Armed Ship Bill was introduced and debated. Congress took up a massive naval bill to build new ships and submarines. It got to conference committee, but then a filibuster in the Senate halted progress.

Largely unnoticed was another action undertaken by Congress on February 5, just two days after the U.S. severed relations with Germany. Congress overrode President Wilson's veto for the very first time, turning the Immigration Act into law. White nationalism was ascendant, and the law—underpinned by the flawed belief in eugenics—banned most Asian immigrants as well as morally undesirable conditions and imposed a literacy test.[14]

Unrestricted submarine warfare had led to the break in diplomatic relations but did not immediately lead to war. Two months of armed neutrality followed. It would take an existential threat, an "overt act," as Wilson called it, for the U.S. to declare war. The act was not long in coming.

Mencken's European Trip

Although his mother was German, H. L. Mencken did not speak the language growing up in Baltimore, nor did he have particular feelings one way or the other about his ancestral homeland. He changed his opinion during the war as he began to notice English propaganda, and he fell in line philosophically with Germans. "I, too, like the leaders of Germany, had grave doubts about democracy. I, too, felt an instinctive antipathy to the whole Puritan scheme of things, with its gross and nauseating hypocrisies, its idiotic theologies, its moral obsessions, its pervasive Philistinism," he recalled later in life. "I was implacably pro-German."[15]

"When World War I actually started I began forthwith to whoop for the Kaiser, and I kept up that whooping so long as there was any free speech left in the United States," Mencken recalled. "That period, unhappily, was not prolonged." After the sinking of the *Lusitania* in 1915, he realized that the U.S. would eventually join the war, and his editors curtailed his pro-German editorials. He made plans to go abroad, "to see something of the German Army in action before it would be too late."[16]

On December 28, 1916, Mencken boarded the Danish ship *Oscar II* in Hoboken bound for Copenhagen (this was the same "peace ship" that Henry Ford had sailed on his ill-fated mission a year before). Denmark was neutral and thus could sail through the contested seas, though the Royal Navy stopped and inspected neutral vessels. Mencken described the polyglot passengers from around the world, and how everyone hated everyone else. He was much bemused by a Russian general with a giant walrus moustache who could put away copious amounts of food. "While he was gobbling away a steward rushed in with the news that a German submarine was in sight, and we all ran on deck to get a look at it, and make our peace with our Maker," Mencken wrote. "Somewhat to our disappointment it merely circled round us twice, and then made off politely. When we got back to the dining-room the Walrus was helping himself to the forequarters of the pig, and excavating another quart of stuffing." The general had probably been in the U.S. to buy munitions for the Russian army.[17]

The North Atlantic was a challenging place for a neutral vessel during the Great War. Not only might German U-boats attempt to sink them, but the Royal Navy was suspicious of anyone on board as being a possible spy. The British boarded the *Oscar II* and briefly detained the ship in Kirkwall, Scotland while they interviewed the passengers and inspected every piece of luggage, searching for German contraband. It took two days to search the ship.[18] Mencken relayed how they intended to search the bags of Glenn Stewart, an American diplomat en route to his post in Vienna. They claimed that Ambassador Walter Hines

Page have given the British permission to search diplomatic baggage, even though this was highly irregular. Stewart refused and supposedly produced a pistol. "If you touch my trunk I shall be obliged to shoot you," Mencken recorded, who was an eyewitness to the confrontation (albeit a rather biased one). The British backed down and sent an admiral to apologize the next day.[19]

It took seventeen days for the *Oscar II* to reach Copenhagen. Once the ship docked, Mencken made his way to Berlin, the German capital. While in Europe, Mencken was to mail his stories to his employer, the *Baltimore Sun*, but the British blockade and their censorship prevented most of his stories from reaching the U.S. He would not be able to file the articles until he reached Cuba in early March on his return journey.

The Imperial German government gave Mencken permission for a press trip to the Eastern Front, where the Germans were pushing the Russians back into what is now Lithuania. It was the dead of winter and unimaginably cold. He returned to Berlin the night before the Germans announced the resumption of unrestricted submarine warfare, and he was there when President Wilson severed diplomatic relations on February 3. For a time he and the other journalists believed they would be arrested, especially after Reuters reported that the U.S. had seized German ships interned in American harbors.[20] Mencken applied to the Foreign Office to allow him to depart with Ambassador James Gerard, and while waiting visited the opera. "No sandwiches between the acts. Not even beer," Mencken complained in his diary. Food shortages were rampant in Germany, with the public often limited to just potatoes and turnips.[21]

The journalists were eventually allowed to travel, which was fortunate: they may well have spent the rest of the war at a German camp. Mencken was luckier than he probably realized. He departed Berlin with Ambassador Gerard. They journeyed to Switzerland, then to Paris together, though neither liked the other (Mencken described the ambassador as "a blatant and very offensive ass").[22] From there, Mencken shivered in unheated trains as he made his way to Spain, then found a ship in La Coruña that would take him to Cuba. It was the first time he was able to make contact with his employer, the *Baltimore Sun*, in over a month.[23]

Mencken landed in Cuba just in time to witness yet another coup on the unstable island. While there he filed his stories from Europe in the form of a travel diary. The *Sun* printed most of Mencken's diary in installments in March, but after war was declared on April 6, the paper stopped publishing Mencken's articles on account of his pro-German views. The *Sun's* editors had been sympathetic to the Allies long before the U.S. entered the war, a position at odds with Mencken's stance.

"When I returned in March, 1917, free speech was completely suspended, and for two years I was pretty well hobbled," Mencken wrote.[24] He published an article profiling Erich Ludendorff, the German quartermaster general who was quietly leading the war effort, in the *Atlantic Monthly* in June. Though Mencken outlined the general's military career and bureaucratic skill, the journalist did not get to meet Ludendorff and acknowledged, "He remains, after nearly three years of war, a man of mystery."[25] Yet it certainly provided American readers with a sense of what they were up against: a military junta that had marshaled every aspect of the German economy to win the war.

Silenced by the *Baltimore Sun* for the foreseeable future, Mencken wrote briefly for the pro-German *New York Evening Mail*, until the owner was indicted for allegedly using German funds to finance his newspaper. Mencken would not return to the *Baltimore Sun* until 1920 when war fever had subsided, and then resumed his irascible writings with a vengeance.

The Zimmermann Telegram

For two and a half years, President Wilson had fought to keep the United States out of the Great War. Germany's resumption of unrestricted submarine warfare was a hostile act that could serve as a cause for war, but Wilson remained reluctant. He continued to seek a way out of the imbroglio. As long as the Germans committed no "overt act," the U.S. would remain with armed neutrality. The Germans immediately stepped over the line.

The overt act came from a bureaucrat, Arthur Zimmermann. A recent appointee as foreign secretary, Zimmermann was pliable to the German war party. He rubber-stamped their efforts for unrestricted submarine warfare and proposed an idea of his own to tie down the U.S. while Germany knocked England out of the war.

On January 19, Zimmermann sent a coded message to Ambassador Bernstorff. He was instructed to forward it to the German ambassador in Mexico City, who was in turn to deliver the telegram to the Mexican government. With the resumption of unrestricted submarine warfare, Germany hoped that the United States would remain neutral, but in the event that war broke out, Zimmermann proposed an alliance with Mexico and Japan to prevent American forces from reinforcing the Allies. The telegram promised: "That we shall make war together and together make peace. We shall give general financial support and it is understood that Mexico is to reconquer the lost territory in New Mexico, Texas and Arizona." It was to be a defensive arrangement—but the U.S. had to make the first move by declaring war. [26]

German diplomats hoped that Mexican President Venustiano Carranza would attack the United States on a much larger scale than Pancho Villa's raid on Columbus in March 1916. Luckily the U.S. had pulled out of Mexico in February 1917. Pancho Villa was still at large, but Wilson had far larger issues to deal with than the Mexican bandit, especially once the president received a copy of the coded telegram.

How the so-called Zimmermann Telegram ended up on President Wilson's desk was one of the great intelligence coups of the 20th century, and it altered the course of the Great War. The Germans had no direct communications link to the Americas once the British cut the transatlantic cables in 1914, so they worked out an arrangement with the U.S. State Department to relay messages to the German embassy in Washington. The German Foreign Office sent two telegrams, both encoded into the same message, via the American embassy in Berlin. The embassy relayed it to the American embassy in Copenhagen, which in turn relayed it to London. The London embassy then forwarded it to the U.S. State Department, which printed the telegram—still encoded—and handed it to Ambassador Bernstorff.

Bernstorff's staff forwarded it to the German embassy in Mexico City via Western Union.[27]

The problem was that not only were the British tracking every German telegram, as they had broken the German ciphers, but that they were listening in on American diplomatic communications, which were easily decipherable. Thus they were able to decode the Zimmerman Telegram soon after it was transmitted. Admiral William Hall, the head of the British naval intelligence unit known as Room 40, knew immediately that this document could bring the U.S. into the war, but he had to protect the fact that his men had deciphered it in London, otherwise the Americans would know their communications were compromised. Hall arranged to intercept the German message sent to Mexico City through Western Union, one that used an older code, and used this second copy to cover his tracks.[28]

British intelligence was hoping that the resumption of unrestricted submarine warfare would draw the Americans into the war on the Allies' side. Instead, President Wilson held fast to armed neutrality. After several weeks, Hall played his trump card. He delivered a copy of the Zimmermann Telegram to the U.S. Embassy in London with the cover story that it had been retrieved in Mexico. The American ambassador, Walter Hines Page, forwarded the message to Wilson on February 24, who read it the next day. The president was stunned.[29]

Admiral Hall understood that Ambassador Bernstorff might have some influence in Berlin over the peace effort, and so arranged to have his Europe-bound ship, the SS *Frederik VIII*, delayed in Halifax for twelve days while the Zimmermann Telegram played out in the States. Bernstorff arrived in Germany too late, and only to find that he had been unfairly scapegoated for leaking the telegram.[30]

After spending several days authenticating the telegram, the Wilson administration released it to the Associated Press, which published it on March 1. It made the front page of newspapers around the country. The Senate engaged in a fierce debate that day. Isolationists like Robert La Follette and William Stone wanted to know the source of the telegram, correctly sensing that the British were trying to manipulate the U.S. into entering the war, while interventionists like Henry Cabot

Lodge saw the note as a provocation. President Wilson refused to tell Congress where he got the telegram, only vouching that it was genuine.

On March 3, Zimmermann confirmed that the telegram was true. He could have denied the telegram, or the German high command might have condemned the message as not reflecting the Kaiser's thinking, but instead the foreign secretary publicly admitted that he had sent it. Secretary of State Robert Lansing breathed a sigh of relief: if the Germans had denounced the telegram as a fraud, he would have had to provide evidence of where the U.S. got it and how they had deciphered it. [31]

For Mexico, the idea of making war against the United States was a nonstarter. It was still fighting a civil war and was in no shape to wage a military campaign against a much stronger neighbor. Germany had no ability to deliver the southwest United States to Mexico. It was an empty promise. The Carranza administration, seeking to remain friendly with the U.S., denied any role in the telegram, only that it was the recipient of the message and had no intention of acting on it. As Treasury Secretary William McAdoo wrote, "The German note eventually reached the Mexican wastebasket." [32]

The Zimmermann Telegram caused a significant shift in American public opinion. People who had been neutral began calling for war. The telegram largely united the country to the threat Germany posed. The Germans made no apology, nor did they back off from unrestricted submarine warfare. More ships were being sent to the bottom of the Atlantic than ever before, and more Americans were being killed. On March 18, three American merchant marine vessels were torpedoed with high loss of life. German aggression made it nearly inevitable that there would be war with the United States. President Wilson certainly recognized the telegram as an "overt act" and began planning accordingly. The telegram proved a fatal miscalculation for Germany.

Among the swirl of debate and outrage over the Zimmermann Telegram, Wilson was quietly sworn in for his second term on March 4, just minutes after Congress adjourned. It being a Sunday, there were no major festivities: the oath was done quickly with little ceremony. The next day would be the more formal public inaugural celebration.

Wilson and his new wife Edith rode in a car to the U.S. Capitol. Security was tighter than any inauguration since the Civil War: special detectives lined Pennsylvania Avenue and soldiers manned machine gun positions along the route. The day was sunny but cold with a gusty west wind, and the president at times held onto his top hat to keep it from blowing away. Some 40,000 people waited outside the Capitol to cheer Wilson and watch the parade—a relatively small crowd. But this was a second inauguration, and the American people already knew their man. [33]

Wilson's second inaugural address made no reference to the Zimmermann Telegram or to the submarine provocation, but clearly the World War was on everyone's mind. He gave a hint to the struggle ahead: "We may even be drawn on, by circumstances, not by our own purpose or desire, to a more active assertion of our rights as we see them and a more immediate association with the great struggle itself." The president began preparing the country not just for armed neutrality, but for the possibility of war. "We are provincials no longer. The tragic events of the thirty months of vital turmoil through which we have just passed have made us citizens of the world. There can be no turning back. Our own fortunes as a nation are involved whether we would have it so or not." [34]

After the Zimmermann Telegram was published, the House of Representatives quickly passed the Armed Ship Bill allowing merchant ships to protect themselves against U-boats. However, isolationist Senator Robert La Follette of Wisconsin (a state with a large German population) led a filibuster to prevent the bill from advancing until the Congressional session expired on March 4. President Wilson denounced these senators in no uncertain terms, calling them "a little group of willful men, representing no opinion but their own." [35] With Congress adjourned and public opinion on his side, Wilson issued an executive order on March 12 to arm the merchant ships. This was an unusual action, as foreign ports of call are reluctant to allow armed vessels to dock. Merchantmen could now engage in an undeclared war against U-boats to protect themselves. More importantly, American ships would now travel in convoys with naval escorts. [36]

Between the publication of the Zimmermann Telegram and the war declaration were five tense weeks. The toll of sunk American ships rose. On March 12, the *Algonquin* became the first American vessel to be sunk without warning under Germany's unrestricted rules of engagement. On March 16 it was the SS *Vigilancia*'s turn, followed by the SS *City of Memphis* on the 17th, and the oiler *Illinois* on the 18th, all torpedoed without warning. The oil tanker SS *Healdton* went down on March 21 under uncertain circumstances. On April 1, the armed steamer SS *Aztec* was sunk, the first such loss since Wilson had authorized merchantmen to arm themselves. There was mounting public pressure on the president to act.

Many factors led to Wilson's decision to seek a war declaration, not just the Zimmermann Telegram, but also the increasing number of American ships that were being sunk and the rising death toll. The Germans were challenging the very basis for the freedom of the seas. But the president, who had literally done everything to keep the country out of the war, had run out of options. War stared him in the face as the only answer.

The Anti-German Hysteria

The United States had a German problem. By the U.S. census undertaken in 1910, the country had ninety-two million people. Of these, 2.5 million were born in Germany. The second generation of German-Americans was nearly 5.8 million people. All told, there were eight million German-Americans in the country, making them the largest ethnic group. There were major centers of German culture and population: Cincinnati, Milwaukee, and St. Louis were the best known, but also in Baltimore, Chicago, New York, Pittsburgh, and countless small communities. The risk of war with Germany was rising by early 1917, but no one knew how German-Americans would respond.[37]

The great wave of German immigrants had come to the U.S. in the 1840s and 1850s after a failed political revolution, concurrent with the potato blight in Ireland that sent millions of impoverished Irish to

American shores. The Germans fought for the Union in the Civil War and were model citizens. Another major wave of Germans came in the 1880s, largely farmers who were squeezed out by modernized farming. The Germans were festive, fond of carousing and culture, dancing and drinking in beer gardens—even on Sundays, much to the offense of Sabbatarians. Count von Bernstorff, the German ambassador, recognized that Americans were fond of stereotyping the German-American as a "Beer-Philistine, whom they disdainfully called a 'Dutchman.'"[38]

With the great wave of 19th-century immigration also came the idea of dual ethnic identity: people who were both English *and* American, German *and* American, or Irish *and* American. They were pejoratively called "hyphenates." Hyphenates came under fierce criticism during the Great War for perceived disloyalty to the United States, their fiercest critic being Theodore Roosevelt. "I do not believe in hyphenated Americans," Roosevelt denounced in a letter. "I do not believe in German-Americans or Irish-Americans; and I believe just as little in English-Americans."[39] Neither German-Americans nor Irish-Americans had a fondness for Great Britain, and so when the war broke out, many of them sided with the Central Powers. Identity politics was at the core of the American divide over the war.

The Germans were criticized—as virtually every immigrant community has been—for not assimilating fast enough into American society. There were so many Germans that they could remain in German-speaking pockets for longer than other immigrant groups could hold out. By the time of the Great War, most German-Americans were second generation and the process of assimilation was well underway.[40] People like H. L. Mencken maintained pride in their heritage (sometimes in the guise of chauvinism), even as they saw themselves as being fully American. Mencken wrote, "The fact is that my 'loyalty' to Germany, as a state or a nation, is absolutely nil."[41]

German-Americans had insisted that the U.S. remain neutral in the war, even to the point of not selling munitions or providing financing to the Allies. But their loyalty was called into question once the Germans resumed unrestricted submarine warfare in February 1917. When the U.S. severed diplomatic relations with Germany, National Guard units were called up to protect vital facilities, factories, and plants against German saboteurs. Troops now guarded the ninety-one German ships interned in American harbors.

The publication of the Zimmermann Telegram on March 1 left the German-American community reeling in disbelief that the telegram was real. Once Foreign Secretary Zimmermann acknowledged that he had in fact sent the message, German-Americans hastened to distance themselves from it. Bernard Ritter, the publisher of the *Staats-Zeitung*, issued a statement: "Viewed from any angle, Dr. Zimmermann's instructions to the German Minister in Mexico constitute a mistake so grave that it renders the situation almost hopeless." George Sylvester Viereck, who published *Viereck's The American Weekly* (formerly the *Fatherland*, but still an arm of German propaganda), cast his suspicion on the British while denouncing former president Theodore Roosevelt for warmongering, and defended the German Foreign Office for making a sound defensive strategy should the United States enter the war. That said, he acknowledged that the two countries would likely part ways, and German-Americans knew where they stood: "We are Americans before we are pro-Germans."[42]

A wave of anti-German hysteria swept over the country after the Zimmermann Telegram was released to the public. Every German-American was now viewed with suspicion; any one of them could be a traitor, a saboteur, a seditionist, or a spy. There was the terrifying prospect of a homegrown German army rising up to sabotage American industries, and people feared another incident like the catastrophic Black Tom explosion the summer before. Soon German-Americans would be branded as Huns—or the *Boche*, as the French called them.

Earlier in the war, German Foreign Secretary Gottlieb von Jagow had supposedly made a threat to the American ambassador, James Gerard, as Josephus Daniels recorded in his diary: "If there is war between Germany and the U.S., you will find there are 500,000 German reservists ready to take up arms for [the] mother country and you will have civil war." Gerard responded, "I do not know whether there are 500,000 or not. But we have 500,001 lampposts and every man who takes up arms against his country will swing from a lamppost." As the likelihood of war approached, many feared that this German shadow army actually existed. [43]

Taking a break from the White House during the crisis, President Wilson and his wife Edith sailed down the Potomac River aboard the presidential yacht *Mayflower* and into the Chesapeake Bay. They visited Tangier Island, a small island populated by a little fishing village. The Wilsons rowed ashore, only to find the town seemingly deserted. They finally found a man, who confessed that they thought they were a party of "Germans coming to blow up the island." The townsfolk swarmed out of their homes, once they realized it was the president rather than the Germans, and everyone wanted to shake hands with Wilson. [44]

The Department of Justice fielded a Bureau of Investigation (the predecessor to the FBI), but it was a small unit and unprepared for the great task ahead. With tacit approval of the president's cabinet, Attorney General Thomas Gregory organized 250,000 volunteer spies to keep an eye on German-Americans and dissenters in March 1917, through an organization known as the American Protective League. They were given badges and ranks. The APL thrived on conspiracy, leaked innuendo, and contributed greatly to the hysteria. Its actions had the whiff of vigilantism. As the war progressed, the APL would turn from rooting out German spies to intimidating and stifling American dissidents to hunting down draft dodgers.

German-Americans quickly found themselves marginalized and under suspicion. Many popular food items were renamed to remove their German association. Frankfurters became hot dogs. Sauerkraut became liberty cabbage. Kaiser rolls became liberty buns. Countless streets with German names were renamed, and even towns were Anglicized. The Germania Life Insurance Company changed its name to the Guardian Life Insurance Company. Orchestras were forbidden from playing music composed by German artists like Beethoven. Schools banished German from being taught. In 1917, there were 522 German-language journals and newspapers being published in the United States; many of these publications folded, under pressure to conform to English. By the end of the war, only twenty-six German-language dailies were still being published. [45]

H. L. Mencken wrote a friend, "The other day the German Hospital in New York was raided by armed police on the ground that some one was signaling Zeppelins from the roof. It turned out that a couple of Low Dutch orderlies were cleaning brass spittoons."[46] In Washington, D.C., a fifteen-year-old boy named Daniel Roper tore down and helped destroy a portrait of Kaiser Wilhelm that his German teacher, Miss Siebert, had hung in the classroom. The teacher dismissed the defacement as "an act of a child." But many people viewed the Kaiser as the enemy now and applauded the vandalism. A year later, a crowd at Baraboo High School in Wisconsin burned a pile of German books.[47]

Even the popular habit of sipping suds in German beer gardens was frowned upon as unpatriotic. Christian Heurich ran the largest brewery in the nation's capital and witnessed a sharp downturn to his business. As the country debated going into war, he was put in a difficult position, as German-born citizens like him were immediately suspected of disloyalty. An article in the *New York Times* claimed he had nefarious, even murderous motives. "Reports from Washington, amply confirmed, assert that a native-born German has caused foundations for German cannon to be laid on his farm, so placed that they can destroy the Capitol. Questioned on the matter he makes the excuse that he is installing a fish hatchery." Heurich's farm was in Maryland a few miles east of Washington.[48]

The *Times*, the country's newspaper of record, had engaged in rumormongering, likely planted by the APL. The concrete foundations that the reporter "amply confirmed" as an artillery battery was actually the family vault that Heurich was building. And it defied logic that somehow the Germans, without an army, would erect an artillery battery to shell the city, but there was a fear that German-Americans would serve as a fifth column in the country.

Heurich fell victim to a rumor that had plagued the country since the war broke out—that German-Americans were planning attacks on the nation's cities. In November 1914, Edward House recorded a conversation with President Wilson: "He told me there was reason to suspect that the Germans had laid throughout the country foundations for great guns, similar to those they laid in Belgium and France." Wilson ordered General Leonard Wood, who may have been the source for the rumor, to investigate discretely. This was twenty-eight months before Heurich was accused of supporting an artillery attack on the capital. It was an unfounded fear, yet clearly one that circulated over the years and reached its peak in March 1917.[49]

Heurich wrote disdainfully of the damage done to his reputation. "It was also reported that a wireless station had been established to transmit important news to the enemy," he wrote. "After the public got tired of hearing and reading about such crimes, the report circulated that I had committed suicide. This ended the entire affair."[50] His wife Amelia noted the suicide article in her diary on March 23. Heurich did not end his life—in fact, he would live until 1945, just shy of his 103rd birthday.[51]

On March 14, a Department of Justice agent came to Heurich's Dupont Circle mansion to interview him and Amelia, then told them he would have to search their home. After finding nothing suspicious, he notified them that he would inspect the brewery and the family farm in Maryland, where the foundations for the German artillery battery were supposedly under construction.[52] The family accompanied the federal agent to the farm two days later. "I think he will feel ashamed of himself!" Amelia penned in her diary, knowing that the family had done nothing wrong.[53]

Amelia Heurich, who was twenty-seven years younger than her husband, was born in Richmond, Virginia and was the granddaughter of German immigrants. "The people's minds seemed to be diseased. They do not seem to have any regard for the Truth," she recorded on March 19.[54] "All these things were and are brought out by the English," she penned ten days later. German-Americans like Amelia often believed that England was the source of the propaganda in the hope that the United States would enter the war on her side—an intuition that was in fact true. "They say when a man or country is down then they resort to almost anything in order to gain assistance," she noted.[55]

On April 3, a federal agent inspected the Heurich brewery again. It was coincidentally the same day that the Senate voted on the war resolution. German-Americans such as Heurich were in a difficult position. "Germany was and is my mother, and I was against the war," Heurich wrote. "But America is my bride, and if I have to choose between the two, then I must leave my mother and go with my bride. My whole existence is with my bride, America."[56] Heurich's statement was not original; many German-Americans used it, most famously Carl Schurz, the highly influential early immigrant, Civil War veteran, and U.S. Senator who had remarked, "Germania is our mother, and Columbia is our bride."[57]

As the country teetered on war, prominent German-Americans felt compelled to issue statements that they were loyal to the United States. In Washington, D.C., Germans working in the hospitality industry issued a statement that they stood behind the president in the pending crisis. Christian Heurich, still piqued at his rough treatment in the press and by federal agents, stated that the firebrand rumors of his disloyalty were "beneath his notice."[58]

Newspaper magnate William Randolph Hearst was outspoken in his desire to keep the U.S. out of the war, and so pro-German in his editorials that the Bureau of Investigation scrutinized him for possible treason. Investigators never charged him with a crime;[59] however, New York City mayor John Purroy Mitchel publicly called Hearst the "spokesman of the Kaiser in this country."[60] As the nation teetered toward war, Hearst slightly changed his tack, ordering his editors to "print nothing but pro-American editorials" to downplay his German sympathy. Hearst became intensely unpopular during the war for his criticism of the Allies, but his reputation would recover.[61]

The *Morning Olympian* recognized that war was likely at hand, but counseled caution at blaming German-Americans. "Americans must not forget that this nation with the German people or with the loyal, patriotic American citizens of German extraction . . . The German people are not responsible for the Kaiser and his dupes."[62]

German-Americans largely closed ranks behind their adopted home country. They registered for the draft, and many young men served in the armed forces and fought in the trenches against the Kaiser's army—or in the skies, like Eddie Rickenbacker. But March 1917 only marked the beginning of the anti-German hysteria, which would marginalize and even terrorize German-Americans throughout the war.

The War Declaration

Although the United States had been involved in many wars, Congress had only explicitly declared war on three occasions before 1917: against England in 1812, against Mexico in 1846, and against Spain in 1898. The president can argue in support of war, but only Congress can declare war.

After revealing the Zimmermann Telegram to the nation on March 1, President Wilson spent several weeks agonizing over the proper course of action—and if the United States was justified in going to war. He came down with a terrible cold on March 7, one that he likely caught at the inauguration two days earlier. Wilson remained relatively secluded in the White House for ten days while he nursed himself back to health. It gave him time to think and plan.

Wilson had understood that the country was not ready for war in the previous two years, and it was not much better prepared now. He could have declared war in 1915 after the sinking of the *Lusitania*, but there was little credible force to defend the country, and the president well knew of serious societal divisions about getting involved in the conflict. He could lead, but the people could only move so fast.

The decision for war was never forced on Wilson. It was something he had pondered greatly for long periods of time, even years. The entry of the U.S. into the Great War would be a contentious issue, not a decision reached easily or lightly. Wilson knew there were many dissenters.

If the U.S. entered the war on the side of the Allies, it expected to champion democracy and fight Prussianism. One major obstacle was that not all of the Allies were democracies: Russia was ruled by an autocrat, Czar Nicholas II, who did not tolerate dissent. That obstacle was supposedly swept away on March 19 when the czar was overthrown. Wilson wrongly believed that Russia was on the road to liberalism. In fact, Russia's experiment in democracy would be short-lived. Nonetheless, the overthrow of the czar made it more palatable to join the Allies.

On March 20, Wilson summoned the cabinet to debate the war question. He posed a number of questions to his cabinet secretaries, and a freewheeling debate followed with Wilson listening to their counsel without expressing his own opinion. He finally asked if the cabinet supported declaring war on Germany. All were in favor except the two doves, Postmaster General Albert Burleson and Secretary of the Navy Josephus Daniels. Burleson stated that he believed the two countries were already in a state of war, but if Congress did not declare it, the people might force the declaration. The president responded, "I do not care for popular demand. I want to do right, whether popular or not."[63]

Daniels then spoke up. ("I had hoped and prayed this cup would pass," he wrote in his diary that day.) He believed that arming and convoying merchant ships was inadequate and would be dependent on the Royal Navy protecting them, pushing the Americans ever more into the Allied camp. If America wanted to protect its right to the sea, war would be the only option. The consequence of the Allies losing the war could be dire. "If Germany wins, we must be a military nation," putting the Americans in a permanent state of military preparedness and setting the stage for future conflicts. Daniels reluctantly favored war. With this, the cabinet recommendation was unanimous: the U.S. should declare war on Germany, and the president should summon Congress for a special session to deal with the question.[64] Wilson ended the meeting with the remark, "I think that there is no doubt as to what your advice is." The president left the meeting sullen, knowing the decision he had to make.[65]

The next day, Wilson called Congress into special session, summoning it to convene on April 2. The president's chief political adviser, Edward House, knew Wilson's mind better than almost anyone. "As far as we are concerned, we are in the war now, even though a formal declaration may not occur until after Congress meets," he wrote Ambassador Walter Hines Page on March 21.[66]

Wilson asked House to come to Washington to discuss the situation. They met on March 27. "The President asked whether I thought he should ask Congress to declare war, or whether he should say that a state of war exists and ask them for a necessary means to carry it on," House wrote in his diary. He suggested the latter, and in fact this is what Wilson would do. House then tactfully spoke his mind, pointing out that Wilson was not cut from the cloth to be a wartime president, an assessment that Wilson shared. "I thought he was too refined, too civilized, too intellectual, too cultivated not to see the incongruity and absurdity of war," House wrote. "It needs a man of coarser fibre and one less a philosopher than the President, to conduct a brutal, vigorous, and successful war."[67]

The president met with the cabinet on March 30 to present ideas for his upcoming war address. Josephus Daniels recorded in his diary that, "He wished no argument and no feeling in his message, but wishes to present facts, convincing from evidence, justifying position." Wilson had heard absurd stories whipped up in the press about the Germans. "There's a German in the cellar!" complained a housekeeper in the White House about a German who tended fires, as if that were grounds to dismiss him. Wilson's response showed his reluctance to panic, as well as a fundamental assumption that people were good: "I'd rather the blamed place should be blown up than to persecute inoffensive people."[68]

On April 1, Edward House visited Wilson in the White House. The president read a draft of his war address to House, seeking advice on phrasing and wording. House later asked Wilson how long it took him to draft the war address. Ten hours, the president responded. "I write with difficulty and it takes everything out of me," he said.[69]

Wilson also asked Frank Cobb from the liberal *New York World* to visit. Cobb was a staunch supporter of the president's administration (some called Cobb "Mr. Wilson's Organ"). Cobb got the message late and did not arrive at the White House until after 1:00 A.M. on April 2. Wilson looked exhausted, having hardly slept the past several days. He pointed to his typewriter and the sheets of paper that were his war declaration speech. He clearly was searching for a way out. "What else can I do?" the president asked. "Is there anything else I can do?"

"I told him his hand had been forced by Germany, that so far as I could see we couldn't keep out," Cobb recalled.

Wilson went on a harangue. The war would transform America from a neutral, pacifist country into something else. "It would mean that we should lose our heads along with the rest and stop weighing right and wrong," he said. "It would mean that a majority of people in this hemisphere would go war-mad, quit thinking and devote their energies to destruction." He lamented that, "There won't be any peace standards left to work with. There will be only war standards." The president feared this would be the end of tolerance, the onset of an age of brutality, and the end of the Constitution. "If there is any alternative, for God's sake, let's take it," Wilson said.[70]

It rained the evening of April 2 in the nation's capital. The Capitol dome was lit up against the dark sky. About a thousand pacifists protested on the Capitol grounds, but police and soldiers guarding the building kept them at bay. The Emergency Peace Federation had planned a parade to protest the war vote, promising to bring trainloads of pacifists to lobby Congress. An opposing group of war supporters vowed a "pilgrimage of patriotism" to support the war vote. Washington police banned both parades on the grounds of public disorder.[71]

Pacifists staged protests at senatorial offices. A Swiss-born former baseball player, Alexander Bannwart, confronted slight, sixty-six-year-old Senator Henry Cabot Lodge. "Anyone who wants to go to war is a coward," Bannwart shouted at the senator, who got so angry that he punched the protestor in the face. Bannwart swung back at Lodge before being arrested. The man was released after apologizing.[72]

Inside the Capitol building, the House of Representatives hosted the joint session of Congress. The chamber was filled to capacity with congressmen, senators, Supreme Court justices, cabinet secretaries, and diplomats, while the galleries were packed with observers. Most congressmen and senators carried small American flags or wore them in their lapels. It was a solemn occasion, and a quiet hush ruled over the chamber as the assembly awaited the president.

The presidential motorcade arrived from the White House. At 8:32 P.M., President Wilson was announced in the House of Representatives. The chamber erupted in thunderous cheering as everyone jumped to their feet, and even the Supreme Court justices stood. Wilson made his way through the boisterous crowd and stepped up to the podium. He pulled out his carefully typewritten sheets of paper and began his war address, the most important speech he would deliver in his career. The room fell into a hushed silence as the audience collectively held its breath.

The president began by denouncing German actions since February 1, calling the submarine campaign "warfare against mankind." It was indiscriminate, sinking neutral as well as British ships, even hospital ships and vessels bound for Belgian relief. Wilson called not for revenge, "but only the vindication of right, or human right, of which we are only a single champion." He criticized the armed neutrality of the past two months—something that he had promoted—as being ineffective.

The chamber remained quiet for several minutes as Wilson spoke calmly, reading from his speech. However, when president spoke the words, "There is one choice we cannot make, we are incapable of making: We will not choose the path of submission," Supreme Court Chief Justice Edward White raised his arms and began clapping, which in turn led to a booming, defiant cheer throughout the chamber. Congress would repeatedly interrupt the speech with sustained applause on numerous points.

Wilson then called for Congress to accept that Germany had behaved as a belligerent, and thus it was America's duty to declare war. The president noted that the country would have to engage in a serious military buildup, and it would be an enormous national effort. Even so, he cautioned against blaming the German people—and tangentially, German-Americans. "We have no quarrel with the German people," he declared. "We have no feeling toward them but one of sympathy and friendship." Rather, it was the military junta that ran the German war effort that was Wilson's target, the autocratic government that was not accountable to its people, and that conspired to turn Mexico against the United States. And then he arrived at the most famous phrase from the speech, perhaps Wilson's most famous line of his presidency: "The world must be made safe for democracy." It was not an evangelical call to extend democracy to every country, as it has often been interpreted, but rather a call to defend democratic countries from autocratic ones, and to allow people to choose self-governance. He added an assertion that would place the U.S. squarely at odds with its soon-to-be allies: "We desire no conquest, no dominion. We seek no indemnities for ourselves, no material compensation for the sacrifices we shall freely make."

Wilson had already extended a fig leaf to the German people. Now he addressed the question of German-Americans, whom he knew had undoubtedly been under a great trial for the past month. "They are, most of them, as true and loyal Americans as if they had never known any other fealty or allegiance." But he threatened, "If there should be disloyalty, it will be dealt with a firm hand of stern repression" As it turned out, it would not be the German-Americans who would face the worst repression, but rather the most outspoken domestic opponents of the war: the pacifists and the socialists.

Wilson concluded the war address by acknowledging the terrible truth about the war that the United States was about to join. "It is a fearful thing to lead this great peaceful people into war, into the most terrible and disastrous of all wars, civilization itself seeming to be in the balance," he said. "But the right is more precious than peace." In calling the nation to arms, Wilson's ambitious and far-reaching speech foretold American intervention as a catalyst for global peace—a fair peace that would be one once militarism had been defeated and the rule of law restored.

Wilson brought his speech to a close, summoning the sacred duty of the American people. "To such a task we can dedicate ourselves and our fortunes, every thing that we are and everything that we have, with the pride of those who know that the day has come when America is privileged to spend her blood and her might for the principles that gave her birth and happiness and the peace which she has treasured. God helping her, she can do no other." The president concluded his thirty-six-minute address. [73]

A long silence overtook the room as the words sunk in, followed by a thunderous applause as the members of Congress and people in the galleries rose to their feet. The president made his way to the chamber exit through the phalanx of cheering congressmen and senators, who waved their miniature flags. One exception was Senator Robert La Follette, the shock-topped isolationist, who stood hostilely with his arms crossed, "chewing gum with a sardonic smile," the *New York Times* observed.[74]

After the speech, Wilson returned to the White House. He was silent for a long time, lost in thought about the consequences of war. He finally remarked to Joe Tumulty, "My message to-day was a message of death for our young men. How strange it seems to applaud that." The president put his head down on the table and wept.[75]

The War Address was Woodrow Wilson's finest speech, one that ranks with Abraham Lincoln's Gettysburg Address and Franklin Roosevelt's Infamy Speech. It summoned the nation to war and provided a moral direction to the cause. For a brief moment, the country was nearly unified. The United States was ready to follow Wilson into war. Even in the West, the region most far removed from the German submarine threat, echoed the president's idealism. "The President has resisted war until he could resist no longer," the *San Francisco Chronicle* opined. "There remains but one course for any loyal American to take, and that is to carve out a peace that will be lasting."[76]

The Senate took up the war resolution on April 4. It passed by a vote of 82 to 6. The debate was more heated in the House of Representatives, which debated the resolution for two more days. Pacifists attempted to amend or derail it. The House finally voted at 3:05 in the morning on April 6, passing the resolution by a vote of 373 to 50. Among the No votes was House Majority Leader Claude Kitchin and Representative Jeannette Rankin of Montana, the first woman to serve in Congress. (Rankin would be the only member of Congress to vote against the war declaration in World War II.) Two-thirds of the no votes were from the Midwest, home to anti-industrialists, farmers, and German-Americans. Wilson signed the resolution just after lunch. America was at war.[77]

FOUR

Mobilization

"At last the declaration of war was made. The solemn instruments which made legal the condition, were all signed, and then we found ourselves, as English-speaking people always do, wholly unprepared for the event."[1]

—Vice President Thomas Marshall

T he United States had taken steps to improve its military preparedness in 1916, but it was nowhere close to being ready to fight in the Great War. The country would have to make a colossal effort to build a fighting force that could take on the vaunted German army. President Wilson had his work cut out to put the nation's economy on a wartime footing. He had to mobilize the country for war. The federal government was small in size, and its role was still small. Federal power had to increase to fight this global conflict, power that would never be relinquished. America would never be a small-government society again.

The U.S. had not fought a major war in more than fifty years since the Civil War concluded in 1865. It had a small military. True, there had been conflicts such as the Indian Wars on the Great Plains, but these had involved no more than a few thousand soldiers. The country fought the lopsided Spanish-American War in 1898, a war that only lasted four months and left the U.S. with a global empire. John Hay famously congratulated Theodore Roosevelt for his part in a "splendid little war."

There was nothing splendid about the Great War—nor was it little. It was a horrendous war of attrition. A single battle would never decide the outcome. The combatant nations threw their entire industrial production into winning and drafted generations of young men who were pulverized in the muddy trenches with artillery shells, machine gun fire, and poison gas. Individual, personal gallantry amounted to little in the Great War. What counted in this war of attrition was firepower, industrial production, and the will to persevere.

Despite his own reservations, President Wilson proved an unexpectedly gifted wartime leader. He made the mission—stopping German militarism—into a righteous cause. He leveraged the American economy and the country's considerable manpower to face the enemy far more than anyone thought possible. That was the big picture. The small picture was clouded with infinite details, countless logistical problems, and the question of how to arm the force. Every waking hour of the president's time was now dedicated to the war effort, and Wilson often worked well past midnight on the constant flow of paper and decisions that had to be made. He told his wife Edith, "You see, everything that comes to me is a problem. Things that go right take care of themselves."[2]

With the war declaration, both the Allies and the Germans expected the U.S. to supply financing, ships, and supplies to the war effort. But soldiers? The Americans had little army to speak of. Wilson would make a bold move and propose sending a large field army to fight in Europe.

The U.S. had 103 million people in 1917 and could conceivably field a large army. The size of the Regular Army on April 1 stood at 121,797 soldiers and 5,791 officers. The standing army was small, its regiments broken up into small forts on the former frontier where the Indian wars had ended. The National Guard had 101,174 guardsmen under state control, while another 80,446 guardsmen had been activated for duty, largely because of the Mexican crisis. That totaled 309,288 soldiers, none of whom were ready for the European trenches. The challenge was to build up a sizable army, equip it with modern weapons, train it, ship it overseas, and put it into battle against the vaunted German army—and in less than a year. Even then it was only half-trained.[3]

The U.S. Navy was in better shape than the army, thanks to the efforts of naval secretary Josephus Daniels, who had beefed up ship-building during the Preparedness campaign. However, many of the ships under construction were heavily armed dreadnaughts, designed to challenge English and German primacy on the seas, when in fact the real threat came from submarines. "O for more destroyers! I wish we could trade the money in dreadnaughts for destroyers already built," Daniels lamented in his diary shortly after the war declaration. The Allies would ask the Americans to halt construction of battleships, which were of limited use, and instead build a fleet of nimble destroyers to escort convoys and fight the U-boat menace.[4]

The U.S. Navy continued its rapid expansion to a two-ocean fleet that operated in both the Atlantic and Pacific. The U.S. would no longer rely on British naval supremacy to protect its shores. To get the army safely across the Atlantic, ships would now travel in escorted convoys that assembled in harbors like New York. Many ships were painted in cubist dazzle camouflage designed to confuse U-boat commanders about a ship's size and speed. These measures significantly reduced losses from U-boats. By the end of the war, the U.S. Navy had mined a 240-mile stretch of the North Sea against U-boats, a pet project of Franklin Roosevelt's.[5]

H. L. Mencken had traveled to Germany in early 1917, shortly before the declaration of war, and witnessed how General Erich Ludendorff has commandeered Germany's industrial might. He wrote in the *Atlantic Monthly*: "The doctrine of Ludendorff is simple: the whole energy of the German people must be concentrated on the war," Mencken wrote. "All other enterprises and ambitions must be put out of mind. All business that is not necessary to the one end must be abandoned."[6] By summer 1917, German chancellor Theobald von Bethmann-Hollweg, who had objected to the renewal of unrestricted submarine warfare, was ousted from his position. He was replaced by the ineffective Georg Michaelis, a pliable Prussian who rubber-stamped Ludendorff's decisions. Mencken called Ludendorff "the real boss of the country."[7]

Although no military junta would lead the United States, the country would mobilize to a high extent, and even run roughshod over civil liberties as it pushed to win. One of the first actions Wilson took after signing the war declaration on April 6 was to order the ninety-one German ships interned in American and Philippine harbors seized. Treasury Department officials removed ship crews and placed heavy guard on the ships. They relocated the 1,100 officers and crewmembers in New York to Ellis Island before a more permanent solution could be found. There had been a fear that the Germans might try to blow up or scuttle their ships, but the crews offered no resistance (although they had sabotaged their engines). Only the enormous liner *Vaterland* was still operational. The engines were repaired and the German ships appropriated for the American war effort, many of them carrying thousands of soldiers to Europe and back.[8]

Shortly after the war declaration, a string of diplomatic missions from America's new allies visited the United States as a sign of goodwill and to discuss the war effort with the president. British Foreign Secretary Arthur Balfour asked for money and ships, while French Marshal Joseph Joffre asked for American ground forces to help steady his wavering country. Other delegations arrived from Italy, Japan, Russia, and Serbia. The meetings revealed the dour plight of the Allies.[9]

In his April visit to the U.S., Balfour met with Edward House. He discussed territorial realignments in Europe with an eventual peace. Alsace-Lorraine and Belgium would need to be removed from German control. Poland would need to be resurrected as a country, its territory coming from Germany and Russia. The Austro-Hungarian Empire would be split into at least three states. Bulgaria, Romania, and Serbia would each get lands. Balfour told House of the secret treaties that had enticed Italy and Romania into the war, and how the British, French, and Russians planned to carve up the Ottoman Empire and seize much of the land for themselves. "It is all bad and I told Balfour so," House wrote in his diary. "They are making it a breeding place for future war." Balfour sent copies of the secret treaties to President Wilson after going over them with House.[10]

Four days after the U.S. declared war on Germany, Theodore Roosevelt called on the White House to volunteer his services. He told President Wilson with much enthusiasm that he could quickly assemble a division of volunteers that he could lead into battle. It would be like the Rough Riders, only a far larger force. After Roosevelt left, Wilson remarked to Joe Tumulty, "Yes, he is a great big boy. I was, as formerly, charmed by his personality. There is a sweetness about him that is very compelling. You can't resist the man." But Roosevelt was no professional soldier, he was in bad health, overweight, diabetic, and partly blind, and he had little understanding of how much warfare had changed. Wilson declined his appointment, as well as that of Roosevelt's outspoken ally General Leonard Wood.[11]

Roosevelt sought an appointment through the War Department, but Secretary of War Newton Baker likewise objected. Roosevelt's popularity might siphon off too many good officers into his volunteer division, and these officers were urgently needed to train the large army that would be drafted. A well-trained professional army, not an army of ill-trained volunteers, would be needed for the coming combat mission.

Pershing Takes Command

On May 18, President Wilson signed the Selective Service Act, creating the first national draft since the Civil War, and announced that the country would send an army to Europe. He appointed Major General John Pershing to lead the army, which became known as the American Expeditionary Forces.[12] Born in 1860, Pershing had graduated from West Point in 1886. He had served as First Captain in the corps of cadets, a position later held by one of his corps commanders, Charles Summerall, and later by Douglas MacArthur, who led an infantry brigade in Europe. While in France, Pershing solemnly told MacArthur, "We old First Captains, Douglas, must never flinch."[13]

Known as "Black Jack" among his soldiers for serving in an African-American cavalry regiment, Pershing was tall and ramrod straight with a powerful square jaw and mustache. He looked every bit the general. Pershing was formal, disciplined, and valued appearances and precision. He was stone-faced and impersonal around his officers and men. That he was a general was a bit of a controversy: He was a favored officer for President Roosevelt, who promoted him to brigadier general from captain, skipping three ranks. Pershing was an observer to the Russo-Japanese War in 1905 and served as a military governor in the Philippines until 1913.

An unspeakable tragedy struck Pershing in 1915 while he was in Fort Bliss, Texas: he received a telegram informing him that his wife and three daughters were killed in a house fire in San Francisco's Presidio. Only his six-year old son Warren survived. The general buried himself in his work to distract himself from the devastating grief, and soon found himself leading the futile Punitive Expedition into Mexico to chase Pancho Villa.

The favored candidate to lead the AEF was General Frederick Funston; however, he died of a heart attack in February 1917. The Wilson administration needed to select a new commander who could not only lead a large force in combat, but also be politically adroit with the Allies. There were six major generals on active duty at the time, and Pershing was the junior-most. He was a Republican and politically well-connected, married to the daughter of Wyoming Senator Francis Warren. Pershing had vocally supported the president's call for conscription, and that certainly helped his career.

The other major candidate for the position of AEF commander was General Leonard Wood. Wood was a physician-turned-army general. He had won the Congressional Medal of Honor fighting against the Apache chief Geronimo and had led the Rough Riders during the Spanish-American War, with Theodore Roosevelt as his second-in-command. He was an outspoken, opinionated Republican with a forceful personality who had openly criticized the president. He was far too political for his own good. Wilson chose Pershing over Wood.

Likewise, Pershing did not want Wood in his command. Wood may have been eager to lead troops in Europe, but Pershing knew that Wood would likely grandstand and attempt to run his own show. Wood was too much of a politician promoting his own interests, and he carried a sense of entitlement that the AEF command should have gone to him. Assigning Wood a command in Europe would have posed certain trouble for Pershing, and President Wilson ensured that Wood spent the war in the states, though it cost him politically. Pershing sidestepped the question of Leonard Wood in his memoirs.[14]

Just as the Americans entered the war, the French army launched a spring campaign, the Nivelle Offensive, against the Germans. The French were seriously mauled, and thousands of soldiers mutinied. Though a new general, Philippe Pétain, took command, there was a genuine fear that France would collapse. President Wilson came under strong pressure to bring American troops into the fight before the Allies sued for peace. The Americans quickly readied a small force of 14,000 men to be the spear tip, untrained as it was. Pershing combined four infantry regiments and one artillery regiment into a combat division, later renamed the 1st Division. He sailed for Europe on May 28 aboard the British steamer *Baltic*, well ahead of the division that was still being organized, and just ten days after his promotion to army commander. Pershing and his staff, which included Captain George Patton, spent the voyage busily laying out the organization of the AEF and how it would operate in France.

Building the Armed Forces

The Wilson administration recognized that an all-volunteer army would not provide the numbers necessary to win the war. In a war of attrition, every able-bodied soldier counted. The United States would have to conscript an army from its large population of young men. The war simply could not be won without the draft.

Within weeks of the war declaration, the Selective Service Act passed the House of Representatives on April 29, but then stalled in the

Senate as Theodore Roosevelt's allies attempted to carve out a provision for the former president to raise and command up to four volunteer divisions. The compromise bill that President Wilson signed into law on May 18 gave him the choice whether to take up Roosevelt's offer. Wilson soundly rejected the option—this was not a time for amateurs. Secretary of War Newton Baker set about greatly expanding the army. Draft boards were created around the country, and the draft moved forward.

The Selective Service Act required American men aged twenty-one to thirty to register by June 5. That day, ten million men registered at more than 4,000 draft boards around the country. This represented nearly ten percent of the country's population. Once registered, men could apply for an exemption, such as a conscientious objector, family dependency (the most common form of exemption granted), medical, or for working in an industry vital to the military effort. The intention was to call up an initial tranche of 625,000 men, followed by successive waves. Altogether, about 4.7 million American men served in the military, and of these two million were sent to France. The American soldiers became known as "doughboys."[15]

Although Theodore Roosevelt was rejected for service, he ensured that all four of his sons served. He appealed to Pershing to allow two of his sons into his command, Archie and Theodore, Jr. Both served in the 1st Division. Kermit volunteered with the British army, then transferred to the American Expeditionary Forces once the U.S. declared war. Finally, the youngest, Quentin, volunteered to be an aviator. Sending four sons to war was a notable contribution, but it would also end tragically when one son was killed, and two others were terribly wounded.[16]

The U.S. Army was woefully unprepared for a modern war, lacking manpower, firepower, tanks, aircraft, and combat doctrine. It faced a steep learning curve—and it had to quickly train millions of men and get them into the fight. Thirty-two army camps were established around the country to train the new army, essentially one per army division. At 28,000 men, the typical American army division was twice the size of an Allied division, a decision made because of the shortage of qualified officers and NCOs. The division would train together for an average of six months, then be shipped to Europe, where it would be equipped with heavy weapons like artillery and undergo several more months of training with the Allies before seeing the front line. But first the officers had to be trained during the summer, and in September the first 687,000 draftees—a larger contingent than initially expected—reported to basic training camps.[17]

On September 4, a parade was organized in Washington, D.C. to honor the drafted soldiers who would soon go to fight Germany. Cabinet members and many congressmen volunteered to march with the soldiers. When Josephus Daniels asked Wilson, "Are you going to march in the parade?" the president responded with a twinkle and said, "I understand they wished good-looking men and so I agreed."[18]

Along with the basic training for drill, rifle shooting, bayonet fighting, throwing hand grenades, donning a gas mask, and infantry maneuvering, the army provided sex education for its budding army. Prostitution was still fairly common, especially among poor families, and soldiers on leave might seek sexual relief. The availability of sex for hire increased the risk of sexually transmitted diseases. A soldier infected might as well be a battlefield casualty. The federal government needed to keep its soldiers healthy. In 1918, Congress appropriated $2 million to create a Venereal Disease Division in the Public Health Service. Sex education largely focused on abstinence.[19]

One of the more novel infantry units created during the war, the 42nd Division, was composed of National Guardsmen from twenty-six states. It became known as the "Rainbow" Division. The idea came from Major Douglas MacArthur, who served on the army's General Staff. He proposed the idea to Newton Baker, suggesting that, "we take units from the different states so that a division would stretch over the whole country like a rainbow," MacArthur recalled. Baker promoted MacArthur to colonel and appointed him as the division's chief of staff. The Rainbow Division trained at Camp Mills on Long Island, New York, and sailed for Europe in October 1917.[20]

In the nation's capital, American University donated 650 acres of land that became Camp Leach. There the army conducted tests on chemical weapons. On August 3, 1918, a mishap at one of the labs released a mustard gas cloud that wafted over a nearby neighborhood. Former senator Nathan Scott lived just a few hundred feet away, and he, his wife, and sister-in-law were sitting on the porch when a green or yellow cloud swept toward the house, killing small animals in its path. They began to choke, their eyes ached, and the senator's face blistered. The family fled inside the house and called the camp, which sent over the post's surgeon, and later dropped off gas masks. "It is an outrage that a citizen cannot enjoy his home without being made to suffer like this," the senator complained to the *Washington Times*, noting that this was the second such incident at Camp Leach. The area later became a residential neighborhood known as Spring Valley, and its chemical weapons history forgotten until the 1990s, when a contractor uncovered a canister, which led to the discovery of many more buried artillery shells. This began the long process of clean up by the U.S. Army Corps of Engineers.[21]

For the first time in American history, the U.S. government provided term life insurance to soldiers while they were serving through the War Risk Insurance Act. The typical soldier was paid $33 per month during the war, and the insurance premium was $6.50 per month. It was a hefty premium, but it guaranteed a payout to families and survivors should the soldier be killed. Treasury Secretary McAdoo, whose department was responsible for the insurance, noted that more than ninety percent of soldiers signed up for the protection, which was voluntary.[22]

Soldiers were issued "dog tags" to wear around their necks. Most American casualties were thus identified. Starting in the Great War, American families began flying flags and banners on their homes with a blue star for each son who was serving in the armed forces. If a son was killed, a gold star replaced the blue star. Mothers of these sons became known as Gold Star Mothers.

Most but not all Americans accepted the draft—and some dissenters plotted against it. The Socialist Party openly opposed the draft, a stance that placed a bull's-eye on the organization. Shortly before the national draft began, anarchists Emma Goldman and Alexander

Berkman organized the No Conscription League. They published materials encouraging young men not to register. Federal authorities kept the two on their watch list, and on June 5—draft registration day—they arrested the two anarchists, charging them under the new Espionage Act. They were sentenced to two years in prison. It was the beginning of President Wilson's war against dissenters.

The day after the Americans declared war, a young author, painter and poet named E. E. Cummings volunteered for ambulance service in France, as did his friend from Harvard, John Dos Passos (some 348 Harvard graduates volunteered in this way).[23] Cummings came from a line of pacifists, and driving an ambulance meant not having to serve in the military—plus the term of service was only six months. In France, Cummings met a Columbia University student, William Slater Brown, who was likewise a pacifist. Neither of the young men liked the other Americans in their ambulance unit, who were uneducated, and they did not get along with their superior, who did not want them fraternizing with the French. Both young men did so anyway.

Brown and Cummings enjoyed gossiping with French soldiers. They learned about the spring 1917 mutiny after the failed Nivelle Offensive, an event the French did not want broadcast. Brown unwittingly wrote about the mutiny in a letter, which French censors caught. He and Cummings were arrested on September 21. Cummings faced no charges— his crime was his friendship with Brown, which landed them in a prison camp. He might have been released had he answered "yes" to the question a French tribunal asked him: *Est-ce que vous détestez les boches?* (Do you detest the Boche?—as the English and French referred to the Germans.) Cummings answered evasively that he only loved the French. A French minister responded, "It is impossible to love Frenchmen and not to hate Germans," and that sealed Cummings's fate. He was held for three months in a French detention camp while his father used every means, including intervening with the American ambassador and writing President Wilson, to secure his son's release. Cummings was finally returned to the United States in December, where he was drafted into the army, but the war ended before he returned to Europe.[24]

Every eligible man was required to register for the draft, including those who were conscientious objectors—that is, those who refused to bear arms. The military usually provided means for COs to serve in noncombat roles. Many COs were from religious traditions that taught pacifism, such as the Amish, Mennonites, or Quakers. One peculiar conscientious objector was Ernest Meyer, the son of German immigrants who enrolled at the University of Wisconsin in 1915. Meyer was an atheist, so had no religious objection to war, but he was a humanist who saw the U.S.'s role as helping secure the peace, rather than engaging in combat. He wrote, "I, as a free-man, deliberately chose the other course, believing that a million men in each nation could achieve more toward peace with folded arms than with all the world's guns and gas."[25]

While Meyer attended college, a German professor uttered a joke in private to a colleague, who reported him to authorities. The professor was branded a spy and fired. Meyer penned an editorial defending him, which in turn got Meyer blacklisted. The dean of the faculty demanded that he sign a loyalty pledge. The young man resigned from the college magazine instead. Meyer was eligible for the draft, and he registered as required, but he never filled out the questionnaire. This eventually drew attention, and he was put on trial at college and expelled.

Meyer was conscripted into the U.S. Army in July 1918 and sent to Camp Taylor, Kentucky—but once there, he refused to put on the uniform. "Everybody was dying, everywhere," he wrote in his diary. "Better to go under of one's own choice, with one's head up, than be dragged away against one's reason and conscience to slaughter and be slaughtered in a fantastic and meaningless war."[26] He was forced to work in the kitchen (known as kitchen patrol or KP) and was segregated in the camp with about sixty Mennonites. Soldiers taunted them, "Yellowback, yellowback, we'll get you when we get back!"[27]

Meyer's group of conscientious objectors was moved to Camp Sherman, Ohio, in August, and was combined with another group of 160 men. There they waited for the military justice system to decide what to do with them. Meanwhile they camped in tents in the mud, the Mennonites engaging in constant theological debates, praying, singing, and Bible reading. Numerous times army officers sought ways to provide Meyer a noncombatant role, such as working in a base hospital, where he would never have to go overseas or carry a gun, but he stubbornly refused. Any such enlistment, even as a noncombatant, aided the war effort, and he would have no part of it. It was an extreme stance, one modeled on Henry David Thoreau's refusal to pay taxes during the Mexican-American War. Most of the conscientious objectors agreed to perform farm labor and were shipped out. Meyer remained with a small band of refuseniks.

On September 12, Meyer noted in his diary: "This morning, after we were lined up, we were given the opportunity of hearing a patriotic address of Governor [James] Cox, who was a visitor at Camp Sherman. We elected, instead, to go out and shovel manure."[28] Soon he and thirteen Mennonites were transferred to Fort Leavenworth, the army's maximum-security prison. They only spent one night at the soul-crushing prison, then were dispatched to Fort Riley, Kansas, where three hundred conscientious objectors were given hearings, including socialists, Wobblies (aka Industrial Workers of the World), and various pacifist religious sects. Meyer and the Mennonites still had not faced a court-martial. They were lodged in a former stable, from which they first had to clean out the piles of manure before they could move in.

Then came the Armistice on November 11, which changed the fate of the conscientious objectors. There was no reason to hold them anymore, and the military had less of a desire to punish the young men. They were dispatched once more to Camp Grant, Illinois, their final stop. There Meyer and the other COs finally faced a military judge. "He asked me a few hurried questions," Meyer wrote. "'And what do you wish to do now?' he ended. 'Join the Quakers in their French Reconstruction Unit.' 'Good. So recommended,'" and the hearing was over. He was released on December 14—five months after reporting for duty—and was perhaps not fully aware of how fortunate he was never to be court-martialed and sentenced to prison. He never served in France, as the Quaker reconstruction unit would not accept him on account of his German parentage. Instead, he was handed his discharge papers that read, "Not recommended for reënlistment!"[29]

Financing the War

After fighting for nearly three years, the Allies were near financial and military collapse by spring 1917. Private American banks like J.P. Morgan had supplied credit in the early years of the war, but that was not enough to keep the Allies financially afloat. Shortly after America entered the war, the federal government offered a lifeline to the Allies, extending $1 billion in credit, as they were nearing default. Over the course of the war, the U.S. would loan $9.5 billion to its allies—and the allies would spend $11.9 billion on food, munitions, and supplies, more than $2 billion beyond what they borrowed. The U.S. went from being a net debtor to a net creditor during the war. Most of the profits went to bankers and munitions factory owners. New York now challenged London as the world's leading financial center.[30]

By the war's end, England was no longer the dominant global financial power: that title now belonged to the United States, and the dollar was solidly entrenched as the favored global currency of trade. The remarkable success of American finance during the war can be largely attributed to Treasury Secretary William McAdoo, the son-in-law to the president. McAdoo was one of Wilson's most competent cabinet secretaries, a man who seemed to succeed at every task Wilson threw at him. That list piled up. McAdoo proved a wizard at finance and statistics who could quickly see into the heart of a problem, but who also knew how to delegate to trusted subordinates. He hired the best talent.

Immediately after the war declaration, McAdoo went to Congress to request an initial $7 billion in bonds and debt certificates, and to loan $3 billion to America's new allies. These were enormous sums of money, and many were shocked by how expensive this war would be. But this was only the beginning. Congress gave Treasury the desired authorization on April 24, 1917, which Wilson signed the next day.[31]

To pay for the war, McAdoo proposed both raising taxes and borrowing. Most of the war effort would have to be financed, as taxes alone could never cover the war's cost. War is expensive. The Great War would cost the country $50 billion, and the federal budget went from $742 million in 1916 to $14 billion two years later.[32]

The Sixteenth Amendment created the income tax in 1913. President Wilson signed the law implementing the tax, which began on October 3, 1913. Initially it was a small tax, topping out at seven percent for high-income earners. Most people paid nothing at all. But with the entry of the country into the Great War, the administration pushed through a massive income tax increase. It was a tax that largely impacted the wealthy—even with the higher rates, most people still paid little in taxes. The highest income tax rate was sixty-five percent in 1917 and rose to seventy-seven percent in 1918. In addition, the Wilson administration convinced Congress to levy taxes on war profiteering, a tax paid by industrialists. [33]

The Treasury Department needed to borrow vast sums of money to finance the war. Worried that McAdoo would have unlimited powers of borrowing, Congress created a debt ceiling in 1917 so it would have a say in how much debt the country issued. McAdoo drafted a loan campaign targeted not just at bankers, but at everyday citizens, asking for their contribution toward the war effort. He wrote later, "We went direct to the people; and that means to everybody—to business men, workmen, farmers, bankers, millionaires, school-teachers, laborers. We capitalized the profound impulse called patriotism." He called them Liberty Loans, and Liberty Bonds could be purchased in denominations as low as fifty dollars. [34]

The first Liberty Loan campaign kicked off in May 1917 McAdoo went on a four-week cross-country tour to sell the idea to the public in order to raise $2 billion at 3.50%. He used mass advertising to publicize the war bond campaign and arranged to have the Liberty Bell rung in Philadelphia on Flag Day. McAdoo was a suffrage supporter, and the Treasury Department hired thousands of women through the National Women's Liberty Loan Committee to sell government bonds. After a slow start, the public responded positively, and the campaign was oversubscribed by $1 billion. [35]

The second Liberty Loan campaign took place in October 1917, netting $4.6 billion in subscriptions. The third campaign was six month later, yielding $4.2 billion. The fourth campaign was held starting in late September 1918 and took in nearly $7 billion. By this point, inflation was high, and to entice people to lend their money McAdoo raised the bond yields to 4.25 percent. A postwar Victory Loan campaign ("Sure, we'll finish the job" was its slogan) raised even more money, though the public enthusiasm for the war effort had waned after the Armistice. Over the course of the war, the Treasury Department raised $21.4 billion in the five loan campaigns. This paid for the bulk of the American war effort.[36] More than eleven million people subscribed to war bonds.[37]

Inflation, then known as the "high cost of living," or HCL, spiked during the war because the economy was overheating, and that amounted to a form of a tax increase that impacted every American. The Federal Reserve was only four years old when the U.S. went to war, and it had not yet sharpened its tools as an inflation fighter. Author Willa Cather noted that HCL kicked in even before the war declaration, as she complained to her mother in February 1917 from New York: "It is costing us fifty dollars a month more to live than it did last winter, and we have cut out the opera altogether, and most concerts."[38] As a result of inflation, the federal government created the Consumer Price Index in 1917, which measured inflation that year at 19.77 percent. The country would suffer double-digit inflation until 1920.[39]

Mobilizing the Economy

The American economy was an enormous industrial machine that would be harnessed for the war effort. Millions of workers would work even harder in factories and mines to sew uniforms and stitch boots, extract coal, fabricate munitions, manufacture gunpowder, slaughter cattle, mold bullets, and render molten iron into steel plates for warships. However, little of American industry had been retooled for military equipment production, and thus with the war declaration, the U.S. Army became reliant on the English and French for much of its heavy equipment.

Coal powered American industry and was critical to fueling the wartime economy. President Wilson appointed Harry Garfield, the son of President James Garfield, to run the vital Fuel Administration. The administration had the power to fix energy prices—notably for coal—and to demand reduced civilian usage. Cities were blacked out at night, including New York's Great White Way. The brutally cold winter of 1917–18 led to coal shortages, as well as widespread theft. On January 16, Garfield ordered restricted coal use for non-wartime related industry east of the Mississippi River.[40]

Eight months after the war declaration, it was clear that American industry had a number of roadblocks, some of which could prove fatal to the war effort if they were not solved. Besides coal shortages, the next lead problem was the railroads. The nation's railroads consisted of hundreds of companies, each with varying, often aging equipment and inefficient commercial models. The Pennsylvania Railroad was particularly inefficient, with trains hitting bottlenecks as they passed through the Keystone State on their way to the Atlantic harbors. When the national railway network nearly ground to a halt in late 1917, the federal government stepped in.

On December 26, Wilson issued an executive order assuming national control of the railroads for the duration of the war. It was a major government incursion into the private sector, but necessary to keep the full mobilization on track. It did not, however, assume ownership of the railroads, which remained in private hands. Wilson appointed Treasury Secretary William McAdoo as director-general of railroads. With the stroke of a pen, 240,000 track miles and two million railroad workers were now under government control. Wilson would issue similar executive orders for critical areas, including the Cape Cod Canal and telegraph lines.[41]

McAdoo quickly recognized the sources of trouble. He brought aboard the heads of railroad companies to run the national railway network as if it were one system. The executives pointed out that two key problems existed: wages for railroad workers were excessively low, meaning that experienced workers were jumping the tracks for better pay in munitions factories, and freight rates were far too low, and thus railroads lacked the capital to modernize. McAdoo raised railroad wages by an average of forty percent to account for the rising cost of living, and he ensured that wages for women and minorities equaled that of men in similar tasks. [42]

Armaments, soldiers, supplies, and everything imaginable bound for Europe came by railroad to the East Coast. New York City and the Hampton Roads area were particularly vital, as they were the embarkation points for most of the American forces bound for France. The railroads were critical for the war effort. McAdoo noted that over the course of the war, the nation's railroads carried nearly 6.5 million soldiers—625,000 people per month—on 9,000 troop trains. [43]

The War Department likewise came under scrutiny. Senator George Chamberlain, a Wilson ally, accused the administration of incompetence and in particular criticized Secretary of War Newton Baker. Baker offered to resign. Secretary of the Navy Josephus Daniels conferred with Baker, telling him that the president would not allow his resignation, which would only stir up the administration's political opponents like Theodore Roosevelt and Leonard Wood. No, he advised, sit tight and Baker would be proven right. [44] On January 28, 1918, Baker testified before Chamberlain's committee for more than four hours, more than holding his own, and explained that the greatest challenge was in finding enough shipping to transport the army to Europe. Baker continued in his role, as Wilson retained confidence in him. [45]

To improve the economy's bottlenecks, President Wilson created a "war cabinet" in February 1918. It consisted of Bernard Baruch of the War Industries Board, Harry Garfield of the Coal Administration, food administrator Herbert Hoover, Treasury Secretary William McAdoo, Edward Hurley of the Shipping Board, Vance McCormick of the War Trade Board, and the president himself. The war cabinet met weekly at the White House. Noticeably absent from the list was Vice President Thomas Marshall, who was left out of much of the president's business.

The War Industries Board proved fairly ineffective. It had no power to control prices, and its board governance meant that decisions were slowly decided. Wilson attempted to beef up its powers by promoting Bernard Baruch to chairman in March 1918. Baruch was a wealthy financier, the type of Wall Street speculator whom Wilson instinctively distrusted. But the country needed the private sector's skills in the time of war. Baruch was tall and handsome, gregarious and well liked. He became known as "the czar" for his wartime portfolio.

Baruch brought in his fellow financiers and industrialists, tycoons who understood how to run large organizations. These were dollar-a-year men who essentially volunteered their management skills for the wartime needs of their country. Most of these men were Republican businessmen who set aside partisanship to aid their country. Wilson had spent much of his career in academia and had no keen understanding of the business world. Humorist Will Rogers joked about Wilson being taken aback that Baruch had recruited so many Republicans. Baruch responded, "You told me to get prominent men from every industry, and I did. Now I can go and get you some Democrats, but they won't be very prominent, and won't have any industries with them. Besides, Mr. President, I doubt if you can get a Democrat to work for $1.00 a year. They are used to getting at least $1.00 a day." [46]

Daylight saving time was established during the Great War, a tool that most European combatants used as a fuel conservation measure. Congress adopted it as well, and DST in the U.S. began on March 31, 1918. Many believe that its purpose was to give farmers more daylight hours to work, but that was patently untrue: farmers rose well before dawn anyway, and they protested the loss of early morning light. It was retailers and the chambers of commerce who wanted the longer evening hours of sunlight so people could shop later. DST proved so unpopular that Congress repealed it in August 1919 over President Wilson's veto. The U.S. did not attempt national daylight saving time again until 1942, although cities like New York imposed their own spring forward-fall back schedule soon after the Great War. [47]

During the war, labor unions were greatly strengthened, in part because Wilson was pro-labor. Workers agitated for higher pay, especially with the rising cost of living, and the demand from factory owners that they work overtime, often twelve-hour days, six days a week. The War Labor Board, co-chaired by former president William Howard Taft, recognized that workers had the right to organize.

Membership in the American Federation of Labor doubled from two million to more than four million between 1916 and 1920. Samuel Gompers, head of the AFL, played a significant role in working with the Wilson administration to keep labor at peace while winning major concessions on pay and working hours.[48]

Earlier in the war, American industries began recruiting low-skilled African-American laborers from the South to work in factories and sometimes unwittingly serve as strikebreakers. White workers went on strike in East St. Louis, Illinois, and the companies brought in cheaper black labor to replace them. Black workers had flooded into the city, causing both racial animosity and resentment at blacks being scabs. Once the strike ended, the white workers struck back with a vengeance. July 2, 1917 marked one of the worst race riots in the nation's history. Whites rampaged through a black neighborhood, killing thirty-nine blacks, while nine whites died. Thousands were left homeless. The police and state militia proved unable to halt the violence, and in some cases joined in.[49] President Wilson wondered if federal intervention was necessary to stop the East St. Louis rioting, as he asked Attorney General Thomas Gregory. Wilson ultimately took no action, other than to meet with four black leaders to condemn mob violence.[50]

More racial violence broke out the following month. When Houston police beat up three black soldiers, one hundred soldiers from the 24th Infantry mutinied on August 23. They armed themselves and headed downtown, shooting indiscriminately at policemen, streetcar conductors, and white people. An armed white mob fought back, and eventually an army battalion was deployed to stop the violence. By the time the fighting subsided, seventeen whites and three blacks were killed. Many of the black soldiers were court-martialed, and the army hanged thirteen of them on December 11. Another forty-one were sentenced to life in prison. Sixteen more black soldiers were later sentenced to death, though Wilson commuted some of the sentences.[51]

The violence directed toward African-Americans was as disturbing as it was one-sided. In August 1917, one of the guiding thought leaders in the black community, Howard University dean Kelly Miller, published an open letter to President Wilson pleading for greater civil rights for blacks who were sacrificing much for their country during the war, yet were denied basic protections from the law. "As long as the black man is excluded from participation in the government of the nation, just so long will he be the victim of cruelty and outrage on the part of his white fellow citizens who assume lordship over him," Miller wrote.[52]

It took more than industry to win the war. It also took an army of bureaucrats to produce the paperwork for purchase orders, promotions, draft assignments, death notifications, and far more. Thousands of people headed to the nation's capital to find employment in the War Department and other agencies. The U.S. census recorded 331,069 residents in 1910, but the population soared to 437,571 a decade later. Many single women flocked to the capital to be part of the burgeoning bureaucracy for the war effort. They lived in cramped and expensive boarding houses, as the population rise created a severe housing shortage. Nothing like this had been seen since the Civil War. Even First Lady Edith Wilson chipped in, often helping her husband decrypt cables sent to him, part of his voluminous daily correspondence.[53]

The State, War, and Navy Building (now the Old Executive Office Building) adjacent to the White House proved inadequate to the bureaucratic needs. A major construction program was undertaken to add temporary office space. The National Mall was taken over by dozens of temporary office buildings for the War Department, the Food Administration, the Treasury, and other federal agencies. These buildings, containing several million square feet of office space, were constructed to handle the massive influx of workers. Known as "tempos," these ugly buildings were to be torn down after the war, but in fact they remained standing. More were added on the other side of the Reflecting Pool during the Second World War, when pedestrian bridges were added to connect the buildings over the water. Many of these buildings remained until the 1970s, when they were finally torn down for the nation's bicentennial, making room for Constitution Gardens.[54]

Food, Beer, and Whiskey

Conscripting several million men and sending them to fight in Europe required an enormous amount of food. The Food Control Act (also known as the Lever Food and Fuel Control Act, or simply the Food Bill) passed Congress in August 1917, giving President Wilson broad powers over the national food supply. It established the U.S. Food Administration.

The Food Bill had been discussed since June, but prohibitionists attempted to amend the bill to ban all alcoholic beverage production. Wilson convinced them to drop their demands to halt brewing, and the bill passed on August 8. The prohibitionists won a partial victory: the Food Bill put an end to the distillation of alcoholic beverages as of September 9. Whiskey makers still had vast reserves aging in their rickhouses and could continue selling their stockpiles. This chafed prohibitionists like Senator Morris Sheppard, who wanted alcohol sales stopped altogether. Sheppard went on to sponsor the Sheppard Act, which made the District of Columbia a dry fiefdom on November 1. This began the incremental efforts to cut off the alcohol supply during the war—an effort that would lead to national Prohibition in 1920. The law also gave Wilson the authority to decide alcohol by volume in beer and wine.[55]

Wilson appointed Herbert Hoover to be the nation's Food Administrator (known colloquially as the "food dictator"), as the president had been suitably impressed with the man's leadership of the Commission for Relief in Belgium. Hoover continued to oversee CRB even after the war declaration; Holland and Spain, both neutral countries, assumed responsibility for the food shipments. Hoover was a whiz of a technocrat, and before he was officially sworn in as the Food Administrator he already had a firm grasp on the nation's food production and the challenges, especially speculators who were rapidly driving up the cost of food. But he first he had to stand up an organization from scratch—and find suitable real estate. Along with other wartime administrations, the Food Administration ended up on the National Mall in Washington, D.C. in temporary buildings. He hired part of the bureaucracy, but he also took on several thousand volunteers, altogether about three thousand people. The administration adopted the slogan "Food Will Win the War." It encouraged many ways to conserve food, such as breadless and meatless days, and people signed pledges to conserve food. There were price controls, but no food rationing in the U.S. during the Great War.

The Food Administration regulated the nation's food supply. The U.S. not only had to feed its own population, but it also had to partly feed the Allies. The Russian grain that the Allies depended on was cut off. Fortunately the U.S. had long enjoyed a grain surplus. American farmers ramped up wheat production for the war effort. The Food Control Act set a price of $2 per bushel—a record high, though Hoover had discretion to adjust the add-on for freight. He quickly raised the average freight price by twenty cents. When Congress tried to impose a new price guarantee at $2.40 in summer 1918, Hoover encouraged Wilson to veto the bill, which the president did, a key action that cost Democrats the farm vote in the midterm election in November. Farmers quickly added new acreage, including the southern plains that would become the Dust Bowl in the 1930s (during the war, cultivated acres nationally grew by twenty-eight million to 432.6 million[56]). Hoover's bureaucrats targeted speculators and farmers who withheld crops from the market, the idea being to eliminate the threat of a black market by offering farmers a more than fair price for their grain. He proudly reported to the president, as any technocrat would, "The farmer is today receiving 40% of the price of the loaf against under 20% in pre-war times—the result of total elimination of speculation and extorinate [sic] profits."[57]

During the war, civilians were encouraged to plant "War Gardens" in every available plot of land. To economize on food became known as to *Hooverize*. Eleanor Roosevelt, the wife of Franklin, was publicized as an early model for food conservation with her large household of seven family members and staff. "Making the ten servants help me do my saving has not only been possible but highly profitable," she remarked. "Since I have started following the home-card instructions prices have risen, but my bills are no longer."[58]

Prohibitionists had to compromise with the president on the food bill, but they continued to hammer the point that barley for brewing and corn and wheat for distilling were better used for the war effort—even though the spent grain could be used to feed farm animals. The point was, they wanted alcohol production ended. They went about choking off the supply through a series of food-related bills that restricted grain for the alcoholic beverage industries.

In November 1917, Herbert Hoover recommended that beer be capped at three percent alcohol so as to cut grain consumption used in brewing by half. Wilson thought the reduction "too severe," fearing that a reduction in the supply of beer would raise prices "and so be very unfair to the classes who are using it and who can use it with very little detriment when the percentage of alcohol is made so small."[59] Wilson consistently pushed back against efforts to halt brewing altogether, knowing that his working-class supporters would rebel. If beer was cut off, drinkers would simply turn elsewhere, giving distillers a "whiskey monopoly," as Hoover called it, since the distillers had plenty of whiskey stored up. No, beer was what the workingman drank, and Wilson allowed the brewers to continue producing low-alcohol beer for the time being. The public had a handy name for this low-alcohol brew: they called it "war beer."[60]

However, Congress passed the Eighteenth Amendment in December 1917, banning the manufacture, sale, and transportation of intoxicating liquors, and sent it on to the states for ratification. The following month, under pressure from prohibitionists, Wilson reduced beer to 2.75 percent alcohol and required brewers to reduce grain use by thirty percent. Brewers may have thought they had won a victory in excluding themselves from excessive wartime restrictions, but it was a rearguard action. The Eighteenth Amendment was now on the table and a very real threat to their business.

In a cabinet meeting in March 1918, Attorney General Thomas Gregory asked what he should do with all of the whiskey seized from illegal sales. The cabinet found this hilarious and offered many suggestions. The president chimed in with a joke about a mule that got its head stuck in a bucket full of whiskey. It drank and drank until it was stumbling drunk, "but it did not kick the bucket." Even teetotaling Josephus Daniels thought this was funny, as he recorded the story in his diary.[61]

As the war pressed on, prohibitionists continued to push to halt brewers' access to grain, and made a legislative move known as war-time Prohibition. Wilson opposed the effort, which had little to do with food conservation, but was a way to force the country to go dry by Congressional fiat. Wilson wrote Senator Morris Sheppard, stating that he did not see the need for it, given that banning beer production would simply shift Americans to whiskey, as there was plenty of whiskey in storage.[62]

President Wilson meanwhile issued an executive proclamation on September 16 ordering the brewers to halt brewing as of December 1. They were to be cut off entirely from the grain supply. They could brew low-alcohol beer until their stockpiled grain ran out, or once December 1 arrived, whichever came first. It would be superseded by a wartime Prohibition law that Wilson signed a week after the Armistice.[63]

Although they served together on the war cabinet, Treasury Secretary William McAdoo and Herbert Hoover evidently had their moments of conflict. Hoover publicly slammed the state of the nation's railroads in a February 1918 interview with the *New York Times*, stating that the food program to feed the Allies was falling seriously behind on account of railroad bottlenecks.[64] McAdoo's ego was pricked. He insisted that the problem was overstated, that the railroads were rapidly improving, and that such talk only encouraged the country's enemies. He demanded that Hoover tell him exactly where the stalled food was so his staff could address the issue, but Hoover vacillated. When they finally met, Hoover brought his attorney, who did all the talking, explaining that Hoover regretted the *Times* interview.[65]

McAdoo later dismissed Hoover's efforts in Belgium relief, writing that, "the job of giving away things requires very little wear and tear on one's ability." It was a harsh and unfair judgment of Hoover, who had in fact saved millions from starving. Then again, when McAdoo penned that damning sentence in 1931, Hoover was president, the Great Depression was well underway, and McAdoo (a Democrat) was likely making a partisan snipe at the Republican president.[66] Hoover struck back in his 1951 memoirs by describing McAdoo's appointment as director general of the country's rails. "Because of McAdoo's lack of railway experience, it was not well done," he wrote, dismissing a rival who had likewise done an exceptional job in organizing the American economy for war.[67]

Shipping

The United States had a large population, a huge industrial base, and a great surplus of agriculture. But all of these would be useless for the Allies if the troops, supplies, and food could not be shipped to Europe. And that was the problem: the U.S. had a tiny merchant marine, having been dependent on British shipping for decades.

With his wartime executive powers, President Wilson appointed a Shipping Board to address the question and nominated Edward Hurley to lead it. Hurley was serving on the War Trade Board and had no experience and declined the appointment. Wilson's personal secretary, Joe Tumulty, relayed a conversation he had with the president over this: "You tell Hurley this is personal." Hurley accepted the chairmanship.[68]

In August 1917, there were 431 ships under construction in American shipyards, many of them contracted by foreign countries. Hurley ordered that all of these ships be requisitioned for the American war effort, and henceforth shipyards would only build American ships. This raised howls of protest from foreign governments, especially the British, who counted on the ships to replace losses from German U-boats. Hurley likewise requisitioned all American-flagged steel vessels weighing 2500 tons or higher for the war effort.[69]

Interned German ships in American ports were put to use. The massive liner *Vaterland* was rechristened as the SS *Leviathan*. Among its notable crewmembers was a young helmsman named Humphrey Bogart, who would become one of Hollywood's leading actors of the 1940s and 1950s. Chairman Hurley chartered every neutral ship he could get his hands on. Even with these measures there still was not nearly enough shipping capacity. The Americans would have to ramp up shipbuilding.

Under Hurley's direction, the U.S.-chartered Emergency Fleet Corporation built numerous new shipyards, the largest of which was constructed at Hog Island near Philadelphia. The facility was an 846-acre yard that could build fifty ships at a time (it is now the site of Philadelphia International Airport). Hog Island was a city in itself, employing more than 34,000 workers. The first ship christened there was the *Quistconck*, named by Edith Wilson, who smashed a champagne bottle against its hull the day it was launched.[70]

Hurley's staff advocated the mass production of ships using prefabricated, interchangeable parts that only needed to be welded together. He had an aggressive goal: to build six million tons of shipping by the end of 1918. He recruited an outspoken Republican executive, Charles Schwab of Bethlehem Steel to oversee shipbuilding operations. In 1918, American shipyards produced 533 ships—and the next year more than doubled that to 1,180 ships, even though the war was over by then.[71]

When the war started, the U.S. only employed about 50,000 shipyard workers, but by the conflict's end, the nation's shipyards employed 350,000, and were churning out one hundred ships a month. Shipyard workers were vital for the war effort, and thus they were exempt from the draft (many draft dodgers, or "slackers," found jobs in shipyards). In addition, the country had quickly trained 42,000 merchantmen to staff the ships. By the end of the Great War, the United States had a large merchant marine and was no longer dependent on Great Britain for its shipping needs.[72]

Wartime Propaganda

The United States had witnessed much foreign propaganda in the three years since the war broke out, as both the Allies and the Central Powers attempted to influence the Americans. President Wilson recognized the value of propaganda as a wartime tool. A week after the war declaration, he created the Committee on Public Information by executive order. He appointed journalist George Creel to lead it, and CPI soon became known as the Creel Committee.

George Creel was a journalist and public relations genius. A moral crusader, he had advocated against child labor and supported women's suffrage. Creel rehabilitated Navy Secretary Josephus Daniels's stodgy public image after alcohol was banned on ships, and then penned a short book, *Wilson and the Issues*, which served as an apology for the president during his 1916 reelection campaign, defending Wilson's stances and neutrality. The book was a bestseller. Creel had proved useful as a skilled propagandist. He was also an unabashed cheerleader for the war effort, idealism and all.

Creel opposed censorship but believed that propaganda offered an alternative tool to steer public opinion. Creel biographer Alan Axelrod wrote about CPI, "It did not rely on the censorship so much as the total monopolization of information, shaping news, shaping images, shaping emotions to create a reality in which President Wilson's war emerged as not merely desirable but inevitable."[73]

A week after CPI's creation, Creel issued a directive for newspaper editors on how they should cover the war—and how they should not disclose anything that would threaten national security or put sailors and soldiers in harm's way. It was a form of voluntary censorship. CPI became a clearinghouse for all information about the war effort. It hired twenty-three journalists and sent them to France with Pershing's army.

Some 75,000 volunteer "Four Minute Men" preached for the war effort in communities around the country in churches, civic associations, and nickelodeons. These citizens were there to sell the war—and Liberty Bonds—and the peace that was sure to follow. The name came from the four minutes that it took to change a film reel in a movie theater. The Four Minute Men delivered 7,555,190 speeches during the war.[74]

Creel hired artist Charles Dana Gibson to lead the Division of Pictorial Publicity, and he in turn roped in three hundred artists and illustrators to create propaganda posters supporting the war effort. These were inexpensive to produce, easy to distribute, and many of them became iconic. Most famous was James Montgomery Flagg's self-portrait as a stern Uncle Sam, dressed in red, white, and blue, pointing directly at the viewer and saying, "I want YOU for U.S. Army." The posters highlighted the war as an idealist crusade of good against evil.

In New York's Union Square, CPI erected a life-size wooden battleship replica known as the USS *Recruit* as an enlistment tool. CPI promoted patriotic movies like *Pershing's Crusaders*, and movie stars like Fatty Arbuckle, Charlie Chaplin, Douglas Fairbanks, and Mary Pickford were pressed into service to help sell Liberty Bonds. Preachers like Newell Dwight Hillis spoke to national audiences, describing the Germans in the most horrific terms: their barbarity, their inferiority, their rapaciousness. This God-fearing man believed the Germans should be exterminated.[75]

Wartime Civil Liberties

Woodrow Wilson often looked to Abraham Lincoln for his leadership as a wartime president. In any war, civil liberties are curtailed, and perhaps that is a natural outcome, to be restored after the conflict ends. Lincoln committed his share of violations, including revoking habeas corpus, holding pro-Confederates indefinitely, and preventing the Maryland legislature from meeting to vote on secession.

The Wilson administration committed serious civil liberties violations, all in the name of winning the war. One could be imprisoned for speaking against the war or the draft. The mail was censored against dissenters, which in turn placed pressure on the press to censor itself.

Wilson had thought through the war declaration in the weeks before the actual event with Robert Lansing, the secretary of state. Within minutes after signing the war declaration on April 6, he issued a proclamation that addressed the question of enemy aliens in the United States. It called for German aliens to respect the law and remain at peace; however, they were forbidden from owning firearms or from coming within a half mile of military facilities. Wilson also opened the possibility of internment, a tool that he would use with his executive privilege as commander in chief.[76]

There was in fact a large population of German aliens in the U.S. Many of the early immigrants had never been naturalized, even though thousands had fought for the Union in the Civil War. They simply took up residence and assumed citizenship, but without the papers to prove it. The lack of citizenship came to haunt these older men in 1917. Thousands were arrested or put under house arrest. Any weapons they owned were confiscated per Wilson's executive order.

On Flag Day, June 14, 1917, Wilson addressed a crowd of about one thousand people, diminished by a heavy thunderstorm, at the outdoor Sylvan Theater near the foot of the Washington Monument. A Secret Service agent held an umbrella over his head. The federal workforce was released at midday, and 40,000 of them were expected to attend his speech, but the rain kept the crowds at bay. Instead, many government employees went to banks to buy Liberty Bonds in response to the federal appeal.[77]

Though the crowd was small, Wilson's Flag Day address was widely reproduced and fed the anti-German hysteria. The country clearly feared the presence of spies. "The military masters of Germany denied us the right to be neutral. They filled our unsuspecting communities with vicious spies and conspirators and sought to corrupt the opinion of our people in their own behalf," he said, adding that the German embassy had conspired to sabotage American industry. "Men began to look upon their own neighbours with suspicion and to wonder in their hot resentment and surprise whether there was any community in which hostile intrigue did not lurk." After planting this seed of sedition, he then toned down his argument, stating that "we are not the enemies of the German people and that they are not our enemies . . . They are themselves in the grip of the same sinister power that has now at last stretched its ugly talons out and drawn blood from us."[78]

An even larger assault against seditionists and spies came in the form of the Espionage Act, which Wilson signed the day after his Flag Day speech. The government assumed broad powers to prosecute people for treason, insurrection, or resisting U.S. law, among other offenses. It was now a crime to share information about national security that might injure the United States. The law went far beyond spying: in fact, it was a tool to silence domestic opponents of the war, largely on the left. Censorship was not mentioned in the Espionage Act, but self-censorship was implied. The law gave the postmaster general the authority to halt treasonous mailings, however interpreted. It meant that the government could keep tabs on dissenters and prosecute them. The Espionage Act was the legal beginning of America's surveillance state. [79]

The July 1917 edition of the *Atlantic Monthly* included an article by Frank Perry Olds that denounced German-American newspapers for disloyalty. (This was the month before H. L. Mencken's article appeared in the same magazine about German General Erich Ludendorff.) The newspapers argued "America first!" but then passive aggressively argued that no money should be provided the allies, no food or supplies should be shipped overseas, and certainly no soldiers should be sent to fight the Kaiser's army. "Confidently expecting a German victory," Olds wrote, "they wish to hasten that desirable event by withholding our weight from the Allied offense." The editors of the *Atlantic*—a publication that defended itself against censorship (and perhaps missing the irony)—argued, "The remedy is a sane war-time censorship upon enemy propaganda, and a substantial war-time tax on the printed use of the enemy language." [80]

H. L. Mencken wrote a fellow German-American, Louis Untermeyer, promising that, "All men with names like yours and mine will be jailed before Sept. 1918." In fact, Mencken would never be jailed, as he never criticized the war effort in print, though he privately assailed the attack on freedom of speech. The war certainly curtailed his own editorials, as he significantly curbed his criticism. During his three years in journalistic exile, he focused on writing books. [81]

The most obvious source of possible spies was the ninety-one German-flagged ships that were interned in American harbors. Once the country declared war, the ships were confiscated and repurposed as merchant marine and troop transports. Their crews were detained. First Lady Edith Wilson helped come up with new names for most of the ships. Several ships kept their original names, including the *George Washington.*

To house the German sailors and other detained enemy aliens, the United States opened four internment camps, known as War Prison Barracks. These were at Fort McPherson and Fort Oglethorpe, Georgia; Hot Springs, North Carolina; and Fort Douglas, Utah. More than five thousand detainees were held between these four camps. The largest detention camp was at Hot Springs, which housed about 2,200 Germans. The Mountain Park Hotel in the resort town housed officers, while the crew constructed barracks and Swiss-style houses for themselves and held weekly concerts. As the war dragged on, Fort McPherson became the central point for German prisoners of war, while detained aliens were transferred to other camps.[82]

Fort Oglethorpe's most prominent detainee was Boston Symphony Orchestra conductor Karl Muck, who was actually a Swiss national. False rumors swirled that he refused to play "The Star-Spangled Banner" at a concert in Providence, Rhode Island, in October 1917. Federal authorities arrested him in March 1918, along with twenty-nine members of his orchestra.[83]

In July 1918, Erich Posselt, an Austrian who had emigrated to the U.S. four years earlier, was arrested after Department of Justice agents found a poem in his house (they had searched his home a dozen times). He was placed in solitary confinement in a Brooklyn jail, then moved to New Jersey, where without a hearing he was told he would be confined at Fort Oglethorpe in War Prison Barracks No. 2 for the rest of the war. The camp was divided in two: one for wealthier Germans who could afford to hire servants, such as among the many sailors and stewards, and a much larger barracks for everyone else. The Germans had difficulty pronouncing Oglethorpe and so called it "Orgelsdorf." The prisoners were only allowed to write two short letters a month, which were heavily censored, but they were well fed and entertained themselves with athletics, classes, gardening, and music, and printed a camp newspaper in German called the *Orgelsdorfer Eulenspiegel.* In these tight quarters, the influenza of 1918 sickened more than half of the prisoners.[84]

One of the country's staunchest opponents of the war, Senator Robert "Fighting Bob" La Follette of Wisconsin, remained outspoken in his criticism. On September 20, 1917, he addressed the Nonpartisan League in St. Paul, Minnesota. When asked about his opposition to the war declaration and the *Lusitania* sinking, La Follette responded, "I don't mean to say we hadn't suffered grievances. We had, at the hands of Germany. Serious grievances." Despite extensive press coverage at the event, his statement was misquoted and widely circulated. His words were turned around to read, "I was not in favor of beginning this war. We had no grievance," a statement that falsely implied that he defended the German sinking of the *Lusitania*. There was an immediate national outcry. Many accused La Follette of sedition and demanded that the Senate expel him. [85]

La Follette's fellow senators ordered a response from the accused. On October 6, he stood before the Senate, its galleries packed with onlookers, and spoke for three hours. He went far beyond just setting the record straight. La Follette defended the right to freedom of speech in wartime. The ongoing campaign against dissenters was suppressing "discussion of the great issues involved in this war," he said. Free speech was "necessary to the welfare, to the existence, of this Government to the successful conduct of this war, and to a peace which shall be enduring and for the best interest of this country." Without free speech, La Follette continued, "we may well despair of ever again finding ourselves for a long period in a state of peace." Fellow senators loudly denounced La Follette; however; the Senate put off its vote to expel him after his son, future senator Bob Jr., fell ill. After the war, cooler heads prevailed and La Follette survived a vote to expel him. The Senate even reimbursed him for his legal fees. Fighting Bob remained in Congress until his death in 1925. [86]

On November 19, 1917, Wilson issued a sweeping executive order directing all German aliens in the country to register with the federal government. They were forbidden to travel without permission. Enemy aliens were required to leave Washington, D.C., and the Panama Canal Zone, areas considered to be sensitive, and were forbidden from being within one hundred yards of any port facility or railroad facilities. The attorney general would be responsible for enforcing the executive order, giving him broad latitude to pursue and detain Germans in the country. More than five thousand German aliens were forced to leave the nation's capital. In the New York City area alone, there were an estimated 130,000 German aliens—and this was likewise the chief port from which American doughboys, munitions, and supplies sailed to Europe. It was impractical to expel so many people, so the government kept a sharp watch on the population for treasonable activity.[87]

The executive order decreed that any non-naturalized German men over the age of thirteen had to report to a U.S. attorney's office or post office to register and be interviewed by February 4, 1918. There they would be fingerprinted and photographed and, if deemed loyal to the U.S., receive a special identity card that would allow them to remain free. In April, the federal government ordered German women to register as well. Some 480,000 German aliens registered that year.[88]

Congress passed another law targeting German resources in October 1917: The Trading with the Enemy Act, which gave the president broad powers to seize belligerent-owned property. Wilson appointed Mitchell Palmer as custodian of alien property to handle confiscated assets. Palmer considered it fair game to go after any German-born American citizen who was in Germany during the war. Palmer was narrowly deterred from seizing the considerable property of Lilly Busch, wife of brewer Adolphus Busch, who had come to the States as a six-month old and who was stranded in Europe at the war's outbreak. When Busch returned to America in early 1918, Palmer ordered her estate confiscated and subjected the frail seventy-four-year-old woman to interrogation. Palmer seized the estate of another brewer, George Ehret, who was likewise stranded in Germany.[89]

"All aliens interned by the government are regarded as enemies, and their property is treated accordingly," Palmer wrote in *Munsey's Magazine*. Property held by legal aliens was untouchable—but property or investments in America that were owned by Germans in Germany was liable to be seized. His office seized hundreds of millions of dollars in assets: "The kinds of industry now under the direction of the custodian include pencil-making in New Jersey, chocolate manufacturing in

Connecticut, beer-brewing in Chicago, mining in Mexico, sawmills in Florida, real-estate offices and retails stores, commission house and public utilities in all parts of the country," he wrote, noting that the office had seized significant miscellaneous property that would be auctioned. "In this respect, the alien property custodian keeps the biggest general store in the country," Palmer bragged. The property would be held in trust until the end of the war, at which point the government would decide what to do with it. [90]

In July 1918, Palmer ordered newspaperman Edward Rumely arrested, charging with him with violating the Trading with the Enemy Act. Palmer provided evidence that Rumely had purchased the *New York Evening Mail* with $735,000 that was allegedly provided by the German government in 1915 for the purpose of printing German propaganda. This was the same newspaper that H. L. Mencken briefly wrote for after leaving *Sunpapers* in 1917. Rumely was convicted and sentenced to a year in the Atlanta Penitentiary. Palmer seized the *Evening Mail* as enemy property and offered to sell it to Arthur Brisbane, who declined. Palmer would later instigate a Senate investigation against Brisbane for his brewery-financed purchase of the *Washington Times*. [91]

As the alien property custodian, Palmer became known as the "Fighting Quaker." His bureau seized more than a billion dollars in assets, including those of the aspirin producing pharmaceutical Bayer, the Orenstein & Koppel Company, nearly twenty German insurance companies, the Bosch Magneto Company, the Hamburg-American shipping company, and the German-American Lumber Company. After the war ended, Palmer ordered seized German property auctioned off. Bayer lost its American patent for aspirin. Although plaintiffs sued Palmer to stop the auctions, the U.S. Supreme Court ruled that he was within his wartime rights. [92]

The Trading with the Enemy Act imposed a form of censorship overseen by Postmaster General Albert Burleson, who alerted editors that the administration would not tolerate criticism of the draft or Liberty Bond sales. He also mandated that German language newspapers translate into English any article or editorial mentioning the American government or the war effort and submit these articles to the local postmaster for review. The U.S. Postal Service used its powers with some discretion, allowing many publications to continue without much interference. Burleson largely directed his censorship powers against the socialist press, outspoken opponents of the draft and the war.[93]

One such socialist critic was Oscar Ameringer, a prominent writer, humorist, labor organizer, and German-American who came to the United States in 1886 and made his name in Oklahoma and elsewhere in the Midwest. Socialists argued that the war was being fought for capitalism. "We knew from history that every war had been a rich man's war and a poor man's fight," he wrote. The Great War would prove disastrous for the socialist movement in the U.S., as it was especially targeted and silenced by wartime measures.[94]

Shortly before the war, Ameringer moved from Oklahoma to Milwaukee, where his German-speaking skills were needed as a columnist for the Milwaukee *Leader*, a socialist, English-language newspaper. The *Leader* had a large local subscription base but was also mailed to 18,000 households around the country. Because the newspaper opposed the war, Burleson revoked the newspaper's second-class postal privileges, which meant it could only be mailed at the more expensive first-class rate, something the publisher could not afford. The newspaper called a public meeting, and Ameringer carried out a washtub, which readers filled with cash, jewelry, and Liberty Bonds to keep the newspaper afloat.

Burleson then invoked the Espionage Act to revoke the *Leader's* ability to use the mails entirely, while federal authorities pressured the newspaper's advertisers. Without advertisers, the *Leader* would have folded, save for the generous support of local businesses and readers who donated money and more than $150,000 in Liberty Bonds to keep the paper solvent. Ameringer's future wife, Freda Hogan, surreptitiously mailed small batches of the *Leader* in the hope that they would get through. He called Burleson "mail-robber number one" and "censor-in-chief."[95]

When the *Leader* refused to fold, federal authorities arrested its editor, Socialist Party cofounder Victor Berger, in February 1918 and charged him with violating the Espionage Act for obstructing the draft through his writings. He was released on a one million dollar bond on the condition that he would no longer write or serve as editor. His trial would not begin until December, so Berger filled the time by running for Congress. He had served a term in the House of Representatives beginning in 1910, the first socialist to be elected to Congress. Berger won the 1918 election, then went to trial, where he was convicted and sentenced to twenty years in prison. He immediately appealed. Congress meanwhile debated whether a convicted felon should have a seat, and ultimately decided to unseat Berger. Milwaukee voters immediately reelected Berger in a special election, but Congress again refused to seat him. In January 1921, the Supreme Court overturned his conviction, and the following year he was elected to Congress, serving three consecutive terms.

Ameringer likewise attempted to run for Congress in the adjacent district in 1918, as did a number of other antiwar socialists around Wisconsin. However, the U.S. Postal Service was off limits to these activists, and authorities served them indictments in November for obstructing the war effort. Ameringer was charged on four counts, including for publishing the antiwar poem "Dumdum Bullets" four years earlier, a poem that was frequently republished in opposition newspapers. The indictments came at the end of the war, but then were quietly dropped without going to trial. This was little consolation for Ameringer, who lost his quest for a congressional seat and likewise learned that one of his sons had been badly injured in the brutal fighting in the Argonne Forest.[96]

While the largely skilled workers of the American Federation of Labor under Samuel Gompers backed the war effort, the more radical Industrial Workers of the World—the Wobblies—stood in violent opposition, representing unskilled, poorly paid farmworkers, loggers, and miners. Its leader, radical socialist William "Big Bill" Haywood, espoused violence against capitalism and openly promoted class warfare. Many Americans considered the Wobblies a threat and met them with violence in return. Phelps Dodge, a mine operator in Bisbee, Arizona, took action against the IWW, rounding up more than a thousand miners at gunpoint, locking them in railcars, and deporting them to New Mexico without food or water in the summer heat of July 1917.

The Wobblies were frequently accused of taking German subsidies to weaken America's industries and war machine. The charges were unfounded, but many thought the Wobblies were traitors. Big Bill Haywood was a thorn in the side of the Wilson administration, a boisterous presence in the press who seemed to relish being arrested in support of the cause. The president was reluctant to make a martyr out of him. However, the attorney general moved against the IWW. The Bureau of Investigation raided dozens of IWW offices and meeting halls around the country, as well as Socialist Party headquarters in Chicago, on September 5, 1917, indicting 165 IWW members under the Espionage Act. One of those charged was Big Bill Haywood.[97]

The IWW members were put on trial in April 1918 in the Chicago court of Judge Kenesaw Mountain Landis. The trial lasted five months, and Haywood's testimony lasted three days. The trial resulted in the conviction of 101 IWW members. Haywood and fourteen others were sentenced to twenty years in prison. He appealed and was released on bail. In 1921, he jumped bail and fled to the Soviet Union. Haywood died there in 1928 and some of his cremated remains were buried in the Kremlin Wall. During the Great War, the IWW was essentially defeated because of wartime measures to curtail radicalism. Foreign-born IWW members were often interned in the War Prison Barracks.

More than just radicals and socialists suffered under censorship and the tightening noose of the super patriots. Many newspapers adopted a rabidly anti-German tone, referring to the Germans as "the Hun." "After the United States entered the war their editorial pages and their news columns were alike filled with grotesque and indeed almost idiotic fulminations against the Germans," H. L. Mencken complained.[98]

The anti-German hysteria intensified in 1918 as the war effort grew. German-Americans showed their loyalty by buying Liberty Bonds, but sometimes were bullied or coerced into purchasing them. When pressed by an angry, sometimes drunken mob, German-Americans were forced to kiss the flag and sing the national anthem. It was an act of humiliation, one that would do little to foster loyalty.

This was an era when angry mobs could silence critics and intimidate dissenters through the threat of violence.

Evangelist and former baseball star Billy Sunday spoke before a large audience in New York's Carnegie Hall, painting the war against Kaiser Wilhelm in black-and-white terms. "I tell you, it is Bill [Kaiser Wilhelm] against Woodrow, Germany against America, hell against heaven," he thundered. "Germany lost out when she turned from Christ to Krupp, and from the Cross of Calvary to the Iron Cross." He strongly insinuated that German-Americans were traitors: "Either you are loyal or you are not, you are either a patriot or a black-hearted traitor. There is no sitting on the fence at this time."[99]

Others denounced the anti-German hysteria for how it alienated foreign-born Americans who had shown no disloyalty. Author Edward Steiner noted that in his home state of Iowa, a mob dragged a man out of bed, whipped him, and forced him to kiss the American flag. "Frankly, I am fearing for the future of our country after the war, not while it lasts," he penned in *Outlook*. "I fear that the breach will grow the greater as the war proceeds and as it exacts from us greater sacrifices. I fear that we who are alien-born, and were born again into Americans, will be made into aliens again."[100]

In an era of mob violence, particularly directed against African-Americans, it is perhaps surprising that only one German-American was lynched. Robert Prager was executed in Collinsville, Illinois on April 5, 1918, nearly the anniversary of the war declaration. His fellow miners thought Prager to be a German spy. The police took him into protective custody, but a 200-person mob stormed the jail and hung him from a tree.[101] The lynching made national news, and not all of it denounced the violence. The *Washington Post* published an editorial saying that some lynchings were justifiable: "Enemy propaganda must be stopped, even if a few lynchings may occur."[102]

President Wilson condemned lynching on July 26, 1918, a statement that was buried in the back pages of newspapers. He equated mob violence with Germany's unlawful behavior and concluded that the rioter "has adopted the standards of the enemies of his country, whom he affects to despise." Beyond that, the president took no further action.[103]

In the backdrop to the Prager lynching and the IWW trial, super patriots believed that the nation needed a tougher law to deal with dissenters. The Espionage Act did not go far enough. Congress amended it on May 16, 1918 with the Sedition Act. It provided the attorney general broad powers to target seditionists, even idle talk that might be perceived to criticize the war effort. One could not speak out against Liberty Bond sales, nor denounce the draft, nor criticize the flag, the military, nor soldiers in uniform. It was a law designed to curtail freedom of speech by imposing de facto censorship.

Brewer Christian Heurich, who had experienced the anti-German hysteria firsthand, was critical of how the Sedition Act silenced the opposition. "This amendment to the espionage act completely muffled freedom of both speech and the press—far more than was ever done in the civil war and far more than was being done in any of the European countries then at war," he noted.[104]

The Espionage Act and the Sedition Act together made it illegal to interfere with the mobilization of the armed forces and the draft. Combined with the Trading with the Enemy Act, the trifecta of laws stifled freedom of speech and basic civil liberties. Well known pacifists such Kate Richard O'Hare, Scott Nearing, and Rose Pastor Stokes were convicted for speaking out against the war. Anarchists Emma Goldman and Alexander Berkman were sent to jail for denouncing the draft. The most famous incident involving the Sedition Act came on June 16, 1918, a month after the law went into effect, when Socialist Party leader Eugene Debs gave a speech in Canton, Ohio, urging resistance to the draft. He was arrested two weeks later and charged with sedition and sentenced to ten years in prison. President Wilson called Debs a "traitor to his country" and refused to pardon him after the war.[105]

Another controversial issue during the Great War was the draft. The country had not seen conscription since the Civil War. Although most young men registered as required, there was substantial opposition from pacifists and socialists. The question of conscientious objectors came to the fore—that is, those who opposed violence on religious grounds. The National Civil Liberties Bureau (precursor to the American Civil Liberties Union) formed in summer 1917 in part to protect conscientious objectors. In what would become an ACLU trademark action, it employed a small army of lawyers in cities around the country to defend those who had been arrested.[106] The *New York Times* opined, "Jails Are Waiting for Them."[107]

In the early months of the war, people could still protest, though not always peacefully. When eight thousand socialists held a peace parade in Boston on July 1, 1917, a mob of sailors and soldiers descended on them on Boston Common, stripped them of their red flags, and beat up many. Though the military had stoked the violence, the only people arrested were socialists.[108] In Neu Ulm, Minnesota, a crowd of ten thousand German-Americans protested the draft on July 25. Three days later, a huge Silent Parade of African-Americans marched through Manhattan to protest the East St. Louis race riot. As war mobilization picked up steam, however, the government increasingly took action against dissenters. Pacifists either converted to supporting the war or fell silent. By the end of the year, the *New York Times* declared the "Ebb of Pacifism in America."[109]

A week after the Armistice, New York City mayor John Hylan banned the display of the red flag. When the socialists met at Madison Square Garden on November 25, some five hundred sailors and soldiers formed a mob to storm the place. Heavy police protection prevented the mob from entering the building. The next night, a gathering of communists at the Palm Garden caused another riot as soldiers beat people up while attempting to storm through a police cordon to disrupt the meeting.[110]

The question of the draft became even more contentious on August 31, 1918, when Congress expanded the age range of men eligible for the draft to eighteen to forty-five (twenty-four million men were now eligible for conscription). "As a bachelor, I am eligible under the new draft, and may soon be toting a gun," H. L. Mencken wrote a friend. "There will be few worse soldiers." He was never drafted.[111] To enforce registration, Attorney General Thomas Gregory ordered the mass arrest of "slackers" (draft dodgers). The volunteer super patriots of the American Protective League (APL) orchestrated a three-day enforcement action in the New York City area and other cities beginning on September 3. It became known as the "slacker raid." Agents fanned out to places of employment, restaurants, subways, and theaters. Every eligible-looking man was ordered to present papers showing that he had registered for the draft, and if he could not, he was detained on the spot and sent to police stations and local armories. In New York, 60,187 were rounded up, while across the river in New Jersey, 88,875 were held until they could prove that they had registered. For all of the storm and stress of the detainments, only a few hundred draft dodgers were actually caught. Most American men had in fact registered but had neglected to carry documentary proof.[112]

The slacker raid was a blunt-force instrument intended to bully dissidents. Nothing like this—a mass police action against the country's own citizens—had happened in American history before. Senators were up in arms, loudly condemning the action. Democratic Senator George Chamberlain of Oregon denounced the raid as "Prussianism."[113] *The Nation* declared "Civil Liberty Dead" after the slacker raid.[114]

Shortly before the slacker raid, the Department of Justice raided National Civil Liberties Bureau offices on August 30 and arrested founder Roger Baldwin for refusing to submit to physical examination in accordance with the draft law. Baldwin was thirty-four years old and eligible for military service, but he refused to be conscripted. He was sentenced to a year in the Atlanta federal penitentiary.[115]

Up to this point in American history, the First Amendment had rarely come before the judiciary. The amendment protected freedom of speech and the press, a freedom that was sorely challenged by American involvement in the Great War. The federal government de facto curtailed free speech, which dissenters challenged. It would be up to the judiciary to decide if freedom of speech had limits.

The U.S. Supreme Court took up one of the most significant 20th century legal cases in January 1919 called *Schenck v. United States*. Pacifist Charles Schenck had distributed fifteen thousand leaflets in Pennsylvania, comparing the draft to involuntary servitude and suggesting that young men avoid registering. He was arrested and charged under the Espionage Act, as he was interfering with the wartime mobilization. He in turned sued the federal government for violating his First Amendment rights.

Justice Oliver Wendell Holmes wrote the opinion in the unanimous decision, issued on March 3. Holmes was an old man now, but he had fought for the Union in the Civil War and had been wounded twice. The earlier war had informed his views on patriotism and the experience of a nation at war, and that conditions really were different in wartime. He argued that the government has the right to limit free speech when there is a "clear and present danger"—in this case, to the war mobilization. He wrote, "The most stringent protection of free speech would not protect a man in falsely shouting fire in a theatre and causing a panic." Holmes would likewise declare that the Eugene Debs case was the same as Schenck's, and the Supreme Court upheld Debs's conviction. [116]

American democratic values and civil rights were significantly undermined during the Great War. Ethnic groups were pressured to conform and protesters were silenced. In fact, things would get even worse after the war when Attorney General Mitchell Palmer attempted to mass-deport the country's radicals and keep the country safe from communism during the Red Scare.

FIVE

The Yanks Are Coming

Over there, over there
Send the word, send the word over there
That the Yanks are coming
The Yanks are coming

—"Over There" by George M. Cohan, 1917

I n March 1917, the German army in northern France retreated a short distance to newly prepared fortifications known as the Hindenburg Line. This was designed to shore up its defenses in preparation for the American entry into the war. Germany planned a defensive strategy on the Western Front while its U-boats sank British vessels and its army knocked Russia out of the war. As the United States marshaled its forces, the Allies teetered on collapse.

The German resumption of unrestricted submarine warfare that winter was brutal. In its first three months, U-boats sank 470 ocean-going vessels. By fall 1917, they had sunk 4.25 million tons of Allied shipping, most of it British. One in four British ships was being sent to the bottom of the sea. The Germans were sinking shipping faster than the Allies could build it, though American shipyards were now churning out vessels. Compounding this was the fact that most of the Allies were near bankruptcy, propped up only by American financing.[1]

It was the crisis of spring 1917 that compelled President Wilson to dispatch a small force with General John Pershing to France to shore up Allied morale. Few in France had heard of Pershing. That would not matter for long once he arrived on the continent in June 1917. The French were thrilled, and huge crowds gathered for the general. *Chicago Tribune* journalist Floyd Gibbons quipped, "Paris took Pershing by storm." The American presence had greatly boosted French morale, even if American doughboys would not be ready for combat for another year.[2]

James Harbord, a marine officer who accompanied Pershing, recorded the general's impression on the French in his diary: "General Pershing certainly looks his part since he came here. He is a fine figure of a man; carries himself well, holds himself on every occasion with proper dignity; is easy in manner, knows how to enter a crowded room, and is fast developing into a world figure. He has captured the fickle Paris crowd at any rate, and could be elected King of France to-morrow if it depended on Paris."[3]

Shortly after arriving in France, Pershing prescribed the Sam Browne belt for officers, a leather belt that passed over the right shoulder and attached to a waist belt. It was a way to distinguish officers from enlisted men without being ostentatious.

Never before had the U.S. sent an army overseas. Pershing knew that the American army would not be ready for combat until spring 1918 at the earliest. The Allies would have to wait a year before the American presence began to be felt on the battlefield. He realized that the American Expeditionary Forces he was to command was merely a "theoretical army," as he called it. The country still faced the massive task of creating a modern army, training and equipping it, transporting it overseas—and only then could Pershing lead it into battle. At the same time, he would also play coalition partner and diplomat to keep the Allies from co-opting the American army and amalgamating it into their own forces. The British and French were eager to enlist Americans directly into their decimated armies, but Pershing declined to be a "recruiting agency" for the Allies, as he called it. He fought hard to preserve an autonomous American army that would be responsible for a sector of the front—a battle he would fight for much of the war. [4]

Likewise, President Wilson wanted the AEF to remain independent. An independent American command, if it could sway the cause to victory, would earn Wilson a prominent place at the peace table. Edward House seconded Pershing's policy of not intermixing American forces with Allied units. "If once we merge with them we will probably never emerge," he reported to the president. [5]

Pershing had his orders from Secretary of War Newton Baker: "The underlying idea must be kept in view that the forces of the United States are a separate and distinct component of the combined forces, the identity of which must be preserved." Pershing had latitude in an emergency to reinforce the Allies with American troops, but he was to do everything possible to keep the American army independent. [6]

At Christmas 1917, Secretary of War Baker relayed to Pershing the president's belief that, should Allied forces be in desperate straits, American forces could be dispatched to various points on the front to support them. "We do not desire loss of identity of our forces *but regard that as secondary* to the meeting of any critical situation by the most helpful use possible of the troops at your command," Baker wrote. Pershing would retain command of the troops and would coordinate their deployment with the Allies. The secretary reminded him that he was authorized "to act with entire freedom to accomplish the main purposes in mind." [7]

President Wilson would never allow the U.S. to become one of the Allies—it simply declared war against Germany without signing an alliance treaty with England and France—and he always referred to American's allies during the war as "associates." It was a legalistic term. Wilson pushed back against Herbert Hoover, showing how he sensitive he was toward the question. "I have noticed on one or two of the posters of the Food Administration the words 'Our Allies.' I would be very much obliged if you would issue instructions that 'Our Associates in the War' is to be substituted," Wilson wrote. Wilson was taking a principled stance that the U.S. was not part of any formal alliance. Although conceptually true, the Allies were de facto America's allies, and the British and French would have been insulted if they were only considered associates. [8]

Pershing had capable staff organizing the mostly raw recruits of the 1st Division, including thirty-seven-year old Captain George Marshall. Marshall, who had graduated from the Virginia Military Institute in 1901, was assigned as operations officer to the new division. The 1st Division mustered at Hoboken to embark on former German merchant vessels, which would take them to Europe. Marshall watched the thousands of men board the ships in the middle of the night, the men saying nothing and there being little noise but their footsteps. Marshall finally remarked to the embarkation port commander, "The men seem very solemn." The commander responded, "Of course they are. We are watching the harvest of death."[9]

The initial fourteen-thousand-man division was sent to Europe with little training—most of the soldiers were enthusiastic recruits who would get much of their experience in France. This would be a notable characteristic of the U.S. Army: it would learn how to fight in the trenches in a trial by fire.

The 1st Division landed in France in late June 1917, and Pershing was thoroughly unimpressed with their appearance and bearing. These soldiers were not ready for war, and they would not be deployed to the front until that autumn. But knowing the importance of boosting French morale, Pershing allowed an infantry battalion to parade through Paris on July 4. Most of the men still behaved like recruits. Pershing was concerned about their conduct, but he need not have worried: the French were so excited that they showered the doughboys with affection. "On the march to Lafayette's tomb at Picpus Cemetery the battalion was joined by a great crowd, many women forcing their way into the ranks and swinging along arm in arm with the men," the general recalled. "With wreaths about their necks and bouquets in their hats and rifles, the column looked like a moving flower garden." Arriving at the Marquis de Lafayette's tomb, the officers gave impromptu speeches. It was Pershing's aide, Colonel Charles Stanton (not Pershing himself), who uttered the famous line, *"Nous voilà, Lafayette!"* ("Lafayette, we are here!"). In the American Revolution, French forces had helped turn the tide against the British and win the war. Now American forces were coming to France's aid. [10]

Seeing only desperation and low morale in France, Pershing cabled Washington, asking for a million American doughboys to be sent to Europe by the next May. This stunned the War Department, but Baker accepted his general's verdict. The first soldiers would soon be drafted. This would require massive amounts of shipping, supplies, and upgrades to ports and railroads. The War Department would send not just one million, but two million soldiers to fight in France. [11]

The War at Sea

"The one all-absorbing necessity now is soldiers with which to beat the enemy in the field, and ships to carry them," noted General Tasker Bliss in December 1917, the former army chief of staff who now represented the Americans on the Allies' Supreme War Council. [12] Though devastating to British shipping, the German renewal of unrestricted submarine warfare proved unable to force England to the peace table. Germany underestimated the amount of assistance the U.S. could provide in making up the shipping and supply shortfall. But how to get the promised million doughboys over to Europe, given that the Germans were sinking Allied shipping faster than replacement vessels could be built? The U-boats might cause huge manpower losses.

The British refused to convoy their ships, and as a result the North Atlantic had become a shooting gallery for U-boats. Britain may well have been knocked out of the war in 1917 had the U.S. not intervened and insisted that all American supplies and soldiers be transported in convoys. This helped keep the U-boats at bay and reduced shipping losses. A merchant marine convoy would assemble in an American port, then steam for Europe with a flotilla of destroyer escorts. They proved so effective that the U.S. only lost ninety-four ships to U-boats during the nineteen months of hostilities.[13]

The Royal Navy ruled the waves—and the merchant marine—and it would initially fall to British steamers to bring the U.S. Army to Europe and to supply it, at least until sufficient tonnage could be built at American shipyards. Even as American ships were launched in greater numbers, half of the American Expeditionary Forces were transported to Europe in British vessels.

Transporting the million doughboys across the Atlantic Ocean through U-boat infested waters was a huge and risky undertaking, and it is a marvel that so few transports were sunk. On October 17, 1917, the *Antilles* became the first troop transport to be torpedoed, claiming sixty-seven lives. Convoys reduced but did not eliminate the risk. The SS *Tuscania* went down in February 1918 with the loss of two hundred soldiers. Most of the troop ships sunk, however, were sailing home with empty holds.

In addition to the open seas, the American coastline proved largely defenseless. Most of the U-boat attacks were in waters off Great Britain, leading many to believe incorrectly that the submarines had a short range. The Germans disproved that with a succession of brazen U-boat attacks in American waters in 1918. In late May, the *U-151* laid mines off the Virginia coast and cut two undersea cables, then attacked and sank three schooners on May 25. On just one day, June 2, it sank six ships off New Jersey, including the small liner SS *Carolina*. Over the next several days the submarine continued to attack and sink ships, engaging twenty-three ships altogether and sinking 58,028 tons of shipping on its cruise. The U-boat was never caught and it cruised back to Germany. The brazen attacks caused a sensation in the United States. It was a major embarrassment to the navy and to Secretary Daniels.[14]

On July 19, the cruiser USS *San Diego* struck a submerged mine off Fire Island, New York, and went down, the only major American warship lost during the war. The mine signaled a new threat on the American coast from the German U-boat *U-156*. Two days later, the submarine attacked the tugboat *Perth Amboy*, which was pulling four

coal barges along the Cape Cod shoreline near Orleans, Massachusetts. The Germans fired three torpedoes, but all missed their target,
so the submarine surfaced and fired its deck gun at the American
vessels. It sank three barges and set the tug on fire. A large crowd
of summer vacationers gathered on the shore to watch the one-sided
battle as shells exploded dangerously close. Some shells landed in a
nearby marsh. Members of the local United States Life-Saving Service, which normally rescued floundering ships, rowed through the
shellfire to rescue the tugboat crew. Meanwhile, two navy airplanes
attempted to sink the U-boat by dropping dynamite. The submarine
submerged and got away. It was a reminder how vulnerable the U.S.
shoreline was to attack—and how unprepared American civil defenses
were. It was also the only time during the Great War that American
soil came directly under attack.[15] President Wilson ordered the Cape
Cod Canal nationalized four days after the attack to ensure that coal
supplies continued and that vessels stayed out of the shipping lanes
where German submarines could attack them.[16]

The Allies were never able to eliminate the threat from U-boats,
but they found ways to mitigate it. Despite sinking more than a half-
million tons of shipping per month, Germany was unable to knock
England out of the war. Escorted convoys had significantly reduced
shipping losses. In addition, the Allies began deploying countermea-
sures, such as mining the Strait of Dover in 1917. Late in the war, the
Royal Navy and U.S. Navy erected a submarine "barrage" across the
North Sea, a heavy zone of mines and underwater nets that largely
curtailed U-boats from reaching the open Atlantic and the shipping
lanes. The American intervention had kept England supplied and
in the war.

Training the American Army

By 1917, the Germans occupied most of Belgium and a large portion
of northern France. They held a large salient that bulged toward Paris,
but curved back north near the English Channel, as the Belgian and

British armies protected the vital ports along the Channel. The bulk of the French army defended Paris. The Western Front continued through Lorraine to the Swiss border, but that front was fairly quiet during the war, as the Vosges Mountains protected France's eastern flank. Somewhere along this long front, Pershing intended to carve out a zone for independent operations. Lorraine would be a good place to start, as the American army could train there in safety while also threatening vital German industries. He organized a General Headquarters (GHQ) at Chaumont, modeled on the British and French armies.

Supporting the American Expeditionary Forces in Lorraine posed a logistical problem not just for the United States, but also for France. Supplies and troops came through the ports of Bassens, Brest, La Pallice, Saint-Nazaire, and others on the French west coast. Many of these harbors needed significant upgrades to support the volumes that Pershing projected would be needed from America. From these ports, the Americans required a lengthy railway network to transport supplies to northeastern France, more than four hundred miles away. These lines had to be upgraded, and the Americans were reliant on French locomotives and railway cars until they could bring sufficient carriages from American factories.[17]

Often there were no barracks where the Americans were to be stationed, so soldiers were billeted in towns across the countryside, in farmhouses and haylofts—wherever there was room. Most of the troops arrived in France with their training only partly complete. This would not do against the most powerful army in Europe. It took months to train the American recruits into fighting soldiers with English and French assistance—and the Allies were desperate to have the doughboys get into the trenches, ready or not.

The Allies were eager to train the American forces, as they had gained much experience fighting the Germans to a standstill for three years. "If the Americans do not permit the French to teach them, the Germans will do so at great cost of life," said French Prime Minister Georges Clemenceau to Edward House.[18] However, Pershing was disappointed that this focused on trench warfare. He wanted the soldiers trained for "open warfare," which would be necessary once they broke through German lines. The Allies were overly reliant on artillery, he believed, whereas Pershing wanted his men to be experts with a rifle. "I am making every effort to inculcate a strong, aggressive, fighting spirit among our forces, and to overcome a more or less perfunctory attitude engendered by years of peace," Pershing wrote to Secretary of War Newton Baker. Baker supported his decision to relieve brigade and division commanders whom Pershing believed were not aggressive or fit enough. Pershing preferred young commanders with a boundless sense of energy and confidence. Any commander who led from behind would soon be sent back to the States. One of the first to go was General William Sibert, the commander of the 1st Division. Pershing would fire more than a thousand officers over the course of the war. [19]

In addition, Pershing believed that training with the British and French was bad for his soldiers. "The morale of the Allies is low and association with them has had a bad effect upon our men," he wrote Baker. "To counteract the talk our men have heard, we have had to say to our troops, through their officers, that we had come over to brace up the Allies and help them win and that they must pay no attention to loose remarks along that line by their Allied comrades." [20]

Pershing's open warfare doctrine butted against the more experienced British and French, who understood that trench warfare was siege warfare, that artillery and the machine gun were the keys to overwhelming firepower, and that the rifle was secondary to the greater weapons of mass killing. Pershing somehow believed he knew better, that the American fighting spirit would prevail against a well-emplaced machine gun nest with a clear field of fire.

Open warfare meant long waves of infantry rising up out of the trenches to assault an enemy position frontally. It was a costly tactic, one that would take the army time to learn to undo (the Americans used open warfare tactics in their initial battles at Château-Thierry, Belleau Wood, and Soissons, three battles with very high casualties among the infantry). The Allies had learned from the disaster at the Somme in 1916 how to use the rolling artillery barrage, and the need for smaller teams of infantry to advance, take cover, and provide supporting fire while flankers took out a strongpoint. The rifle was certainly paramount to the infantryman, but infantry was almost defenseless against artillery and machine guns if caught in the open. Even infantrymen had to specialize: some would carry machine guns, others trench mortars and flamethrowers, while others would specialize in launching grenades. Being an infantryman was more complicated than just charging forward with a bayonet affixed to a rifle. The Americans had much to learn, and Pershing's adherence to his flawed open warfare doctrine would cost many young men their lives.

Although American industry produced prodigious amounts of steel, and American farms grew bountiful surpluses, American weapons-making capacity was sorely lacking. The American Expeditionary Forces became heavily dependent upon Allied production for automatic rifles, masks, machine guns, munitions, trench mortars, and even mules. The Americans requisitioned airplanes, artillery, light tanks, railroad equipment, and trucks from the French, and bought gas mask and heavy tanks from the British. "Pershing commanded a beggar army," noted army historian David Woodward.[21]

American artillery batteries were outfitted with French guns, often manufactured with American steel: the heavy 155mm howitzer, and the light but devastating 75mm cannon, better known as the French 75. This little howitzer was revolutionary: a top-secret hydropneumatic design allowed it to remain in place after firing. It was lightweight and rapid-firing, and thus was an extremely lethal weapon on the battle-field. The Germans called it the Devil Gun. In honor of the nimble little gun, a New Orleans bartender invented the French 75 cocktail.[22]

The 1st Division would prove the guinea pig for the rest of the army. George Marshall called it the "only child," as it was initially on its own in France.[23] By October 1917, the division's initial training was complete. Pershing agreed to test it by deploying it with the French army on a quiet sector of the front. The battalions rotated in and out of the trenches to gain experience. On October 23, doughboys fired the first artillery shell directed at German lines. The honor went to Sergeant Alex Arch of South Bend, Indiana, who pulled the lanyard of a French 75mm howitzer from Battery C of the 6th Field Artillery. The brass casing was saved and presented to President Wilson.[24]

A second American division, the 26th "Yankee" Division, arrived in the fall. By the end of 1917, American forces in France numbered about 175,000, organized in four divisions, with another forty-five divisions being trained in the U.S. The question of training and transportation loomed over all.[25] The winter was severely cold and there was too little fuel to warm the soldiers, who froze in their billets and haylofts. In February 1918, however, the army created an independent newspaper for the doughboys, known as the *Stars and Stripes*. Pershing authorized publication of the newspaper to give doughboys patriotic news of the war effort and news from the home front.

Much of the American Expeditionary Forces would not arrive for a year or later after war was declared. It took the U.S. a considerable time to assemble and train an army nearly from scratch, as well as construct the ships that would carry them to Europe. Part of the U.S. Army was shipped over by the British, and they assumed responsibility for training these units in trench warfare. The British were eager to have the American troops amalgamated into their army, but Pershing would have none of that: American soldiers had to be under the American flag. Although he intended for these troops eventually to be transferred to the American zone in Lorraine, the springtime crisis of 1918 left several divisions in place in Flanders, and there they fought in support of the British and Belgians for the duration of the war.

The American soldiers serving in Flanders shared rations with other Allied countries. The Belgians were particularly fond of fried potatoes, which they called *frites*, named after a Parisian restaurant owner named Fritz who perfected how to cook the potatoes known as pommes frites in French. The doughboys came to call the delicacy French fries.

A crucial part of training was how to fight while wearing a gas mask, a necessary implement of war since the Germans began gassing the Allies in 1915. War correspondent Floyd Gibbons, who wrote for the *Chicago Tribune*, described the claustrophobia of wearing a gas mask: "Our heads were topped with uncomfortable steel casques, harder than the backs of turtles. Our eyes were large, flat, round glazed surfaces unblinking and owl-like. Our faces were shapeless folds of black rubber cloth. Our lungs sucked air through tubes from a canvas bag under our chins and we were inhabiting a tree top like a family of apes." Soldiers might have to spend six hours or longer wearing a mask after a gas attack, or risk an excruciating, choking death.[26]

Captain George Patton had accompanied Pershing to Europe in 1917 after serving with the general in Mexico. He spent much of the year 1917 in boredom, running a motor pool and conspiring to get his wife Beatrice to Europe for a visit. Patton came from a wealthy family and spent a large sum, $4,386, buying a Packard Twin Six automobile so he could drive himself around northern France. That fall, an opportunity presented for him to establish an American tank school. It was a fateful decision for the young officer, who wrote his father, "I have a hunch that my Mexican Auto Battle was the fore runner of this," referring to his time battling *Villistas*. "Who can say?"[27]

It was an opportune time for Patton, just as tanks were proving their worth on the battlefield. On November 20, the British army attacked at Cambrai with hundreds of heavy tanks, briefly breaking through the German lines and showing what massed tanks could do in combat. Patton established the American tank school in Bourg. He borrowed ten French light tanks to train his men in March 1918. "When the procession of ten started across the fields I was delighted as I have been living on hopes for the last four months," Patton wrote his wife. Patton would eventually train two battalions of tankers, and he would lead them into battle as the 1st Tank Brigade.[28]

Douglas MacArthur was one of the more charismatic, flamboyant, and handsome officers in the American army. Often at odds with the army headquarters, he had a knack for casual insubordination. When his Rainbow Division reached France in late 1917, he soon learned that it would be broken up to reinforce other divisions. He called in a favor with Pershing's chief of staff, and the division remained together. MacArthur served as the division chief of staff and later commanded a brigade, always placing himself on the front line. He developed his own modified field uniform: a crushed cap instead of a helmet, a scarf knit by his mother, a turtleneck, and a riding crop. He never carried a weapon or a gas mask, and as a result he was gassed twice.[29]

Another soldier who would rise to prominence after the war was Harry Truman of Independence, Missouri. He was thirty-three years old, had terrible eyesight, and was the sole breadwinner for a farming family—yet he volunteered to serve. He signed up, as he felt it was his patriotic duty, and was elected a lieutenant in a Missouri field artillery battery. It was the first position he would ever be elected to. Truman led Battery D of the 2nd Battalion, 129th Field Artillery Regiment. It was largely an unruly, Irish Catholic unit. Truman was strict but fair, and the men came to appreciate him. Many became lifelong friends.

Truman and an advanced party of his battalion sailed from New York on March 29, 1918, aboard the *George Washington*, the converted German ocean liner. Truman's eyesight was so bad that he took six pairs of eyeglasses with him.[30] In France, Truman was run through a French artillery school to learn about the French 75mm howitzer, which his unit would be equipped with—and then had to train the other officers of his unit. His unit was first deployed in August 1918 to the Vosges Mountains in Lorraine, a quiet stretch of the front, in order to experience the front line. The first rounds that his battery fired were poison gas shells, though the inexperienced soldiers panicked and ran when the Germans fired back.[31]

Some 367,710 African-Americans enlisted in the armed forces during the Great War; of these, about 200,000 were sent to France, though most ended up being relegated to traditional roles in hard labor. Only 50,000 black soldiers saw combat. Army training was a major challenge in the segregated Deep South, where black soldiers always had the worst camps and facilities and were discriminated against whenever they attempted to patronize businesses. Much of the South still could not accept blacks as fellow citizens and cringed at the idea that blacks in uniform might demand equality for serving their country.[32]

Two infantry divisions were composed of African-Americans: the 92nd and 93rd. The War Department dispatched the 92nd Division to train with the British, who in May 1918 protested having black troops assigned to them. Pershing wrote back to the British commander, Field Marshal Douglas Haig: "You will, of course, appreciate my position in this matter, which, in brief, is that these negroes are American citizens. My Government, for reasons which concern itself alone, has decided to organize colored combat divisions and now desires the early dispatch of one of these divisions to France. Naturally I cannot and will not discriminate against these soldiers." The British continued the protest, and the War Department eventually backed down, assigning the division to train with the French.[33]

The 93rd Division likewise trained with the French, its four regiments broken up so that each supported a French division, rather than fighting as a cohesive unit or under the American Expeditionary Forces. Pershing claimed in his memoirs that he had asked the French to return the division, but they did not. Pershing was known to get his way when it came to having his men assigned to the American army, but his protest was either feeble or nonexistent. That fact is, it was a relief to Pershing for the French to keep the black soldiers, as he was well aware of the intrinsic racism in much of the American army. Many white doughboys did not see black soldiers as equals, and this created antagonisms that would continue well after the war.[34]

And as supportive as he was toward black soldiers— he had led them for years and was probably more tolerant than most officers and soldiers—Pershing viewed their role best as enlisted men. "Under capable white officers and with sufficient training, negro soldiers have always acquitted themselves creditably," Pershing wrote.[35]

The War Department protested to Pershing when it heard that black troops were placed in dangerous areas of the front but had not received adequate medical care. Pershing noted that this was likely from German propaganda, and that the black troops were in fact stationed on quiet fronts. He cabled back, "Only regret expressed by colored troops is that they are not given more dangerous work to do. They are especially amused at the stories being circulated that the American troops are placed in the most dangerous positions and all are desirous of having more active service than has been permitted so far." In fact, most of the black units were used as labor battalions, rather than combat forces. It was likely a disappointment for many of the black soldiers who hoped to be part of the fighting.[36]

Of the black units, none achieved the fame of the 369th Regiment, known as the "Harlem Hellfighters." Commanded largely by white officers, the unit was organized as the 15th New York, comprised of urban soldiers. It had one of the finest regimental bands around. After a period serving as dock workers helping upgrade St. Nazaire's port facilities, the unit was unceremoniously renamed the 369th and assigned to the French sector. The regimental commander, William Hayward, pleaded with Pershing to allow his men to fight in the trenches, but Pershing was leery of having a black combat unit among white infantry. Placing the 369th with the French solved that problem: the French *poilu* (the rank-and-file infantrymen) were more egalitarian and there were fewer discipline problems over race. The French equipped the Hellfighters as one of their own units, down to helmets, rifles, and uniforms. Colonel Hayward wrote a friend, "Our great American general simply put the black orphan in a basket, set it on the doorstep, pulled the bell, and went away."[37]

On May 11, 1918, the Hellfighters won their first recognition for gallantry during a deployment to the front. Two privates, Henry Johnson and Needham Roberts, were sent forward to a listening post, and there they were attacked by a platoon-size German raiding party. Roberts was shot but continued fighting, while Johnson killed four Germans, including one with a bolo knife, and wounded several others, forcing the raiders to retreat. The two soldiers were awarded the French Croix de Guerre.[38]

Women at War

Women had long been left behind to tend the home fires while men went off to fight wars, but the Great War was different. Because of the nature of total warfare, every citizen was involved in the conflict, like it or not. Not only did American women replace men in industry and shipbuilding, serve in the vast military bureaucracy, and work as nurses, they even joined the armed forces. Encouraged by Secretary of the Navy Josephus Daniels, some eleven thousand women served in the navy and received the same pay as men, while another 350 women joined the marines. It was women's contribution during the war that would directly lead to them getting the vote. [39]

The American Red Cross undertook a massive expansion during the Great War, mostly guided by women. Women set up and staffed thousands of local Red Cross stations in the U.S. and in Europe, rolled bandages, and volunteered in countless ways. First Lady Edith Wilson and the president's daughters sewed bandages during the war and volunteered for the American Red Cross. Edith worked at the canteen at Washington's Union Station, where trainloads of hungry soldiers passed through daily en route to New York, where they would sail to Europe.

Eleanor Roosevelt, wife of the assistant navy secretary, volunteered at the same Red Cross canteen as Mrs. Wilson. Like her husband, Eleanor spoke with the Yankee lockjaw that Northeasterners affected. She had not yet gained the self-confidence and independence that she would exercise as First Lady in the 1930s. But the Great War gave her an opportunity to serve, and she loved it. Like many American women, she took up knitting during the war. "No one moved without her knitting," she noted. [40]

The American Red Cross furnished fifty hospitals in France, all privately funded, with staffs of doctors and thousands of women nurses. Other women served as communications specialists and telephone operators with the AEF. Some worked for the Young Men's Christian Association (YMCA), staffing canteens, providing hot beverages and a place for doughboys to relax while they were away from the front. The Salvation Army sent a contingent to France, where they developed a mobile kitchen that produced doughnuts. The women became known as the "Doughnut Girls." [41]

As hundreds of thousands of American soldiers prepared to ship off to Europe, Isabel Anderson volunteered to serve at Red Cross canteens in France. She was a wealthy woman who combined her considerable fortune with her husband Larz. She published her memoirs of the experience in 1918, before the war had even ended, donating the proceeds to the American Red Cross. The book was called *Zigzagging*, a phrase generally associated with the zigzagging that ships used to foil submarine attacks. In this case, Anderson zigzagged across Europe. When asked about her time in Europe, she explained casually, "Well, I worked with an American Red Cross canteen in the army zone for a time, and assisted for several weeks in an operating-room with the Queen of Belgium, and among other things I had the good fortune to dine with General Pershing at headquarters at the American front."[42] On that latter occasion, she arrived so late because of automobile trouble that the general had already eaten. "The only thing which I remember General Pershing's saying was that he was very much troubled by the lack of ships," Anderson recalled.[43]

The War in the Air

One of the first American officers to arrive in France was Lieutenant Colonel William Mitchell, better known as Billy, a brilliant and flamboyant member of the general staff who would become one of the leading innovators in the American armed forces. His father was a U.S. senator from Wisconsin. The opinionated young man had an independent streak and an outspoken tongue that would land him in trouble. Mitchell talked incessantly, a trait that earned him few allies. As an army officer, he was intrigued by aviation, a technology that was only a decade old. However, the War Department spent precious little money on developing American aviation. Mitchell was stationed in Washington, D.C., but the army would not pay for flight school. He enrolled and paid for it out of his own pocket.

Mitchell landed in Europe just as the U.S. declared war in April 1917. He was assigned to the American embassy in Paris, but he spent almost no time there, instead traveling to British and French lines to observe how they conducted wartime aviation. Three years of warfare had led to startling developments in flying. New specialty airplanes were developed: interceptors, day bombers, night bombers, reconnaissance, even torpedo bombers. Most of the planes were biplanes, twin-winged aircraft constructed of wood, though the Germans developed a Fokker triplane late in the war, best associated with the "Red Baron," Manfred von Richthofen.

Colonel Mitchell's assignment was to build an air service to support Pershing's army. He had to create this literally out of nothing, as no American air service existed. "Our air force consisted of one Nieuport airplane which I used myself and that was all," he wrote. His first pilots were American members of the French Foreign Legion. Mitchell arranged for French airplanes and mechanics. [44]

Mitchell eventually ditched his obsolete Nieuport for a speedy French Spad, a single-engine biplane that became the backbone of the American air service by summer 1918. Mitchell flew himself around the battlefield in northern France and though he avoided dogfights, he often reconnoitered the area. He soon observed how the two sides operated in the skies overhead: the French tended to use constant air patrols along the front lines, whereas the Germans left the skies open, massing their planes to dominate the skies in support of a particular mission. The Germans had excellent aircraft and experienced pilots. This made them tough to beat.

By April 1918, just as the bulk of the American Expeditionary Forces began to arrive in France, Mitchell had assembled his air service command and numerous pursuit (fighter) squadrons. His men would support the U.S. Army in every major battle from the air. The Americans focused on pursuit aircraft, relying on the Allies to provide bombers when needed.

Billy Mitchell recalled a prank that his pilots played on a hospital. The infirmary was near his aerodrome, and many hotshot pilots took to spending their downtime there on account of the pretty American nurses. The chief surgeon ordered the pilots to stop fraternizing with his staff. The pilots stated their objections by bombing the hospital with toilet paper rolls. Mitchell called it "the funniest sight I had seen in a long time. Of course I knew who had done it but took no action beyond telling them to cut out all foolishness in the future." [45]

There was a great deal of chivalry and respect among pilots, even among enemies. If a pilot was shot down and killed over enemy territory, they were given a funeral with honors, and the opposing air service was notified of the last rites. Such was done with both Manfred von Richthofen and Quentin Roosevelt.

Both sides sent up observation balloons, heavily protected by antiaircraft batteries, to keep track of enemy movements and to adjust artillery fire. Despite being filled with hydrogen, these balloons were difficult to blow up, even with incendiary bullets.

One of the young men Mitchell recruited to become a fighter pilot was an Ohioan with a slight accent named Eddie Rickenbacher. His parents were German-speaking Swiss, and during the war he changed the "h" to a "k" in his last name so it sounded less German. Rickenbacker came from a modest, working-class family. Before the war, he was road tester for automobile companies, and soon found himself racing cars. Over the years of high-speed driving, he developed instincts for daring maneuvers and anticipating an opponent's move—skills that would serve him well as a combat pilot.

Rickenbacker joined the army and became a driver in Pershing's motor pool, as he was not only a skillful driver but also knew how to fix engines. It was not what he had signed up for. One day he fixed a broken-down car on the side of the road in France, which drew the attention of Colonel Billy Mitchell. Rickenbacker let Mitchell know that he wanted to fly, and Mitchell in turn got Pershing to release Rickenbacker for the French flight school at Tours.

Rickenbacker joined the 94th Pursuit Squadron in March 1918, known as the "Hat-in-the-Ring" squadron for its logo of Uncle Sam's stovepipe hat surrounded by a ring. The nickname came from the idea that America had thrown its hat in the ring by entering the European conflict. The squadron included the famed pilot, Raoul Lufbery, who had flown with the Lafayette Escadrille for two years. The squadron was issued old French Nieuport fighters. The Nieuport was speedy and climbed quickly, but it had one major flaw: the wing fabric stripped away during a steep dive. The Americans had to make do with surplus aircraft, as the U.S. had virtually no combat aircraft manufacturing.

April 14 dawned cloudy with low-lying fog obstructing visibility. The sound of approaching German aircraft could be heard as they crossed the front lines, and two American pursuit craft, flown by

Douglas Campbell and Alan Winslow, scrambled from the aerodrome near Toul to intercept them. The pilots flew up through the fog just as two German fighters descended through the clouds. The dogfight was on, directly over the airfield where much of the squadron could see the action. American machine guns tore through the German aircraft, forcing both to land, their pilots taken prisoner and their aircraft seized as prizes. One of the pilots was badly burned and died, while the other, a Pole, survived. They admitted they were lost. Billy Mitchell was impressed by the speed with which his men had acted, as "our pilots were back on the aerodrome within four and one-half minutes after they left it." These were the first two German planes that the budding American air service had shot down. [46]

Fifteen days later, Eddie Rickenbacker shot down his first German plane, a Pfalz fighter. "At 150 yards I pressed my triggers. The tracer bullets cut a streak of living fire into the rear of the Pfalz tail," he wrote in his 1919 memoir. "Raising the nose of the airplane slightly the fiery streak lifted itself like the stream of water pouring from a garden hose. Gradually it settled into the pilot's seat." The enemy aircraft began its death spiral to the earth. By May 28, Rickenbacker had shot down five planes, officially making him an ace. Over the course of the war, Rickenbacker shot down twenty-six German airplanes and balloons, more than any other American pilot, and became America's "ace of aces." [47]

Drinking Doughboys

Influenced by the Anti-Saloon League—the organization pushing for national Prohibition—Congress made it illegal to serve alcohol to a soldier in uniform. Soldiers were expected to be upstanding examples of sobriety, although drinking and soldiering had long gone hand in hand. However, the law could not be enforced outside the United States. American doughboys fighting in France discovered that French soldiers regularly drank in uniform. Wine and cognac were simply part of their rations, which they often shared with Americans. George Cassiday, an American tanker from West Virginia, noted how normal it was for soldiers to drink. "We saw liquor being used in all the allied countries and when we were at the front, detailed with French troops, I received rations of cognac along with the other men." [48]

Colonel Billy Mitchell noted the French supply columns that fed the troops. "Long trains of trucks, each carrying three small hogsheads of wine or beer ran up behind the lines every day, were emptied of their contents and returned for more," he wrote. "The French soldiers are as used to their wine as ours are to their coffee." [49]

Similarly, Captain (and future president) Harry Truman had billeted with the French army and experienced their hospitality. With the news of the pending Eighteenth Amendment, which would enact national Prohibition, Truman noted that some of his soldiers were discussing future plans. "It looks to me like the moonshine business is going to be pretty good in the land of the Liberty Loans and Green Trading Stamps, and some of us want to get in on the ground floor," he wrote his fiancée Bess Wallace. "At least we want to get there in time to lay in a supply for future consumption." [50]

Edwin Parsons, who flew fighter planes for the Lafayette Escadrille, observed that pilots often drank to quiet their nerves. There were no abstainers in his squadron. A favorite beverage was the Lafayette Cocktail, a blend of brandy and champagne "with the kick of a mule," as he called it. After his first dogfight, Parsons landed and was so trembling with fear that he could barely stand. He made his way to the squadron bar. "I swallowed half a glass of brandy neat, in one gulp, without even a shudder," he wrote. It had little effect, so he continued drinking until he had consumed most of the bottle and his nerves finally settled down. After that, Parsons drank a couple shots before each patrol and sipped from a hip flask to warm himself in the frigid high altitudes. When they received complaints that upright American flyers were spoiling their lofty reputation by drinking, the squadron shifted their bar to a neighboring squadron's fifty feet away, and continued business as usual. [51]

General Pershing turned a blind eye toward American soldiers drinking wine when they were billeted with the French. He understood that barring beer and wine consumption by American forces while in France was impractical. However, he could not ignore the greater disciplinary problems that ensued when soldiers drank liquor. Pershing placed any bar or restaurant near a cantonment area off limits if it served distilled spirits. He expected his officers to enforce this order.[52]

Pershing recalled a meal with a French general who had traveled across the United States and stopped in Iowa, then a dry state. "If there is any one thing that a Frenchman cannot understand it is that any people should deliberately enact a law to deprive themselves of taking a glass of wine," he observed. "To have heard him describe how he suffered while in Iowa one would have thought he was telling of a trip across the Sahara Desert."[53]

George Patton, who led the American tank school at Bourg, noted with dismay that four of his officers were arrested for drinking. "We are getting full of virtue here," he wrote his wife sarcastically. "The French do as they please so why not we. People who are going to be killed deserve as much pleasure as they can get."[54]

In his memoirs, Colonel George Marshall noted over and over how he and his fellow officers toasted with champagne after each battlefield success. On a victory parade of American soldiers in London after the war, the Prince of Wales remarked to him, "What a magnificent body of men never to take another drink." Most would likely continue drinking during the dark days of Prohibition ahead.[55]

The War in Fall 1917

In October and November 1917, the Austrians and Germans leveled a decisive defeat against Italy at the Battle of Caporetto, sending the Italian forces reeling and capturing more than a quarter million prisoners. The British and French quickly sent reinforcements before Italy was knocked out of the war.

Things were even worse in Russia. The Germans had captured Riga in August, a heavy blow to Kerensky's Provisional Government. The Germans continued their offensive northward along the Baltic, marching ever closer to the Russian capital, Petrograd (formerly

St. Petersburg). The Kerensky government prepared to evacuate to Moscow in October. The army had lost faith in the government and deserted en masse, stoked by revolutionary fervor and land reform promised by the Bolsheviks.

The Bolsheviks overthrew the Provisional Government and seized Petrograd on November 7. (The second Russian Revolution of 1917 is often called the "October Revolution," as the Russians still used the pre-Gregorian calendar, although it was more a coup than a popular revolt.) Russia was desperate to remove itself from the war, and the Bolshevik leaders, Vladimir Lenin and Leon Trotsky, promised bread, land, and peace. American socialist journalist John Reed witnessed the Bolshevik coup in Petrograd. He published his account of the takeover in early 1919 in his book *Ten Days That Shook the World*, which became an instant bestseller as Americans were eager to learn what was happening in Russia. When Reed died of typhus the following year, his ashes were buried in the Kremlin Wall.[56]

The Bolsheviks promised not just political but economic revolution as well, ending private ownership of land and turning factories over to workers' committees. According to Marxist ideology, the proletariat would rise spontaneously to overthrow capitalism, uniting workers around the world and forming a working-class utopia worldwide, what Karl Marx called the "dictatorship of the proletariat." Communism promised a classless society, one based on factory workers and farmers, sailors and soldiers. Led by Lenin, who soon renamed the Bolsheviks as the Communist Party, the Russians expected the working class to rise across Europe in support of the October Revolution. Though there were uprisings in numerous countries, the proletariat revolution largely remained confined to Russia.

The expected workers' utopia in Russia instead found itself in a brutal civil war. The czarist and anti-communist forces, known as the Whites, counterattacked against the communist Red Army. Fearing that Czar Nicholas would be rescued, the Bolsheviks executed him and his family in July 1918. The conflict would last more than four years before the communists emerged victorious, having conquered much of the former Russian Empire at the point of the bayonet. The Russian

Civil War cost millions of lives. Millions more would die from starvation during the communist land reforms.

The United States had recognized Kerensky's Provisional Government, as it was founded on a democratic basis; however, when the Bolsheviks overthrew the Russian government in November 1917, the U.S. did not recognize the radical new government. The U.S. would not establish diplomatic relations with the Soviet Union until 1933.

Just as Russia was undergoing upheaval, France too experienced political turmoil. In November 1917, Prime Minister Paul Painlevé's coalition government collapsed, and Georges Clemenceau took over. Clemenceau was seventy-six years old but fiercely energetic and a devout German-hater. He was known as "the Tiger." Having experienced the humiliating defeat at the hands of the Prussians in 1871, Clemenceau was determined to rescue France from the German foe and secure the country's borders.

When the U.S. declared war against Germany, it opted not to make war against Austria-Hungary, as it hoped to drive a wedge between the Central Powers by negotiating a separate peace. This effort failed. The Austrians and the Turks recalled their diplomats in support of their German ally. The U.S. declared war on Austria eight months later, on December 7, 1917. As it turned out, the question of the Central Powers would all be dealt with in the Treaty of Versailles, including the breakup of the Austro-Hungarian Empire.

America's War Aims

On September 2, 1917, President Wilson asked his political adviser Edward House to put together the Commission of Inquiry, or simply the "Inquiry" as it became known. It was a chance for Americans to gather independent facts free of the Allies. House brought in two key figures to lead the Inquiry: Sidney Mezes (House's brother-in-law), and liberal journalist Walter Lippmann of the *New Republic*. The commissioners—in particular Lippmann—had a strong influence in drafting what would become Wilson's Fourteen Points. As House lived in New York, the Inquiry was headquartered in New York and organized under the American Geographical Society. The Inquiry gathered huge amounts of data, historical documents, and maps for an eventual peace conference. Wilson also instructed House to gather ideas for a how a League of Nations might work.

The twenty-seven-year-old Lippmann soon irritated the intellectuals providing the materials for the Inquiry with his demanding and critical tone. In spring 1918, he took a commission in the army, went to France, and worked as a propagandist. He got in trouble with President Wilson for acting beyond the authority of George Creel's Committee on Public Information. He was dispatched home in early 1919, his outspoken views removing him from the scene of influence just as the Paris Peace Conference began.[57]

Wilson sent House to Europe in late October 1917 to head the American delegation to the Supreme War Council. It included General Tasker Bliss, who would take a permanent seat on the council, among numerous other experts who could coordinate armaments, industrial output, shipping, and supplies with the Allies. The council would coordinate the war effort. However, no one wanted to give up sovereignty over their armies, nor could the Allies agree on war aims. In his report to the president, House wrote, "The Supreme War Council as at present constituted is almost a farce."[58] House quietly left France without most realizing he had gone. He was like a ghost, a man who eschewed the limelight and preferred to work behind the scenes. Wilson gave House few instructions; House was his alter ego, and he trusted the man implicitly.[59]

The Bolsheviks took control of Russia just as the Supreme War Council met in France. The communists demanded peace without territorial annexations; anything otherwise was imperialist. The Russian economy was imploding, the population was starving, and the country desperately needed peace. The Bolsheviks sent out peace feelers to the Germans, and likewise insisted that the various belligerents state their war aims. The failure of the Supreme War Council to unite on Allied goals, combined with the Bolshevik call for peace, led President Wilson to respond.

Wilson had spent years calling for a peaceful adjudication between the combatants. Only after nearly three years of neutrality had failed, he led the country into war when the Germans acted belligerently through unrestricted submarine warfare and by goading Mexico into a hostile alliance. "The world must be made safe for democracy," he had proclaimed in his war address. Now as 1918 began the global conflict was entering its fourth year. American armed forces were preparing to ship out for Europe as the fighting raged with no end in sight. As American lives would soon be at stake fighting on the ground, Wilson poignantly laid out the country's war aims—and called for other countries to do the same, as he understood it would be a crucial for eventual peace negotiations.

On January 8, 1918, Wilson stood before a joint session of Congress and delivered America's war aims in what became known as the Fourteen Points Address. Peace talks between Germany and Russia had just commenced at Brest-Litovsk, and Wilson was hopeful that a just peace could be concluded. The Fourteen Points were a mixture of idealism and realism: Wilson called for "open covenants of peace" rather than secret treaties and alliances, freedom of the seas, the resumption of trade, arms control, resolution of colonial claims, the restoration of Belgian and Russian territory, the return of Alsace-Lorraine to France, a redrawing of the Italian border, a breakup of the Austro-Hungarian Empire and autonomy for its people, territorial integrity of the Balkan states, many of which were newly freed from either the Austrians or the Turks, the breakup of the Ottoman Empire, the establishment of Poland, and "a general association of nations" to help secure the peace, what would later be known as the League of Nations. This was what the United States was fighting for. In fact, most of Wilson's Fourteen Points would be enacted, some of them to the lasting embitterment of the nations affected.[60] The *New York Times* gushed that the speech was a smashing success. "The resolve to make the foundations of the world's peace sure is one and irrevocable."[61]

The Fourteen Points were developed in part to rein in more extreme Allied demands at the peace table. The Allies never fully embraced the Fourteen Points, though they were willing to negotiate with the

Germans using the American war aims as a foundation for an armistice. Many of the countries viewed the points as restricting their actions, even as they had dreams of expanding their empires. England would have to abide by the American interpretation of the "freedom of the seas"; Italy would be denied Tyrolia and the Adriatic coast; England and France would be prevented from land grabs in the Middle East.

With its fair and balanced terms, the Fourteen Points were designed to appeal to German liberals, driving a wedge between them and the militarists running the war effort. Wilson made clear that the fight was with Germany's military leaders, not its people, as his Flag Day speech in 1917 demonstrated. The Fourteen Points Address had an impact in Germany: on January 28, a general strike broke out across the country as a million industrial workers walked off the job. Germans were tired of the war, the food shortages, and the deaths of their sons. Wilson's policy of encouraging German democrats and socialists would ultimately succeed.

A month later, on February 11, Wilson addressed Congress with a major foreign policy speech, the Four Points Address. He declared that, "self-determination is not a mere phase. It is an imperative principle of action which statesmen will henceforth ignore at their peril." He outlined four points in addition to the Fourteen Points that would be necessary for peaceful negotiations. They included resolving conflicts with justice in mind; that peoples and territories were not simply to be bargained away like "pawns in a game"; that territorial settlement should benefit the people living there, rather than the states that were eager to claim them; and that new countries had the right to emerge based on their national aspirations. [62]

In his Four Points Address, Wilson specifically rejected a Congress of Vienna–style settlement that would restore the balance of power, as was done after the Napoleonic Wars in 1815. "The method the German Chancellor proposes is the method of the Congress of Vienna," Wilson stated. "We cannot and will not return to that. What is at stake now is the peace of the world. What we are striving for is a new international order based upon broad and universal principles of right and justice—no mere peace of shreds and patches." That is to say, the Germans proposed a series of negotiations between individual countries, such as the German-Russian negotiations at Brest-Litovsk, one that would in essence leave the balance of powers intact. Wilson rejected that process; he wanted a grand settlement among all the combatants that would resolve all of the issues and lead to a general peace. "All the parties to this war must join in the settlement of every issue anywhere involved in it; because what we are seeking is a peace that we can all unite to guarantee and maintain and every item of it must be submitted to the common judgment whether it be right and fair, an act of justice, rather than a bargain between sovereigns."[63]

Even as Wilson hoped for a democratic victory over autocracy, he was stunned to learn how cruelly the Germans treated the Russians at the peace table. But what choice did the Russians have? The Bolsheviks were desperate for peace and signed the unfair accord, known as the Treaty of Brest-Litovsk, on March 3, 1918. Germany claimed the Baltic States; Ukraine was declared independent and made a German fiefdom, a buffer state that would protect Germany from Russia while providing food from its vast breadbasket. Russia was to pay six billion German gold marks in reparations. President Wilson was livid and said so publicly in Baltimore on the one year anniversary of the war declaration. "They are enjoying in Russia a cheap triumph in which no brave or gallant nation can long take pride," he railed. "A great people, helpless by their own act, lies for the time at their mercy." Wilson called the German empire an "empire of force," one that would lead to an "empire of gain and commercial supremacy" and no autonomy for the conquered peoples. The strong would rule the weak. "Germany has once more said that force, and force alone, shall decide whether Justice and peace shall reign in the affairs of men, whether Right as America conceives it or Dominion as she conceives it shall determine the destinies of mankind."[64]

The Bolsheviks opened the czar's archives and published many of the Allied "secret treaties" to embarrass Russia's erstwhile allies, whom the communists viewed as imperialists and therefore no better than the Germans. To the communists, imperialism was the highest and most malignant form of capitalism, as it allowed governments not only to exploit their own workers, but those of foreign countries as well. The publication revealed the extent of Allied territorial ambitions. When President Wilson sent a sympathetic note to the Soviet Congress, promising that the injustice of Brest-Litovsk would not stand, the Soviets responded, "the happy time is not far distant when the laboring masses of all countries will throw off the yoke of capitalism and will establish a socialistic state of society, which alone is capable of securing just and lasting peace." They berated the president, who led the leading capitalist country in the world, promising that the proletariat revolution would happen there just as Karl Marx had foretold. [65]

As Wilson developed his postwar plans for peace, he became ever more convinced that the League of Nations must arise out of the ashes of war to adjudicate national differences before they resulted in war. Secretary of State Robert Lansing was not a supporter of the league concept. He wrote Edward House in April 1918: "Until Autocracy is entirely discredited and Democracy becomes not only the dominant but the practically universal principle in the political systems of the world, I fear a League of Nations, particularly one purposing to employ force, would not function." Lansing saw the war in more practical yet high-minded terms: defeating Germany. "We must crush Prussianism so completely that it can never rise again, and we must end autocracy in every other nation as well." House was undeterred by Lansing's opposition: he had the president's support and drafted an initial constitution, known as the Covenant, for the League of Nations that summer as the war reached its climax. [66]

On May 27, President Wilson addressed a joint session of Congress to raise taxes to help pay for the war effort. He pleaded for the sake of the wave of sailors and soldiers reaching European shores. "We are not only in the midst of the war, we are at the very peak and crisis of it," Wilson stated. "Hundreds of thousands of our men, carrying our hearts with them and our fortunes, are in the field, and ships are crowding faster and faster to the ports of France and England with regiment after regiment, thousand after thousand, to join them until the enemy shall be beaten and brought to a reckoning with mankind." It was the country's duty to rise to the challenge. The president added a line that would come back to haunt him: "We must meet it without selfishness or fear of consequences. Politics is adjourned." High-minded words, no doubt, but in a democracy, politics are never adjourned.[67]

Having knocked Russia out of the war in early 1918, the Germans could now shift hundreds of thousands of veteran soldiers to the Western Front for the spring offensive and inflict a decisive defeat on the Allies. The double defeats of Italy and Russia did not bode well for the Allies, who teetered on collapse. All eyes looked west to the Americans. Would the doughboys arrive in time and in sufficient strength to stop the Germans from winning the war?

SIX

Into the Breach

German General Ludendorff's plan for spring 1918 was not to capture Paris, but rather to demolish Allied armies before American forces could intervene on the battlefield. He hoped a bold stroke would conclude the war in Germany's favor. On March 21, the Germans opened their spring offensive. They targeted the juncture between the English and French armies along the Somme River to drive a wedge between the two allies. The Germans had spent the winter retraining part of their army for "storm trooper" tactics to bypass strong points and break through enemy lines, just as the Russians had used in the previous year against Austria. They severely mauled the British Fifth Army and broke through to the open countryside.

The moment of crisis had arrived. The Allies requested American soldiers to take control of part of the front line. Pershing yielded to the emergency and allowed American units to be interspersed among Allied units wherever they were most needed, as his Christmas orders from Secretary Baker had allowed. The most combat-ready force

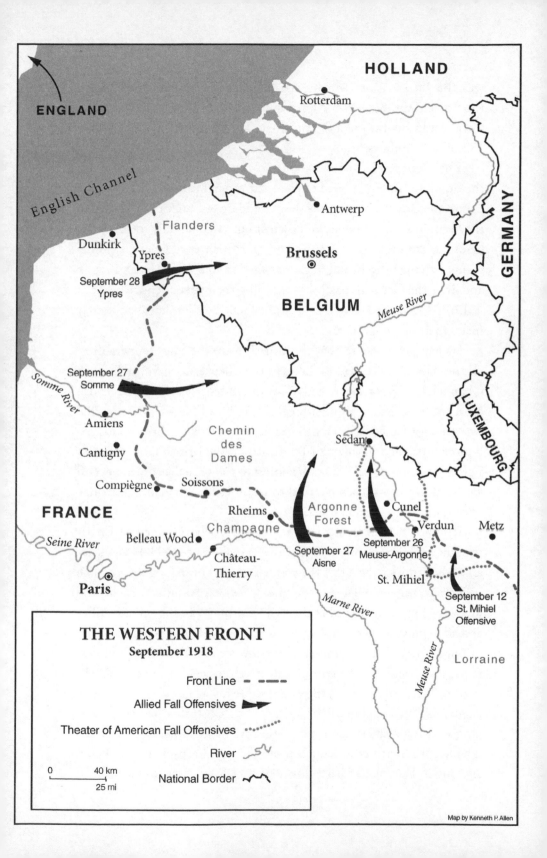

HOLLAND

Rotterdam

ENGLAND

English Channel

Antwerp

Flanders

GERMANY

Dunkirk

Ypres

Brussels

September 28
Ypres

BELGIUM

Meuse River

Somme River

September 27
Somme

Amiens

Cantigny

Chemin
des
Dames

Sedan

LUXEMBOURG

Compiègne

Soissons

Cunel

FRANCE

Rheims

Argonne
Forest

Verdun

Metz

Champagne

Seine River

Belleau Wood

September 27
Aisne

September 26
Meuse-Argonne

Château-
Thierry

St. Mihiel

Paris

Marne River

September 12
St. Mihiel
Offensive

Meuse River

Lorraine

THE WESTERN FRONT
September 1918

Front Line	– – –
Allied Fall Offensives	▶
Theater of American Fall Offensives	•••••
River	∿
National Border	∿

0   40 km
25 mi

Map by Kenneth P. Allen

was the 1st Division, which was shifted west by train to reinforce the French. Other units occupied quiet sectors of the front so French forces could join the main fight. Altogether, Pershing loaned the Allies 132,000 doughboys.[1]

The Germans lacked the ability to exploit their breakthrough on the Somme. If they had had tanks, their momentum might have fully cut off the British army, just as they would do at Dunkirk in 1940. But the Germans had no tanks, and their infantry could only travel so fast before outrunning artillery and supplies. British and French reinforcements arriving by train and truck managed to contain the breakthrough and drive the Germans partly back, ending their first offensive by April 4. But the crisis was far from over; in fact, the Germans had merely made their opening move.

Ludendorff believed that the British were the most vulnerable of all the Allies. All he had to do was drive their army into the English Channel. Ludendorff launched his second offensive against the British on April 9, achieving another breakthrough in Flanders, but one that was soon contained. The French heavily reinforced the British, making it more difficult for Ludendorff to finish off the British Expeditionary Forces. He would redirect his attention to the French army to peel off the reinforcements, then planned to resume the attack on the British once they were vulnerable again.

It took this emergency for the Supreme War Council to finally appoint an Allied commander in chief to make battlefield decisions for all of the armies. Given that the war had mostly been fought on French soil, the command fell to a Frenchman: General Ferdinand Foch. And given the high casualties that the British army had suffered, the Allies agreed to provide far more shipping to bring American doughboys over in huge waves. The million-soldier commitment the Americans had made soon doubled to two million. Pershing cabled back to Washington, "Send over everything you have ready as fast as you can. The responsibility for failure will be ours."[2] The British allocated more shipping to bring soldiers across the Atlantic, while American shipyards doubled their efforts to launch more ships. The pace of doughboys arriving in Europe had been slow, but now it quickened significantly, rising by several hundred thousand each month until the American Expeditionary Forces reached two million men in France. This tipped the manpower scales in favor of the Allies. The downside was that most of the soldiers were shipped out with only partial or even minimal training, and none of the doughboys were well armed. The Americans would rely on the Allies to provide heavy weaponry, including artillery and machine guns.[3]

British Prime Minister David Lloyd George expressed his frustration with how the Americans were building up their army. He was a leading advocate for "amalgamation," allowing British and French forces to train and fight alongside the Americans, believing there was too little time to bring the doughboys to a combat-ready state. The Americans had been in the war a full thirteen months already and with little to show. Pershing refused to take advice from the Allies nor scatter his precious untested forces. "The result was that an amateur army was fighting a professional army," Lloyd George complained with much justification.[4]

After mauling the British army in Flanders and along the Somme, Ludendorff uncharacteristically delayed his next offensive until late May, possibly because of high rates of influenza in the German army. During the lull, Pershing agreed to send the 1st Division into a limited battle to test its combat readiness—and to prove American resolve to fight. The target was the German-occupied town of Cantigny, a small salient that cut into Allied lines. The attacked was staged on May 28 and quickly captured the town. Colonel George Marshall, who fractured his ankle when his horse fell, described the battle: "The general artillery bombardment opened with a tremendous roar and Cantigny itself took on the appearance of an active volcano, with great clouds of smoke and dust and flying dirt and debris, which was blasted high into the air."[5] The Germans unleashed a furious counterattack, pounding the doughboys with heavy artillery even as the supporting French artillery pulled out to counter the latest German offensive. Still, the Germans failed to push the Americans out of Cantigny, and the 1st Division remained in the sector for the next two months. The 28th Infantry Regiment, which bore the brunt of the fighting, suffered more than 1,600 casualties in the three-day battle. One of the Americans who fell during the battle was author Willa Cather's cousin, Lieutenant Grosvenor Phillips Cather, who was leading his men against a German counterattack. Another participant in the battle was Major Theodore Roosevelt, the former president's son. He would later land in the first wave at Utah Beach on D-Day in 1944, dying a month later from a heart attack. Captain Clarence Huebner, who led an infantry company at Cantigny, commanded the 1st Division at adjacent Omaha Beach.[6]

Artillery was the big killer during the war, and as one historian noted, "The Great War was, in reality, the Great Artillery War."[7] The term "shell shock" was coined to describe the psychological and physical outcome from high explosives. George Marshall noted how shell shock would impact even the strongest soldier: "A 3-inch shell will temporarily scare or deter a man; a 6-inch shell will shock him; but an 8-inch shell, such as these 210-mm. ones, rips up the nervous system of everyone within a hundred yards of the explosion." It left men trembling uncontrollably and sometimes comatose with a thousand-yard stare for hours or even days. Every man had a breaking point. Some men never recovered psychologically.[8]

As the Battle of Cantigny was unfolding, the Germans opened a new offensive against the French army on May 27. Thirty German divisions broke through the Chemin des Dames region and pushed toward the Marne River. If Paris was sufficiently threatened, the Allies would reinforce this sector, and Ludendorff could then concentrate on wiping out the English army in Flanders. In four days, the Germans drove the French back thirty miles and took 60,000 prisoners. They now had a foothold on the Marne, where they were turned back from Paris in 1914. They rapidly approached the river crossing at Château-Thierry.

Red Cross volunteer Isabel Anderson had just returned to Paris for some rest when the latest German offensive commenced. She packed her belongings into an overstuffed trunk. "Thinking I might never get a hot bath again, I took two, one at midnight, the other at three in the morning," then departed at five after a brief rest.[9] She and the other volunteers departed for the front, where they helped set up a hospital near Compiègne, northeast of Paris. "Just as soon as we were ready to receive the soldiers, they began to come in from the trenches. They were terribly shot to pieces, and many had head wounds, which were perhaps the worst of all." The Germans were bombing Paris by airplane, and a giant artillery piece known as Big Bertha was trying to destroy a nearby railroad bridge. It was a scene of considerable excitement as the wounded poured in to triage. "From my window at the hospital I counted seven balloons hovering over the trenches, and saw airplanes constantly passing," both French and German. [10]

Big Bertha, as it became known, was actually a half-dozen giant cannons that the German firm Krupp manufactured. They could lob artillery shells seventy-five miles, though not always accurately. "This gun was a marvelous product of technical skill and science," Ludendorff wrote, who admired the gun's ability to hit Paris from far away. "Part of the population left the capital and so increased the alarm caused by our successes," he bragged. As the Germans advanced toward the Marne River, hundreds of thousands of French refugees fled toward Paris. [11]

German success meant another Allied crisis. The French lacked the reserves to stanch the German tide, and General Philippe Pétain called Pershing for help. Pershing yielded the 2nd and 3rd Divisions to confront the Germans at the apex of their advance. The 3rd Division took up a defensive position at Château-Thierry, the vital Marne River crossing, on May 31. A fierce battle ensued at Château-Thierry, with the Americans holding the south bank while the Germans continually attacked from the north. German artillery plastered the town, but doughboys took up positions in the rubble and, armed with machine guns, repulsed wave after wave of German infantry attacks. The German advance faltered and a seven-week stalemate resulted while both sides peered over the river from their respective sides of the wrecked town. [12]

While the 3rd Division held off the Germans at Château-Thierry, the 2nd Division moved into the dense Belleau Wood on June 4, just to the northwest, to close a gap in the French line. The 2nd was a composite division of regular army and marine brigades. Commanded by General James Harbord, the Marine 4th Brigade pushed into the thick forest and engaged the Germans. They had little artillery support, so the battle was a straightforward infantry fight with rifles, bayonets, hand grenades, and machine guns. Embedded American journalist Floyd Gibbons accompanied the marines into the hellish forest and recorded the most famous line from the battle when Gunnery Sergeant Dan Daly led his platoon forward on a suicidal attack across an open field, shouting, "Come on, you sons-o'-bitches! Do you want to live forever?" [13] The marines eventually drove the Germans out of Belleau Wood after five weeks of horrific fighting. More than five thousand marines became casualties in the fierce battle, which had taken on four German divisions. The French renamed Belleau Wood as *Bois de la Brigade de Marine*. The high casualties revealed flaws in Pershing's open warfare doctrine, as many casualties could have been avoided if the marines had proper artillery support. [14]

Gibbons was shot twice and suffered a compound fracture to his skull at Belleau Wood. He recovered in a hospital ward with fourteen soldiers from a wide range of ethnic backgrounds. "There was an Irishman, a Swede, an Italian, a Jew, a Pole, one man of German parentage, and one man of Russian extraction," he wrote. "Here in this ward was the new melting pot of America . . . They are the real and new Americans—born in the hell of battle." [15]

With the German offensive and American concentration near Château-Thierry, Billy Mitchell brought his aircraft brigade to assist in the battle from above. They faced off against the best fighter pilots the Germans had, including the Flying Circus, the famed squadron once led by the famed Red Baron, Manfred von Richthofen. (Richthofen was shot down and killed over the Somme on April 21.) The Germans flew in large formations of Fokker fighters that dominated the skies, while the more inexperienced Americans flew the obsolete Nieuports. Mitchell desperately asked for the more modern, nimble Spads to take on the faster Germans. His command suffered a heavy loss of pilots, including Theodore Roosevelt's youngest son Quentin, who was shot down over German lines on July 14. The following month, the French began equipping the American squadrons with Spads.

The Germans gave the young Roosevelt a funeral with military honors, and a photographer forwarded a photograph of the plane wreckage showing Quentin's lifeless body. It might seem a morbid gesture, but it was sent out of respect for the former president so that he and his family would know that Quentin had served and died honorably—and that he was killed instantly. The former president was devastated at the loss of his youngest son. His own health rapidly declined in coming months. [16]

The American air service focused on pursuit aircraft. It had a few bombers as well, though they were not well equipped or well led. A squadron of six American bombers led by Major Harry Brown took to the air on July 11, got lost, landed at a German airfield, and were captured. The Germans dropped a cheeky message on an American aerodrome, "We thank you for the fine airplanes and equipment which you have sent us, but what shall we do with the Major?" Mitchell came to rely on British, French, and Italian bombers instead. [17]

In one month, the 1st, 2nd, and 3rd Divisions had taken part in some of the heaviest fighting of the war and held their own against the Germans. Though the Americans had lacked experience and suffered high losses, they proved their fighting mettle. Pershing reinforced his bloodied frontline soldiers with two divisions, the 26th and 42nd, forming the 1st Corps under Hunter Liggett facing the German salient on the Marne River that now bulged toward Paris. It was the first step toward an independent American army in France.

Ludendorff launched his final offensive on July 15—the day after the French Bastille Day holiday—in an attempt to break out of the Marne salient and capture Reims. It became known as the Second Battle of the Marne. The French 4th Army was expecting it and had made significant defensive preparations. The German attack east of Reims was halted with heavy losses, but west of the city they crossed the Marne River on pontoon bridges and briefly broke through French lines before reinforcements contained the advance. About 85,000 American troops hurriedly reinforced the French. In the path of the German advance now stood the American 3rd Division, which held Château-Thierry and a key ridge overlooking the Marne River crossings.

Hearing that the Germans had commenced their offensive, Colonel Billy Mitchell took to the air personally to scout the front line. It was a cloudy day with a low ceiling, forcing him to stay close to the ground, but fortunately he did not run into German pursuit aircraft. He flew along the Marne, following the river's course when suddenly a great volume of German artillery fire landed on the south bank, which the 3rd Division was defending. He flew in closer and discovered five bridges that the Germans had thrown over the river. Columns of infantry were marching across. "Looking down on the men, marching so splendidly, I thought to myself, what a shame to spoil such fine infantry," Mitchell wrote.[18] But this was war. Landing at his aerodrome, Mitchell ordered his brigade of pursuit aircraft to take to the air and strafe the German infantry. The French sent bombers to hit the pontoon bridges. The 3rd Division held its position, blunting the German offensive, and earned its nickname, "Rock of the Marne."

Three days into the latest German offensive, Ferdinand Foch, the supreme Allied commander, marshaled forces for a counterattack on the German Marne salient. The American 1st and 2nd Divisions, along with a French colonial division, were placed on the vulnerable western part of the German bulge. They were to counterattack directly into the salient, their goal to take Soissons, a vital supply route. Their attack was to begin on July 18. The 2nd Division had trouble assembling, as the roads were so crowded with vehicles that they could not reach the area until the middle of the night, and numerous units got lost in the dark. Colonel Paul Malone, commander of the 23rd Infantry Regiment, got the men to the front with the help of his entire staff and a French regiment's runners. Many men did not reach the front until after the artillery bombardment began, and they had no opportunity to reconnoiter: they simply went straight into the battle. Malone noted, "The Second Battalion leading the attack had gone over the top at H hour (4:35 A.M.), but to reach its position it had been necessary to advance during the last ten minutes at a run, the men reaching the jumping-off trenches breathless and exhausted." The Americans were in luck: despite the lack of reconnaissance, their attack smashed through the German line. The Battle of Soissons took the Germans by surprise.[19]

Over the next four days, and Americans advanced seven miles and took thousands of prisoners, but at a high cost. The 1st Division suffered 7,500 casualties, while the 2nd Division—only engaged on the first two days of the counterattack—had 5,000 casualties. The attack threatened the German supply lines, and Ludendorff not only halted his final offensive, but also began evacuating the Marne salient.[20]

Fifty-three years earlier, General Ulysses Grant had attacked Robert E. Lee's army at Cold Harbor and in a single afternoon lost 7,000 men. The 1st Division's casualties at Soissons were greater than the entire Union Army had experienced at Cold Harbor. Colonel George Marshall was saddened at the horrific combat losses. All of the division's colonels, except for three, had been killed, and every battalion commander was a casualty. These had been Marshall's friends.[21] The Battle of Soissons was so costly in part because of Pershing's open warfare doctrine. It was too reliant on riflemen attacking with limited or no artillery support. Time and again the inexperienced doughboys charged machine gun nests frontally, positions that artillery could have eliminated. The result was unnecessarily high casualties.

The Battle of Soissons was a victory for the Allies and proved the turning point of the war. They had seized the initiative from the Germans, who would never regain it. Ludendorff advanced reinforcements to prevent the Marne salient from collapsing, and in turn the Germans canceled their planned attack on the British in Flanders, as they had deployed their reserves. The last German offensive had ended. Chancellor Georg von Hertling said, "We expected grave events in Paris for the end of July. That was on the 15th. On the 18th even the most optimistic among us understood that all was lost. The history of the world was played out in three days." Hindenburg wrote how it dashed the Central Powers' hopes: "The effect of our failure on the country and our allies was even greater, judging by our first impressions. How many hopes, cherished during the last months, had probably collapsed at one blow!"[22]

By early August, Franco-American forces had pushed the Germans out of the Marne salient and back to their starting point, the Hindenburg Line. The Second Battle of the Marne was a clear Allied victory but a costly win: some 300,000 American troops were engaged in the fight, and more than 50,000 were casualties. But even more important, the German army was spent. Morale plummeted as soldiers grew tired of the fighting, the poor rations, life in the muddy trenches, and propaganda aimed at them to go home—or to make common cause with the Bolsheviks. With a growing number of American soldiers in France, the Allies seized the initiative to drive the Germans from France. Pershing's dream of fielding an independent army under American command would soon become a reality. The spring crisis for the Allies was finally over—but for the Germans, their crisis was just beginning.[23]

While Ludendorff evacuated the Marne salient, the Australians and Canadians struck back against the denuded German lines along the Somme River on August 8, completely surprising their foe. British Field Marshal Douglas Haig executed a brilliant combined arms operation at Amiens that penetrated deep into German lines, demolished six German divisions, and took thousands of prisoners. Ludendorff called August 8 the "black day of the German Army." He realized that the army's losses and morale had declined to a point beyond salvaging. Germany had lost the war, even though the soldiers were still fighting.[24]

The Influenza

Another enemy was lurking that would kill millions, one even deadlier than German machine guns: the 1918 influenza pandemic. With conscription, millions of young men were brought together in cramped barracks. The close proximity became a breeding ground for infectious diseases. Measles struck the U.S. Army in late 1917, killing 5,741 soldiers from secondary infections, mostly pneumonia. But this paled in comparison to one of the deadliest pandemics that would ravage the world: the so-called Spanish flu.[25]

The influenza probably began in Haskell County, Kansas, in January 1918, then soon spread to Camp Funston (now part of Fort Riley) in March. It quickly overwhelmed the camp, and the contagion soon spread to other military bases when soldiers were transferred.

Nearby cities and towns witnessed people falling sick as well. From there, soldiers carried the flu aboard ships to France. The British, French, and German armies soon had it. When the King of Spain got sick, newspapers reported on the illness, and since Spain was not at war, their press was not censored. The flu took on the name history assigned it: the "Spanish influenza," though it did not originate there. The virus moved quickly, but this initial variation was not deadly. Most people recovered after three days. [26]

Viruses are constantly evolving, and this particular strain of influenza mutated into a far deadlier pathogen over the summer. In fact, the worst period for the flu was during the final phase of the Great War, from mid-September to December. This lethal strain first appeared at Camp Devens near Boston. People suffered severe headaches and bodily pain. Bodies turned blue like they were being strangled, while victims coughed up blood and their eardrums ruptured. Many became delirious. The deadly influenza could kill someone in half a day. The flu was especially lethal for young adults, whose vigorous immune systems filled their lungs with fluid and white cells, resulting in a higher number of deaths from pneumonia.

The influenza struck terror. People isolated themselves and avoided human contact. Those who ventured outside wore gauze masks that proved useless: they still got sick. Influenza hit the cramped steel mills and shipyards hard, and many others stayed home to avoid catching the contagion. The dead overwhelmed hospitals and morgues, and there was hardly a house in the country that did not have a sick person in it. Cities ran out of coffins. Some resorted to mass graves to bury the dead, the trenches dug by steam shovels. Troop transports witnessed crew and passengers reeling from the pandemic. Many ships buried scores of the dead at sea. The September draft was to call up 142,000 men, but authorities postponed it because the cantonments were too full of sick soldiers. [27]

Assistant Secretary of the Navy Franklin Roosevelt went on an inspection tour of Europe in summer 1918, visiting battlefield sites and naval facilities. He returned to the U.S. in September on the *Leviathan*. Like many on board, he caught the influenza and was deathly ill with double pneumonia, such that he was carried off the ship on a stretcher when it reached New York. Once he returned to the family's Hyde Park residence, his wife Eleanor unpacked his suitcase and there found a bundle of love letters from Lucy Mercer—Eleanor's former social secretary—to Franklin. FDR had been having an affair with the woman for two years. It devastated Eleanor. Faced with the threat of divorce and the end to his political career, Franklin stayed with Eleanor, but the intimacy in their marriage was over. They continued as political partners. [28]

Influenza struck the nation's capital with a vengeance in fall 1918. Thousands were sickened, and authorities banned public gatherings, including church services and concerts, knowing that the disease was highly contagious. Still, hospitals soon ran out of space—and morgues soon ran out of coffins. Gravediggers were in short supply as well, since people were fearful of coming into contact with those who had died from the flu. Herbert Hoover noted that the influenza epidemic struck the Food Administration hard: half of his employees got sick, and many of them died. About 3,500 people in Washington, D.C. died from influenza. [29]

And then abruptly in December, shortly after the war ended, the virus began to weaken. The death count dropped. A third wave of influenza would strike as the virus mutated again, but it was not nearly as deadly. President Wilson would fall ill to this wave in April 1919 at the Paris Peace Conference. People continued getting sick into 1920 and even beyond, though the virus was losing its virulence.

The influenza of 1918 killed at least twenty-one million people worldwide, more than the combat deaths from the Great War. Later estimates ranged from fifty to one hundred million deaths worldwide. In the U.S. alone, an estimated 675,000 people died from the flu. The influenza was the deadliest plague in human history. [30]

Hemingway's War

The United States had just entered the war when Ernest Hemingway graduated from high school in the Chicago suburb of Oak Park. After

Woodrow Wilson in 1912, the year he won election to the presidency. *Image courtesy of the Library of Congress.*

Former president Theodore Roosevelt was Woodrow Wilson's strongest political opponent and fiercest critic. *Image courtesy of the Library of Congress.*

ABOVE: When the Great War broke out in 1914, American public opinion was divided over which side to support. German ambassador Johann von Bernstorff understood that Americans naturally sympathized with the Allies, but a neutral America was better than a belligerent one. He worked until 1917 to soften German diplomacy to keep the U.S. out of the war. *Image courtesy of the Library of Congress.* BELOW: A German submarine torpedoed the ocean liner RMS Lusitania on May 7, 1915, causing international outrage and 128 American deaths. An artist's rendering falsely showed a second torpedo hitting the ship, a British cover story designed to hide that the vessel was carrying munitions. *Image courtesy of the Library of Congress.*

Three-time presidential candidate and secretary of state William Jennings Bryan differed with President Wilson over how to respond to the Lusitania sinking and resigned. He continued to loudly support pacifism from the sidelines. *Image courtesy of the Library of Congress.*

With the resignation of William Jennings Bryan, the main pacifist remaining in Wilson's cabinet was Secretary of the Navy Josephus Daniels. A newspaper man from North Carolina, Daniels kept a detailed diary of the Wilson administration. *Image courtesy of the Library of Congress.*

ABOVE: German saboteurs blew up the Black Tom arsenal on July 30, 1916, the largest act of sabotage in American history. The explosion was felt several states away, broke windows in Brooklyn and Manhattan, and damaged the Statue of Liberty. *Image courtesy of the Library of Congress.* BELOW: Women's suffrage supporters began picketing at the White House in January 1917, just weeks before the country severed diplomatic relations with Germany. The pickets continued during the war, leading to arrests and counterprotests. *Image courtesy of the Library of Congress.*

ABOVE: Woodrow and Edith Wilson rode to the Capitol for Wilson's second inauguration ceremony on March 4, 1917. A month later, the country was at war. *Image courtesy of the Library of Congress.* BELOW: Woodrow Wilson delivered his War Address to both houses of Congress on April 2, 1917, the most important speech of his presidency. The U.S. declared war against Germany four days later. *Image courtesy of the Woodrow Wilson House, a National Trust Historic Site, Washington, D.C.*

George Creel invented modern propaganda when he took charge of the Committee on Public Information soon after the war declaration. *Image courtesy of the Library of Congress.*

The best known of all Great War propaganda posters was James Montgomery Flagg's self-portrait as Uncle Sam, appealing to patriotic duty. *Image courtesy of the Library of Congress.*

The American Red Cross's "Greatest Mother in the World" poster showed a nurse cradling a wounded doughboy similar to Michelangelo's *Pietà*. Thousands of women worked for the Red Cross during the war. *Image courtesy of the Library of Congress.*

General John Pershing led the two million doughboys of the American Expeditionary Forces in France. *Image courtesy of the Library of Congress.*

ABOVE: Artillery was the biggest killer during the Great War. Artillery barrages turned a forest near Cantigny, France into a moonscape of shell holes and tree trunks. *Image courtesy of the Library of Congress.* BELOW: Doughboys practice going "over the top" from the trenches, a dangerous maneuver that exposed them to enemy machine gun fire. *Image courtesy of the Library of Congress.*

Doughboys rest in the obliterated landscape of the Argonne Forest, a German strongpoint during the Meuse-Argonne Offensive. *Image courtesy of the Library of Congress.*

Doughboys cheer the Armistice announcement the morning of November 11, 1918. *Image courtesy of the Library of Congress.*

ABOVE: The Big Four Allied negotiators at the Paris Peace Conference: from left, David Lloyd George of the United Kingdom, Vittorio Orlando of Italy, Georges Clemenceau of France, and Woodrow Wilson of the United States. *Image courtesy of the Library of Congress.*
BELOW: Edward Mandell House—better known to history as Colonel House—was President Wilson's key political advisor, occupying a singular role in American history: a private citizen who had the president's ear. *Image courtesy of the Library of Congress.*

Republican Senator Henry Cabot Lodge of Massachusetts became the Senate majority leader after the November 1918 midterm election and demanded reservations be placed on the Treaty of Versailles. *Image courtesy of the Library of Congress.*

Attorney General Mitchell Palmer led the roundup of leftist radicals after a bombing at his house nearly killed his family in June 1919. *Image courtesy of the Library of Congress.*

ABOVE: Radicals bombed Wall Street on September 16, 1920, killing dozens, but the culprits were never caught. *Image courtesy of the Library of Congress.* BELOW: Though fallout from the Red Scare ended Attorney General Mitchell Palmer's political career, J. Edgar Hoover's career was just getting started. He was appointed to lead the Bureau of Investigation in 1924—the precursor to the FBI—a position he held until his death in 1972. *Image courtesy of the Library of Congress.*

ABOVE: New York City police commissioner John A. Leach oversaw beer being poured into the sewer in the early days of Prohibition. *Image courtesy of the Library of Congress.* BELOW: National Woman's Party leader Alice Paul raised a glass to celebrate the ratification of the Nineteenth Amendment, giving women the right to vote. *Image courtesy of the Library of Congress.*

President Wilson's successor, Warren Harding, had the looks of a Hollywood leading man, but he was a second-rate Ohio senator with little moral compass who oversaw one of the most corrupt administrations in American history. *Image courtesy of the Library of Congress.*

Former president Woodrow Wilson attended the unveiling of the Tomb of the Unknown Soldier at Arlington National Cemetery on the third anniversary of the Armistice in 1921. *Image courtesy of the Library of Congress.*

After leaving the White House, Woodrow Wilson lived at 2340 S Street, Northwest for less than three years before his death in February 1924. His wife Edith donated the house to the National Trust for Historic Preservation upon her death in 1961. *Image courtesy of the Library of Congress.*

Woodrow Wilson never recovered from his October 1919 stroke during the campaign to ratify the Treaty of Versailles. His manservant Isaac Scott was constantly at his side to help the invalid former president. *Image courtesy of the Woodrow Wilson House, a National Trust Historic Site, Washington, D.C.*

a short stint working on a farm, he went to work as a cub reporter for the *Kansas City Star*. Hemingway wanted to serve in the war, but he had terrible eyesight and was only eighteen, so could not be drafted. In March 1918, he enlisted as an ambulance driver in Italy. If the U.S. Army would not have him, the American Red Cross would.

Hemingway traveled to New York to await transport to Europe. He was issued a full set of uniforms and was commissioned a lieutenant. Hemingway explored Manhattan with his friends in uniform—a proposition that soon became tiresome, as he wrote his family: "We thought at first it would be fun because all privates and non commissioned officers have to salute us. But by the time we had returned about 200 salutes it had lost all its fun."[31]

On May 18, 1918, President Wilson was to review a Red Cross parade in Manhattan, but instead he decided to lead the parade, marching at the head of 70,000 people down Fifth Avenue. The *New York Times* fairly gushed about the president: "For the thousands of the city who had never seen the President, this was an opportunity for which their gratitude yesterday knew no bounds." Among the participants marching in that same parade was young Hemingway.[32]

Hemingway was strikingly handsome and a talented wordsmith, and he was always falling in or out of love with a woman. By the time he shipped out to Europe in May, the eighteen-year-old was broke, having spent $150 on an engagement ring for a girl he would never marry. However, he would eventually have four other wives.[33]

Hemingway briefly made his first visit to Paris—a city he would return to after the war and would forever be associated with—before being sent to Italy to his assignment, an American hospital in Milan. On his first day he helped retrieve body parts from a munitions plant explosion that had killed thirty-five people, mostly women. He would later describe the incident in his 1932 book, *Death in the Afternoon*: "I remember that after we searched quite thoroughly for the complete dead we collected fragments." In June 1918, he met a Red Cross ambulance driver, John Dos Passos, a fellow Chicagoan and writer he would befriend after the war.[34]

Hemingway quickly grew bored at the hospital and asked for a transfer to a Red Cross canteen closer to the front. Even that was not close enough to the action, so he began delivering chocolate and cigarettes to the Italian troops in the trenches, riding to the front on a bicycle. The Italian troops referred to the smiling young man as the *giovane Americano*—the young American.[35] He wrote a high school classmate, describing the sound of artillery and mortar shells. He was "sitting out in front of a dug out in a nice trench 20 yards from the Piave River and 40 yards from the Austrian lines listening to the little ones whimper way up in the air and the big ones go scheeeeeeeek Boom and every once in a while a machine gun go tick a tack a tock." He was amazed that he had graduated high school just a year earlier.[36]

One July 8, one of those mortar shells nearly landed on him. An Italian standing between him and the shell was killed, while another nearby had his legs blown off, and a third soldier was badly wounded. More than two hundred shell fragments peppered Hemingway's legs, and he was also shot twice. For this the Italians would award him the Silver Medal of Bravery.[37]

Hemingway was the first American to be wounded in Italy, a fact that made him particularly proud and earned him much notoriety in the press. He faced a long recovery in the hospital and multiple surgeries, and it took months before he was able to walk again. While he was in the hospital, he fell in love with an American nurse, Agnes von Kurowsky, a blond beauty who was seven years older than him.[38]

After completing his convalescence, Hemingway returned to the States in January 1919 after nine months away. He continued writing Agnes, who remained in Italy as a nurse, planning their life together. However, she wrote him in March 1919 to say that she no longer loved him and was engaged to an Italian officer. Hemingway was heartbroken. But he would also rebound and marry his first wife, Hadley Richardson, in 1921 and they would decamp for Paris. He would write about his affair with Kurowsky in his 1929 novel *A Farewell to Arms*.

The Allied Fall Offensive

French Marshal Ferdinand Foch had seized the initiative from the Germans in summer 1918. He was now faced with a significant choice: continue the offensive or wait until more trained American troops were on hand. By the following summer, the War Department planned to have eighty American divisions in Europe, numbering 3.2 million soldiers. A tidal wave of doughboys was coming, and after sufficiently training the rookie soldiers, the Allies could prepare for a knockout blow to Germany in 1919.[39]

That was one option. The other, riskier option was to continue the offensive with the troops that were on hand, including the partly trained American Expeditionary Forces. It was a gamble to begin an offensive in the fall, as the weather would no doubt turn foul. But there were political benefits as well: Germany's allies were abandoning ship, and the French knew that German morale was low. Likewise, the Allied populations were weary of the war and wanted peace. As thousands more partly trained American reinforcements arrived in France each day, Foch deemed it time to strike.

The great Allied offensive of fall 1918 would commence on September 26 and involve armies from many nations attacking the German army along much of the Western Front. The German position was a crescent-shaped bulge, stretching from Flanders in the west to the Vosges Mountains to the east. The Belgian and British armies would push east through Flanders, driving the Germans back into Belgium, while the French would pressure the center of the enemy line in Champagne. Foch ordered the Americans to attack the German left flank along the Meuse River east of the Argonne Forest, aiming for the vital railhead at Sedan. It was a massive undertaking designed to crush the German defenses that ran through northern France.

After the battles of the summer, American units were scattered across northern France, supporting the British and the French. Pershing finally concentrated most of his men on a single front in Lorraine and under a unified command to attack the Germans. He activated the 1st Army on August 10 with himself as its commander and moved headquarters to Neufchâteau to be closer to the front.

Before the fall offensive commenced, Pershing had one major task to accomplish: to pinch off the Saint-Mihiel salient. The Germans had occupied this triangular salient in 1914 and held it against repeated French attacks. The city of Verdun sat in its shadow to the west, and as the Americans drove deeper in the Meuse-Argonne region, the salient would expose them to ever greater flank attacks. Pershing wanted to eliminate the salient while also testing his newly unified army. Saint-Mihiel would become the first American-led battle in France.

Staff officer George Marshall was tasked with developing the plan to reduce the Saint-Mihiel salient. But before the offensive could commence, he was redirected to plan how to move most of the American army up to the front for the pending Meuse-Argonne Offensive. This was a massive coordination effort. The bulk of the army would shift over from Saint-Mihiel, displacing some 200,000 French soldiers who occupied the zone north of Verdun. And to complicate matters, there were only three roads to supply the Meuse-Argonne front. It would take two weeks to reposition the army sixty miles to the northwest in time for the joint allied offensive on September 26. Marshall called it the "hardest nut I had to crack in France," but one that "represented my best contribution to the war." His operational planning ensured that more than a half-million American soldiers got into place on time for the expected offensive. [40]

For the Saint-Mihiel Offensive, Pershing assembled a powerful force of 550,000 American troops and 110,000 French soldiers to attack the German salient. The army borrowed 267 light tanks from the French, and behind the lines were more than 3,000 artillery pieces, mostly British or French-made and partly manned by American gunners. The preparations for Saint-Mihiel were done in the dreary, cold downpour, as the autumnal rains had come, turning the battlefield and trenches into muck. [41]

For his support at Château-Thierry and the Marne, Billy Mitchell was promoted to chief of air service for the 1st Army. He assembled a force of nearly 1,500 planes to challenge the Germans over

Saint-Mihiel. He offered to take Pershing's staff on an airborne reconnaissance, but he only got one taker. "I could have taken them myself and protected them so that there would have been ninety-nine chances out of a hundred of their getting back unscathed (even if they did get killed, there were plenty of people to step into their shoes)," he wrote, probably with some irony. [42]

The American attack on the Saint-Mihiel salient began on September 12. In the past, the Allies had used lengthy, days-long bombardments to destroy German defensive positions and barbed wire entanglements in advance of an attack, but often all this did was give the enemy enough time to gather reinforcements for a counterattack. The preliminary bombardment at Saint-Mihiel was only four hours, designed to soften the German position but without giving them time to bring up reinforcements. This was a method that the Germans themselves used with their storm trooper tactics. In addition, the shorter bombardment meant fewer shell holes for the tanks to drive through.

With such a short bombardment, there was no guarantee that the German barbed wire guarding the trenches would be breached. American engineers came up with several solutions to mitigate this: they carried wire cutters to cut lanes and used Bangalore torpedoes to blast holes in the wire. In some places, they constructed contraptions made of chicken wire that they simply lay over the barbed wire, allowing the doughboys to walk over it.

The main attack fell on the south side of the salient. On its west side, a steep ridge confronted Allied forces. Their job was to hold the Germans in place while the main body delivered a right-punch to their rear. The main body of infantry attacked at 6:00 A.M., quickly breached the German lines and swept the enemy back miles. Colonel Douglas MacArthur led a brigade of the 42nd Rainbow Division in the assault. A brigade of French-built light tanks commanded by George Patton supported him; in fact, the two men met on the battlefield. "I joined him and the creeping [German] barrage came along toward us, but it was very thin and not dangerous," Patton wrote about meeting MacArthur. "I think each one wanted to leave but each hated to say so, so we let it come over us." The tanks did well, advancing with the infantry until the vehicles ran out of gas. [43] The next day, the attacking force linked up with a column that had pushed through the German heights to the west. The Saint-Mihiel salient was now closed just a day after the battle had commenced. Some 16,000 prisoners were captured and 450 guns seized. American casualties were 7,000 men killed or wounded. [44]

Despite the massed air power, Billy Mitchell was unable to provide much airborne support for the Saint-Mihiel Offensive because of the low cloud ceiling and rainy weather. Eddie Rickenbacker managed to take off with another pilot to scout the battlefield. They flew over the retreating German lines and spotted countless fires: the Germans had torched equipment and supplies that they could not carry. Rickenbacker spotted a horse-drawn German artillery battery stretched out along a road. The two pilots zoomed in at low altitude and sprayed the column with bullets, killing horses and men and throwing the battery into chaos. [45]

On September 15, a U.S. Army air serviceman named Lee Duncan was scouting for a new airfield in the newly liberated Saint-Mihiel salient. He came to the village of Flirey and there found a demolished kennel. There were no surviving dogs except a female German shepherd who had recently given birth to a litter of five pups. All were on the brink of starving. Duncan took the dogs back to his unit, which quickly adopted the canines and brought them back to health. Duncan gave four of the dogs away but kept a male and female puppy. They were named Rintintin and Nénette, after the good luck charms that French children gave to doughboys. After the war Duncan returned home with his dogs, although Nénette would succumb to pneumonia. Changing the spelling of the male dog's name, he trained Rin Tin Tin to do tricks, and got the dog into Hollywood movies in 1922. Over the next decade, Rin Tin Tin would wow movie audiences in twenty-seven films and win international fame. [46]

With the success at Saint-Mihiel, a rich enemy target lay just over horizon: the strategic manufacturing center and German fortress city of Metz. It was only lightly defended. But Ferdinand Foch had his timetable for the fall offensive, and the Americans were expected to attack on the Meuse-Argonne in a matter of days. The Allies missed an opportunity to capture a strategic asset at low cost. Douglas MacArthur wrote later, "I have always thought this was one of the great mistakes of the war."[47]

The Saint-Mihiel Offensive turned into a deceptively easy victory for the Americans. They had not faced a resolute enemy, as the Germans had already pulled their best soldiers from the salient. As Pershing prepared the army for the Meuse-Argonne Offensive, the Americans would confront a far more determined foe. Their commander still believed his troops could sweep through the German lines and avoid a war of attrition. In this Pershing would be tragically mistaken. The bulk of American forces were still not combat tested. In fact, much of the army was only partly trained.

Meuse-Argonne

Following Colonel Marshall's logistical plan, Pershing quickly repositioned the American 1st Army from Saint-Mihiel for the Allied fall offensive, scheduled to begin on September 26. His objective was the city of Sedan, a strategic logistical point for the Germans near France's border with Belgium, as the main railroad line supplying the German army in France passed through the city. The Prussian army had encircled French Emperor Napoleon III at the town in 1870 and forced his surrender and abdication. It was also the town where the Germans broke through the French lines during the blitzkrieg in May 1940 that led to the capitulation of France. If the Americans could capture Sedan in 1918, it would cut off much of the German army from resupply in northern France. But first they would have to fight their way through forty miles of German-held territory.

Some 600,000 doughboys were concentrated along a twenty-four-mile stretch of the front between the Argonne Forest to the west and the Meuse River to the east. Here Pershing would land his main blow, pushing the army to the northwest toward Sedan. He organized three corps on the front lines, each composed of three infantry divisions totaling 225,000 men who would assault the Hindenburg Line on day one. The French 4th Army would attack the Germans just west of the Argonne Forest.

Billy Mitchell was promoted to lead the air service for the army's 1st Corps under General Hunter Liggett, whom he would support for the duration of the war, commanding larger air groups as Liggett took command of the 1st Army. Liggett was perhaps a surprising choice; he was past sixty years old, nearing retirement, and overweight. "We are too old to make war," he told Pershing, who was three years younger. "If I were fifteen years younger I should not be sitting here before a map; I should be out on a horse all over the Front." Perhaps that was true, but he was also an effective and energetic leader, and above all, Pershing had faith in him. Liggett steadily rose from brigade to division to corps to army commander during the war. He proved a skilled tactician who quietly abandoned Pershing's open warfare doctrine in favor of combined arms operations, a leader who adapted himself and his men to the realities of the modern battlefield. [48]

The Meuse-Argonne Offensive was the largest military offensive in American history, a tremendous logistical feat as the soldiers and supplies moved up in long night marches. "To call it a battle may be a misnomer, yet it was a battle, the greatest, the most prolonged in American history," Pershing wrote proudly after the war.* The offensive would last forty-seven days, ended only by the Armistice. [49]

Facing the American 1st Army were three formidable German defensive belts that comprised the Hindenburg Line. The Germans actually called it the Siegfried Position, and the three lines were named after female characters in composer Richard Wagner's operas: Giselher, Kriemhilde, and Freya. The German commander in the region, Max von Gallwitz, was an experienced general who initially had just 24,000 men along the front, deceptively deployed six kilometers behind the main line. The Germans were well dug in, though they

---

* The Meuse-Argonne Offensive took place due south of the largest battle that the U.S. Army fought in World War II, the Battle of the Bulge.

expected the main American blow to fall at Metz, as it was so close to Saint-Mihiel. [50]

Shortly before Meuse-Argonne, Eddie Rickenbacker was promoted to commander of the 94th Pursuit Squadron. He was already an ace pilot, but most of his kills were still ahead of him. On his first day of command—September 25—he alone attacked a German squadron of seven aircraft, shooting down a Fokker and a photography plane. For this he would be awarded the Congressional Medal of Honor in 1930.

At 2:30 A.M. on September 26, a massive artillery bombardment began of German lines. At the same time, American pilots took to the air in their Spad fighter planes and blew up ten observation balloons, their giant hydrogen-filled gas bags exploding in a rain of incendiary bullets and crashing to the ground. (The Germans sent up new balloons within days.) [51] Three hours after the bombardment began, the guns shifted to a rolling barrage as American infantrymen advanced just behind it for the German trenches. The Germans were heavily outnumbered but well entrenched, and the fighting was murderous. The American army advanced slowly through the devastated landscape.

The first day was foggy, which provided some cover for the advancing Americans. The French had supplied light tanks to protect the infantry. Tanks had proved useful as mobile gun platforms during operations. However, German artillery easily knocked out the tanks. On the opening day of Meuse-Argonne, Lieutenant Colonel George Patton, who commanded a brigade of light tanks, advanced several miles into the German position in heavy fog. He was pinned down by machine-gun fire. When he attempted to charge the position on foot, a bullet struck him in the thigh. The war was over for the man who would become a legendary tank commander in World War II. [52]

The key to the first German line was Montfaucon, a lofty, 1,122-foot-tall citadel where the German crown prince had led the campaign against Verdun in 1916. The French dubbed it "Little Gibraltar." The rookie 79th Division assaulted the fortress frontally. They got no help from General Robert Bullard's III Corps to the east, which had advanced eight miles on the first day and could have swung around behind the fortress to capture it, preventing a bloodbath.

Instead, German machine guns inflicted heavy casualties on the massed doughboys. The 79th finally captured Montfaucon after two days of fighting that cost the division 3,500 casualties.[53]

Pershing had achieved strategic surprise over the thinly held German line, but he entertained unrealistic expectations for the offensive: the objective on day one was to reach Cunel and Romagne at the center of the Kriemhilde Line (the second of the German defensive belts), nine miles north of the American jumping-off point. Instead, it would take the Americans nearly three weeks to get there, fighting the entire way. By the second day of the offensive, the 1st Army had penetrated part of the first German line, but the Americans were still far short of Pershing's objectives. General von Gallwitz brought up reinforcements and the fighting intensified. The Germans were well trained and dug in, and the terrain heavily favored their defense. The Germans concentrated much of their best aircraft and pilots to challenge Billy Mitchell's fighters for command of the skies, and the airborne fighting was fierce. Casualties among pilots were high on both sides.

Pershing's doctrine of open warfare would prove a costly failure. The frontline divisions were a mixture of veteran and virtually untrained units, the latter of whom rose up in waves to assault machine gun positions and were mowed down, rather than pinning the enemy down with suppressive fire while other troops worked around the machine gunner's flanks to take him out. As the doughboys moved forward, the artillery struggled to keep up. Poor coordination existed between artillery and infantry in many divisions, resulting in infantry making unsupported attacks with heavy losses and coming under withering German artillery fire.

The autumnal skies opened with cold rain. What passed for roads were a muddy mess, especially after four years of artillery bombardment that had devastated the landscape. Enormous traffic jams clogged the only three roads to the Meuse-Argonne as the Americans brought up immense quantities of munitions and supplies. The logistics of resupplying such a large field army broke down in the mud. Pershing had not allocated military police to direct traffic, nor engineers to continuously repair the roads. It made for a stupendous mess, such that soldiers on the front line were not always fed.

After a week of fighting that had captured the first German "Giselher" defensive line, Pershing ordered a pause to reorganize his exhausted army. The Meuse-Argonne Offensive had stalled and the casualties were high. Some of the infantry divisions needed to come off the line already, as they were disorganized and spent. This was the first combat experience for most of the soldiers, and many of the divisions lost their effectiveness after just a couple days in battle. Veteran divisions replaced the raw frontline troops, such as the 1st Division, which took the position of the disorganized 35th. Pershing renewed the attack on October 4.

Most of the initial offensive took place on the plain east of the Argonne Forest, which represented the American 1st Army's western boundary. Combat was challenging in such heavily wooded terrain, and so Pershing decided to avoid the forest until the army outflanked it. The Germans took advantage of the woods, hiding artillery batteries and machine guns that fired upon the Americans advancing to the east. German artillery fired from the heights above the east bank of the Meuse River, catching the Americans in a crossfire.

Only one division, the 77th (known as the "Liberty" Division because it was largely made up of New Yorkers), was assigned to pin down the Germans in the Argonne Forest. As the division advanced into the woods on October 2, one battalion of 550 soldiers under Major Charles Whittlesey advanced ahead of its regiment and was cut off and surrounded. German machine gunners pinned down the Americans for five days and prevented relief forces from rescuing the battalion, while both American and German artillery pummeled the doughboys' position. Whittlesey refused to surrender, despite running out of food and water. The story of the "lost battalion" became one of the most dramatic of the war and spurred much press coverage.[54]

By this point, the Americans had gained a solid foothold east of the Argonne Forest and could outflank the German position in the woods. The 1st Corps commander, Hunter Liggett, ordered the 82nd Division to assault the forest obliquely from the east, threatening to cut off the enemy line of retreat, while the 77th Division advanced from the south. The plan worked and the Germans abandoned the forest. The Lost Battalion was soon rescued. More than half of the men had been killed or wounded. Whittlesey was awarded the Congressional Medal of Honor. The Germans retreated to a formidable position at Grandpré.[55]

On October 7, the same day that the Lost Battalion was rescued, Private First Class John Barkley was in a forward observation post near Cunel when a German battalion launched a counterattack against the 3rd Division. He took shelter in a nearby disabled French tank and rounded up an abandoned German machine gun and 4,000 rounds of ammunition. From this sheltered position, he mowed down hundreds of German soldiers and blunted two counterattacks. For this achievement he was awarded the Congressional Medal of Honor. That same day, two American divisions attacked east of the Meuse River to drive off the artillery that was firing into the flanks of the advancing 1st Army. The attack was also intended to pin down more Germans so they could not reinforce their defensive lines protecting Sedan. The attack quickly bogged down and made little headway.[56]

One of the more astonishing incidents of the war occurred on October 8 as the Americans were cleaning the Germans out of the Argonne Forest. When his unit became pinned down, a corporal from Tennessee named Alvin York infiltrated his seven-man squad into enemy lines, killed at least twenty-five Germans, destroyed thirty-five machine guns nests, and captured 132 prisoners. He was awarded the Distinguished Service Cross, and later the Congressional Medal of Honor for the feat. It was particularly remarkable given that York had initially registered for the draft as a conscientious objector before a friend convinced him of the rightness of the American cause. York's story was published in the *Saturday Evening Post* in 1919, making him a national hero.[57]

To the west of the Argonne Forest, the French 4th Army was slowly pushing back the Germans. It had notable American reinforcements, including the 369th Infantry—the Harlem Hellfighters—and the experienced 2nd Division, now under General John Lejeune. The Second captured a key German stronghold in early October, the Blanc Mont ridge, helping drive the Germans out of the Champagne region.

East of the Meuse River, the Germans prepared a counterattack on October 9. Airborne reconnaissance spotted the enemy concentration of forces, and Billy Mitchell ordered a major air attack. The French sent 322 airplanes, wave after wave of bombers that pounded the German position while American fighters held off pursuit aircraft. "Just think what it will be in the future when we attack with one, two or three thousand airplanes at one time; the effect will be decisive," he mused, foretelling the carpet bombing of World War II and Vietnam.[58] Mitchell would go on to suggest to Pershing that they assign the 1st Division to the Air Service, equip each man with a parachute, load them on bombers, and drop them into the rear of German lines to attack the enemy from behind. His 1918 suggestion foreshadowed the airborne infantry of the next war.[59]

Despite the October rain and supply difficulties, American forces were slowly driving the Germans back. George Marshall wrote, "The transportation of ammunition and supplies was rendered difficult over the water-soaked ground; the long cold nights were depressing to the troops, who were seldom dry and constantly under fire, and the normally leaden skies of the few daylight hours offered little to cheer the spirits of the men." Being a soldier was miserable, as the doughboys were constantly wet and cold.[60]

Soldiers in France had their letters censored. They were instructed not to give away American military plans, nor reveal casualties or the conditions on the battlefield. Doughboys generally wrote glowing words to their families, probably in the hope that they would not worry. The public had no idea how terrible the conditions were in the trenches, nor what it was like to endure an artillery bombardment to the point of broken nerves, nor what it was like to witness an infantry company get ripped apart by an enemy machine gun, nor what it was like to watch a man choke to death from poison gas, nor what it was like to see a man have half his face shot off by a sniper.

While the fighting raged in the Meuse-Argonne, deadly influenza indiscriminately ravaged the armies. Pershing noted 16,000 cases the first week of October, and eventually 70,000 soldiers would be stricken—and a third of them would die from it. More American troops were killed by influenza than by German bullets. Even Pershing caught the flu, though he stayed on duty and continued leading the army from his train, parked in a wooded siding near Souilly.[61]

By the second week in October, Pershing was exhausted, as was every man in the army. At one point the commander broke down in tears. He had such high hopes for breaking through the German lines quickly, when in fact the brutal fighting was inflicting devastating casualties. Pershing had not been able to fight the open warfare campaign he hoped for. Instead, the advance was a slog, and the army was losing over five hundred men a day as the Germans tenaciously held on.

Pershing ordered a halt to offensive operations while he regrouped the army and the soldiers rested. On October 12, he announced a reorganization, splitting the American Expeditionary Forces into two armies: the 1st Army west of the Meuse River under General Hunter Liggett, and the 2nd Army east of the river under General Robert Bullard. The 1st Army would continue bearing the brunt of the fighting while the 2nd would pin the Germans in place. Pershing would leave command of day-to-day operations to his army commanders, though in truth he was preoccupied with Liggett's 1st Army. That same day, Lieutenant Samuel Woodfill advanced ahead of his infantry company near Cunel and took out a series of German machine guns with just his rifle and pistol. He was awarded the Congressional Medal of Honor.

After a two-day rest, Liggett renewed the attack on October 14. The second German line, known as the Kriemhilde Position, occupied the dominant Romagne ridge, blocking the American advance. On the opening day of the attack, the 32nd Division seized the Côte Dame Marie, the Germans' strongest point on the line. To the east, the 42nd Rainbow Division prepared to assault another strongpoint, the Côte de Châtillon. The V Corps commander, Major General Charles Summerall, told Douglas MacArthur, "Give me Châtillon, or a list of five thousand casualties."

MacArthur, who led an infantry brigade, responded, "All right, General, we'll take it, or my name will head the list." MacArthur split his brigade into two flanking movements to surround the hill, then steadily, platoon by platoon, climbed upward and knocked out the German positions. In two days, MacArthur's brigade finally secured the strategic hilltop. The cost in human lives was high: one battalion of 1,475 men was down to just 306 men by the end of the battle. MacArthur was cited for bravery once again. He emerged from the Great War as the most decorated American soldier with the Distinguished Service Medal, seven Silver Stars, two Purple Hearts, and numerous decorations from Allied countries. [62]

The second German defensive line, known as the Kriemhilde Position, was now breached, three weeks after Pershing hoped to capture it. Only one final entrenched line stood in the way, the Freya Position, before the Americans could break out into the open countryside and capture Sedan. The largely green American army was gaining experience and ground against the battle-tested Germans.

Peace Negotiations and the 1918 Election

President Woodrow Wilson had spelled out America's wartime goals with the Fourteen Points in January 1918. As the year progressed, he added eleven points through diplomatic notes and speeches so that by the end of the war there were twenty-five American conditions for peace. This included a February 11 address that asserted the right of peoples for self-determination. Another speech came on July 4, where Wilson spoke at Mount Vernon. After a rather academic and lawyerly recitation, Wilson reduced the four new points to language that people could understand. "What we seek is the reign of law, based upon the consent of the governed and sustained by the organized opinion of mankind." If the Central Powers wanted peace, they would have to shed their ruling monarchies and adopt democratic governments. This impactful phrase would provide the foundation for Wilsonian diplomacy and American advocacy for democracy abroad. [63]

Wilson spelled out the last of America's war aims on September 27, the day after the Meuse-Argonne Offensive commenced, in a public address at New York's Metropolitan Opera. These were aimed in particular at the military junta that had commandeered the Central Powers at the cost of civilian government. He knew the war would end at some point—sooner in fact than anyone could imagine—and he set the stage for "a *secure* and *lasting* peace," one founded on the League of Nations, an idea that would be baked into the peace treaty. He wanted to build a peace based on "the principle that the interest of the weakest is as sacred as the interest of the strongest." It was one of Wilson's most principled statements, and he expected the league's covenant to be negotiated in the open and without resorting to "alliances or special covenants."[64]

The opera house speech sent a strong signal to the Germans. By October, it was clear that the German army was in trouble. It was being pushed back on all fronts. Key allies like Bulgaria and the Ottoman Empire had sued for peace, opening Austria's southern flank to Allied invasion. Austria-Hungary soon made peace overtures. The German Supreme Army Command signaled that the army faced collapse, and the government of Georg von Hertling resigned. Hindenburg wrote a memo to the government that concluded: "In these circumstances the only right course is to give up the fight, in order to spare useless sacrifices for the German people and their allies. Every day wasted costs the lives of thousands of brave German soldiers." On October 3, Prince Maximilian of Baden formed a new government and was appointed imperial chancellor. He had publicly called for peace and had opposed unrestricted submarine warfare, and his installation as chancellor was a stepping-stone toward an armistice. Maximilian would only serve as chancellor for five weeks, but his term in government would bring a close to the war.[65]

On October 6, Maximilian sent a note to President Wilson asking to begin peace negotiations based on the Fourteen Points and Wilson's subsequent addresses (a total of twenty-five points). A series of diplomatic cables, routed through the Swiss government, followed between the two men. The Germans tried to save their army by appealing directly to the United States, rather than to the Allies, but Wilson deflected that by responding that an armistice was a military matter best decided by the generals—in this case, Marshal Ferdinand Foch.

The question of peaceful terms for the Germans was a contentious debate in late 1918. Famed defense attorney Clarence Darrow came down with the hardliners in the war: "Peace will come when the German military machine is destroyed, and it cannot come before," he wrote in an article.[66] Henry Cabot Lodge, the leading Republican in the Senate, made a speech in late August 1918 demanding German unconditional surrender. "No peace that satisfies Germany in any degree can ever satisfy us. It cannot be a negotiated peace. It must be a dictated peace, and we and our Allies must dictate it."[67] Theodore Roosevelt likewise called for a "peace based on the unconditional surrender of Germany." Both Lodge and Roosevelt stood squarely against a peace negotiated on the Fourteen Points.[68]

Word soon leaked that the Germans were asking for peace, and that Wilson might go soft on them. As the German army retreated, the American press, GOP leaders, and Theodore Roosevelt called for Germany to surrender unconditionally, casting off Wilson's more moderate terms. On October 13, TR denounced Wilson for his efforts for a negotiated peace. "I must earnestly hope that the Senate of the United States and all other persons competent to speak for the American people will emphatically repudiate the so-called fourteen points," which would let Germany too easily off the hook.[69]

Wilson had made it clear that, if the monarchy or the military continued to rule Germany, then the country's only option would be to surrender, rather than negotiate. The message was received: the Kaiser would have to abdicate. When the civilian German government confirmed that it was in fact speaking for its people, and not for the military, another eruption broke out in Congress: senators wondered why Wilson was not consulting with them. On October 14, Senator Henry Ashurst of Arizona paid an unscheduled visit to the White House to meet with Wilson. The senator was highly agitated and denounced any armistice before Germany was totally defeated. "If your reply should fail to come up to the American spirit, you are destroyed," Ashurst warned.

Wilson took umbrage. "So far as my being destroyed is concerned, I am willing if I can serve the country to go into a cellar and read poetry the remainder of my life," he intoned. He reiterated what he had said all along: the United States would make peace on the basis of the Fourteen Points, rather than demanding unconditional surrender. [70]

Josephus Daniels recorded Wilson's exchange with Senator Ashurst in his diary. Wilson told Ashurst, "Why don't you Senators sometimes give me credit with not being a damned fool?" He explained it in terms that the cowboy senator could understand: "If you and I were in a fight and you held up your hands and asked for quit and would agree to all I said, and then I made you disarm, wouldn't that be all right?" Ashurst said that would be fine. Wilson then asked if the senator would prefer the Bolsheviks over the Kaiser—a distinct possibility if the German authorities were overthrown after surrendering unconditionally.[71]

Wilson meanwhile continued exchanging diplomatic notes with the Germans. Encouraged by their positive response to his peace overture, Wilson dispatched Edward House to Europe to lay the groundwork. He had immense confidence in his political adviser, remarking, "I have not given you any instructions because I feel you will know what to do."[72]

Republicans were speaking out against Wilson's goal to bring an early end to the war. The president responded with a statement of his own that would have profound political repercussions. On October 19, Wilson appealed publicly for a Democratic majority in Congress, two weeks before the midterm election. "If you have approved of my leadership and wish me to continue to be your unembarrassed spokesman in affairs at home and abroad, I earnestly beg that you will express yourselves unmistakably to that effect by returning a Democratic majority to both the Senate and the House of Representatives." His reasoning was that the Republicans were undermining his wartime leadership: "they have sought to take the choice of policy and the conduct out of my hands and put it under the control of instrumentalities of their own choosing." Wilson, who only five months earlier had declared, "politics is adjourned," now demanded that Democrats control the levers of power. [73]

Rather than champion national unity as a wartime president, Wilson called for a partisan Congress, one made up of Democrats, to ensure he could get his agenda through. That did not sit well with many voters. There was strong dissatisfaction against the president for the way he had run the war, all but ignoring domestic affairs. Wheat farmers, who had earned a federally guaranteed price, were upset that Wilson had rejected a twenty percent rise in the price floor in a time of high inflation. The pro-Republican business community had a long-standing grudge against Wilson for reducing protectionist tariffs while raising income taxes and war profit taxes. Newspaper editors chafed at self-censorship and the government's monopoly as a news source about the war effort. And, frankly, many Americans sided with the Republicans and wanted Germany to surrender unconditionally. [74]

Wilson had consulted with his political adviser, Edward House, about the speech, but House said nothing, though he sensed it would lead to trouble. House was on a ship bound for France when Wilson gave the speech. A week later, he wrote in his diary that it was "a political error to appeal for a partisan Congress. If he had asked the voters to support members of Congress and the Senate who had supported the American war aims, regardless of party, he would be in a safe position." House regretted that he did not tell Wilson that the partisan speech was a bad idea. [75]

Wilson understood the firestorm that he stoked, and he knew that the talk of an armistice would affect the election. Josephus Daniels penned in his diary that Wilson "might find popular opinion so much against him he might have to go into cyclone cellar for 48 hours." But Wilson also hoped the public understood that no one would benefit from having to fight all the way to Berlin. [76]

Wilson's appeal for a Democratic Congress backfired. The midterm election on November 5—six days before the Armistice—witnessed sizable Republican gains in Congress, and the GOP now controlled both houses. The 1918 election, as it turned out, marked the death knell of the Progressive Era, but no one knew that yet. The last progressive still occupied the White House, for now.

The midterm election of 1918 was a mess of Wilson's own making. The Espionage and Sedition Acts effectively silenced the opposition to the war—especially from pacifists on the left such as Eugene Debs.

Wilson had muzzled a key part of his political base, a fact that helped him lose control of Congress as a consequence.

With the Republican capture of the Senate—commencing in March 1919 when the new Senate met—Henry Cabot Lodge would become the majority leader and the chairman of the Senate Foreign Relations Committee. Republicans now had a narrow command of the Senate with forty-nine seats to forty-seven Democrats. Lodge was Wilson's staunchest opponent in the Senate, and he believed the Republican capture of Congress was a sign that the country wanted a dictated peace on Germany, not a peace of compromise.[77]

The Final Fighting

General Pershing sent a message to the American army on October 17, reminding the soldiers not to let up on the Germans, who were clearly in dire straits: "Now that Germany and the Central Powers are losing, they are begging for an armistice. Their request is an acknowledgement of weakness and clearly means that the Allies are winning the war. That is the best of reasons for pushing the war more vigorously at this moment." Pershing ended, "There can be no conclusion to this war until Germany is brought to her knees."[78]

The Allied Supreme War Council met in late October in to consider what terms should be part of the armistice. Pershing's views were the most strident of the council's: "Germany's morale is undoubtedly low, her Allies have deserted her one by one and she can no longer hope to win. Therefore we should take full advantage of the situation and continue the offensive until we compel unconditional surrender." His views were more in line with the Republicans, who wanted the same thing, not Wilson's peace without victory.[79]

Yet Marshal Ferdinand Foch believed that if France could achieve its military goals without further bloodshed, then why not grant the Germans an armistice? The cease-fire itself would effectively be a German capitulation, even if the words "unconditional surrender" were never written. Having reached Paris on October 26 and apprised himself with the situation, Edward House realized that the war might actually end sooner than anyone expected. He cabled the president on October 28th: "Things are moving so fast that the question of a place for the Peace Conference is on us."[80]

Germany's main ally, Austria-Hungary, was squeezed on two sides: a multinational Allied force moved up the Balkans to attack it from the southeast, while Italy opened an offensive that broke through the demoralized Austrian lines. Austria-Hungary's Emperor Karl I realized that his country was defeated, and the Austrians were granted an armistice on November 3. Germany now fought alone, all of its allies having deserted it.

After taking command of the 1st Army, General Hunter Liggett directed special attention to fixing his army's logistics and supply lines. The army was now better led, its logistical nightmare having largely been solved, and Liggett planned an operation to break through the final German Freya line. He abandoned Pershing's overreliance on infantry and instead concentrated heavy artillery and planned attacks with limited, attainable objectives that would allow artillery and supplies to keep up with the advancing infantry. It was this final assault that showed that the American army had reached fighting parity with the Allies and the Germans. Yet even at this late stage in the war, the army relied entirely on Allied armaments and munitions. "It is interesting to note that during the entire operation [Meuse-Argonne] the First Army did not fire one American gun, except the 14-inch naval guns, nor did it use one American shell manufactured for American use," Liggett noted after the war.[81]

The Americans in the Meuse-Argonne assaulted the last remaining German defensive line on November 1. As usual there was a short, sharp artillery bombardment, then an infantry attack at 5:30 A.M. Within hours the doughboys broke through the German position, and the troops advanced northward quickly toward Sedan through open countryside. Progress was now measured in miles, rather than yards. Part of the 2nd Division made a stealthy four-mile night march through enemy lines, sweeping up many prisoners who were fast asleep.[82] Another American force made a surprise crossing over the Meuse River on November 5, a move to outflank the German defenders on the eastern heights of the Meuse opposing the Second Army. Humorist Will Rogers joked, "The Kaiser was on the verge at one time of visiting the western front then he said, 'No I will just wait a few days till it comes to me.'"[83]

Revolution broke out in Germany. It began with a mutiny in the High Seas Fleet when sailors cooped up in port with bad rations for four years rebelled. Communist revolutionaries, inspired by the Russian Revolution and Bolshevik coup, plotted to overthrow the German government and staged an uprising in Berlin on November 9. On that day Kaiser Wilhelm abdicated and went into exile in Holland.

In his July 4 speech declaring that Germany could not be ruled by an autocratic government, President Wilson effectively demanded that the Kaiser abdicate before peace negotiations could begin. It meant toppling the German aristocracy at a time when the Bolshevik threat was real. Nevertheless, the Kaiser abdicated, while Prince Maximilian stepped down from the German chancellorship after just a brief but vital month. A government formed under Social Democrat Friedrich Ebert once the Kaiser abdicated, handing over the reins of the government to civilians as Wilson required. (Ebert would be elected Germany's first president two months later.) The military cautiously threw its support behind Ebert with the condition that he fight Bolshevism. General Ludendorff resigned and fled to Sweden.

On November 7, German delegates entered French lines to request an armistice, and met with Ferdinand Foch in his railcar parked in Compiègne Forest. The United Press falsely reported that day that the Germans had signed an armistice. GERMANY SURRENDERS; THE WAR IS OVER read headlines of afternoon newspapers. Jubilant crowds gathered at the White House to celebrate. Around the country, judges closed courts, schools ended early, churches rang bells, and thousands of people took to the streets, vacating their jobs and offices, some taking to drinking in celebration. A large crowd gathered at the Liberty Bell in Philadelphia. Even the New York Stock Exchange closed early. Shortly after noon, Secretary of State Lansing issued a statement denying that there was a cease-fire. In New York, the mood turned sour when newspapers reported that the armistice rumor was false. The police stepped up their vigilance and saloons closed early, lest angry, drunken crowds protest.[84]

Foch provided the terms of the cease-fire to the German delegation. The delegates crossed the front line to confer with their country's leaders, then returned to Compiègne to announce that Germany would accept the terms. The Armistice was signed at 5:15 A.M. on November 11, and a cease-fire would commence in six hours. There was a poetic timing to the Armistice: The guns would fall silent for the first time in more than four years on November 11, specifically the eleventh minute of the eleventh hour of the eleventh day of the eleventh month.

On the eve before the Armistice was declared, American forces converged on Sedan, reaching the heights above the vital town shortly before the Armistice. A near tragedy was averted: General Charles Summerall was determined that the 1st Division should capture the town, and he sent the division in front of the 42nd Division at night, a maneuver that could have led to fratricide. American troops under Douglas MacArthur intervened before the two divisions started shooting at each other. (During the nighttime march 1st Division soldiers briefly arrested him.) George Marshall called it a "grandstand finish," but Hunter Liggett was furious that his commanders were willing to risk their men's lives just for bragging rights.[85]

Under the terms of the Armistice, the Germans were required to withdraw immediately from Belgium and France and completely across the Rhine River, including returning Alsace-Lorraine to France. The Allies would militarily occupy the west bank of the Rhine and demanded that the Germans hand over much of their railroad rolling stock. Germany would disband most of its army and surrender the High Seas Fleet, which would be interned in Scapa Flow in the Orkney Islands off Scotland and wait there until the Allies decided how to distribute the ships among the victors. The intention of the Armistice was not to disarm Germany completely—the Allies understood the threat posed by the Bolsheviks—but to reduce Germany's offensive capabilities. Should the Allies need to invade if the Armistice collapsed, they wanted the German army weakened such that it could offer little resistance.

Captain Harry Truman wrote his fiancée Bess Wallace the morning of the Armistice as artillery bombarded German lines, trying to use up all of their ammunition before the cease-fire began. "I knew that Germany could not stand the gaff. For all thier [sic] preparedness and swashbuckling talk they cannot stand adversity," he wrote. "France was whipped for four years and never gave up and one good licking suffices for Germany."[86]

Colonel George Marshall had gone to bed at 2:00 A.M. on November 11 at army headquarters, but he was soon woken to deal with orders for four divisions, which were to begin a march northward that morning. He canceled their march from his bed and went back to sleep, not getting up until 10:00 A.M., an hour before the Armistice began. The officers gathered for a late breakfast when a huge explosion knocked them out of their chairs. Fortunately no one was hurt. A pilot soon ran in to survey the damage; he had just landed on an adjacent field from a bombing run when his final bomb fell out of the rack near the officer's quarters on his landing approach.[87]

General John Lejeune, who led the battle-hardened 2nd Division, had thrown his division across the Meuse River shortly before the Armistice while the two sides lobbed artillery shells at one another. "A few minutes before eleven o'clock, there were tremendous bursts of fire from the two antagonists and then—suddenly—there was complete silence," he wrote. "It was the most impressive celebration of the Armistice that could possibly have taken place." That night the cold, soaked doughboys and marines lit campfires and set off fireworks while automobiles and trucks turned on their lights. Lejeune heard many a cheering soldier shout, "It looks like Broadway."[88]

Most American pilots remained on the ground that last day, not willing to risk their lives when peace was so near. But not all pilots. Captain Eddie Rickenbacker, commander of the 94th Pursuit Squadron, took to the air in his Spad fighter late in the morning to witness the cease-fire from above. He flew just one hundred feet over the front lines. A few Germans shot at him, "but at the appointed hour all shooting ceased, and then slowly and cautiously, soldiers came out of the German and American trenches, throwing their rifles and helmets high into the air," he told an interviewer. "They met in no-man's land and began fraternizing just as a group of school kids would after a football game—happy in the realization that they would not be killed in this terrible conflict."[89]

Marine general James Harbord, who led the AEF's services of supply, recalled two doughboys discussing the peace. One had lost an arm, the other a leg. "Well, after all, this is worth losing an arm for." His friend responded, "Well, I don't mind leaving my leg over here so long as I can take the rest of my body home."[90]

After the Armistice began, Pershing drove to Paris, which he discovered was in bedlam. A huge weight had lifted over the city, which had lived in a state of siege for four years. "It looked as though the whole population had gone entirely out of their minds," he recalled. "The city was turned into pandemonium. The streets and boulevards were packed with people singing and dancing and wearing all sorts of costumes." He was trapped in the Place de la Concorde for two hours when an enormous crowd surrounded his car. He was finally rescued by a group of American soldiers who were partaking in the festivities, and who rescued their chief by helping push the crowd aside so the automobile could move. "If all the ridiculous things done during those two or three days by dignified American and French men and women were recorded the reader would scarcely believe the story," Pershing concluded. "But this was Paris and the war was over."[91]

Similarly, General Billy Mitchell drove to Paris and his car got stuck in a celebratory crowd. A group of French airmen spotted him and almost literally carried his sedan through the crowd. It had been less than three years since he took his first flying lesson, but Mitchell had commanded thousands of American aviators and bested the Germans, and he would become a leading proponent for an independent air force. He was satisfied with the support the French had provided for the budding American Air Service. Their training had allowed green American pilots to challenge German dominance of the skies. Mitchell counted his aircraft by the end of the war: Of his 740 airplanes that were flying, 528 were built by the French, just sixteen by the British, and only 196 were American made. Mitchell was disappointed that the American aviation industry built such poor aircraft. "We did practically all our fighting with foreign machines, the airplanes manufactured in America being inferior," he wrote. "There was no excuse for this."[92]

Future author Ernest Hemingway was recuperating in an American hospital in Milan when the war ended. He wrote his family that day that he was planning big adventures: "Because about next fall I am going to commence the real war again. The war to make the world Safe for Ernie Hemingway and I plan to knock 'em for a loop and will be a busy man for several years." He planned to travel Europe with the money he had saved—and naively thought he had a large pension coming from the Italian government (a sum that turned out to be $50 per year). In fact, Hemingway would return home in January.[93]

The Armistice began in the middle of the night in the U.S., just after 5:00 A.M. on the East Coast. Many people rose from bed to mark the occasion, including the president and his wife. Edith Wilson recalled, "Many persons have asked me what we did, and all I can answer is, we stood mute—unable to grasp the full significance of the words."[94] Secretary of the Navy Josephus Daniels learned at 2:45 A.M. that the Armistice would begin within hours, and soon after that newsboys began shouting that they had special newspaper editions for sale.[95] Americans took to the streets to celebrate, shouting, cheering, and throwing confetti. Cars honked their horns. It was cheerful bedlam in every city. President Wilson gave the federal workforce the day off, de facto declaring this to be a holiday. (It lived on, first as Armistice Day, and now Veterans Day.) Shopkeepers hung signs, CLOSED FOR THE KAISER'S FUNERAL, and many effigies of the Kaiser were burned that day.[96]

Author Willa Cather noted the excitement of the Armistice in New York. She immediately wrote her Aunt Franc, who had lost a son at Cantigny. New York was "mad with joy and all the church bells are ringing." She expressed her idealism at the nation's cause for war: "Think of it, for the first time since human society has existed on this planet, the sun rose this morning upon a world in which not one great monarchy or tyranny existed," she wrote, overlooking that the British and Ottoman monarchies still sat on their thrones, nor could she know that the Bolshevik coup would create enormous tyranny and human suffering for decades. "I like to feel that G.P. and the brave boys who fell with him, who went so far to fight for an ideal and for that only, became and are God's soldiers. Whatever the after life may be, I know they have a glorious part in it."[97]

From Paris, Edward House wired President Wilson a short but congratulatory cable: "Autocracy is dead. Long live democracy and its immortal leader. In this great hour my heart goes out to you in pride, admiration and love."[98] That morning, the president issued a short, moving statement, even as he prepared to address Congress. "My Fellow Countrymen: The armistice was signed this morning. Everything for which America fought has been accomplished. It will now be our fortunate duty to assist by example, by sober, friendly counsel, and by material aid in the establishment of just democracy throughout the world.[99]

Historian Frederick Lewis Allen brilliantly analyzed Wilson's Armistice Day proclamation: "Never was a document more Wilsonian. In those three sentences spoke the Puritan schoolmaster, cool in a time of great emotions, calmly setting the lesson for the day; the moral idealist, intent on a peace of reconciliation rather than a peace of hate; and the dogmatic prophet of democracy, who could not dream that the sort of institutions in which he had believed all his life were not inevitably the best for all nations everywhere." But was the world now safe for democracy? Had the United States in fact achieved its goals in the war, as Wilson promised?[100]

That afternoon, Wilson drove the one mile from the White House to the Capitol along Pennsylvania Avenue, the way crowded with 300,000 people celebrating the American victory in the war. The adulation continued when Wilson addressed both houses of Congress, the Supreme Court, and the Cabinet. He read aloud the terms of the Armistice, then added his own remarks about the way forward. "The war thus comes to an end," he started to say, though was immediately interrupted by applause before continuing, "For, having accepted these terms of armistice, it will be impossible for the German command to renew it." He called the conflict "this tragical war whose consuming flames swept from one nation to another until all the world was on fire." He announced that "armed imperialism is at an end." He concluded that what would follow would be a just peace. "The great nations which associated themselves to destroy it," meaning German militarism, "have now definitely united in the common purpose to set up such a peace as will satisfy the longing of the whole world for disinterested justice, embodied in settlements which are based upon something much better and much more lasting than the selfish competitive interests of powerful States." Wilson was already informally discussing that he may go to Europe for the peace conference.[101]

Secretary of War Newton Baker immediately suspended the draft, sparing 300,000 young men who were to be called up by the end of the month.[102] Three days after the Armistice, the government announced an end to voluntary censorship. The work of George Creel and his Committee on Public Information was done. CPI had been remarkably effective in its job in uniting public opinion while quietly squelching naysayers. Nothing like it existed for Wilson's later campaign to ratify the Treaty of Versailles.[103]

American intervention shortened the Great War by helping to defeat Imperial Germany. As the war ended, General Pershing was proud of the American army's accomplishments. This semi-trained army had gained combat experience and bested the German army. Meuse-Argonne was an American victory, but a costly one: some 117,000 American men had been killed or wounded in the forty-seven-day battle. The general estimated that they had faced 470,000 German soldiers and inflicted more than 100,000 casualties. He also discovered that the Germans no had more reserves: they had placed every unit in line to stop the Americans.[104]

Some 116,516 Americans were killed in the Great War (more than half were killed by the 1918 influenza), and more than 200,000 were wounded. American involvement had shortened the war and prevented a German victory. Germany's defeat came unexpectedly fast. Wilson's willingness to negotiate an armistice—rather than push the military offensive until Germany unconditionally surrendered—prevented much destruction and gave peace a chance.

Though the war was not fought on German soil, the Germans were far closer to collapse in 1918 than anyone realized. Mutiny, revolution, and strikes plagued the country, even as an Austrian-born corporal, Adolf Hitler, was recovering in a hospital from a British mustard gas attack that left him temporarily blind. The future dictator's voice would be raspy for the rest of his life. In 1929, Erich Maria Remarque wrote hauntingly of his experience as a German soldier in *All Quiet on the Western Front*: "Had we returned home in 1916, out of suffering and the strength of our experience we might have unleashed a storm. Now if we go back we will be weary, broken, burnt out, rootless, and without hope. We will not be able to find our way any more."[105]

The German army, thoroughly beaten and in headlong retreat, was not required to surrender. The Allies feared that, without an army to protect the German government, the Bolsheviks would seize the country. In fact, a German army column marched on Berlin and bloodily put down a communist revolt. Most of the soldiers then simply went home. Revisionists such as Adolf Hitler later argued the myth that the army had not been beaten, but rather that the starving civilians, communists, and above all the Jews stabbed them in the back. It was a fabrication, but it gave Hitler internal enemies to blame during his rise to power. Germany took on the role of victim, and from there it would seek vengeance. When France surrendered in June 1940, the Germans took their revenge by forcing the French to sign the humiliating surrender documents in Ferdinand Foch's railcar in Compiègne Forest—and then blew it up.

The Rhineland Occupation

On November 17, more than a million Allied soldiers advanced from their Armistice positions and began the march to occupy the German Rhineland. The terms allowed the Allies to establish bridgeheads at major Rhine River crossings: the British at Cologne, the Americans and French at Coblenz, and the French at Mainz. The newly created American 3rd Army, a composite force numbering 150,000 soldiers, would occupy the middle stretch of the river. The army was under command of Major General Joseph Dickman, the former commander of the 3rd Division and later the 1st Corps after Hunter Liggett's promotion. On December 13, the three Allied armies crossed the Rhine and occupied their respective bridgeheads, which they would inhabit for the next seven months. Pershing established his headquarters in the ancient city of Trier, founded by the Romans two millennia earlier.[106]

The Allied occupation of the Rhineland expelled the Bolshevik-leaning soldiers' and workers' councils that had usurped civilian authority during the uprising that had led to the German collapse. Though the Rhineland was now beyond the German government's control, the occupation stabilized the region by preventing communist trouble.[107]

General John Lejeune's 2nd Division was part of the Rhineland occupation, as was Douglas MacArthur's Rainbow Division. MacArthur's brigade headquarters was in Sinzig, just south of Remagen where American troops would storm across the Rhine River in March 1945. The Harlem Hellfighters (the 369th Infantry) remained attached to the French 4th Army and moved into the Rhineland. It was given the honor of being the first American unit to cross the Rhine River at Mainz on December 1.

An anti-fraternization order prevented the doughboys from socializing with the Germans, but soldiers being soldiers, this rule was soon ignored. Just as in France, many doughboys were billeted not in barracks, but in farms and houses. It was impossible for soldiers not to fraternize with their host families, and not a few doughboys came home with German brides. The order was revoked in September 1919.[108]

In early January 1919, Billy Mitchell received word that Edward, the Prince of Wales, would pay him a visit in Coblenz. Mitchell was not eager to entertain the royal but was surprised when Edward arrived with only an aide and an orderly—and had driven himself. "It took only a few minutes of conversation for us all to be delighted with the personality of the Prince," Mitchell recalled. "He seemed just a nice big overgrown boy with all the instincts of a healthy young fellow." Mitchell added, "He is the most democratic young man belonging to the crown families of Europe that I have ever met." Indeed, as King Edward VIII he would abdicate in 1936 so that he could marry American divorcée Wallis Simpson.[109]

Prince Edward was very interested in taking a flight with Mitchell. The two men took off in a two-seater Spad on a rare sunny January day. They flew up the Moselle River, passing castles and wineries built along the steep banks, then looped back to the Rhine. They flew over the Lorelei, the massive rock that legend held lured sailors to their deaths. Mitchell circled back to Koblenz, noting the statue of Kaiser Wilhelm that stood where the Moselle and Rhine met. "With one turn over the city of Koblenz, I landed on the airdrome after one of the most enjoyable air trips I have ever taken."[110]

In April 1919, Hunter Liggett assumed command of the occupying 3rd Army. That army was disbanded on July 2 after the signing of the peace treaty and replaced titularly by the American Forces in Germany. Most of the army was sent home, leaving behind a much smaller occupying force of about 19,000 men by end of year. Two years later, the force numbered only 8,710 men. General Henry Allen served as U.S. military governor in Germany, commanding the dwindling force. Part of his task was to restrain the French, who still hoped to split off the Rhineland into a neutral buffer state. Unfortunately, the Harding administration ordered the remaining occupying force to return to the States in January 1923, just as the Ruhr crisis reached its peak. The Allied occupation of the Rhineland would continue until 1936, when Adolf Hitler marched in unopposed just months before the Berlin Olympics where American athlete Jesse Owens won his fame.[111]

SEVEN

The Prophet of Democracy

The Great War having been won, President Wilson set his mind to winning the peace. Around the time of the Armistice, he had suggested to his cabinet that he would go to Europe personally to negotiate the peace treaty and build the framework for the League of Nations. "I want to go into the Peace Conference armed with as many weapons as my pockets will hold as to compel justice," he told Josephus Daniels. A week later he let it be publicly known. In messianic fashion, he claimed to speak for all the world's peoples who wanted a peace of justice rather than one of revenge.[1]

Wilson's war aims were not necessarily the Allies'. They paid lip service to the Fourteen Points and reluctantly agreed to negotiate the peace with the points in mind. They had their own goals centered around punishing Germany, demanding an indemnity, and seizing territory from their enemies. England also wanted the U.S. to end its aggressive shipbuilding program so that the Americans would not challenge the Royal Navy's command of the seas.

The president would personally lead the American Peace Commission. In addition to including Secretary of State Robert Lansing, Wilson appointed three others: Edward House, General Tasker Bliss, and Henry White, the commission's one Republican. White was a former diplomat, not a high-ranking politico. Wilson himself would be the country's chief negotiator, rather than delegate the task to trusted subordinates. This would remove him from the domestic stage for many months while in Europe. Wilson was immediately criticized for his choice of peace commissioners, as well as criticized from both the left and the right for removing himself from domestic affairs.[2] Will Rogers, who kept up on current events and commented on them nightly in his vaudeville act, noted, "Of course there was a lot of dissatisfaction against the President going, mostly by people whom he did not take along."[3]

Wilson refused to share power with Republicans in war and in the peace effort. This came to haunt him: Republicans had just seized control of Congress in the midterm elections a week before the Armistice. He blundered when he did not take into account how much political ground he lost in the 1918 election. Many historians have argued that not including a senator on the negotiating team alienated Wilson from the Senate. The treaty ending the Spanish-American War in 1898 included three senators at the negotiating table. Yet obviously Wilson could not pick Henry Cabot Lodge, who might undermine him, so he selected no senators. Certainly there were other Republicans whom Wilson could have chosen, such as former Senator Elihu Root, who had served as Theodore Roosevelt's secretary of state, won the Nobel Peace Prize in 1912, and who was a firm supporter of the League of Nations. Then there was former president William Howard Taft, who led the League to Enforce Peace. Adding a higher-profile, respected Republican to the American Peace Commission—even if not a senator—may have paid political dividends for Wilson.[4]

But is this long-standing historical assumption accurate? The Senate's responsibility is to provide advice and consent to treaties, not to negotiate them. Negotiating treaties falls to the executive branch and is most often carried out by the State Department. Even Senator Lodge admitted publicly, "I have no fault to find with his not appointing Senators as delegates to the conference. There is no obligation whatever upon him to make such appointments."[5]

It may have been wiser for Wilson to help kick off the peace conference, then delegate the actual negotiations to the diplomats or to a high-profile politician who was aligned with Wilson's views toward peace. With the Republicans now in control of Congress, Wilson needed to keep his political enemies close and shape the debate. Instead, he effectively left the country for six months. It was a mistake. Wilson's going to Paris turned the peace process into a partisan issue.

Much of Wilson's cabinet and his closest friends were concerned that the president was taking on more than he could handle by attending the Peace Conference. Many were worried that Wilson's vision was too grand. It went far beyond just ending *this* war, but in attempting to end *all* war. Bernard Baruch, Herbert Hoover, Edward House, and Robert Lansing all voiced opposition to Wilson going to Paris.[6] Secretary of State Lansing had been a little too vocal about Wilson's peace efforts, and he came to realize that the president had lost confidence in him.[7] Likewise, Secretary of Agriculture Houston believed Wilson's participating in the Peace Conference was a mistake. He believed it was fine to travel to Europe, meet with the Allied leaders, then return home, but Houston believed Wilson needed to keep his distance from the negotiations. "His voice would be mightier going across the ocean," he wrote.[8]

Other cabinet secretaries remained silent, possibly because they were bowing out. Treasury Secretary William McAdoo and Attorney General Thomas Gregory announced their resignations soon after the Armistice. McAdoo was now fifty-five years old and had exhausted his financial resources serving in a position that cost him $35,000 a year in expenses, far beyond his income. Wilson replaced them with David Houston at Treasury, and Mitchell Palmer as attorney general.[9]

Many contemporaries pointed out that Wilson could have served as a mysterious oracle if he had stayed in Washington, delivering pronouncements and overruling treaty terms that were too harsh. By going to Paris, Wilson lessened his authority. He became just another politician wallowing in the heated negotiations, something he was not particularly astute at. "If he remained in Washington and carried on the negotiations through his Commissioners, he would in all probability retain his superior place and be able to dictate such terms of peace as he considered just," Lansing told Wilson the day after the Armistice, but the president dismissed the suggestion. [10]

Frank Cobb of the *New York World*, a Wilson administration ally, wrote Edward House once he learned that Wilson intended to go to Paris. "The moment President Wilson sits at the council table with these Prime Ministers and Foreign Secretaries he has lost all the meaning that comes from distance and detachment," he warned. "Instead of remaining the great arbiter of human freedom he becomes merely a negotiator dealing with other negotiators." [11]

Wilson ignored the advice of his cabinet and friends. He went to Paris anyway, determined to build his beloved League of Nations. "Well, Tumulty, this trip will either be the greatest success or the supremest tragedy in all history; but I believe in a Divine Providence," the president told his secretary. "If I did not have faith, I should go crazy." Wilson's hubris—his belief that only he could negotiate the peace treaty—would be his costliest political mistake. [12]

Theodore Roosevelt had personally negotiated a peace treaty after the Russo-Japanese War ended in 1905. For his efforts he won the Nobel Prize. Wilson would one-up him: he could go to Europe and negotiate a peace treaty that would end war altogether. Wilson had in mind an international framework, a League of Nations, which would arbitrate future conflicts.

Why did Wilson intend to negotiate in person, rather than delegate his authority? Part of it was that he believed his personal involvement would better secure the peace, as he knew the Allies would be vindictive toward the Germans, and he believed he could lessen this through his personal presence. Another factor was that Wilson did not think highly of his secretary of state, Robert Lansing. Lastly, Wilson believed that only he could negotiate the Covenant of the League of Nations into the framework of the peace treaty itself, a document that he and Edward House had jointly drafted. Wilson had a high motive:

engendering a lasting peace. Herbert Hoover, who considered Wilson and House to be his close friends, noted their naivety: "Both President Wilson and the Colonel were living in a stratosphere far above the earthly ground on which the war was being fought."[13] What Wilson did not understand was how strong European ethnic hatreds were, with centuries of grievances beyond remembrance. After the blood-bath of the World War, he naively hoped people would lay down their arms. The reality was something different: they wanted the other side punished. It was irrational, no doubt, yet Wilson never quite fathomed how deeply the French hated the Germans. Though he would make fast friends with Clemenceau, he never understood that Clemenceau's goal was to gut Germany, not to restore it to friendship.

Wilson effectively removed himself from the United States for six months during the treaty negotiations, with a short visit home in the middle. It became nearly impossible for him to shape public opinion in his absence and he had minimal contact with Congress at the time. Congress was left out of the loop and ultimately seized control of the narrative.

Wilson's quest for peace became a personal crusade, one that blinded him to political realities, especially once the Democrats lost control of the Senate. And it became intensely personal: he had to be the one to negotiate the treaty—a treaty that turned out to have enor-mous flaws—then sell it to the Senate, and ultimately to the American people. It was too much for one person to do. Wilson paid the price politically, and it destroyed his health.

The president's political enemies were already working to under-mine Wilson's peace efforts. Theodore Roosevelt published a statement on November 27 that denied Wilson's role in the negotiations. "Our allies and our enemies and Mr. Wilson himself should all understand that Mr. Wilson has no authority whatever to speak for the American people at this time," as Wilson's party had lost control of Congress. "He is President of the United States. He is a part of the treaty-making power; but he is only part. If he acts in good faith to the American people, he will not claim on the other side of the water any represen-tative capacity in himself to speak for the American people. He will say frankly that his personal leadership has been repudiated and that he now has merely the divided official leadership which he shares with the Senate." This was a statement that likewise echoed Senator Lodge's sentiment. That Roosevelt worked so hard to undermine the president and engaged in such partisanship did not speak well for what turned out to be his twilight years. He no doubt would have bullied anyone who criticized him in public in such a fashion, especially in the face of sensitive negotiations. But Wilson was no bully. He simply ignored Roosevelt. [14]

Wilson delivered the annual State of the Union Address on December 2, 1918, to a Congress that was still controlled by Democrats, at least for another three months until it adjourned. After that, Republicans would assert control over both houses. He praised the two million soldiers who fought overseas to defeat the Germans, and the women who shouldered much burden during the war. He also said that the federal government would continue to operate the railroads for the foreseeable future and noted that the Treasury would need $6 billion to draw down the military. Wilson then explained why he was going to the Paris Peace Conference: "It is now my duty to play my full part in making good what they offered their life's blood to obtain. I can think of no call to service which could transcend this." [15]

Wilson's speech did not go over well with Republicans. The war had only been over for four weeks and partisan squabbles had already broken out. They refused to applaud the president, not even his references to the brave sailors and soldiers who had won the war. Senator Henry Ashurst of Arizona noted the poor reception in his diary: "The disgruntled Senators trooped over to the House. When the President appeared the applause was meager; his message was long, and surely he must have felt the chilliness of his reception." [16] Irked by the icy Republican reaction, the president remarked privately to Josephus Daniels, "When I get out of this office, I will tell them what I think of them." [17]

The next day Ashurst paid a visit to the president in the White House. Wilson started the conversation with a rare word of profanity. "What are those ***** on the hill doing today?" he asked.

"Mr. President, the House of Representatives would impeach you and the Senate convict you if they had the courage," the senator responded. "Their lack of nerve is all that saves your removal from office; Congress opposes your going to Europe."

The president turned icily cold—and Ashurst could tell he was upset—in one of those moments where Wilson controlled his temper by speaking slowly and deliberately. "Congress has a brain-storm but as soon as I am on the high seas they will recover," he said emphatically. In this Wilson was profoundly wrong. His political opponents were angry at his going to Europe, and they would do much to undermine his efforts.[18]

American idealism from the war soon broke down in the weeks and months after the Armistice. Wars provide a rare instance of national unity that often proves fleeting. After the victory over Mexico in 1848, a heated debate emerged over whether to allow slaves in the newly-acquired territories. After the Civil War, Congress and the president fought over how best to reconstruct the country, resulting in the impeachment of President Andrew Johnson. And after World War II, partisans would ask, "Who lost China?"

Theodore Roosevelt was fond of playing backseat president. He was one of the few who truly enjoyed the office, and he hoped to occupy it one day again—possibly as early as 1921, once Wilson's second term ended. He parsed Wilson's State of the Union Address, attacking the president's lack of transparency in developing the country's war aims and for daring to go to Europe. Roosevelt decried the Fourteen Points, saying that these were Wilson's policies, not the American people's, since Congress had never voted on them—and that the November 5 election had repudiated Wilson's leadership. "He says the American Army was fighting for them. Why, there was not one American soldier in a thousand that ever heard of them," Roosevelt claimed with great exaggeration, but he then got to the heart of what motivated the soldiers: "The American Army was fighting to smash Germany. The American people wanted Germany smashed."

Roosevelt hoped that Wilson would not try to play umpire in Paris. "It is our business to stand by our allies," he wrote. He was willing to let the British keep their interpretation of the freedom of the seas, as well as retain Germany's colonies. It was clear from Roosevelt's statement that, if he were president, he would negotiate a substantially different peace treaty, one that smashed Germany and gave the prizes to America's allies. Republicans like Roosevelt wanted a more limited peace treaty, one that addressed the specific reason why the country went to war: to thwart German aggression.[19]

The Republicans in the Senate, led by Henry Cabot Lodge, wanted to separate the peace treaty from the League of Nations. The league could wait, they argued. In a December 21 speech, Lodge reminded the president that the Senate had to consent to any treaty, power given to it in the Constitution. He also called for German indemnities—and believed that the U.S. should receive some.[20]

No sitting president had ever left the United States before, so Wilson's trip to Paris was a controversial first. Tradition held that the president was forbidden from leaving the country, though that was nowhere spelled out in the Constitution. No one was certain how the president would perform his executive duties from so far away. His political opponents hatched a plan to declare that he was temporarily out of office since he would be out of country, allowing Vice President Marshall to assume the position until Wilson returned. The plan went nowhere, but it was a clear signal that the Republicans were displeased with Wilson going to Paris.[21]

The day after the State of the Union address, Edith and Woodrow left Washington on a midnight train bound for Hoboken. Wilson left behind most of his cabinet secretaries to continue the business of running the country. His private secretary Joe Tumulty would stay behind and be his key contact in Washington. The two were in regular contact, often cabling each other daily.

The next morning the Wilsons boarded the *George Washington*, the same German-built ocean liner that had carried Harry Truman to France in March, and subsequently tens of thousands of American doughboys. Joining Wilson were two dozen members of the Commission of Inquiry, or "The Inquiry," as they called themselves, a group of experts Edward House had organized. The commission had loaded three truckloads of data onto the ocean liner.[22] The president also took his leading public relations man, George Creel. Will Rogers joked, "Mr. Creel went along to suppress any scandal that may crop up."[23]

The *George Washington* set sail for Europe on December 4, escorted by the battleship USS *Pennsylvania*, five destroyers, and the transport USS *Orizaba* carrying eighty journalists to cover the Peace Conference.[24] The ships were in constant communication with the United States, thanks to new technology developed during the war: powerful radio transmission towers had been built in Annapolis, Maryland that could communicate with ships far out to sea.[25]

Wilson had caught a cold a few days before in Washington, and Dr. Grayson insisted that he rest while aboard the ship. The president caught up on his sleep, a rare luxury for any president. As the ocean liner steamed across the Atlantic, Wilson addressed the Commission of Inquiry on December 10, a group that he viewed as vital to assisting with the peace negotiations. He provided his thoughts on the upcoming conference, then boldly concluded, "Tell me what's right and I'll fight for it; give me a guaranteed position." Instead, Wilson would largely fight for the position that he and Edward House had staked out, while often disregarding the other American Peace Commissioners and Inquiry members.[26]

Larz Anderson, a wealthy former diplomat, political observer and Taft supporter, noted in his diary that Wilson went to Paris "taking over with him hundreds of 'expert advisers' with whom he never advised." Anderson did not get everything right in his assessment of Wilson's presidency—he believed that Wilson was planning to take the country to war before the election in 1916, and thought he was a Johnny-come-lately to the idea of a League of Nations—but he was correct in that Wilson did not effectively use his cadre of advisers at Paris. The president served as his own secretary of state. He tried to do too much and delegated too little.[27]

As Wilson was sailing to France, another American was returning home from Europe. Journalist and poet Carl Sandburg, who wrote for the *Chicago Daily News*, was sent to Stockholm to cover the end of the Great War, the civil war in Finland, and the Bolshevik takeover of Russia. He returned to the States in December 1918 with two steamer trunks full of information, some of which he unwittingly accepted from Bolshevik spies, along with two bank drafts that were allegedly for friends but were really for Bolshevik operations in the U.S. Sandburg had been duped. Customs officials and American and British intelligence officers grilled him for days in New York upon his return. He was finally released without being charged, though authorities confiscated the Bolshevik material.[28]

Wilson in Europe

The *George Washington* docked in Brest on December 13, where the docks were crowded with thousands of cheering French, and the city bedecked with red, white, and blue. Everywhere Wilson traveled in Europe he was met by huge crowds. He was an exemplar to millions and was treated like a conquering hero. Woodrow Wilson was perhaps the most famous man in the world in his day. When the Wilsons arrived in Paris, they paraded through jubilant crowded streets. "Every inch was covered with cheering, shouting humanity. The sidewalks, the buildings, even the stately horse-chestnut trees were peopled with men and boys perched like sparrows in their very tops," Edith Wilson recalled. "Roofs were filled, windows overflowed until one grew giddy trying to greet the bursts of welcome that came like the surging of untamed waters."[29]

The crowds may have convinced Wilson that his mission was destiny, that he spoke for the people of the world, and that the European people wholeheartedly supported his efforts toward peace without victory. This belief proved delusional: they cheered him for sending an army that had helped win the war. Few of the Allies had Wilson's idealism. They wanted concrete rewards owed for their sacrifice.

Wilson set up shop in Paris, ready to get to work on the peace treaty. He quickly discovered that he had arrived a month too early: the British insisted on waiting until after their December 14 parliamentary elections, so the Peace Conference could not begin until January. England was not physically ravaged like Belgium or France; still, it had suffered battlefield casualties, and the losses to its merchant marine were enormous. Prime Minister David Lloyd

George returned to Paris politically strengthened, his Labor Party government reelected on the campaign promise that they would make the Germans pay for the war.

Wilson was nearly sixty-three years old when he arrived in Paris. His health was not great, as the war had reduced his ability to exercise with the countless meetings and voluminous correspondence that never ended. While he waited for the Peace Conference to begin, Wilson undertook travels to visit the Allies. After Christmas, he and Edith journeyed to England, meeting King George and Queen Mary. After returning to France, they traveled to Rome, where they met with the king and queen of Italy and Prime Minister Vittorio Orlando. They had an audience with Pope Benedict XV, who gave Wilson a mosaic of St. Peter created in the Vatican workshops. Wilson was the first president to ever meet with the pope, a controversial step at the time, given that many Americans still considered the Catholic Church a cult. He and Edith visited hospitals to see the wounded, many with mangled bodies and faces. However, Wilson would not set foot in any of the countries that the U.S. had been at war with, not even the occupied German Rhineland.

Shortly before the Peace Conference was set to begin, an unexpected death rocked the United States: Theodore Roosevelt died in his sleep on January 6, 1919 of a pulmonary embolism. Vice President Thomas Marshall quipped, "Death had to take him in his sleep, for if Roosevelt had been awake, there would have been a fight." The former president was only sixty. Roosevelt was the presumed Republican candidate for the presidency in 1920, but his surprise death opened the question. Woodrow Wilson's greatest political rival and fiercest critic was no more.[30]

The day before Roosevelt's death, a workers' revolt known as the Spartacist uprising broke out in Berlin. Chancellor Friedrich Ebert called in the military and the right-wing militia, the *Freikorps*, to crush the uprising. Germany was temporarily saved from the Bolshevik threat. Ebert was elected to the presidency a month later in the small city of Weimar, where representatives were drafting a new constitution away from the chaos of Berlin. Germany became known as the Weimar Republic during the period between the Great War and Hitler's rise to power in 1933.

Meanwhile, Seattle dockworkers struck in January to protest the high cost of living and lack of pay raises. They were soon followed by more than one hundred other labor unions. It was the beginning of a calamitous year as waves of strikes hit the United States. The public was largely unable to separate the motives of the striking workers—who were for the most part calling for higher wages in a time of high inflation—from those of the bomb-throwing anarchists and communists. The uneducated public feared the whole country was going Red.

On January 15, a tank holding 2.3 million gallons of molasses collapsed in Boston's North End. The molasses wave flooded the streets in the surrounding blocks, knocking buildings off foundations and killing twenty-one people while injuring 150 more. The sticky syrup thickened in the cold New England air, trapping more people in the ooze and making rescue far more difficult. People feared that it was an explosion set by anarchists, as the molasses was distilled into industrial alcohol that was used extensively in munitions manufacturing. In fact, the tank collapsed from structural deficiencies.[31]

On January 10, President Wilson addressed the American Peace Commissioners. He stated that lawyers could not draft the peace treaty. Robert Lansing was stung by this criticism—he was the one lawyer on the commission—and hence he withdrew from offering Wilson further advice about the League of Nations. Lansing later complained that Wilson "was prejudiced against any suggestion that I might make, if it in any way differed with his own ideas even though it found favor with others."[32]

Wilson was soon beset by countless petitioners. It seemed everyone wanted to meet the president in Paris. Representatives from small countries. Ambassadors, royalty, committees, politicians, petitioners, veterans, farmers. Wilson spent every waking moment in meetings with little respite. He also had to deal with domestic affairs, cabling instructions to Tumulty at home. Wilson's press secretary in Paris, Ray Baker, wrote soon after the peace conference, "I found him looking utterly worn out, exhausted, often one side of his face twitching with nervousness," he wrote. The president's hair turned visibly grayer at Paris, and his face notably aged with sleeplessness and worry.[33]

The war and subsequent peace treaty radically redrew Europe's map as new countries emerged from the wreck of empires. Several countries organized themselves even before the Peace Conference began, including Czechoslovakia and Yugoslavia. Czechoslovakia included a minority of three million Germans who lived in the bordering Sudetenland. Yugoslavia was a pan-Slavic country with Serbia at its core; Serbia had marched into the power vacuum as the Austro-Hungarian Empire fell, seizing Bosnia, Croatia, and Slovenia. Yugoslavia would prove a thorny problem: despite being Slavic, there were vast cultural problems, as the Croatians and Slovenians were Catholic and used the Latin alphabet, while the Serbs were Orthodox and used Cyrillic. To further complicate things, Bosnia had a large Muslim population.

To the east and north of Germany, Finland and the Baltic States—Estonia, Latvia, and Lithuania—had won their independence from Russia. Poland was created in the military vacuum after the war with undetermined borders. Polish independence fighters would carve out as much as they could take from Germany, Austria-Hungary, and Russia. The new state included several million Germans, and it surrounded a German enclave on the Baltic, East Prussia. Its access to the sea—as Wilson promised in the Fourteen Points—would be Danzig, a German city that would be declared independent but with a Polish customs union.

The American Relief Administration

Herbert Hoover had done such exceptional work, first in Belgian relief and then leading the Food Administration, that President Wilson tapped him to lead the American Relief Administration after the Armistice. Like Wilson, Hoover would decamp for Paris for much of the next year. There were many American officers in France idly waiting to depart for home, and General Pershing granted permission for Hoover to recruit officers for relief work. He took 2,500 army and naval officers to assist. The troops fanned out across Europe, helping to reopen coalfields and ports, deliver food, set up temporary housing, even negotiate between warring militias. They deloused the population of entire regions in Eastern Europe to stem the spread of typhus.

Congress had appropriated $100 million toward feeding European children after the war, as there were millions of orphans. Its charter expired on June 30, 1919, but there was still great need for food relief, so Hoover reorganized the administration as a private charity. He enlisted banks for their help and enabled Americans to send food aid to European relatives by depositing bank drafts. This continued into 1921, as there were still millions of hungry European children.

Hoover was particularly proud of a December 1920 dinner in New York City that he hosted with General Pershing. Donors paid one thousand dollars a plate to attend, and a thousand people attended, raising a million dollars for the charity. Unprompted, a man stood up and announced, "There is a million dollars here for the asking," and demanded that the audience be allowed to make additional contributions, which raised another million. Then John D. Rockefeller Jr. added yet another million, raising the evening's total to three million dollars.[34]

Hoover estimated that the American Relief Administration helped between fifteen and twenty million children. When starvation loomed in the Soviet Union from the collectivization of farms, he stepped in to feed millions more. Hoover's work was a tremendous humanitarian gesture that saved millions of lives during and after the war.[35] He was especially proud that the charitable food program that had fed malnourished children was entirely American financed.[36]

Herbert Hoover's efforts after the war kept much of Europe from starving. "The ungrateful Governments of Europe owe much more to the statesmanship and insight of Mr. Hoover and his band of American workers than they have yet appreciated or will ever acknowledge," wrote British economist John Maynard Keynes.[37]

The Paris Peace Conference Begins

The Paris Peace Conference opened on January 18, 1919 at the Quai d'Orsay. The conference was an incredibly rare event: political leaders from twenty-seven countries gathered to discuss and deal with the world's problems. It was a chance to alter the world order. Wilson nominated French Prime Minister Georges Clemenceau to chair the conference, a courtesy since France was hosting the conference and had borne the brunt of fighting on its soil.

Woodrow Wilson found himself an outlier at the conference: he was the only head of state on the Supreme Council: the others were prime ministers, the heads of parliamentary governments. Wilson was highly ignorant of European affairs and public opinion. He never quite understood what motivated the men he negotiated the peace with. For him, it was about principle. But for others, it was about compensation for war damages, national security, or territorial gains.

Little of the Great War was fought on German soil. The country's industry and transportation network were intact, though its economy was near collapse and its people almost starving. Trade had ground to a halt thanks to the blockade. The Royal Navy maintained the blockade against German ports, even after the Armistice was reached, exacerbating the economic and humanitarian crisis in Germany during a cold winter. The German government resorted to massive deficit spending to keep its economy going, which in turn fueled hyperinflation in the early 1920s.

France had suffered probably more than any other country. The Germans had damaged or destroyed French coal mines as an economic weapon, as coal was the key energy source for much of industry. France's chief concern—argued through Prime Minister Georges Clemenceau—was for its security against Germany. Clemenceau was seventy-eight years old. He had lived in the U.S. in the 1860s, spoke fluent English, and had married an American. He had severe eczema on his hands, so he wore gloves, even indoors. He and Wilson became quite fond of each other, despite their many arguments.

Clemenceau stood decidedly for the balance of power. It was realistic, and it had long worked. This required alliances and ensured that powerful nations and empires could dictate to smaller countries. Wilson sought to end this system; he wanted self-determination for countries emerging from the former empires, not more colonization. He desired that all countries be treated as equals.

At the end of the Great War, the United Kingdom had essentially gotten what it wanted. Germany's powerful navy sat guarded in British harbors, the German African colonies were in English hands, and England had captured much of the Ottoman Empire's territory in the Middle East. The Royal Navy commanded the seas, but it viewed with caution a possible naval rivalry with the Americans and Japanese. Above all, England wanted to resume international trade, a key reason for its global empire.

The December parliamentary victory had strengthened the negotiating hand of British Prime Minister David Lloyd George. He was charming and an excellent public speaker. He was also verbose and a bit of a demagogue. Lloyd George was cheerful but slippery, with no fixed position, unlike Clemenceau. Ray Baker observed, "One knew where Clemenceau stood and what he intended to do; one never knew where Lloyd George stood: he never stood twice in the same place." Yet Wilson increasingly saw eye to eye with Lloyd George. Their national interests were aligning, especially as they fought to tone down France's more extreme demands at the negotiating table. [38]

Another key player at the peace talks was Italian Prime Minister Vittorio Orlando, as well as his foreign minister Sidney Sonnino. Orlando led a weak coalition government. To strengthen his position at home, Orlando had promised that he would win territory beyond that promised in the Treaty of London: he would win the eastern Adriatic for Italy, shutting out the newly established Yugoslavia from the coast. Italian honor demanded it.

One of the key Allies was not present in Paris. Russia had already signed a separate peace with Germany, and in any case who would represent the country? Russia was divided into Red and White factions as a cruel civil war raged. There was another factor as well why the Russians were not invited: the Bolsheviks had repudiated Russia's foreign debt, worth billions.

The Allies occupied Russia's ports—Archangel, Murmansk, Odessa, Sebastopol, and Vladivostok—to secure supplies dispatched to the Russian government and to help evacuate the Czechoslovak Legion. No one was sure what to do with Russia. It was an enormous country—the largest geographically in the world—and the civil war was raging over a vast landscape. Americans soldiers occupying Russian ports were stranded during the sub-zero winter of 1918–1919, unsure of their mission while staving off the arctic cold and skirmishing with the Bolsheviks. The Allies had no clear strategic objective. Their intervention was haphazard, uncoordinated, and pointless, and it failed.

Edward House had been first on the scene in Paris, and he initially issued the public pronouncements about American policy. Secretary of State Robert Lansing, who attended the Peace Conference, probably felt squeezed out, knowing he did not have Wilson's confidence. Realizing the slight, Wilson appointed journalist Ray Baker to act as the public affairs official to the American Peace Commission. Baker had spent most of 1918 as a State Department special envoy in Europe, and Wilson thought highly of him. Baker was a muckraking journalist and popular novelist who wrote under the pen name David Grayson.

It was House who got the Allies begrudgingly to accept the Fourteen Points as a basis for negotiating the peace treaty. Yet in coming months, they would casually disregard it—and Wilson would negotiate away numerous points in order to reach a final peace agreement. Germany had accepted the Armistice with the assumption that the subsequent peace treaty would be negotiated along the line of the Fourteen Points. The Allies had begrudgingly agreed to most of the points as well, though they saw this merely as a basis for what they intended to extract from Germany.

House was sick with a kidney ailment for two weeks in January 1919, just as the Peace Conference got underway. The initial days of the conference were chaotic, as there was no real plan or organization. Many small countries had petitions for grievances. Under Clemenceau, the conference finally organized a Council of Ten, consisting of the main representatives from the five key allies (France, Great Britain, Italy, Japan, and the U.S.) plus their foreign ministers. These would decide what should be in the peace treaty. The Central Powers were not invited to attend.

English and French were the two official languages of the Peace Conference. Complicated issues were delegated to the small army of specialists each side had brought to Paris. They formed commissions to study an issue and provide recommendations, which the council usually accepted. While the Peace Conference was underway, so was demobilization of the armies. Smaller armies meant less leverage against the Allies, so it was a race against time to reach a settlement before the Allies lost their ability to coerce the Germans to sign a peace treaty. There was much talk initially about hanging the Kaiser, but that waned over time, and in any case the Dutch refused to hand him over for trial. He died there in 1941.

The Armistice signed on November 11, 1918, was extended every thirty-one days until a peace treaty could be reached. A peace treaty could have been quickly concluded. The Allies and the Germans had largely accepted the framework of Wilson's Fourteen Points, itself a foundation for a peace treaty, and the military questions were largely decided in the Armistice terms. Ending the war quickly would allow the world's commerce to resume and prevent more human suffering caused by the blockade. However, the Allies wanted so much more, as did President Wilson.

Wilson set urgently to work on his key priority: the League of Nations. He had been in Europe for more than a month now. Edith recalled, "The month lost after our arrival he felt was a great waste, and so he was driving every hour to try to make up this loss."[39] Europe urgently needed peace, yet Wilson effectively hijacked the Peace Conference by demanding that the commissioners draft the covenant for the League of Nations first. He might have promoted a more general framework that a later commission would organize in detail, but instead Wilson expected the peace treaty to bring the League fully to life. It took the first month for the Peace Conference to address this question, considerably delaying the restoration of peace.[40]

On January 25, a week into the Peace Conference, Wilson achieved an early victory: he convinced the Allies that the draft peace treaty should include the covenant for the League of Nations. A commission of nineteen people from various countries was put together to hammer out the details, including House and Wilson. The committee then met for the next two weeks in House's chambers to edit the covenant.[41] Ray

Baker called the League of Nations commission "the hardest-driven commission at Paris," as Wilson was the driver behind it. [42]

Wilson sought to smash the old order of diplomacy that relied on alliances, the balance of power, land grabs, and secret agreements, often to the detriment of smaller countries and marginalized populations. Instead of a balance of power, nations would have collective security through the League of Nations. He envisioned a brave new world of diplomacy based on principle and conflict resolution. [43]

While Wilson was engaged with drafting the League of Nations covenant, the British dominions made a move to annex the German colonies. Australia in particular wanted German colonies in Papua New Guinea. Wilson headed them off by insisting that they be governed by League of Nations mandates. Mandates were largely assigned on non-European countries with the intention that they would be preparing for independence in line with Wilson's views on self-determination. However, Wilson never defined the term "self-determination," a key phrase in the Fourteen Points, and the phrase was eventually removed from the League of Nations covenant. The key phrase had been launched on the world, however, and the idealistic promise of self-determination stoked ethnic nationalism.

On February 13, the league commission completed the draft covenant. The permanent members of the League of Nations were the five key allies, now constituting its executive council: England, France, Italy, Japan, and the United States. They had won the war, and they carved out advantageous roles for themselves in the League. (The United Nations Security Council would follow a similar format in 1945.) Although the peace treaty affirmed that all countries were equal, it was clear that some were more equal than others—and some were more important. The League of Nations had a fatal flaw: it required all decisions of the executive council to be decided unanimously. A single dissident nation could prevent the others from taking action on a global issue.

Clemenceau was not enthusiastic about the League of Nations, given that his goals were more severely practical: assuring French security against Germany. However, the Peace Conference accepted the League covenant the next day. Wilson was so enthusiastic that he met with American reporters for an hour at noon, eagerly talking up the covenant. Wilson wired Joe Tumulty, asking him to set up a dinner with the Senate Foreign Relations Committee so he could explain the points of the covenant upon his return to the U.S. [44] He then departed Paris for Washington, for the end of the Congressional session. Edward House took over the American delegation as the Peace Conference addressed the peace treaty, hoping to have it ready for discussion when Wilson returned in March.

Wilson's Trip Home

Wilson steamed home aboard the *George Washington* with many wounded soldiers, Ray Baker, and Eleanor and Franklin Roosevelt. He had been absent from the U.S. for more than two months, but Democrats still controlled Congress until March 4. He was thrilled at how much he had accomplished thus far at Paris. His plan was to sign bills and meet with senators to eagerly share the plan for the League of Nations, then return to Paris after ten days to resume negotiations. He was destined for disappointment.

On February 19, as Georges Clemenceau traveled in a car through Paris, a communist gunman attempted to assassinate the prime minister. He fired seven shots at Clemenceau at nearly point-blank range, all but one of them missing the mark. Doctors decided that removing the bullet would be too difficult, so Clemenceau carried it for the rest of his life. The prime minister's recovery delayed the negotiations by several days, but he was soon back at work.

The *George Washington* made landfall at Boston, rather than New York. Wilson gave a speech on February 24 at Boston's Mechanics Hall, stressing the need for the League of Nations in Henry Cabot Lodge's hometown, an action that irritated the Republican senator. It was hardly a conciliatory move on Wilson's part to offend the chief person who needed to approve the peace treaty.

As Edward House had requested, Wilson dined with the members of the Senate Foreign Relations Committee two days after his

Boston speech. No liquor was served, much to the senators' annoyance. Washington had technically been dry since November 1917, but that was just a technicality to the thirsty senators. Wilson was too principled to offer liquor or wine in a legally dry city, though it may have lightened the mood. The senators expected to hear about the peace treaty; instead they got two hours of questions-and-answers about the League of Nations. They left disappointed. "Your dinner to the Senate Foreign Relations Committee was a failure as far as getting together was concerned," Wilson told House testily when they met in France several weeks later. Lodge was present but said nothing, a silent figure of looming opposition.[45]

On February 28, Lodge made his first public pronouncement about the League of Nations. The Senate was packed, as were the galleries, when Lodge delivered his long-awaited speech. "Party considerations and party interests disappear in dealing with such a question as this," he declared, then made clear that he opposed the League of Nations as it currently stood. The treaty would infringe on American sovereignty and violate the Monroe Doctrine. He made a salient point: the peace treaty was still under negotiation, and therefore it could be amended.[46]

Lodge feared that the League of Nations would impose on national sovereignty and the Monroe Doctrine, particularly Article X, which was designed to protect the territorial integrity of all countries through collective security. He seized on the idea that the League of Nations would force the United States to get involved in a war, even when it had no desire or interest. Lodge wanted the league covenant separated from the peace treaty while imposing a harsh settlement on Germany.

Contrary to received wisdom, Lodge was not an isolationist; he saw the country's role in more realistic (and less idealistic) terms than Wilson. However, he was a partisan Republican with a "festering dislike" of Woodrow Wilson, as his biographer called it. Lodge found Wilson mean, selfish, vacillating, and weak, but this was in part because the president was a Democrat. Lodge was in fact willing to allow the country enter the League of Nations if certain protections were built to safeguard American sovereignty.[47]

During his short visit to the U.S., Wilson met with important Republican statesman, including former president William Howard Taft, Senator Elihu Root, and Judge Charles Hughes to get their feedback on the draft covenant. Wilson incorporated almost all of their suggestions into the treaty's text, including an explicit mention of the Monroe Doctrine. But even knowing that Article X would be a sticking point for ratification, Wilson still made no move to alter the language. Will Rogers joked, "They seem to think the President took the Monroe Doctrine in his pocket and is liable to lose it over there."[48]

Wilson had missed virtually the entire session of Congress, returning only for the final days in late February. There was considerable resentment about this fact from both political parties. Republicans demanded that he call Congress back in session, just as he did during the war, to deal with the peace. Wilson did not want to do this, as he was set to return to Paris, and he knew that the GOP would now be running Congress in his absence. Wilson announced that he would summon Congress when he returned from Paris with the final peace treaty. In a speech at the Metropolitan Opera in New York on March 4, he offended senators on both sides of the aisle by claiming that senate Republicans had "such a comprehensive ignorance of the state of the world. These gentlemen do not know what the mind of men is just now. Everybody else does."[49] He also signaled his unwillingness to compromise on the question of the league: "When that treaty comes back, gentlemen on this side will find the covenant not only in it, but so many threads of the Treaty tied to the covenant, that you cannot dissect the covenant from the Treaty without destroying the whole vital structure."[50]

William Howard Taft took the stage with Wilson to defend the League of Nations, but it was Wilson's condescending words that ignited a firestorm in the Senate with his injudicious criticism. On that closing day of Congress, Senator Henry Cabot Lodge delivered a preview of what would happen once he was in charge of the Senate in the next session. He presented a resolution that stated, "the constitution of the League of Nations in the form now proposed to the Peace

Conference should not be accepted by the United States." Thirty-seven senators had signed the resolution, known as the "round robin," enough to block ratification of the peace treaty. Lodge made it clear that he believed that the final peace and the League of Nations should be separate treaties—and that the peace should come first and immediately. It was an opening shot that signaled the senator's intentions: he had declared war on the president's peace plan. Congress then adjourned on March 4, its session finally over.[51]

Wilson was only home for ten days, then he returned to Paris for four months. He landed at Brest on March 13 and was soon back in the thick of the Peace Conference. Negotiations for a preliminary peace were at a point where all sides would have to compromise to secure a treaty. American idealism at Paris came face-to-face with political reality: all of the Allies had agendas for their own security, often at odds with other countries. House realized this, and so hoped for a preliminary peace that would then punt the deep-seated issues to the League of Nations for resolution.[52]

The Return to Paris

President Wilson returned to France politically weakened. His party no longer controlled Congress, and his League of Nations message was not well received by the majority Republicans. But Wilson plowed ahead despite the warning signs. He was unwilling to separate the peace treaty from the League of Nations. The two remained intertwined.

During the month that Wilson was away from Paris, the Allies worked on the preliminary peace treaty with Germany. House was in frequent communication with the president about progress. Some French diplomats and officers attempted to steer around the League of Nations. They did not want to kill it but went after it obliquely. Ray Baker, who accompanied the president on his voyage home and back, wrote: "Thus while it is too much to say that there was a direct plot, while Wilson was away, to kill the League or even cut it out of the Treaty, one can affirm with certainty that there was an intrigue against his plan of a preliminary military and naval peace—which would have indirectly produced the same result."[53]

On March 13, the *George Washington* docked in Brest. Wilson and his party disembarked, where Edward House met them. The party boarded the night train for Paris. House briefed the president on what had transpired in the past month, in particular the diplomatic maneuverings. What happened next was controversial and conflicting for historians, especially as the main sources had differing accounts.

According to Dr. Grayson, Wilson's physician, House briefed Wilson on developments, "including the apparent desire on the part of the French authorities to have the League of Nations covenant side-tracked and a preliminary peace treaty signed which would include the complete disarmament of Germany, the creation of a Rhenish Republic, and would in effect do what the President had declared on a number of occasions he would not countenance." In this version of events, House informed the president that Marshal Foch and other French reactionaries were driving for a buffer zone in the Rhineland, a punitive peace toward Germany, and to separate the League of Nations covenant in the preliminary treaty.[54]

Another account comes from Edith Wilson, who published her memoirs two decades after the Paris Peace Conference. According to her version, Edward House had negotiated away the League of Nations commitment. House had seen Senator Lodge's March 4 "round robin," and thinking that Congress would not support the league, he gave away Wilson's prize. Edith remembered that her husband was furious. "The change in his appearance shocked me. He seemed to have aged ten years, and his jaw was set in that way it had when he was making superhuman effort to control himself."[55]

Edith's memory of the event was biased and unreliable. Her husband was justifiably angry at the news House brought, but she was wrong to blame House. In the intervening years, she had developed a strong prejudice against the former adviser. Edith was increasingly jealous of the attention that House got at Paris, attention that she believed belonged to her husband. She used the alleged League pitfall as a wedge to separate House from Wilson—and after Wilson's stroke in October 1919, she would completely shut House out.

Upon Wilson's return to France and meeting with House, Ray Baker perceived "a coldness between the two men," not based on jealousy, but "based upon far deeper failures in understanding and action." This was the basis for the long-standing myth that Wilson and House had suffered a break in their friendship, one that Edith would later magnify in her memoirs.[56]

Wilson's friendship with Edward House never ended, but it certainly faded. House's biographer, Charles Neu, noted that, "There was no open break or confrontation."[57] He added, "Wilson did not reprimand House, but the trust he had placed in him for so many years now disappeared."[58] Despite Edith Wilson's claim, it was a myth that House gave away the League of Nations—he had done no such thing. There was in fact no plot against the League of Nations, only diplomatic wrangling over the draft treaty, which Wilson may have mistaken as a conspiracy against his treasured league.[59]

When Ray Baker landed in France with the president, a well-informed person told him, "Well, your league is dead."[60] This was not quite true, but it was under threat. House recorded in his diary that day (March 14), "The President comes back very militant and determined to put the League of Nations in the Peace Treaty."[61] Immediately upon returning to Paris, Wilson took action to quell any rumor of the League's untimely demise. He directed Baker to publish a press release saying that the Supreme Council had agreed on January 25 that the League of Nations covenant would be integrated into the final peace treaty. The question would not be reopened for discussion. This settled the matter.[62]

The Doughboys Return Home

After the war, feeding the starving continent—including Germany—was a priority that took much shipping, while the doughboys in Europe were anxious to return home. The Germans had a large merchant marine as well as passenger vessels stranded in their harbors. An idea was floated to use the ships to bring the American soldiers back to the states, freeing up shipping that could then supply the Germans with food. In the January 1919 extension of the Armistice, the Germans reluctantly agreed to allow their ships to be used, but it did not sit well with the German population. And justifiably so: the Allies would confiscate the entire merchant marine as part of the reparations package—and then demand that the Germans build 200,000 tons of shipping for five years to hand over to the Allies in compensation for the U-boat campaigns. This hobbled Germany's ability to export its products and rescue its flailing economy and contributed to the rising resentment.[63]

While the Paris Peace Conference was underway, the U.S. Army began to demobilize. The tide that had swept two million doughboys to France now reversed and the young soldiers were shipped back to the states by the thousands. Many of them arrived in New York City to await transport home. The city held parade after parade for the returning soldiers, and when they returned to their home towns, locals held victory parades again. New York–based author Willa Cather did her best to entertain as many doughboys as she could, as she wrote a relative:

> After dinner I went to the theatre with six of them who had landed that morning—six western boys alone in New York on Christmas Eve. We had some time, I can tell you! No, I don't do anything but run about with soldiers. They come in from Europe now at an average of five thousand a day, and to most of them this city is stranger and more confusing than Paris. On Christmas Eve there were 30,000 soldiers and sailors, on leave from camp, tramping the streets of New York hunting a good time. I wanted to go to the theatre with them all![64]

When George Patton's tanker brigade landed in Brooklyn, several hundred men signed a petition denouncing the presence of newspaper magnate William Randolph Hearst on the welcoming committee. "The protest is registered because of the conviction that he has proved himself to be un-American, pro-German and inhumanitarian," read the petition. Patton himself did not sign the document.[65]

With the signing of the peace treaty in June 1919, the American army of occupation on the Rhine came to an end. General Liggett and his 3rd Army were sent home. General John Lejeune returned to the states in July aboard the *George Washington* with five thousand men of his 2nd Division. The division was celebrated in New York City with a parade up Fifth Avenue, beginning at Washington Square Arch and concluding at the far end of Central Park. Thousands of people turned out to cheer for the returning heroes of Belleau Wood, Soissons, Blanc Mont, and the Meuse-Argonne, a division that had suffered more casualties (23,218) than any other American force in the Great War.[66]

Not all of the returning soldiers were thrown a parade. Douglas MacArthur complained to a friend that once his division returned to New York in April 1919, there was no one to greet them. "Amid the silence that hurt—with no one, not even the children, to see us—we marched off the dock, to be scattered to the four winds—a sad, gloomy end to the Rainbow [Division]." He would soon be given a new assignment to be the superintendent at West Point, and a decade later would serve as the chief of staff of the army. On the eve of World War II, MacArthur commanded the American forces in the Pacific.[67]

Freshly back in the states, the doughboys were sent to their cantonments, and there they were discharged from military service. Every soldier received a $60 bonus and money to pay for transportation home. They faced a weakening economy and struggled to fit back in. Thousands of wounded men were disfigured or maimed. Some had missing limbs, but artificial appendages and plastic surgery came to the rescue to help the veterans retain a semblance of mobility. Some survivors whose faces had been shot away beyond the help of surgery wore plastic masks to hide their gruesome visages. Those permanently disabled received small disability checks. Veterans established American Legion lodges around the country, providing for the veterans lobby and asserting their political power. The lodges provided comradeship but also the ability to commiserate privately with one's fellow veterans over the brutal experience of war, something most Americans simply could not relate to.

When the end of the war came, the estimated five thousand Germans in War Prison Barracks were still held in confinement. Around the time of the Treaty of Versailles signing in June 1919, those who wanted to be repatriated were allowed to return home to Germany. The Department of Justice released small numbers of people, and the detention camps shrank. Most of the sailors went home. Conductor Karl Muck was deported in August. A DOJ employee interviewed Erich Posselt, accusing him of helping to plant bombs on ships, something Posselt adamantly denied. Posselt remained at Fort Oglethorpe until January 1920, when he was finally released. He was never charged with a crime but had been held seventeen months. The War Prison Barracks were finally closed in April 1920.[68]

Negotiations Continue

Wilson returned to Paris and into the thick of the peace negotiations. The Council of Ten was proving burdensome. There were too many people in the room, too many competing agendas, and progress on a preliminary peace treaty had slowed to a crawl. And there were far too many press leaks during the delicate negotiations. Edward House suggested that they reduce the council to the four key Allies: England, France, Italy, and the United States. Japan was politely excluded, as it had not played a major role in the fighting. Clemenceau approved. The Council of Four first met on March 14, the day Wilson returned to Paris. Only four men were in the room, plus their interpreters. The council met in closed-door sessions in Wilson's private study. This would open Wilson to criticism that he had engaged in secret diplomacy and backroom deals, violating his own Fourteen Points.

Intransigent issues faced the Council of Four, and the negotiations turned into a two-month slog. France wanted its security guaranteed by dismembering Germany, in addition to reparations. England wanted deep reparations to compensate for its massive merchant marine losses. Italy wanted part of the Alps and more of the Adriatic coast. In the face of these demands, Wilson held onto his ideals for a just peace, but he would give much away in the ensuing talks, including several of his beloved Fourteen Points, to finalize the peace agreement.

Because of the frequent press leaks, Wilson was hesitant to speak to reporters during the sensitive negotiations. His press secretary Ray Baker believed that Wilson should meet with reporters, as it would combat the intensely negative state-controlled French press that Wilson faced by sympathetically explaining America's goals for world peace. "He never seemed to appreciate the value of mere human contact," Baker lamented. [69]

French reactionaries were out in full force. Marshal Foch pushed for ever more military action, especially in the East against the Bolsheviks, and demanded that France annex the entire German Rhineland. Clemenceau knew this was too far, but France would need some sort of security. He dove into this upon Wilson's return in March, demanding that a separate Rhine Republic be established as a buffer state, carved out from German territory. Lloyd George and Wilson were united in not wanting to give in to Clemenceau on this issue. They offered an olive branch to the French prime minister by promising that England and the U.S. would come to France's relief if Germany ever attacked. Clemenceau considered this—but he also demanded the coal-rich Saar Basin in compensation for the damage done by the Germans to France's coal industry. The problem was that the Saar was ethnically German. Wilson would not go along with this proposal, nor would Lloyd George.

Clemenceau's position hardened. Ray Baker wrote in his diary on March 22: "The President is growing impatient with the French, who are delaying and objecting at every point. The French are suffering from a kind of 'shell-shock' and think only of their security." [70] Six days later, he recorded another exchange between Clemenceau and Wilson. "France must have this for her security, or we have lost the war," the prime minister demanded. Wilson explained to Baker, "We spend an hour reasoning with Clemenceau, getting him around to an agreement, and find when we go back to the original question Clemenceau stands just where he did at the beginning." [71]

Likewise Clemenceau was frustrated with Wilson, his self-righteousness and his idealism, as he remarked to Edward House,

"When I talk with President Wilson, I feel as if I were talking to Jesus Christ." He added: "The Almighty gave us Ten Commandments, but Wilson has given us Fourteen."[72]

The president remained calm throughout the negotiations, though he certainly made numerous passionate speeches. He complained privately to Dr. Grayson that the French wanted him to tour more of the devastated regions to prove just how bad the destruction had been—and therefore the need to punish Germany. "They want me to see red, and I can't afford to see red," Wilson said in exasperation. "To whip myself into a passion of rage would be to unfit myself from the present task. I know well enough the wrong that Germany has done, and Germany must be punished, but in justice, not in frenzy."[73]

One morning Clemenceau angrily accused Wilson of "wearing the Kaiser's helmet" for being too soft on the Germans. After lunch and much thought, Wilson gave a passionate speech, witnessed by Dr. Grayson. Wilson singled out Clemenceau for criticism, and when the prime minister rose to leave the room, the president berated him, "You sit down. I did not interrupt you when you were speaking this morning." Clemenceau did as he was told. Wilson then continued, "Therefore I cannot consent to be a party to the kind of adjustment that you men counsel because it is no adjustment. It is merely laying fire for the future. It is not only the innocent children of Germany that I am thinking of. I am thinking of the children of France, of England, of Italy, of Belgium, of my own United States, of the whole world. I see their faces turn toward us in unconscious pleading that we shall save them from annihilation. I am not asking for a soft peace but for a righteous peace." And thus Wilson arrived at one of the key themes of his campaign to ratify the peace treaty: what the peace would mean to the next generation.[74]

Meanwhile, Bolshevism was a rising threat to Europe, a continent beleaguered by starving people. On March 21, communists under Béla Kun seized power in Hungary, an action that landed like a bombshell at the Peace Conference. (As it turned out, Kun would be overthrown in August). Germany was starving, thanks to being cut off from the world, and a Bolshevik takeover threat was real in a hungry population. However, France would not allow the wartime blockade to be lifted without a peace treaty. Bolsheviks staged an uprising in Bavaria, though this did not last long in the conservative kingdom. It was clear that the continent was in a race against time. The peace treaty was necessary to stabilize European politics and revive the economy.

The Allies grasped that Germany was on the brink of revolution, and should they wish to forestall a communist revolution as witnessed in Russia, they had better keep the population from starving. The situation in Germany deteriorated during the winter of 1919 as the country ran out of food. As the negotiations at Paris continued, there was a genuine fear that the fragile German democracy would collapse under communist revolution if the domestic situation worsened. The Allies agreed to raise the naval blockade and supply Germany with food in March 1919—but the Germans would have to buy it, and their only asset to trade was gold. The country spent half of its gold reserves; much of it ended up in the United States, which had the food.[75]

Wilson protected his prize from being negotiated away: the League of Nations covenant would remain permanently in the final treaty. Secretary of State Lansing composed a memo on March 30 that concluded with his frustration at the president's approach toward peace. "The President's obsession as to a League of Nations blinds him to everything else. An immediate peace is nothing to him compared to the adoption of the Covenant. The whole world wants peace. The President wants his League. I think the world will have to wait."[76]

Secretary of the Navy Josephus Daniels visited Paris in late March. It was still winter-like, but the beautiful palace where the Wilsons resided was unheated. After eating lunch together, the president gave Daniels the tour. "Now come, let me show you the refrigerator where I sleep," he joked about his bedroom. With the lengthy hours at the Peace Conference, "The only exercise I get is to my vocabulary," Wilson said. Lack of exercise had long been a problem in Wilson's sedentary life, an issue that would compound later that year.[77]

The president took to bed with cold symptoms on April 3, symptoms that soon turned out to be the flu. He did not return to the

Council of Four until April 8. Edward House sat in for him, though they met in the next room so Wilson could listen in from his bed. House was not the silent pushover that history has accorded him. He was actively involved in negotiations. His opinion of Wilson lessened during the Paris Peace Conference, as he saw firsthand that the president was a poor negotiator. Observing both Wilson and Clemenceau at the negotiating table, he noted in his diary: "One is an idealist, the other a practical old-line statesman."[78] House was becoming disgruntled with the president's lack of ability to lead a team; instead, he did it all himself. Wilson's tendency to act unilaterally and without consultation blinded him to the fact that he was negotiating the peace treaty into a terrible condition. "His training in all his previous life, it should not be forgotten, had been that of the scholar, the student, not the politician, accustomed to getting his information, not from people, but out of books, documents, letters—the written word," wrote Ray Baker.[79]

The American Peace Commission was not like Wilson's cabinet, where they had freewheeling debates and eventually reached consensus. Wilson seldom subjected his ideas to debate among his fellow commissioners; he and House largely kept their ideas to themselves. One exception was on April 6. While Wilson lay in bed with the flu, he met with the American Peace Commissioners to strategize. They agreed that the president should demand that either the Council of Four agree to build the peace upon the Fourteen Points, or Wilson would insist that they return to the Council of Ten, which would slow the talks to a crawl. None of the Allies wanted that, of course, and they agreed to Wilson's stratagem.[80]

From his sickbed on April 7, Wilson signaled that he would walk out of the peace talks when he inquired how long it would take for the ocean liner *George Washington* to return to France (the navy's answer was ten days). This was in effect an ultimatum that Wilson would return home unless the Allies toned down their demands. It was quickly leaked to the press.[81]

Clemenceau asked Dr. Grayson if the president was bluffing. "If he ever starts for Brest to go aboard the *George Washington*, you and your entire French army cannot turn him back," the physician responded.[82] Once they realized Wilson was serious, the Allies changed their tack and made much progress in the following week—so much that they delivered notice to the Germans on April 13 that the Allies were soon prepared to deliver the terms of peace. Wilson did not walk out of the Peace Conference.

While Wilson was bedridden with the flu, House yielded on one considerable area: reparations. The American position had been that the reparations sum should be spelled out in the treaty, and then divided among the Allies who made claims. House agreed—presumably with Wilson's support—to punt the reparations sum to a commission, rather than to fix the sum in the treaty. On April 8, Clemenceau won a concession on this point: reparations would be decided by a commission that would examine each country's claim, then provide a final bill to Germany. Clemenceau believed France would win more money this way. The British demanded that the Germans not only pay for war damages, but also for pensions for wounded survivors and widows. Wilson went along with this, though it inflated the price tag. Sums as high as $40 billion were bandied about. Germany's colonies, which were a total loss, were never considered in the reparations formula. The Reparations Commission would calculate Germany's bill by May 1921.[83]

Part of France had been occupied during the Franco-Prussian War in 1870–1871, and the country was forced to pay reparations to Germany. When it paid off the indemnity, the German army left France. In 1919, the French believed it was more than fair for Germany to repay France with the same coin. Likewise, the Germans had demanded an ungodly sum from the Russians at Brest-Litovsk the year before and had likewise treated Romania poorly at the peace table. Given this, there was little sympathy for the German argument that their economy was weak. The Allies demanded to be paid.

The Allies wanted Germany to pay for economic reconstruction, but also so they could in part pay down their large war debts, much of which was owed to the U.S. government and American banks. The U.S. had loaned enormous sums and expected to be paid back. Wilson was not willing to address the question of debt forgiveness, which would have relieved much of the economic burden on all sides. The U.S. itself wanted no reparations; however, it did keep the interned German ships that it had seized for the war effort. The country found itself in far better standing regarding global trade at the end of the war and now had a sizable merchant marine.

With Wilson's recovery from the flu, and armed with suggestions from Congress and William Howard Taft, he asked to reopen the League covenant on April 10 to address American political realities. Taft had provided suggestions to Wilson on ways to make the treaty more palatable to Republicans, including a reservation for the Monroe Doctrine. Taft firmly supported Wilson's work at Paris and wrote that the "Monroe Doctrine reservation alone would probably carry the treaty, but others would make it certain."[84] This did not go over well—the Allies wanted their issues revisited as well—though the Council of Four eventually agreed to it after a multi-day fight.

The Allies quickly came to agreement on a number of issues. The Saar issue was resolved on April 13: France would only take title to the coalmines, and the Germans would have to buy them back. The Saar would fall under a League of Nations mandate administered by France. A plebiscite would be held in fifteen years (when Saar residents voted in 1935, they overwhelmingly voted to rejoin Hitler's Germany). Two days later, the council agreed that the Rhineland would be occupied for fifteen years with a phased withdrawal as Germany paid off its reparations. Wilson had yielded in crucial areas while working to rein in Clemenceau's more onerous demands on Germany. And most damning, he had agreed to the war guilt clause, the most controversial aspect of the treaty.[85]

Marshal Ferdinand Foch was not happy with this compromise. He demanded that France have the Rhineland for its security, a claim that he took public, much to Clemenceau's irritation. "The next time, remember, the Germans will make no mistake," he told a British reporter. "They will break through into Northern France and seize the Channel ports as a base of operations against England." He had a point: this was exactly what the Germans did in 1940.[86]

The final treaty could have been far worse toward Germany. Wilson had headed off most of Clemenceau's drastic proposals against Germany, yet not nearly enough of them. France abandoned its idea to carve out a buffer state in the Rhineland, as well as its attempt to annex the ethnically German Saarland. Wilson believed David Lloyd George was of little help, changing positions daily. "Well, I suppose I shall have to stand alone," the president told Ray Baker. [87]

Wilson was not exactly standing alone: he did have some assistance from Lloyd George, who was eager to rekindle England's commercial relationship with Germany, a leading prewar trading partner. Lloyd George had been reelected on the promise to make the Germans pay for the war, but on March 25 he shifted his stance in a published memorandum, warning against treating Germany with too much harshness: "You may strip Germany of her colonies, reduce her armaments to a mere police force and her navy to that of a fifth-rate power; all the same in the end if she feels that she has been unjustly treated in the Peace of 1919 she will find means of exacting retribution from her conquerors."[88]

But now that France had partly resolved its border security issues with Germany, Italy wanted similar security with the soon-to-be-former Austro-Hungarian Empire. Italy had long been at odds with the Austrians, and now felt threatened by the new, pan-Slavic state of Yugoslavia that emerged on its eastern border. The Allies awarded part of the Adriatic coast to Italy, including the port city of Trieste. Wilson yielded to Italy taking over the ethnic German enclave of South Tyrol, including the strategic Brenner Pass through the Alps—a land grab that clearly violated the Fourteen Points. Italian Prime Minister Orlando demanded the Adriatic port of Fiume (now Rijeka, Croatia), which had been promised to Yugoslavia. The three other powers opposed Italy's acquisition, but Clemenceau and Lloyd George were more than willing to let Wilson be the messenger. Wilson consulted with his peace commissioners about the Fiume question, then issued a statement on April 23 that Italy could not have the Adriatic port. Overnight Wilson went from hero to pariah in Italy public opinion. The country went into an uproar, and Orlando walked out of the Peace Conference. It was down to the Council of Three.

Wilson's health suffered from the Peace Conference. His temper flared in unusual bouts of rage. His handwriting grew worse, and he became increasingly belligerent. He suffered severe headaches. He had aged noticeably, his hair turning white from the stress of the negotiations. His health problems may have affected his relations with House—and other members of the American Peace Commission. This could have been the coldness that Baker observed. In fact, Wilson may have had several minor strokes at Paris, including one on April 28 during the Fiume crisis. [89]

Wilson also never addressed the question of the freedom of the seas with Great Britain, the very issue that had brought the United States into the war against Germany. The U.S. and Great Britain had difficulty reaching common ground on what the concept even meant. Edward House had earlier told the British that "we did not intend to have our commerce regulated by Great Britain whenever she was at war." During the World War, the U.S. had greatly enlarged its fleet, and England was worried that the U.S. Navy would reach parity with the Royal Navy. The two allies never resolved the freedom of the seas question at Paris, averting a lengthy fight, and instead agreed that they would work it out later, which in turn led to the Washington Naval Conference in 1921. [90]

As Italy walked out of the peace talks, the Japanese suddenly spoke up. Their representatives had remained virtually silent throughout the peace conference, but now they sensed it was their time to make demands. Japan had wanted a racial equality clause inserted in the treaty, in part because Japanese emigrants to the West Coast of the United States found racial discrimination, but the Europeans and Wilson rejected this. Wilson opposed the clause on the grounds that all nations would be considered equals at the League of Nations. The Japanese then argued for something more concrete: the Japanese wanted the German license to the Shantung Peninsula, which they had occupied during the war. The Chinese rightfully wanted it back. [91]

The Shandong Peninsula (at the time called Shantung) is just south of Beijing, a coastal region with the harbor city of Kiaochow. The Germans had opened coalmines and a railroad, a brewery, and built the port of Tsingtao and a brewery of the same name. The Japanese seized the German colony at the beginning of the war with little effort and demanded (and got) the Chinese government to reassign the German concession to them. Japan sought international recognition for this. It wanted its own version of the Monroe Doctrine for East Asia to keep out interlopers while it exploited China, Korea, and even Russia during its civil war.

The four other American peace commissioners presciently warned Wilson not to allow this land grab, as they wrote him: "If we support Japan's claim, we abandon the democracy of China to the domination of the Prussianized militarism of Japan. We shall be sowing dragons' teeth." Having lost Italy, and fearing that Japan would not join the League of Nations, Wilson caved and let the Japanese keep the Shandong Peninsula, though it was a clear violation of his Fourteen Points. China was betrayed. Some members of the American delegation resigned in protest, including William Bullitt, who would later provide damaging testimony about the peace treaty before Congress. [92]

Edward House and Edith Wilson had a falling-out at Paris when it was revealed that House was leaking information to the press through his son-in-law, Gordon Auchincloss. Edith had her last conversation with the man in Paris. She considered him persona non grata for the rest of her life. Wilson, however, retained House on the American Peace Commission, albeit with diminishing trust, and later sent him to London to hash out final details for the League of Nations. The league would be headquartered in Geneva, Switzerland, a neutral location where the Geneva Conventions were signed.

The Treaty Presentation

Having settled most of the major issues over the League of Nations, reparations, and territorial claims, the Paris Peace Conference was ready to present to the Germans the draft peace treaty—the Treaty of Versailles, it would be called, named after the place it was signed. On May 6, the Allies formally approved the treaty and invited the Germans to the formal presentation the following day, which was coincidentally the fourth anniversary of the sinking of the *Lusitania*. A delegation of 150 German officials arrived on May 7, led by Foreign Minister Ulrich von Brockdorff-Rantzau.

The peace treaty was presented in Versailles's Grand Trianon Palace. It was a highly staged event, designed to showcase France's pageantry while humbling the German delegation. The Allied delegates, including Clemenceau, Lloyd George, Orlando, and Wilson, were arranged on one side of the room, with the Germans on the other, surrounded by a great number of diplomats and observers. Clemenceau rose to deliver his sharp remarks. "It is neither the time nor the place for superfluous words," he declared. "The time has come when we must settle our accounts. You have asked for peace. We are ready to give you peace." It was clear that the Germans' role was to accept the peace, not negotiate for terms. [93]

A copy of the Treaty of Versailles was placed in Brockdorff-Rantzau's hands. It was the size of a book, with 214 pages. Ray Baker called it a "Dickens novel." [94] This was not the first time the Germans had seen the treaty: it had been leaked to the press days before. The French wanted to prevent any changes to the treaty, and believed that leaking it would seal the wording, rather than allow the Germans to ask for alterations. Thus when the Germans appeared in Versailles for the treaty presentation, they knew exactly the conditions they were being dictated. It was no secret.

Brockdorff-Rantzau then delivered a speech. He remained seated, preferring a message of passive defiance over active resistance. He began: "We are under no illusions as to the extent of our defeat and the degree of our want of power. We know that the power of the German arms is broken." He railed against the naval blockade that continued to starve the German people and pointed out that a Germany with a failing economy would be in no condition to pay reparations to the victors.

The foreign minister delivered a bitter denunciation of the war guilt clause. "It is demanded of us that we shall confess ourselves to be the only ones guilty of the war. Such a confession in my mouth will be a lie," he read from his prepared text. "We are far from declining any responsibility that this great war of the world has come to pass. But we deny that Germany and its people were alone guilty."[95] In other words, Germany accepted its responsibility in the war, but it objected to having to accept sole blame for a war that it did not start. This was a nuance lost on most peace delegates at Paris, one that would prove a prime point of contention in the German conscience after the war.[96]

Brockdorff-Rantzau concluded his speech. Clemenceau cut off any further debate. "Has anybody any more observations to offer? Does no one wish to speak?" he asked rhetorically. "If not, the meeting is closed."[97]

The Germans were given fifteen days to review the treaty and submit clarifying questions in writing. This was extended to nearly two months. They were not allowed oral arguments, only written objections and questions. The Allies would respond in writing. The delegation was summoned home to Berlin, and another sent in its place. What could the Germans do? It was either sign the hard peace, or begin the war again, and all sides knew the Germans were in no shape to recommence fighting. Germany was defeated, though not annihilated.

The Germans were shocked by the terms of the treaty. They had hoped that President Wilson would maintain his ideals and negotiate the peace treaty along the lines of the Fourteen Points. Some of the points were honored, but many were not, as Wilson allowed the Allies to inflict retributive conditions on Germany that did not foster peace.

The Germans felt betrayed by Wilson at Paris. Where was the just peace they had been promised? He had preached peace, but inflicted injustice. Germans came to see Wilson as a hypocrite. In his public speeches, he had clearly separated the military government from the German people; however, once the Kaiser and his government had fallen—as Wilson himself had demanded—Wilson allowed the Allies to punish the German people.[98] The president of the National Assembly denounced Wilson: "It is incomprehensible that a man who had promised the world a peace of justice, upon which a society of nations would be founded, has been able to assist in framing this project dictated by hate." Most of the hate in the treaty was Clemenceau's, but Wilson took much of the heat.[99]

Former German Ambassador Johann von Bernstorff laid the blame with his own people, who shunned Wilson's 1917 peace overture in favor of unrestricted submarine warfare. "The President's spiteful censure and treatment of us, both during the war and at Versailles, may be explained psychologically, by the fact that we rejected his efforts as a mediator, and declared the U-Boat war," he wrote in 1920.[100]

Protests broke out in Germany over the Diktat (the dictated peace). President Friedrich Ebert came under intense public pressure to denounce the Treaty of Versailles, but the military was in no condition to renew the war. Germany would have to accept the peace terms, dictated or not.

On May 29, the Germans published *Observations on the Conditions of Peace*, a point-by-point critique of the peace treaty. This had an impact on public opinion, especially with English liberals like David Lloyd George, who now began denouncing the treaty as unfair. This was the same man who had campaigned six months earlier on making Germany pay for the entire war.[101] Despite the public's newfound sympathy for Germany, Clemenceau would not yield when it came to the question of France's security. "The Treaty is not a good one, it is too severe," Edward House concluded in his diary, but did not think it feasible to rewrite it.[102]

General Douglas MacArthur, who had returned to the states in April with his Rainbow Division, noted how unfair the peace terms seemed from the vantage point of a soldier. "They look drastic and seem to me more like a treaty of perpetual war than of perpetual peace," he wrote a friend.[103] The 214-page peace treaty was so long that comedian Will Rogers joked, "I thought the Armistice terms read like a second mortgage, but this reads like a foreclosure."[104] This witticism was probably truer than he knew: Germany would be unable to pay the debts that the treaty demanded. Its economy was wrecked.

The Germans were not alone in believing the peace treaty was unfair: about a dozen members of the American delegation resigned in protest after the treaty was published. They knew this was a bad treaty. On June 3, Wilson met with the American Peace Commission. They all agreed the treaty was too harsh, and that it required too much of

Germany. But the president also understood the need for Allied unity, and so pushed on with the treaty as it was written, knowing Clemenceau would not budge. The Treaty of Versailles was left intact. The Germans would have to swallow it or resume the war.

While the Germans withdrew to discuss the peace treaty, other diplomatic initiatives were underway. Edward House was dealing with the Italian-Yugoslav question over who would control Fiume. "I saw the President in the afternoon and told him what I was doing in the matter of the Adriatic settlement," House wrote in his diary. "He thanked me, but showed no inclination to be conciliatory to the Italians."[105]

While the Allies awaited the German response, President Wilson delivered one of the finest speeches of his career on Memorial Day, May 30, 1919, at the American military cemetery at Suresnes. He spoke to a large group of American soldiers in uniform: "But it would be no profit for us to eulogize these illustrious dead if we did not take to heart the lessons which they have taught us. They are dead; they have done their utmost to show their devotion to a great cause; and they have left us to see to it that that cause shall not betrayed, whether in war or in peace. It is our privilege and our high duty to consecrate ourselves afresh on a day like this to the objects for which they fought."

The American soldiers fought to defeat the Central Powers and everything they stood for: "the sort of power they meant to assert in the world, the arrogant, selfish dominance which they meant to establish; and they came, moreover, to see to it that there should never be a war like this again." In order to prevent a catastrophe like the Great War from destroying another generation, Wilson had worked with the other statesmen to create the League of Nations, which he called "the covenant of governments that these men shall not have died in vain."

Wilson drew a parallel to the many who died during the Civil War. "These men have given theirs in order to secure the freedom of mankind; and I look forward to an age when it will be just as impossible to regret the result of the labor of those who fought for the union of the states. I look for a time when every man who now puts his counsel against the united service of mankind under the League of Nations will be just as ashamed of it as if he now regretted the union of the states."

Recalling the dead, whose spirit still resided in this place, Wilson noted that they would command, "Be ashamed of the jealousies that divide you." America was born "to show mankind the way to liberty. She was born to make this great gift a common gift."

In concluding his remarks, Wilson stated, "There is something better, if possible, that a man can give than his life, and that is his living spirit to a service that is not easy, to resist counsels that are hard to resist, to stand against purposes that are difficult to stand against, and to say, 'Here stand I, consecrated in spirit to the men who were once my comrades and who are now gone, and who have left me under eternal bonds of fidelity.'" Many in the audience were in tears. The Suresnes Memorial Day speech was Wilson's Gettysburg Address.[106] One witness to the ceremony was William Monroe Trotter, an African-American civil rights activist who had trailed Wilson to Europe. He hoped to meet with the president to encourage him to support racial equality in the peace treaty. Wilson refused to meet with him.[107]

Wilson visited many military hospitals, which proved a challenge for him to maintain his composure. Dr. Grayson witnessed him many times in tears at seeing the wounded men. He shook the hand of a blinded man but was so overcome that he could not speak. He responded similarly when he asked a one-legged soldier why there were so many amputees in the ward. "Those who were shot higher up are not here, sir," the soldier responded. The president continued down the line in silence, his lip quivering.[108]

The Wilsons visited Belgium in early June as they waited for the German response, a two-day trip led by King Albert and Queen Elisabeth. The Germans had stripped Belgium of its factories, and the small country emerged from the war with no tangible industry. The Germans had largely marched across the country; only the southwestern corner showed heavy scars of war. Northern France was far more physically damaged than Belgium.

The Allies grew impatient with the Germans and demanded a response. Would they accept the peace treaty or not? Finally, on June 20, the Supreme Council authorized Foch to cross the Rhine

River in force if the Germans did not sign. This would renew the war. The German cabinet deadlocked and resigned that same day. Germany was in no position to fight: it had disbanded its army and its economy was in shambles. A new government formed the next day and begrudgingly accepted the peace treaty. That day, the German navy scuttled the High Seas Fleet in Scapa Flow. This ended the Allied debate over how to divide the ships among them.

The Treaty of Versailles destabilized the German government, and it would undermine the newborn Weimar Republic so that liberal democracy never had much chance of success in postwar Germany. Right-wing nationalists blamed the democratic socialists, who were the governing power, for signing the wicked peace treaty. Their long-standing protest undermined faith in the young democracy. The Weimar Republic would end in 1933 with Hitler's accession to power—one that he conducted legally by stoking Germany's anger during the Great Depression.

The Treaty of Versailles

Germany signed the hard peace on June 28 in the Hall of Mirrors at Versailles. The date was exactly five years after Archduke Franz Ferdinand's assassination, the event that had triggered the war. And the treaty was a revenge play for France: Germany had proclaimed the German Empire in the same room in 1871 after defeating France in the Franco-Prussian War. It was a fitting location—and deliberately designed to humiliate the Germans.

A great crowd lined the roadway between Paris and Versailles, cheering as the motorcades drove past on their way to the signing cer-emony. At the Palace of Versailles, the delegates were dressed in their finest formal wear while the French cavalry paraded on the grounds. Inside the palace, chasseurs dressed from Napoleonic times lined the passageway to the Hall of Mirrors. The formal signing ceremony lasted about an hour. Among the pageantry the German delegates were brought in. "I had a feeling of sympathy for the Germans who sat there quite stoically," Edward House penned in his diary that day. "The affair was elaborately staged and made as humiliating to the enemy as it well could be."[109]

Four treaties were signed that day: the Peace Treaty, a document certifying the return of Alsace-Lorraine to France, an agreement for a phased withdrawal of the Rhineland as Germany paid its reparations, and recognition of an independent Poland. As soon as the treaties were signed, cannons boomed to signal the end of the Great War. The fountains at Versailles were turned on while airplanes passed in formation overhead. The great crowd cheered mightily.

Wilson had successfully included the League of Nations in the peace treaty, but given that there were three other treaties, could the League covenant not have been a standalone treaty? This may have brought peace to the continent sooner and paved over the ratification difficulties that Wilson faced in the senate.

Four empires—Germany, Austria-Hungary, Ottoman, and Russia—had fallen in the Great War, their royal houses scattered to the winds and their territories parceled out. New European countries emerged based on ethnic identity. The old monarchies were overthrown in the defeated countries. Germany surrendered Alsace-Lorraine, which it had annexed in 1871 after defeating France in the Franco-Prussian War, the war that had unified Germany into a country. It handed over territory surrounding East Prussia to the newly reformed country of Poland, including Danzig (Gdansk) to give Poland a harbor. Prussia was left as a separate, isolated pocket on the Baltic. The geographic separation of Prussia from Germany gave Adolf Hitler the excuse he needed to declare war on Poland on September 1, 1939.

The Austro-Hungarian Empire was dismantled entirely. Austria and Hungary each became separate, small, landlocked countries, as was the new Czechoslovakia. The country of Yugoslavia was created in the Balkans, jumbled together from pieces of the Austrian and Ottoman Empires and Serbia. The former Austro-Hungarian Empire yielded territory for the restored Poland, as did Germany. Romania acquired Transylvania, a region largely populated by ethnic Hungarians.

Self-determination only applied to Europe, and even there imperfectly. Millions of Germans were left out of Germany when the borders of Poland and Czechoslovakia were defined. The new German constitution affirmed the right to unite with the newly-established Austria, as the two countries shared a common culture and language, but the Allies nixed this: they were trying to weaken Germany, not strengthen it. The German-speaking Austrians of South Tyrol became Italians when their region was handed over. Self-determination did not apply to ethnic Germans.

The League of Nations assumed authority over former German colonies and much of the Ottoman Empire. It then delegated the power to administer the colonies through mandates, which were intended to prepare the colonies for independence and self-governance. France and Great Britain salivated at the prospect of breaking up the Ottoman Empire and expanding their dominions. In 1916, they signed the Sykes-Picot Agreement to divide the mostly Arabic territories, an agreement that remained secret until the Bolsheviks revealed it the following year. The French staked their claim over the northern region of what became Lebanon and Syria, while the British created Trans-Jordan, Iraq, and Kuwait from their sphere of influence. England was also interested in forming a Jewish state that would guard the flank of the Suez Canal, as well as protect the overland route to India. The route passed through Iraq, home to the strategic oil fields that England wanted from the war. In November 1917, England had published the Balfour Declaration, promising a future Jewish homeland in Palestine that would become the State of Israel in 1948.

The Middle East did not get self-determination; rather, Britain and France artificially drew its borders as these western powers expanded their empires. The western occupation of the Middle East built lasting resentment among Arabs. Arab nationalism had awoken in their rebellion against the Ottomans, and some called for a single Arab state. But the Great Powers had other ideas. Oil had been discovered in Mesopotamia, and the British wanted it. Western occupation led to decades of dictatorships, strong men, and resentment among Arabs for at least the next century. They resented the promises of freedom from

Ottoman rule that the West had made, only to occupy them as League of Nations mandates. Nor were large ethnic groups within these new territories, such as the Kurds, granted unified nationhood. The Kurds to this day are spread across four countries.

Although Wilson was anathema to the Germans, he became a hero to many ethnic groups that emerged from the Great War as independent countries, particularly in Europe. Czechoslovakia named the Prague train station after Wilson in 1919, then erected a statue of Wilson in front in 1928. The Nazis destroyed the statue in 1941; a new statue was cast in 2011. [110]

In Siberia, the so-called Czech Legion of 50,000 Czechoslovaks had seized the Pacific port of Vladivostok, the terminus of the Trans-Siberian Railway. These were men whom the Russians had captured during the war, but who agreed to fight against the Central Powers so they could help their homeland gain independence. When the Russian Revolution broke out, their goal was to return to Western Europe to fight the Germans, but to do so they first had to travel completely across Siberia to the Pacific, board ships, and sail to Europe. They did not make it in time. In fact, they got bogged down in Siberia for two years fighting the Bolsheviks. Wilson sent seven thousand troops to Vladivostok to support the Czechs, while the Japanese sent ten times that number. The president feared that if the Japanese ventured alone into Siberia, they would make territorial claims on Russia.

Wilson had done much to raise awareness of the Armenians' plight during the war because of the Turkish genocide. The Treaty of Sèvres, negotiated in 1920, partly broke up the Ottoman Empire and established Armenia as an independent country. In order to protect the new country from the marauding Soviet Union, Wilson proposed that the United States assume a mandate over Armenia. But this would be expensive and would require the U.S. to maintain a presence in a part of the world where the country had little interest. The U.S. Senate rejected the treaty. The Turks went to war against its Armenian population in late 1920, while the Soviet Union occupied the remaining part of Armenia.

One of the more interesting points of the peace treaty was the mention of champagne, the sparkling wine sipped by French monarchs.

The French insisted that only sparkling wine produced from the Champagne region could actually be called champagne and included a clause in the treaty to protect this exclusive name. Other countries had to come up with new names for their sparkling wine, such as prosecco and spumante in Italy, Sekt in Germany, and cava in Spain. The United States never ratified the Treaty of Versailles, although at the time Prohibition was certain to begin, so little thought was given to the champagne question. Only after Prohibition ended in 1933 did American winemakers begin to produce sparkling wine again, and some of them used the phrase "champagne" to describe their products. A commercial agreement between the European Union and the United States in 2005 ended this use, though it grandfathered several brands that had trademarks.[111]

The Treaty of Versailles was a miserable peace treaty. Edward House noted the day after the treaty was signed, "To those who are saying that the Treaty is bad and should never have been made and that it will involve Europe in infinite difficulties in its enforcement, I feel like admitting it."[112] He penned words in his diary that echoed Frank Cobb's sentiment, the *World* editor who had warned President Wilson against going to Paris. "It may be that Wilson might have had the power and influence if he had remained in Washington and kept clear of the Conference," he wrote. "When he stepped from his lofty pedestal and wrangled with representatives of other states upon equal terms, he became as common clay."[113] Noting the fallout from the peace treaty, House wrote Wilson at the end of July, "The world is in a belligerent mood, and the next ten years will be the most dangerous to its peace."[114]

Robert Lansing, in his 1921 book *The Peace Negotiations: A Personal Narrative*, listed how his views as secretary of state had diverged from President Wilson's. He believed that the president had made a number of mistakes at Paris, starting with going to Paris at all, rather than delegating the negotiations to a peace commission. Lansing believed that incorporating the League of Nations covenant into the peace treaty was an error, as was Wilson's language that ensured it would never get past the Senate. Lansing was offended by the power that the

"Great Powers" (the allies who had won the war) granted themselves, including placing themselves permanently on the league's executive committee. He condemned the backroom deals of "secret diplomacy" that had characterized the Big Four negotiations, rather than allowing an open forum. And Wilson made a tragic error in granting Japan the Shandong Peninsula, as it robbed one country of its own land and fueled another's territorial ambitions. Lansing largely kept quiet about his views until they spilled out before the Senate Foreign Relations Committee in September 1920. Wilson did not trust Lansing and ignored his counsel at Paris. Yet Lansing was correct in much of his assessment of Wilson's errors. [115]

Author Willa Cather wrote presciently in 1914: "I suppose they will patch up a temporary peace and then, in twenty-five years, beat it again with a new crop of men." Indeed, the Treaty of Versailles forged a temporary peace—but only for twenty years. And it did nothing to build trust between countries; Europe remained even more heavily armed after the war than before. At tremendous cost, the French constructed a defensive belt known as the Maginot Line against a future German resurgence. It was a waste of money: German tanks outflanked the line during the blitzkrieg of 1940. The French had prepared to fight the last war and were beaten within a matter of weeks. [116]

The Treaty of Versailles "left sore winners and unrepentant losers," wrote historian John Milton Cooper. [117] Versailles created enormous resentment among Germans and set the stage for Adolf Hitler's rise to power. The fledgling democratic Weimar Republic was hobbled from the beginning, as Germany suffered hard economic times and went through a series of prime ministers, lurching from crisis to crisis. Likewise, the Italians believed they were not given due credit for their part in the war, nor the territory it demanded from Yugoslavia. It seized the port of Fiume in 1924. In the next decade, the Japanese would make war against China and seize vast parts of its territory.

Margaret MacMillan's *Paris 1919*, the definitive history of the Paris Peace Conference, challenged the widely accepted consensus that the peace treaty and subsequent reparations caused the collapse of the German economy. "The picture of a Germany crushed by a vindictive peace cannot be sustained," she wrote. "The Treaty of Versailles is not to blame." She noted that Germany only paid a small fraction of what it was required to pay, and therefore the reparations could not have undermined its economy. She blamed Hitler's rise on the German perception of how they were treated at the peace table when they had been promised a just and fair peace.[118]

The Germans in 1919 believed that they would be treated fairly based on Wilson's Fourteen Points. The peace treaty clearly violated their expectations. Right-wing nationalists like Hitler were able to effectively harness this resentment. That the punitive conditions proved unworkable would not be known for years. But in 1919, all that Germans understood was that they were taking the blame for everything and were facing a massive, unfathomable, and undefined bill for the war. It was an enormous blow to their national pride. The Treaty of Versailles was the key reason why Germans would eventually follow Adolf Hitler.

Edward House and Woodrow Wilson saw each other for the last time in Paris on June 29, the day after the peace treaty signing. House and his wife Loulie were leaving for London to continue the work on the League of Nations. He knew probably better than Wilson that the president faced an uphill battle to convince the Senate to ratify the treaty, and so House suggested that Wilson compromise with Congress. Wilson answered, "House, I have found one can never get anything in this life that is worth while without fighting for it." Wilson would return home for the fight of his life.[119]

The Treaty Outcome

In 1920, George Creel—President Wilson's chief cheerleader and propagandist—published his assessment of the Treaty of Versailles. "Nothing is more certain than that the calm judgment of the future will bear witness to the amazing justice of the Peace Treaty," he claimed. The future quickly changed its mind. The peace treaty was anything but amazing.[120] Creel included a lengthy critique of John Maynard Keynes's book *The Economic Consequences of the Peace*. Creel turned out to be entirely wrong, and Keynes turned out to be not only right, but prophetic for the future of Europe: that the Treaty of Versailles ordained more war, and that the path for peace was European economic union.

Keynes was an insightful economist who was part of the British Treasury and an official representative at the Peace Conference. A brilliant, well-educated but sharply opinionated man, he was contemptuous of nearly everyone at Paris. Keynes resigned in June 1919 once he realized that the peace treaty was far too harsh toward Germany. Over the next six months he composed his thoughts, citing the vast economic data that the peace commissioners had gathered, and published a highly influential critique of the treaty in early 1920. Walter Lippmann published the book as three essays in the *New Republic*.

Keynes was critical of all of the politicians at the Peace Conference, but none more so than of Woodrow Wilson. He observed the president closely over the six months of treaty negotiations and recognized his weaknesses in the council room. "The President was not a hero or a prophet; he was not even a philosopher; but a generously intentioned man," Keynes surmised. Wilson was ideologically wed to the League of Nations, but he had little experience in personal negotiations, especially when pitted against the shrewd machinations of Clemenceau, Lloyd George, and Orlando, all of whom came from parliamentary systems. When it came to negotiations, Wilson was "slow and unadaptable." He was simply outmaneuvered on the question of reparations and war guilt. Clemenceau paid lip service to the League, while his real desire was to contain Germany.[121]

Keynes understood that Germany was the economic engine of Europe. Clemenceau desired to destroy that engine so that Germany could never be a threat again. He drove the harshest aspects of the peace treaty. He believed that as long as Germany remained strong, France would never be safe. "According to this vision of the future, European history is to be a perpetual prize-fight, of which France has won this round, but of which this round is certainly not the last," Keynes wrote. Because of Clemenceau's desire to ruin Germany economically, Keynes called the treaty a "Carthaginian Peace," a reference to how Rome destroyed Carthage at the end of the Third Punic War.[122]

France wanted to seize or put out of commission Germany's coalmines, steel mills, and railroads. Its army was reduced to a paltry 100,000 men, and its navy was shrunk to 15,000 sailors. Major territories were peeled off and given to other countries, including a third of its coal capacity. Germany lost all of its overseas colonies and received no compensation for private or public investment in them. Likewise, the Allies assumed the right to confiscate private German property within their domains. Germany ceded its public investment in infrastructure in Eastern European countries. It could even lose its investments in neutral countries that simply wished to nationalize German property. Despite Wilson's promise of self-determination for all peoples, Germany was expressly forbidden to unite with Austria, which was ethnically German. And most importantly, Germany had to accept responsibility for the war, and thus as the richest of the Central Powers had to take on all of the war's liabilities, including significant reparations. The Allies stuffed their reparations wish-list full of expenses, not just to damages to industry, land, and shipping, but to civilian damages like pension obligations.

The Allies seized Germany's extensive merchant marine as part of the reparations package, a step designed to cripple the country's international trade, one that would particularly advantage Great Britain. The League of Nations placed a mandate over the coal-rich Saar region and allowed France to administer it. The Silesian coalfields were likewise given to Poland, even though the populace was German. Germany also had to deliver coal to the Allies for ten years to make up for the destruction of coalmines in Belgium and France. Germany's major rivers and waterways were handed over to an international commission, meaning the country lost sovereignty even within its own borders.

Keynes took a pragmatic approach toward reparations, calculating actual physical damage and loss of ships at sea, and estimated that the Allies could reasonably charge the Germans about $5.8 billion (£2.120 billion). He believed that this sum should have been settled in advance and included in the treaty, rather than being an open-ended obligation that ultimately allowed the combatants to squeeze Germany for every penny. Some countries wanted Germany to pay for the entire cost of the war, a charge that Germany could never fulfill.[123] American comedian Will Rogers quipped, "Everybody at the table wants a second helping, and Germany the cook hasn't got enough to go around."[124]

The final reparations allocation for Germany was to give twenty-eight percent to England, fifty-two percent for France, and the remainder to countries like Belgium and Serbia. The reparations commission decided in 1921 that Germany's bill would be 132 billion gold marks ($34 billion). In fact, Germany would only pay around 22 billion gold marks ($4.5 billion) by 1932, a fraction of what it owed. Once Hitler came to power, the payments halted altogether.[125]

Keynes recognized that war debts were so high that no one could repay them. Some form of debt forgiveness would need to take place for Europe's economy to recover. He argued presciently for a free trade union that would bind Europe economically and thus help eliminate future wars. His economic ideas were not followed in 1919, but they proved highly influential in the aftermath of World War II, when debt forgiveness and the Marshall Plan were used to resuscitate Europe's economy, followed by the creation of the European Economic Community (the precursor to the European Union) in 1957.[126]

The Treaty of Versailles was not a treaty of reconciliation. It failed to build a framework for lasting peace, and instead drove a deep wedge between nations. World War II was likely inevitable, given Germany's harsh treatment and lasting resentment, but would the outcome have differed had the U.S. remained engaged in global politics? Or might Hitler's rise to power have been averted? Or if Wilson had been willing to strip the League covenant from the peace treaty in order to achieve a quicker peace to restore economic ties? Or if he had directed a shrewder negotiator to handle the peace talks? These are questions we can only ask, but not answer.

EIGHT

Carthaginian Peace

T he former German ocean liner *George Washington* docked in New York City on July 8, 1919, carrying President Wilson and his entourage home from the Paris Peace Conference. He paraded through the city in a victory lap, then took a train to Washington, where 100,000 cheering people met him at Union Station. He carried his copy of the Treaty of Versailles. Like Caesar returning to Rome, the Senate warily awaited Wilson's arrival. Two days later, he presented the sanctified peace treaty to the Senate with the expectation that they perform their duty and ratify it. The dramatic gesture and Wilson's high-toned speech were not well received. Democratic senators cheered, but they were in the minority now. The majority Republicans were respectful but silent.[1]

The president had aged visibly during the Paris negotiations, and his health had deteriorated. Dr. Grayson wanted Wilson to rest, recuperate, and resume regular exercise after the lengthy peace conference. "Give me time," Wilson responded. "We are running a race with Bolshevism and the world is on fire." He promised to return to recreation once the treaty had been ratified.[2]

Wilson had arrived in Paris as the savior of the world in December 1918; however, by the time of the peace treaty signing seven months later, his authority was significantly diminished and he was out of touch with how much the political balance had shifted in the U.S. Wilson had paid little attention to domestic developments, such as the postwar economy, the simmering race question, or how much the country simply wanted to move on after the war.

Once the Armistice went into effect, the excitement of the war quickly wore off, as did the near-sense of national unity that had existed since the war declaration in April 1917. Wartime bipartisanship had broken down. This was partly Wilson's fault: his call for a Democratic Congress near the end of the war was an overt partisan act, negating his promise to put an end to party politics. Additionally, there was much social unrest with the high cost of living, strikes for higher pay, and angry farmers who felt they deserved more money for their wheat. By July 1919, 1.7 million American doughboys had returned home from France. The rest would follow soon, and all would look for jobs.[3]

Censorship had officially ended, but there was still unofficial self-censorship. Journalists began to test the boundaries of the new normal. In 1919, the *New York World* published German General Ludendorff and Admiral Tirpitz's memoirs against much denunciation and protest. The liberal newspaper wanted to reassert press freedoms that had been muzzled. Editorial writer Frank Cobb essentially told the public to deal with it: "The war is over, and anybody who is now afraid of German propaganda is afraid of a ghost."[4]

President Wilson and his peace treaty had a difficult road ahead: the Constitution requires the Senate to ratify treaties by a two-thirds majority. The Republicans now had a slim two-vote majority, and Senate Foreign Relations Committee chair Henry Cabot Lodge was a partisan conservative and no friend to Wilson's liberal cause. There was no way the peace treaty could be ratified without Republican votes. An expert parliamentarian, Lodge had a wealth of senatorial tools at his disposal to delay or even strangle the treaty. Nattily dressed with a gray beard, Lodge was a slender patrician who looked the part of the Boston Brahmin that he was. H. L. Mencken called him "as cool as an undertaker at a hanging."[5]

The Senate Foreign Relations Committee soon held hearings on the treaty. Secretary of State Robert Lansing testified before the committee on August 6 and did the president few favors, as he was quietly against the League of Nations. He admitted that both he and General Tasker Bliss had dissented on the decision to give the Shandong Peninsula to Japan but believed that the treaty overall conformed with Wilson's Fourteen Points. To many of the committee's questions, he simply responded, "Ask the president."[6] When Senator Hiram Johnson of California asked, "You do not know whether there were any treaties made during the war or not?" Lansing responded, "No; because I never paid any attention to that." The secretary offered that the entire treaty was negotiated without secret agreements.[7] Lansing's testimony made it clear that the secretary of state had little hand in crafting the treaty. The peace treaty was Woodrow Wilson's child.

On August 19, President Wilson met with the Senate Foreign Relations Committee for three hours in the White House East Room to answer their questions about the peace treaty. He pointed out that he had addressed the Senate's objections at the March meeting during his brief visit home, incorporating their suggestions and addressing their objections, with the exception of one: Wilson did not split the peace treaty from the League of Nations, which was what Lodge wanted above all else. Although Wilson had committed to negotiating peace based on the Fourteen Points, the final treaty was messy and anything but principled. Wilson had yielded on many of the points, and there was little that would satisfy anyone. Yet Wilson had to sell the treaty to the Senate as if it were perfect. Senators had profound misgivings, and justifiably so.[8]

One of Wilson's Fourteen Points was "open covenants of peace, openly arrived at." Yet the negotiations at Paris had been conducted behind closed doors with little transparency, all designed to prevent press leaks. Some Senators concluded that Wilson's role violated his own principles; in effect, he had negotiated a "secret treaty," just as the

Allies had during the war promising territorial gains. Senator William Borah grilled Wilson on the question of when he learned about the Allies' wartime secret treaties.

Senator Borah: "When did the secret treaties between Great Britain, France, and the other nations of Europe with reference to certain adjustments in Europe first come to your knowledge? Was that after you reached Paris also?"

The President: "Yes, the whole series of understandings were disclosed to me for the first time then."

Senator Borah: "Then we had no knowledge of these secret treaties, so far as our Government was concerned, until you reached Paris?"

The President: "Not unless there was information in the State Department of which I knew nothing."[9] Ray Baker claimed the president knew little about the secret treaties as well—and only that Edward House knew the most. This was disingenuous: James Balfour had informed House and Wilson about the treaties in April 1917, and in any case the Bolsheviks had published them in November 1917 shortly after seizing power, so there was no excuse playing coy. Why did Wilson make this statement? Perhaps he was distancing himself from the treaties, which were made by the Allies, not by the U.S.[10]

Republican senators made it clear that they were uncomfortable with the Treaty of Versailles. The GOP did not want to give the president sole credit for ending the Great War. They wanted their say in the outcome, which they expressed through a number of amendments or "reservations." Wilson was not opposed to interpretive reservations, but to those that would open the treaty to renegotiation.[11]

The Senate divided along lines opposing or supporting the treaty. Nine senators declared themselves "mild reservationists" who would support the treaty if their concerns were addressed, while eight others were "irreconcilables" like William Borah who would attempt to amend the treaty so as to gut it. Wilson found all of the reservations intolerable and believed that the Senate must vote the treaty up or down, not amend it. He would not budge, a mistake as it turned out, as a willingness to compromise would have won over the mild reservationists and ensured treaty ratification.[12]

Senator Lodge's main sticking point was Article X of the League covenant, which he interpreted as requiring American intervention in global conflicts, even if the country had no interest. Wilson believed he had addressed this concern: the U.S. had a permanent seat on the Council, and all decisions made by the Council had to be made unanimously. Thus the U.S. held veto power over interventions. Another consistent Republican criticism of the League was that it undermined the Monroe Doctrine, a foundation of American foreign policy. In fact, Article XXI specifically provided a specific carve-out for the Monroe Doctrine, language that Wilson inserted using William Howard Taft's wording: "Nothing in this Covenant shall be deemed to affect the validity of international engagements such as treaties of arbitration or regional understandings, like the Monroe Doctrine, for securing the maintenance of peace." None of these arguments were convincing to the irreconcilables: their intention was to keep the nation from joining the League of Nations. Senator Lodge was not opposed to the league if he could include his reservations, but his main goal was to keep the divided Republican caucus together. Even League supporter Taft had come out in favor of reservations. [13]

Barnstorming for the League

By late August, Wilson realized that getting the Senate to ratify the Treaty of Versailles was futile. Senate irreconcilables were stonewalling by offering a slew of reservations. The president announced a nation-wide whistle-stop campaign on August 27 to take the message to the American people to pressure the Senate into ratifying the treaty. Senator Lodge was nonplussed: "The only people who have votes on the treaty are here in the Senate," he wrote a friend. [14] Wilson's tour was against Dr. Grayson's advice: the president was exhausted and was suffering from blinding headaches and diarrhea. "Yes, all that is true; but I feel it is my duty, and my own health is not to be considered when the future peace and security of the world are at stake," Edith Wilson recalled her husband saying. He concluded: "I must go." [15]

Sir William Wiseman dropped by the White House for lunch with Wilson before the president set out on his tour. In a 1928 letter, Wiseman recalled being stunned at the president's appearance. "He was obviously a sick man. His face was drawn and of a gray color, and frequently twitching in a pitiful effort to control nerves which had broken down under the burden of the world's distress." Wilson was working himself nearly to death. [16]

After he resigned from the Shipping Board, chairman Edward Hurley paid his respects to the president shortly before the whistle-stop tour began. Hurley noted how exhausted and worn the president appeared. "Hurley, I have just been talking to some more Senators about the Peace Treaty," he said, adding, "They are endeavoring to humiliate me." Hurley could tell the president was defensive about his life's work, which was on the brink of defeat. But knowing the state of Wilson's health, he urged the president not to make the barnstorming campaign. Wilson objected. "Hurley, I feel it is in my duty to explain my views and my position to the people, and I believe they will accept them," he argued. "If they do not, I shall have the satisfaction of knowing that I did the best I could do." [17]

A key figure was missing from the scene: Edward House was wrapping up his League of Nations work in London as Wilson prepared for his national tour, and thus Wilson lacked his chief political adviser. He cabled the president on August 26 that a rumor had emerged that their friendship was at an end. Wilson cabled back, "The best way to treat it is with silent contempt." House's influence and steady hand was sorely missed. [18]

On September 3, the Wilsons set out aboard a special train from Washington's Union Station for the long tour. Edith accompanied him, as did Joe Tumulty and Dr. Grayson, as well as about two dozen reporters who were covering the monthlong campaign. It was a trip that Edith would later call "one long nightmare." The president began the fight already exhausted and with none of his speeches written. [19]

Wilson's nationwide barnstorming tour took him on a giant loop around the country, starting at Columbus, Ohio, then continuing to Richmond, Indiana; St. Louis, Missouri; Bismarck, North Dakota;

and the Montana cities Billings and Helena. In Seattle the president reviewed the Pacific fleet, which fired twenty-one-gun salutes to the commander in chief. The train headed down the coast, stopping in Tacoma, Washington; Portland, Oregon; and California cities Oakland, Berkeley, Palo Alto, and San Francisco. Wilson journeyed down to San Diego, then traveled back north through Los Angeles to Sacramento. Altogether, the Wilsons spent six days in California. From there the whistle-stop tour headed east to Salt Lake City, Utah; Cheyenne, Wyoming; and Denver and Pueblo, Colorado. Huge crowds met the president at every stop, like a victory tour of the country.

Wilson spoke mostly without notes, other than a few documented quotes. Most of the speeches were extemporaneous, something which he excelled at. In his road trip, the president promised a world at peace—and that all parties were eager for it, though in fact most of the Allies were more interested in retribution and evening the score. He painted a picture of a love fest and global unity that did not in fact exist.

On September 19, Wilson addressed the largest crowd of the barnstorming campaign: 30,000 people in the San Diego Stadium. The outdoor venue included microphones and amplifiers—an early use of this technology. Wilson made it clear that there would be another major war in a generation—and the present children would have to fight it. "Because I know, if by chance, we should not win this great fight for the League of Nations, it would be their death warrant. They belong to the generation which would then have to fight the final war, and in that final war there would not be merely seven and a half million men slain. The very existence of civilization would be in balance." He was right on that account. The idea of sparing a future generation from a disastrous war was a theme that he expressed again and again in his campaign to ratify the treaty.[20]

The national tour set a grueling pace. Wilson gave as many as three speeches a day, sometimes from the back of his Pullman car, but other times in crowded, stuffy convention halls in an era before amplification, where he had to shout loudly and breathe the tobacco-infused air. In Salt Lake City, the president addressed thousands of people inside the Mormon Tabernacle. The building had little ventilation and it was incredibly hot, and the smell of so many sweating people was nearly unbearable. The Salt Lake speech was poorly delivered. The pace took its toll on the president. Edith noted that her husband began suffering from headaches from nearly the beginning of the tour. They steadily worsened into migraines, some of them blinding. When Edith counseled her husband to take a break, Wilson objected: "No, I have caught the imagination of the people. They are eager to hear what the League stands for; and I should fail in my duty if I disappointed them."[21]

On September 10, the Senate Foreign Relations Committee approved the peace treaty with Lodge's four reservations, sending the treaty to the Senate floor for debate. Lodge expected a vote in November.[22] He countered Wilson's barnstorming campaign by calling damaging witnesses who would undermine the president. On September 12, the committee heard testimony from William Bullitt, a former State Department official and member of the peace commission. Bullitt had resigned in May in protest of the peace treaty. In his testimony, he recalled a private conversation with Secretary of State Robert Lansing, who had expressed severe doubts about the treaty and the League of Nations. Bullitt reported that Lansing had said, "I consider that the League of Nations at present is entirely useless. The Great Powers have simply gone ahead and arranged the world to suit themselves." He then added damningly about the treaty's ratification prospects: "I believe that if the Senate could only understand what this Treaty means, and if the American people could really understand, it would unquestionably be defeated, but I wonder if they will ever understand what it lets them in for."[23]

Lansing did not deny what Bullitt had said. He wired Wilson, explaining that he had indeed said this, but it had been taken out of context. The president felt betrayed. "Were I in Washington I would at once demand his resignation!" Wilson said. "That kind of disloyalty must not be permitted to go unchallenged for a single minute." Tumulty felt certain that Wilson would soon demand Lansing's resignation for undermining the president, but the break would not come for another six months.[24]

The Pueblo, Colorado speech on September 25 was one of the finest of Wilson's career. It was his thirty-ninth speech of the campaign. Historian John Milton Cooper called it "a final burst of eloquence from a dying star."[25] Wilson admitted that he, as president and commander in chief, bore a heavy responsibility for going to war, no less to future generations of children as to the parents who lost their sons in the war. "I advised the Congress of the United States to create the situation that led to the death of their sons. I ordered their sons overseas. I consented to their sons being put in the most difficult parts of the battle line, where death was certain, as in the impenetrable difficulties of the forest of Argonne." He continued with both eloquence and emotion:

> Why should they weep upon my hand and call down the blessings of God upon me? Because they believe that their boys died for something that vastly transcends any of the immediate and palpable objects of the war. They believe, and they rightly believe, that their sons saved the liberty of the world. They believe that, wrapped up with the liberty of the world, is the continuous protection of that liberty by the concerted powers of all civilized people. They believe that this sacrifice was made in order that other sons should not be called upon for a similar gift—the gift of life, the gift of all that died.

Wilson offered a vigorous defense of the League of Nations. He called Article X "the heart of the whole matter." The same article that Senator Lodge objected to "provides that every member of the League covenants to respect and preserve the territorial integrity and existing political independence of every other member of the League as against external aggression." It was never intended to address internal dissent, not give the League a veto over a nation's sovereignty. Nations could still go to war, but they would submit their dispute for adjudication first. The Monroe Doctrine was still the bedrock of American foreign policy, and Wilson had specifically negotiated with the other powers to ensure that it remained legal and recognized.

Wilson struck a blow against hyphenates. "And I want to say—I cannot say it too often—any man who carries a hyphen about with him carries a dagger that he is ready to plunge into the vitals of this republic whenever he gets the chance," he said to applause. "If I can catch any man with a hyphen in this great contest, I will know that I have caught an enemy of the republic." This was almost a year after the war had ended, and the president was still criticizing German-Americans. He had seemingly taken on Theodore Roosevelt's role. [26]

Back at the train, Wilson's splitting headache returned. About twenty miles outside of Pueblo, Dr. Grayson ordered the train stopped. Accompanied by Edith and the physician, Wilson stepped out for an hour-long walk. They ran into an elderly farmer, who shook the president's hand and gave him apples and a head of cabbage. On the way back to the train, they stopped at a house where an ailing soldier was sitting on the porch, and the president expressed his sympathy to the young man and to his family. [27]

The fresh air and the walk seemed to improve Wilson's condition and he ate dinner. The train continued its journey toward Wichita, Kansas. There were just five speeches left in the whistle-stop campaign. Later that night, however, the unbearable migraine redoubled. The president was up all night, unable to sleep, until he finally dozed off at 5:00 A.M. He slept for only two hours while the train rolled into Wichita.

Wilson was in no condition to give a public address, though he insisted that he could. It took Edith, Dr. Grayson, and Joe Tumulty considerable effort to convince him to cancel the speech. "Don't you see that if you cancel this trip, Senator Lodge and his friends will say I am a quitter and that the Western trip was a failure, and the Treaty will be lost," Tumulty recalled him saying. They reminded him that his very life was at stake and that the trip needed to end. Wilson grudgingly agreed. [28] "This is the greatest disappointment of my life," he said as tears streamed down his face. [29] The train now made a beeline for the nation's capital. It arrived two days later, the nation anxiously wondering what had happened to its leader. Rather than take the president to a hospital, he was driven back to the White House, where he could rest in his own bed.

The Stroke

Woodrow Wilson was diagnosed with hypertension in the 1890s, a situation compounded by stress and his sedentary lifestyle. The symptoms of a stroke were building for weeks after his return from Paris—in fact, he may have even experienced small strokes while at the Peace Conference. Stress from the treaty whistle-stop tour had compromised his health until he finally suffered a stroke at the White House on October 2. He woke to realize that he had no feeling in his left arm. Edith helped him to the bathroom, then called Dr. Grayson. When she returned, she found her husband passed out on the floor.[30]

Philadelphia neurologist Francis Dercum was summoned to Washington to examine the president. He diagnosed what we call today an ischemic stroke: a blood clot in the brain leads to gradual onset of symptoms, and finally a full arterial blockage and sudden stroke. The common wisdom among medical professionals at the time was to isolate stroke victims. The doctors advised Edith to keep any kind of stressful information from the president, as it might exacerbate his condition. Edith and Dr. Grayson did exactly that, even as they misled the public about the president's condition. He was to rest in isolation, taking few visitors, such as the King Albert and Queen Elisabeth of Belgium, who presented eighteen hand-painted plates of historic Belgian sites. Another later visitor was the Prince of Wales. A bladder infection compounded Wilson's recovery.[31]

"So began my stewardship," Edith wrote in her autobiography. She lacked political instincts, and all she knew was to protect her husband. Even the vice president and the cabinet were left in the dark for crucial days. The White House simply fell silent. Edith became the president's gatekeeper. The chief of military intelligence at the British Embassy, Sir William Wiseman, sought an audience with Wilson, but Edith did not like the man, and the president declined to see him. It was an unusual rejection: both House and Wilson considered Wiseman a friend and opened their doors to him at all hours. "This was the only instance that I recall having acted as an intermediary between my husband and another on an official matter," Edith wrote, adding an important caveat, "except when so directed by a physician."[32]

In the years since Wilson's stroke, historians have wrestled with the question of whether Edith served as the nation's de facto first female president. Edith called the lengthy period her "stewardship" and denied that she was acting president. However, she controlled and limited access to her husband, and in that she certainly exercised some executive powers. Few people got to see the president during the first month, and even loyal Joe Tumulty was refused admission until mid-November. Edith and Grayson isolated the president from human contact and refused to publicly acknowledge what had happened. Instead, they lied. They did this to protect Wilson, but ultimately it did nothing to help his presidency. It was certainly bad for the country.

When a visiting delegation demanded time with the ailing president, Edith remarked, "I am not thinking of the country now, I am thinking of my husband." And that was exactly the problem.[33] Edith was doing her best, but her behavior was shortsighted. Her actions helped undermine the president's authority and inadvertently ensured that the Treaty of Versailles would fail its Senate vote. Edith's biographer, Kristie Miller, called her decisions in the wake of Wilson's stroke "disastrous."[34]

Against the backdrop of Wilson's stroke was the 1919 World Series—the famous baseball championship that was "fixed." The Chicago White Sox squared off against the Cincinnati Reds. Gambler and racketeer Arnold Rothstein had paid White Sox players to intentionally lose the World Series in what became known as the Black Sox Scandal. Baseball Commissioner Kenesaw Mountain Landis, who had overseen the trial of Big Bill Haywood and the Wobblies, expelled eight members of the White Sox for their role. The second game of the World Series was played on October 2, the day of Wilson's stroke. The Reds won the game that day by a score of 4 to 2.[35]

A few days after Wilson' stroke, Secretary of State Robert Lansing visited the White House to speak with the president's secretary, Joe Tumulty. He reminded Tumulty that the Constitution required the vice president to assume the powers of the presidency if the president dies or proves unable to perform the office. He suggested that either Dr. Grayson or Tumulty certify that Wilson was incapacitated. Tumulty erupted at the suggestion. "You may rest assured that while Woodrow Wilson is lying in the White House on the broad of his back I will not be a party to ousting him." Grayson likewise refused. Lansing was correct to raise the issue—the president was indeed unable to perform the office—but his loyal followers would not countenance action against him. Lansing was always an outsider to Wilson's closest associates. Tumulty later told the president about the exchange, which no doubt vexed Wilson.[36]

On October 6, the cabinet met at Lansing's prompting and without the president. They discussed what they should do. Lansing was in favor of calling upon Vice President Marshall to assume the presidency, even temporarily. Others like Josephus Daniels were reluctant to take this step. Dr. Grayson paid a visit to the cabinet meeting, informing them that Wilson was on the mend but could not take any visitors. He pointedly mentioned that the president was not happy that the cabinet was meeting without him—and wanted to know who authorized them to meet. In hindsight it was a ludicrous question: the president was seriously incapacitated. Was the government simply to stop functioning because the president could not make it to his own cabinet meeting? Lansing had called the meeting, and his days in office were now numbered (he would in fact stay on until the following February, as the president was in no condition to vet new cabinet secretaries).[37]

Dr. Grayson was deliberately vague, even misleading, about the president's health, only saying that the president suffered from "nervous exhaustion" and needed rest. He did his best to deflect the public and inquiring reporters. When Senator George Moses of New Hampshire, an irreconcilable to the peace treaty, speculated about the health of the president, Grayson asked whether the senator was a physician, adding pointedly, "Senator Moses must have information that I do not possess." At an October 12 press conference, Grayson refused to comment on whether the president had suffered a stroke. "In the absence of any official statement of a definite character regarding the President's illness, rumor and gossip have run wild in Washington and all sorts of stories have been current for more than a week," the *New York Times* reported. It was not like the public had no clue that something was medically wrong with the president. Most of Congress knew, as did the press corps. The strongest rumor was that the president had had a stroke, a rumor that turned out to be on point.[38]

Two months passed without anyone seeing President Wilson in public. Finally, two senators, Albert Fall and Gilbert Hitchcock, visited the White House to check on the president's condition, what Wilson called a "smelling committee."[39] The Republican Fall was a noisy critic of the president. He told Wilson, "Mr. President, I want you to know that I am praying for you."

According to Edith, Wilson remarked, "Which way, senator?" and the meeting concluded on a humorous note.[40] However, the president was offended at Fall's line of questioning. "If I could have got out of bed, I would have hit the man," he told David Houston, an unusual statement if true, showing how much the stroke had changed Wilson's personality. "Why did he want to put me in bad with the Almighty? He must have known that God would take the opposite view from him on any subject."[41]

Wilson's stroke did not affect his speech, nor did he have much facial drooping, but walking was now nearly impossible for him. He lost the use of his left arm and left leg. He was blind in his left eye, and his mind was prone to wander. The great voice that had once filled stadiums and halls was now weak. After his stroke, Wilson did not shave for six weeks, and his beard grew long and shaggy.

The stroke effectively ended Wilson's presidency seventeen months early, even though he remained in the White House until his successor was sworn in. Wilson should have stepped aside, at least temporarily, once it became clear that he could no longer serve. It was obvious by November—a month after his stroke—that he was incapable of the rigorous workload that every president faces. Historian John Milton Cooper called Wilson's stroke "the worst crisis of presidential disability in American history." He concluded, "Out of a dynamic, resourceful leader emerged an emotionally unstable, delusional creature." He became obstructive and self-destructive, even against his own interests.

He was unwilling to compromise on the peace treaty, though compromise might have saved it. [42]

Wilson and his vice president, Thomas Marshall, were never particularly close. Marshall was not prepared to assume the president's duties, nor was he personally inclined to do so. The Constitution was not clear about what to do in the event of presidential disability. Had Marshall stepped into the power vacuum, would it have made a difference? Could he have pushed the Treaty of Versailles through the Senate? Marshall knew the senators quite well, as he spent much of his official time there, and he believed that the lines were fairly fixed about the treaty, and that neither side was likely to change their mind. "It was pride of opinion, as I saw it," he recalled. [43]

The fall of 1919 was a crucial moment in American history. Not only was Wilson fighting for his life while clinging to the Treaty of Versailles, the country had experienced violent race riots, persistent strikes, and anarchist explosions. Edith probably convinced her husband not to step aside, though it would have been the right thing to do. [44] Had Wilson resigned, he might have taken the nobler course that would have ensured ratification for his peace treaty. He would then be a martyr for peace, one who gave his health and perhaps even his life for humanity. But Wilson stubbornly clung to the office, believing that only he could see the treaty through. This truly was delusional.

At the time of Wilson's health crisis, Edward House was sailing home to the United States. He too took ill with a recurring kidney ailment and was bedridden for several weeks. Despite his major role at the Paris Peace Conference, he never got to testify before the Senate Foreign Relations Committee in favor of the peace treaty, nor did Wilson summon him to the White House to meet at his sickbed (and certainly Edith was not going to ask House to come). However, House did write Wilson on November 24, offering advice through the treaty mess. Wilson should call up his ally, Senate minority leader Gilbert Hitchcock, and "advise him to ask the Democratic Senators to vote for the Treaty with such reservations as the majority may formulate, and let the matter then rest with the other signatories of the Treaty." In other words, compromise. House realized it was more important to get the treaty ratified, period, than to let it fail altogether, which seemed Wilson's path. "To the ordinary man, the distance between the Treaty and the reservations is slight." He wrote Wilson again three days later. The president never wrote back. [45]

Even the president's wife Edith counseled him to accept the Senate's reservations. He responded, "Little girl, don't you desert me; that I cannot stand. Can't you see that I have no moral right to accept any change in a paper I have signed without giving to every other signatory, even the Germans, the right to do the same thing?" [46] Nor would Wilson entertain stepping down. The League of Nations was the culmination of his life's work.

The Treaty of Versailles in the Senate

To some credit, Senate Majority Leader Henry Cabot Lodge did not try to kill the Treaty of Versailles outright, which he might have readily done. He understood that there was strong public support for the treaty. Instead he weakened it politically through reservations while casting doubt by questioning if the treaty obligated the U.S. to intervene in foreign affairs. He called the League of Nations covenant a "deformed experiment" on the Senate floor to a cheering audience. [47]

As the fall progressed, Lodge expanded his initial four reservations to fourteen. President Wilson contacted Senator Hitchcock. "I trust that all true friends of the treaty will refuse to support the Lodge resolution," he wrote (or more likely dictated to Joe Tumulty), and with Lodge's reservations voted down, he hoped they would then vote for the treaty. Wilson, deluded, uncompromising, and still in his sickbed, would have none of Lodge's reservations. There was no ground for compromise. [48]

On November 19—the last day of the special Congressional session—the Senate debated the peace treaty for twelve hours, then finally voted. It first voted on the treaty with Lodge's reservations attached: 39 for (largely Republicans) and 55 against (mostly Democrats and irreconcilables), followed by a vote on the treaty without reservations. This latter vote was 38 for and 55 against. No vote came close to reaching the two-thirds majority needed to ratify the Treaty of Versailles. The vote fell on predicable partisan lines. With that, Congress adjourned. Josephus Daniels noted in his diary that day, "Senate defeated the treaty. Lodge has one passion—hatred of Wilson."[49]

A month after the vote, Joe Tumulty privately consulted with navy secretary Josephus Daniels. Tumulty was despondent over the treaty's defeat and the president's health. "If he had [died] when he brought the treaty home it would have let him loom larger in history," Daniels recorded the secretary saying. He could not bring himself to write the word "died," and instead left the space blank. But Daniels probably shared the same sentiment: had the president died, he would have been a martyr for the cause of peace, rather than an invalid.[50]

Unable to lobby or speak for his interests after the stroke, Wilson's political power and influence evaporated. His principles demanded that he not yield, and this ultimately sank him. "Woodrow is now almost forgotten," H. L. Mencken crowed in January 1920. "His collapse has been stupendous."[51] Wilson considered resigning when it became clear that his health would not recover. It might have given the Treaty of Versailles a fairer chance of passage if he stepped out of the way and allowed the vice president to handle it. Dr. Grayson advised Wilson to resign, but Edith objected to the idea. She believed in part that Wilson needed to see through the League of Nations. Her husband remained in office for another painful and largely useless year.[52] The country did not have an immediate answer to the question of presidential incapacitation; however, the Twenty-fifth Amendment was finally ratified in 1967 to address the question.

Wilson did not want his cabinet meeting without his being present. However, the cabinet had much business to conduct in the wake of the war. It met frequently and informally at least twenty times during Wilson's incapacitation, according to Josephus Daniels's diaries. The president got wind of these meetings and sent a strongly worded note to Robert Lansing on February 9, 1920, telling him that the cabinet was not to meet unless the president authorized it. He accused the secretary of state of disloyalty. Lansing resigned four days later. He had overstepped the line in organizing the cabinet meetings, but he had also done his part keeping the government functioning while the president recovered. The cabinet continued to quietly meet, often by alleged accident and always far from the White House.[53]

Lansing's sensational resignation backfired against Wilson. Though the stated offense was unauthorized cabinet meetings, the true offense was that Lansing had long undermined Wilson's peace efforts. The public soon learned the truth of Wilson's incapacity and of his increasingly erratic behavior. He began to be blamed for the impasse over the peace treaty, not the Republicans.[54]

But the fight for the peace treaty was not over. The treaty failure did not sit well with public opinion. During the winter of 1920, a bipartisan working committee, including senators Hitchcock and Lodge, took up the Treaty of Versailles with the understanding that Lodge's reservations would remain attached to it. President Wilson had a second opportunity to secure its ratification if he was willing to compromise. Senate Democrats negotiated one hundred sixty reservations down to fourteen. By March 1920, it became obvious that the only way the treaty could pass was with the reservations. Had Wilson compromised earlier with the Republican reconcilables, he may have softened these. Now it was too late.

On February 28, Josephus Daniels spoke with Joe Tumulty. Tumulty believed that it would be better to accept Lodge's reservations and keep the treaty alive rather than to throw the entire peace away—advice that many had given Wilson, including Edward House and Edith Wilson. His argument failed to win over the president. Wilson was unwilling to yield.[55]

The president attempted to head off Lodge's reservations with an open letter to Senator Gilbert Hitchcock on March 8. His health had improved enough that he drafted it himself. The correspondence was Wilson's last word on the treaty and the League of Nations, and with it he dug the treaty's grave. He adamantly defended the treaty as not violating American sovereignty. He denounced the reservations that would, as he saw it, gut the treaty. "I have been struck by the fact that practically every so-called reservation was in effect a rather sweeping nullification of the terms of the treaty itself," he wrote. "I hear of reservationists and mild reservationists, but I cannot understand the difference between a nullifier and a mild nullifier." With that, Wilson burned his last bridge. The letter severed any chance of compromise, as it vaulted any senator who might have voted for compromise right into Senator Lodge's camp.[56]

The Senate voted again on the Treaty of Versailles on March 19. Even most Democrats voted for the treaty with Lodge's reservations. The vote was 49 in favor, and 35 against, seven votes short of the two thirds necessary for ratification. The peace treaty was now officially dead in Congress. The United States would never join the League of Nations. In fact, the U.S. remained technically at war with Germany, which Congress attempted to address by declaring that the war was over without a peace treaty. Wilson promptly vetoed the bill on May 27.

Nowhere was there the spirit of compromise. Lodge held to his reservations, which Wilson refused to accept. The fault lay squarely with these two men, yet more so with Wilson, who needed to recognize that the peace treaty could not be ratified without Republican support. Wilson's peace plan failed. His inability to compromise cost him dearly. The world moved on, and the League of Nations was established, but it was notably weaker without the United States. Wilson's propagandist George Creel wrote in 1920: "Wherever one looks, democracy is hemmed in on one side by Trade Imperialism and on the other by Bolshevism. And America, the nation that called the democratic aspiration into life and passion, refuses aid and stands aloof! Must another world war be fought to drive home the fact that humanity's one hope is in an international concert?"[57]

Herbert Hoover, his wife Lou and son Allan sailed home from Europe in September 1919, just as Wilson's peace treaty barnstorming campaign was underway. They returned to their cottage at Stanford University, where they hoped to relax after the busy war years. It was not to be. Hoover found himself bombarded by media requests and speeches. His sojourn in California was short, and he was soon swept back to the East Coast. The Hoovers would not reside in California again until after leaving the White House in 1933.

Hoover supported the League of Nations despite the obvious flaws in the peace treaty but hoped that the league would be able to address the treaty's injustice. He believed that Wilson should have ultimately accepted the reservations: once the U.S. entered the league, conditions could be renegotiated. Hoover described the ultimate outcome from the peace treaty: England, France, and Italy would now dominate Europe. "Their domination was better than German domination; but it was 'balance of power,' not 'collective security.'"[58]

Noting the failure of the peace treaty, Will Rogers asked, "I wonder if we quit fighting too quick and dident sign peace quick enough." In other words, what if the country had continued fighting until Germany was so defeated that it surrendered unconditionally and the Allies made quick work of the peace talks, rather than the messy negotiations that led to partisan discord? The partisan split was likely inevitable, given Wilson's insistence on including the League of Nations within the peace treaty framework. Wilson's failure to compromise destroyed his dream of a world at peace.[59]

NINE

Unintended Consequences

Like the Greek fable of Pandora's box, the Great War unleashed a stream of unexpected and unintended consequences, not all of them good. Race riots broke out in the summer of 1919, a hot season called the Red Summer, an angry response from the white community that believed blacks were attempting to rise to equality. This was soon followed by the country's first brush with communism, known as the Red Scare. The Progressive Era was rapidly coming to a close, but not before progressives won two final victories, both outcomes from the war. Women won the right to vote thanks to their contribution to the war effort, while the temperance movement enacted national Prohibition. Both of these victories required Constitutional amendments; they went into effect in 1920. All of these consequences left a legacy through the 20th century.

A forgotten and disturbing part of American history were the race riots that shook the country in the summer of 1919. This was a direct outcome from the war—and the unsettled question of race relations.

African-Americans had proudly fought for their country and were demanding ever-greater protections and equality in an era marked by Jim Crow laws. Whites were resentful at black demands and lashed out with violence.

Tens of thousands of African-Americans had enlisted in the military and fought in France to make the world safe for democracy. But would their own democratic country be safe for them? Activist W.E.B. Du Bois witnessed the soldiers returning home to confront segregation. He wrote in his magazine, *The Crisis*, in May 1919: "Make way for Democracy! We saved it in France, and by the Great Jehovah, we will save it in the United States of America, or know the reason why." [1]

Race riots broke out in twenty-five cities around the United States in the summer of 1919, and in almost every circumstance it was whites who initiated the violence. The riots were especially concentrated in the South, though the worst violence occurred in Chicago. It was James Weldon Johnson of the National Alliance for the Advancement of Colored People (NAACP), who dubbed it the Red Summer. The Red Summer was "the worst spate of race riots and lynchings in American history," according to historian Cameron McWhirter. It happened in tandem with the Red Scare, the country's first run-in with communism. Some associated black unrest with the Bolsheviks, but blacks had not developed a class consciousness. They were simply battling for equal treatment and racial identity. [2]

The two million doughboys returning from France sought their old jobs back, only to discover that the American economy was contracting, munitions factories were closing, and that both inflation and unemployment were rising. Black laborers had taken white jobs during the war, jobs that whites viewed as rightly theirs, stoking white resentment. In addition, factories often hired poor black workers as strikebreakers during the massive strikes of 1919, further straining racial tensions.

Resentment went both ways. Whites felt that blacks had grown "uppity" during the war with their demands for equal treatment, while African-Americans believed that their soldiers, who had fought as bravely and contributed just as much as anyone else, deserved to be treated with respect. Much of the country did not see it that way.

Whites largely stuck to racial stereotypes of blacks as dumb, idle, lazy, and half-formed. Most Americans believed blacks were racially inferior and pushed back against black demands for equality. And whites often felt justified in using force against blacks, believing blacks to be violent and needing to be held in check.

At any perceived black provocation, an angry white mob was ready to put them back in their place. It was all driven by the myth of white racial superiority. The violence and property destruction were lopsided: whites almost always had the upper hand. But what emerged from the Red Summer was a transformed black community, one that banded together to defend its interests and neighborhoods, and one that would demand and eventually gain equal rights. For the first time, the black community stood up en masse to resist oppression.

On May 10, 1919, drunken sailors started a race riot in Charleston, South Carolina, though the quick response from the mayor and naval base commander quickly quelled the mob.[3] The next month in Ellisville, Mississippi, a huge crowd of whites gathered to lynch John Hartfield, an African-American man who had supposedly confessed to raping a white woman. The lynching was publicized nationwide days before it happened, yet the governor refused to intervene, and remarked, "no one can keep the inevitable from happening." Hartfield was lynched, shot multiple times, and then burned to ashes. No one was charged with a crime.[4]

Seeing the rising hostility directed toward them in the months after the war ended, blacks began arming and banding together to protect their communities. So many young men had served in the armed forces, and this had given them discipline and teamwork. Many were dressed in their military uniforms as a statement when a white mob threatened to attack a neighborhood.

In Washington, D.C., four days of rioting began on July 19 after an African-American man allegedly insulted a white woman. A white mob consisting mostly of off-duty sailors and soldiers descended on the city's predominantly black neighborhoods. The *Washington Post* irresponsibly stirred things up even more by taunting the crowd on the second day to finish the job. MOBILIZATION FOR TONIGHT read the headline.[5] In the prosperous black neighborhood Shaw, many young African-American men in uniform blocked the roads near the Howard Theatre. The police intervened to keep the two sides from coming to blows.

Woodrow Wilson had returned to Washington from the Paris Peace Conference just a week before the riots broke out. His mind was elsewhere, gearing up for the Senate confirmation of the peace treaty. After several days, he reluctantly ordered the military to help local police restore order. A thunderstorm on the fourth day drenched everyone, and the rioters went home, their anger finally spent. Calvin Chase from the *Washington Bee*, a black thought leader in Washington, wrote a scathing headline: THIS NATION'S GRATITUDE with a cartoon of a mob beating a black person.[6]

A week after the Washington riot petered out, violence erupted in Chicago. Carl Sandburg covered the riots for the *Chicago Daily News*, noting the trigger point for the riot. "A colored boy swam across an imaginary segregation line. White boys threw rocks at him and knocked him off a raft," Sandburg wrote. "He was drowned."[7] The incident triggered a violent confrontation that left thirty-eight people dead, hundreds injured, and the destruction of much property. The governor finally called up the state militia to quell the riots. Chicago was the largest and most tragic of the 1919 race riots. Afterward, Sandburg produced a slim volume of his newspaper articles that examined the many sides of the riots. Walter Lippmann wrote the introduction.[8]

Random violence descended on cities as white—and sometimes black—mobs roamed the streets looking for victims to beat or kill. "There's a nigger! Let's get him!" was a too common cry during these dark times.[9] In return, increasing numbers of black men armed themselves and were shooting back. "The race riots in Washington and Chicago have shown a new feature," H. L. Mencken noted in an August letter. "The coons have fought back—and pretty well beaten the whites. They are armed everywhere and apparently eager for the band to play."[10]

Police forces often found themselves overwhelmed, and federal or state troops had to be called in to restore order. That did not always help: in Knoxville, National Guardsmen responding to a race riot opened fire with a machine gun on a black crowd, a weapon designed for mass killing, not crowd control.[11] On September 28, a mob of thousands seized Willie Brown from the Omaha, Nebraska, courthouse and nearly destroyed the building. They shot him multiple times, hanged him, then burned his remains. It was savage. The mob even lynched the mayor, who had pleaded for law and order, but he miraculously survived the hanging.[12]

Charles Evans Hughes, the former Supreme Court justice who ran against Woodrow Wilson in 1916, condemned lynching at the National Conference on Lynching at Carnegie Hall on May 5. Black soldiers had served their country honorably, and because of their sacrifices, "the black man shall have the rights guaranteed to him by the Constitution of the United States." These were bold words championing black equality from a notable conservative.[13]

Yet President Wilson did virtually nothing to stop the violence or appeal for law and order, as he was preoccupied with the Treaty of Versailles ratification. He made only one comment about the riots during his whistle-stop campaign in Helena, Montana in September. "I hope you won't think it inappropriate if I stop here to express my shame as an American citizen at the race riots that have occurred at some places in this country, where men have forgot humanity and justice and ordered society and have run amuck," he remarked.[14]

Wilson came up short on the question of race. But his sin was a matter of omission rather than commission. He allowed his base of Southern Democrats to further cement the gains from Jim Crow laws and he did little to stop it. His minimal efforts to halt the race riots and lynching were ineffectual. He allowed the federal government workforce to become even more segregated, and many black federal workers lost their jobs. He maintained the status quo of a segregated military. Yet Wilson's views were not unusual: most Americans of the era were comfortable with a segregated society and did not yet view African-Americans as equals.

Racial violence was abating on its own by fall 1919. There were eighty-three documented lynchings that year, a number that would soon decline with anti-lynching laws and greater law enforcement. "The year 1919's historic importance was that it was the start of a process—a great dismantling of institutional prejudice and inequity that marred American society," wrote Cameron McWhirter in his definitive study *Red Summer*.[15] A key reason why this took place was that the federal government took on the role of protecting its citizens. The era of voluntary policing and vigilantism was coming to an end.

What was remarkable about the 1919 race riots was how blacks stood together to oppose white violence, and henceforth would become louder in their demands for equal rights. The African-American community was on the road to building racial identity in the 1920s with the Harlem Renaissance, and the children of the Great War veterans would lead the civil rights movement after World War II. The era of mob violence would gradually give way to the rule of law.

The Red Scare

The United States had only been at war for nineteen months by the time the Armistice was signed. But a new menace reared its head: the Red Scare. Historian Frederick Lewis Allen called it a "reign of terror," though the real terror came from the country's reactionary response.[16]

During the Great War, the Wilson administration worked closely with Samuel Gompers of the American Federation of Labor to get better wages for workers. Rising prices and wages in the U.S. had built resentment among businessmen who had to pay their workers extra, and among workers who saw the buying power of their wages shrink. Strikes, walkouts, and sometimes violence were the result. This coincided with the Soviet takeover in Russia, which in turn made Americans fearful that the striking workers would turn Bolshevik and spawn a revolution in the U.S. This overlooked the fact that American organized labor was not communist. The actual numbers of communists and radicals in the country was small, no more than a few thousand people, but suddenly any striking worker calling for higher wages was swept into the broad category of insurgent. The Red Scare was on.

The Red Scare cut as deep as the wartime German hysteria—and lasted far longer. The animosity and suspicion that had been directed at German-Americans for the past two years shifted over to anarchists, communists, radicals, and socialists. The alarm made every leftist a suspect, and the Socialist Party's days were numbered. The Red Scare stifled a democratic movement.

The Red Scare created a culture of fear and paranoia that was in part magnified by the public response. The threat was greatly overblown. A certain part of American society responded to threats to their safety by yielding to authoritarianism; safety was their concern, not civil liberties. "During a war liberty disappears as the community feels itself menaced," journalist Walter Lippmann wrote in 1920. "When revolution seems to be contagious, heresy-hunting is a respectable occupation." [17]

Yet communism failed to roll over Europe after the Great War. The German army crushed a communist revolt in Berlin. Bolshevik takeovers in Bavaria and Hungary were thwarted. Only the Soviet Union had become communist, and there it seemed confined, though it certainly sent out propaganda and spies like an evangelical missionary out to convert the world, believing that the end phase of the class struggle and a workers' utopia was at hand.

The left and the radical left opposed the war on grounds that it only fed capitalism and empire building, while the soldiers and workers bore the brunt. When some radicals took to violence, Attorney General Mitchell Palmer (appointed in March 1919) took action. The Red Scare was a reaction against the radical left. Through fear mongering and quick action, the federal government effectively hobbled the radical movement, but in turn violated civil liberties.

The anarchist movement was multiethnic, composed mainly of Eastern and Southern European immigrants. Anarchy had been around for decades, as shown by the Haymarket Riot in Chicago in 1886 and President McKinley's assassination in 1901. Emma Goldman was one of the best-known anarchists, a Jewish immigrant who had come from Russia in 1885. In 1920, there were 1.4 million Russian immigrants in the U.S., most of them Jews who had fled conscription and pogroms in czarist Russia. Many of them were leftists and socialists, while a small minority were anarchists.[18]

Radicals began a mail bombing campaign to protest the anti-anarchist Immigration Act of 1918. On April 28, 1919, a black servant opened a package that had arrived at Georgia senator Thomas Hardwick's house, a politician who had sponsored the law. It exploded, blowing her hands off. The next a day, a postal clerk in New York City named Charles Caplan pulled out sixteen identically-wrapped packages for having too little postage; all were addressed to major public figures. Once he learned of the mail bombing at Senator Hardwick's home, he called the authorities. Each package contained a bomb. Caplan's diligence had undoubtedly saved lives.

Two days later, leftists staged a May Day parade in Cleveland to protest the jailing of socialist Eugene Debs. Off-duty soldiers confronted the peaceful parade and demanded that they take down their red flags. When the marchers refused, a violent scrum ensued. Two people were killed and dozens arrested before the military and police restored order. After that, the red flag was banned in Cleveland.[19]

As the federal government prepared to deport Italian anarchist Luigi Galleani, his followers struck back. On the evening of June 2, a bomb exploded at Attorney General Mitchell Palmer's house at 2132 R Street, NW in Washington, directly opposite the home of Franklin Roosevelt. One of the bombers tripped on the sidewalk before reaching Palmer's front door and triggered the explosion, killing himself and badly damaging the front of the Palmer residence. Palmer and his family survived, though they were in shock. Eight bombs exploded around the country that night at 11:00 P.M. It was no coincidence: anarchists were attempting to assassinate public figures.

Palmer had largely ignored the Red Scare until the bombing at his house that targeted him and his family. After that it seemed personal. It would become something that he could leverage politically, as Palmer had ambitions to be president. With the 1920 election a year away, a bold stroke against radicals would raise his public profile, even make him a hero. Palmer appointed William Flynn as head of the Bureau of Investigation. Flynn had successfully combated anarchists in New

York during the war and served as head of the U.S. Secret Service, uncovering the German wartime plot to bomb merchant ships at sea.

In giving the commencement address at Georgetown University, Palmer remarked, "The Government proposes to protect itself against attacks from within as carefully and as forcefully as it has shown itself able to protect itself against attacks from without." William Flynn served notice the next day that the Bureau of Investigation would soon swoop down on the anarchists. Flynn got to work rounding up radicals, people the Secret Service had monitored since the war, often without a warrant and often without filing charges. Still, after weeks of following leads, Flynn's men had not cracked the case of who had bombed the attorney general's house.[20]

Based on the 1918 Immigration Act forbidding anarchists, Palmer seized on the idea of rounding up the radicals. He created a Radical Division in the Bureau of Investigation to investigate anarchists. He tapped a twenty-four-year-old attorney, J. Edgar Hoover, to lead the new organization. Hoover joined the Department of Justice fresh out of law school in 1917 just as the nation went to war. His was a draft-exempt job. Hoover immediately began building files on radicals.

Anarchists were willing to resort to violence to achieve their goals, which included overthrowing the U.S. government, while socialists were largely pacifists. In August 1919, the Socialist Party of America evicted its more radical members, including John Reed, who believed that revolution and the dictatorship of the proletariat was at hand. The radicals set up their own organization, the Communist Party of America, dominated by Russians. The next day, Americans split off to form the Communist Labor Party. The far left was seriously split, even at war with itself, and its wounds were in part self-inflicted.[21]

At the same time, strikes around the country escalated. One of the most memorable began on September 9, 1919 when the Boston Police Department walked off the job, prompted by absurdly low pay. When labor leader Samuel Gompers intervened, calling for Massachusetts governor Calvin Coolidge to broker an agreement, Coolidge responded that there was "no right to strike against the public safety by anybody, anywhere, any time." The statement struck a chord at a time when the public was tiring of labor walkouts. The Boston Police Department gradually hired a new police force, effectively breaking the strike.[22]

While in Helena, Montana on his League of Nations barnstorming tour, Wilson addressed the police strike in Boston that had started two days earlier. He called the strike a "crime against civilization," as it left the citizens of Boston unprotected. "In my judgment, the obligation of a policeman is as sacred as the obligation of a soldier. He is a public servant, not a private employee, and the whole honor and safety of the community is in his hands."[23]

The political right blamed Bolshevism for the many strikes, which were nowhere close to being over. Two weeks later, 315,000 steel workers walked off the job, calling for higher wages. Their strike lasted three months with no positive outcome for the workers, and much hardship while they went without wages. H. L. Mencken noted that with the seventy-five percent war profits tax, steelmakers preferred to spend their money breaking the strike, rather than pay the government. "Every dollar they spend on fighting the unions includes 75 cents from the public treasury," he wrote sarcastically. "An altruistic, patriotic lot." The United Mine Workers soon announced they would strike, which would paralyze a coal-fueled economy. Attorney General Palmer got a court injunction blocking the strike, but 400,000 miners still walked off the job on November 1.[24]

During this epic struggle between business and labor, President Wilson became incapacitated from his October stroke. With little oversight, Mitchell Palmer planned a roundup of radicals. What became known as the Palmer Raids began on November 7, 1919. Bureau of Investigation agents, assisted by local policemen and volunteers, conducted raids in fifteen cities targeting the Union of Russian Workers, an organization closely affiliated with the Bolsheviks. "This is the first big step to rid the country of these foreign trouble makers," Palmer's office stated. The following night, it raided other communist organizations. Thousands of people were rounded up in the dragnet, though most were soon let go. Those identified as Reds were dispatched to Ellis Island, which was now serving as a holding pen for radicals. Fearful of the consequences, the coal miners ended their strike. The Palmer Raids lasted three months and arrested up to 10,000 people—many without a warrant. Most were never charged.[25]

On Ellis Island, a single attorney from the National Civil Liberties Bureau represented the reds. While the public applauded the roundup of supposedly dangerous radicals, the federal government pushed through a truncated process to deport them. On December 20, the U.S. Army transport *Buford* steamed out of New York harbor, loaded with 249 radicals. The two most prominent deportees were anarchists Alexander Berkman and Emma Goldman, who had been recently released from prison after inciting young men not to register for the draft. The *Buford* became known as the "Soviet Ark," as the passengers were being deported to the Soviet Union.

After this initial success, J. Edgar Hoover planned another massive dragnet to score more than 3,000 people from the two communist parties. On January 3, 1920, the biggest police raid in American history thus far took place around the country. More than 2,500 people were arrested. Most were never shown a warrant, nor charged, nor told that they had a right to legal counsel. And thus began the problem: mass arrests without warrants overwhelmed local jails, as well as the ability to sort through the good and the bad. A humanitarian crisis developed in jails overly packed with people. Hoover's intention was to deny bail, hold deportation hearings, and expel as many as possible on a far grander scale than the November raids. For many detainees there was too little or no evidence against them. Public opinion began to sour with the realization that many arrested were not radicals and that due process was being denied.

On January 7, the New York legislature suspended five Socialist Party assemblymen, all of whom were democratically elected. "You have been elected on a platform that is absolutely inimical to the best interests of the State of New York and of the United States," Speaker Thaddeus Sweet declared as he arbitrarily suspended them from office.[26] The *New York Times* condoned the action, calling it "an orderly and lawful procedure."[27]

Three days later Congress expelled its one Socialist member, Victor Berger of Wisconsin. The largely pacifist socialists were grouped with the anarchists, communists and radicals. Even conservatives were appalled, such as Charles Evans Hughes, who condemned the assembly's super-patriotic action as "un-American, and if successful must destroy the right of minorities and the very foundations of representative government."[28]

The Red Scare was a knee-jerk reaction; its response was to keep America safe by any means, often extralegal or illegal, and disregarded established civil liberties. The political motivation behind it emerged on March 1, 1920, when Mitchell Palmer announced he was running for president as a Democrat. But public opinion was swinging against the mass arrests, and the fact that detainees were starting to be released on account of insufficient evidence showed that the government did not know what it was doing. The plan to round up the Reds proved too ambitious. Rather than elevate Palmer's platform, the raids discredited him. Judging a trial of communist leaders in Boston, federal judge George Anderson compared the Palmer Raids to the Salem witch trials: "Well, in these times of hysteria, I wonder no witches have been hung during the last six months."[29]

Acting Secretary of Labor Louis Post, whose office handled the immigration and deportation cases, began dropping the cases and releasing those arrested. Simply appearing on a Communist Party list was not enough evidence to deport a person, and far too many had been arrested without warrants or sufficient evidence against them. Post emerged as one of the heroes during the Red Scare by demanding accountability and due process.[30]

As 1920 progressed, the Red Scare ebbed as it faded from the public eye. Unlike the year before, May Day 1920 came and went without incident. Still, Palmer saw fit to detain 360 radicals and hold them for a day without charging them. Palmer was widely criticized for preemptively arresting so many without warrants or provocation. The country was growing tired of the fear-mongering and red-baiting. People were troubled by the massive roundups, the mass incarcerations, the terrible conditions in jails, and the disregard for due process. Organized labor denounced Palmer's raids for smearing them by associating honest workers who simply wanted better pay with radical bomb-throwers.

Palmer quickly worked to dismiss the rest of the cases from the raids. His political ship was sinking, as was his presidential candidacy.

Palmer and J. Edgar Hoover attempted a bit of political payback against Louis Post for betraying the roundups. They arranged for Post's impeachment before Congress. Former president William Howard Taft supported Post publicly, denouncing the extralegal methods that the attorney general had undertaken to deport aliens, and scoffed at the idea that Bolsheviks were about to take over the country. "No matter what a man may say, he should not be punished unless there has been the fullest inquiry into what is done," Taft declared.[31]

On May 7 and 8, Louis Post testified for ten hours before the House Rules Committee. The seventy-one-year-old acting secretary carried the day with humor and a marathon runner's stamina, winning over the congressmen by showing that the entire process of the Palmer Raids was befuddled and the lack of due process was egregious.[32] Within weeks, twelve nationally recognized lawyers, including Felix Frankfurter, signed their names to a report denouncing the judicial mishaps of Palmer's Department of Justice. They published the document on May 28, just days before Palmer had his turn testifying before Congress. It was damning.[33]

Palmer's turn before the House Rules Committee came on June 1. He read a 209-page statement prepared by J. Edgar Hoover defending the propriety of the raids. After listening to this, the congressmen declined to take action against Louis Post. Palmer's credibility was shot just weeks before the Democratic Party Convention in San Francisco. Palmer's role in the Red Scare turned too many people off, dashing his hopes to win the presidential nomination. The attorney general would soon find himself out of a job.[34]

As the Red Scare ended, the public had found new issues to discuss: women's suffrage was at hand, Prohibition had begun, drinkers were busy finding bootleggers, Charles Ponzi had developed a scheme to get rich that quickly collapsed, and the Democratic and Republican Party conventions were held that summer to pick candidates for the presidency. But the spasms from the Red Scare continued, even as it withered away.

In April 1920, a man was killed during an armed robbery at a shoe factory in Braintree, Massachusetts. Two anarchists were arrested, both Italian immigrants: Ferdinando Nicola Sacco and Bartolomeo Vanzetti. The subsequent trial of Sacco and Vanzetti became one of the most sensational trials of the 1920s. They were convicted in 1921 and appealed the death sentence. Author John Dos Passos interviewed both men and published *Facing the Chair*, a book that argued for their innocence while excoriating American racism. He would be arrested twice protesting the men's execution. Sacco and Vanzetti were sent to the electric chair in 1927. An open question remains if they really were guilty of the crime.

On September 16, 1920, an enormous explosion rocked Wall Street. A horse-drawn cart carrying the bomb had been parked in front of the J.P. Morgan building, timed to detonate at lunchtime. Dozens of people were killed on the street, but few workers in the targeted bank were injured. The New York Stock Exchange shut down for the rest of the day, then resumed trading the next morning as if nothing had happened. The culprits were likely anarchists, but the perpetrators were never brought to justice. After the initial shock, the country quickly moved on. The people were over the Red Scare.[35]

H. L. Mencken complained about the "idiotic alarm about Bolshevism, and brought on the wholesale jailing and deportation of innocent men." He noted bitterly that only two newspapers rose to denounce the Palmer Raids—and even then when it was too late: his own *Baltimore Sun* and the *New York World*. "To have horned in at that time would have been to run grave risks, for Wilson was strutting about in his halo and Palmer and company believed themselves invincible—but it would have been to render a public service of inestimable worth," Mencken wrote.[36]

The Red Scare decimated American communists as well as socialists. The Socialist Party went extinct after Eugene Debs's death in 1926, while the communists went underground. Historian Kenneth Ackerman called the Red Scare "one big exercise in guilt by association."[37] Attorney General Mitchell Palmer's political career died in the blowback from the Palmer Raids—but J. Edgar Hoover's career took off. In 1924, he was chosen to lead the Bureau of Investigation, the predecessor to the FBI, a position he held until his death in 1972.

The Red Scare echoed for decades afterward. We see its outcome in McCarthyism and the blacklisting of Hollywood writers in the 1950s. We see it applied viciously to the civil rights movement, when racists accused African-Americans striving for equal rights as being part of a communist plot. We see it with 21st-century race-baiting, where Muslim terrorists have replaced Eastern European anarchists as the enemy. The Red Scare became indelibly imprinted on American memory.

We know the outcome from the rise and fall of communism: The state control of enterprise, the brutal dictatorships, the lack of freedom of expression and religion, and the deaths of millions. With the fall of the Berlin Wall in 1989 and implosion of communist states in Eastern Europe, followed by the fall of the Soviet Union two years later, free markets and societies triumphed over communism. But no American alive in 1920 could have guessed the course of history. All they feared was the rise of communism in Europe would soon spread to their own shores. They feared it was already here.

Suffrage

The framers of the Constitution may have used oblique language in referring to slavery, but they were very clear about voting rights: only men could vote. Women were deliberately excluded. And women had chafed about this for more than a century, finally formalizing their protest at the Seneca Falls Convention in 1848 with the birth of the women's rights movement. It would be a seven-decade-long, multigenerational movement to win the vote for women.

In 1890, Wyoming became the first state to enter the Union with woman's suffrage; as a territory, it offered this benefit to lure more women to join the overwhelmingly male population of miners and ranchers. Shortly after Arizona became a state in 1912, it placed suffrage on the ballot, which was widely approved. Western states tended to be more open-minded on this question. The day before Woodrow Wilson was sworn in as president in 1913, suffragists staged a massive parade in the nation's capital.

There was strong opposition to women's suffrage. The long-standing tradition was that women bore the children and tended the household. The blood sport of politics was for men, while women were above that. Their role was to be nurturing stewards of the family and societal institutions. Besides, the U.S. Constitution clearly spelled out that voting was strictly for men. The suffrage movement set out to change that. But it was also clear that men would have to grant women the right to vote, since only men could vote. It would take a Constitutional amendment to establish a federal right for suffrage.

President Wilson's views on women's suffrage evolved during his presidency. His first wife, Ellen, was an artist and supported suffrage, as did all three of their daughters. But the question was more complicated for the president, who had to balance varying interests within the Democratic coalition, including the chauvinism and misogyny that was commonplace among American men of the era.

The president issued a statement in October 1915 saying that he would vote in favor of woman's suffrage, though as a private citizen, not as a partisan measure. He ducked the question of whether suffrage should be treated as a national issue. "I believe that it should be settled by the states and not by the national government, and that in no circumstances should it become a party question," Wilson said. Suffragists were not pleased with his artful dodge.[38]

Republicans sensed an opportunity in 1916 and embraced suffrage as part of their platform. Former president Theodore Roosevelt threw his considerable clout behind suffrage. Now it was the Democrats—ostensibly the Progressives in the country—who were the main obstacle to providing women the vote. A strong vein of conservatism ran through the Democratic Party's base, and the party was reluctant to embrace suffrage. Meanwhile more states granted women the right to vote.

There were two competing woman-led suffrage groups. The National American Woman Suffrage Association, led by Carrie

Chapman Catt and Helen Gardener, formed in 1890 when two suffrage organizations merged. Its activism was more orthodox as it
sought to educate men that women were worthy of the vote. They
allied with the much larger Woman's Christian Temperance Union
to sway public opinion in favor of Prohibition and suffrage. The other
leading activist group was the more controversial National Woman's
Party. Led by tiny framed but strong-willed Alice Paul, its tactics were
far more confrontational and controversial. The GOP had supported
suffrage, and now activists would confront the Democratic president
until he did the same.

A month after winning reelection in 1916, President Wilson gave
his annual address before Congress on December 5, 1916. Suffragists from the National Woman's Party smuggled a yellow banner
into the House of Representatives gallery, then hung it while the
president spoke. It read, MR. PRESIDENT, WHAT WILL YOU DO FOR
WOMAN SUFFRAGE? The banner was quickly pulled down, but it made
national news. This was just the beginning of the NWP's escalation
in activism.[39]

On January 9, 1917, a delegation of three hundred NWP women met
with the president and demanded his support, but Wilson refrained.
The next day the NPW began its "silent sentinel" vigil: twelve pickets
were stationed around the White House gates in a daily watch, carrying yellow banners that repeated the line he saw in the House of
Representatives: "Mr. President, what will you do for woman suffrage?"
Whenever the president entered or left the White House, he would be
confronted by a suffrage picketer.[40]

The NPW continued its vigil outside at the White House, even as
the country debated and finally declared war against Germany. The
suffragists stepped up their protests, a controversial tactic that many
criticized. The signs grew ever more critical. Some NWP protesters
carried banners denouncing the president as "Kaiser Wilson," heckling
him for supporting democracy abroad but denying it to women at home.
Some of the women chained themselves to the White House fence,
an act that got more than two hundred of them arrested for disorderly
conduct. Many were remanded to the Occoquan Workhouse. On July

14, Washington policemen arrested sixteen NWP members, who were sent to jail for sixty days. The president pardoned them after just two days, though they vowed to continue their protests.[41] In August, a crowd of 3,000 people, including numerous sailors and soldiers in uniform, taunted the suffragists and pelted them with eggs, rocks, and vegetables while wrenching the "Kaiser Wilson" banners from their hands. The police stepped in to protect them but forbade them from carrying the banners. Tensions were high from the war, and many considered the women's behavior seditious. On the other hand, the suffrage arrests were terrible public relations for the White House.[42]

Meanwhile, the other leading suffrage organization, the National American Woman Suffrage Association, refrained from such escalating tactics. This group encouraged the president to support suffrage as part of the war effort. And this became the linchpin that would win his endorsement.

Women played vital roles in the World War. While none were drafted into the armed forces, many volunteered for nursing duty, others took over men's jobs in factories, and sewed millions of uniforms for the doughboys, while thousands went to work for the War Department as secretaries to staff the bureaucracy needed to win the war. Many others served in the American Red Cross, the most visible of the wartime humanitarian organizations. One of the best-known wartime posters was the Red Cross's "The Greatest Mother in the World" poster, which showed a nurse cradling a wounded doughboy similar to Michelangelo's *Pietà*.[43]

H. L. Mencken wrote with a clear eye to human nature in supporting women's suffrage. As a committed atheist, he saw no biblical reason why wives should obey their husbands. The vote would change relationships for the better, he wrote. "Men, facing them squarely at last, will consider them anew, not as romantic political and social invalids, to be coddled and caressed, but as free competitors in a harsh and abominable world." Mencken was hardly a romantic. A committed bachelor, he would succumb to marriage in 1930.[44]

On October 20, 1917, Alice Paul and three women were arrested for picketing at the White House and sentenced to jail for seven •

months. Paul went on a hunger strike and was force-fed. The women were terrorized in prison as the guards tried to break them. Paul was eventually released early. Shortly after that, President Wilson agreed to endorse the Nineteenth Amendment.[45] Wilson had come around to women's contributions as vital to the war effort, and thus they should be awarded with the vote. He returned to the Capitol on January 9, 1918—the day after delivering his Fourteen Points speech—to endorse a Constitutional amendment for suffrage, calling it "an act of right and justice to the women of the country and of the world." He did so in a meeting with the House's suffrage committee. It had been exactly a year since his meeting with the NPW that had triggered the silent sentinel pickets. The next day, the House of Representatives approved the suffrage amendment by a margin of two votes.[46]

Things were different in the Senate, where conservative Democrats opposed suffrage and delayed debate for eight months. The Nineteenth Amendment was finally debated in the Senate in September 1918. The vote was two short of the two-thirds majority needed. Theodore Roosevelt provided public backing, as did numerous cabinet secretaries. Treasury Secretary William McAdoo helped corral some of the wayward senators, but to no avail. He then hit upon the idea of asking the president to deliver a special message in support of the amendment. Wilson was initially reluctant to interfere in a specific bill, but he ultimately decided in favor of it.

On September 30, Wilson made a surprise visit to the Senate, addressing the suffrage question for fifteen minutes, in the hope of swaying two senators to add their votes to the Nineteenth Amendment. He stated, "I regard the concurrence of the Senate in the constitutional amendment proposing the extension of the suffrage to women as vitally essential to the successful prosecution of the great war of humanity in which we are engaged."[47]

McAdoo noted that Wilson's speech was a surprise to most senators—and a rather unwelcome one at that. "It was clear that his appearance was bitterly resented by all those opposed to the amendment and that even those who favored it were influenced by senatorial tradition and the feeling that the Chief Executive should not plead for any particular measure which the Senate had under consideration," he wrote. "Although it had no effect on the Senate's vote, it made a profound impression on the country." The amendment ultimately failed by one vote to secure the necessary two-thirds, but Wilson had planted a seed that would bear fruit. [48]

Vice President Marshall presided over the Senate, where he witnessed endless debate about the Nineteenth Amendment and women lobbyists and protesters who demanded that the issue come to a vote. He later quipped, "The amendment really was submitted to the people in self-defense, to get rid of these women in order that some business might be transacted" in the Senate. Marshall himself opposed suffrage. [49]

In spring 1919, the new Republican-dominated Congress took up the issue of suffrage once again. The House passed the Nineteenth Amendment on May 20 by a vote of 304 to 89. The Senate voted for the amendment on June 4. It passed by 56 to 25. Having cleared Congress, the suffrage amendment went on to the states for ratification. The states lined up, one by one, to vote on the Constitutional amendment for women's suffrage. On August 18, 1920, Tennessee ratified the amendment, putting it over the top. Women could vote for the first time in the upcoming presidential election that November. The Nineteenth Amendment took more than fourteen months to ratify, one month longer than the Prohibition amendment.

With the suffrage amendment, the size of the American electorate nearly doubled. It was "the largest expansion of the electorate in American history," noted suffrage historians Kevin Corder and Christina Wolbrecht. Women had earned the federal right to vote and cast their ballots for the first time in the 1920 national election. Received wisdom is that few women turned out to vote, and those that did voted identically to their husbands. But is that true? There were no exit polls in 1920, and few ways to measure how women cast their ballots. Women initially had low turnout rates, which remained low for decades, but gathered steam as more women embraced their role as political beings. Women voters would play key roles in ending Prohibition and supporting the New Deal during the Great Depression.

Women were working more, free of tight familial and parental control. Sexual liberation went along with independence. Women began using contraceptives for family planning, thanks to birth control pioneer Margaret Sanger, and family sizes began to shrink. Much of this happened in the 1920s.[50]

On February 15, 1921, a new statue was unveiled in the U.S. Capitol Rotunda honoring the women who had fought so hard to win the vote: sculptor Adelaide Johnson's portrait monument of Susan B. Anthony, Lucretia Mott, and Elizabeth Cady Stanton. Suffrage leader Alice Paul commissioned the statue for the National Woman's Party. It soon earned the disparaging nickname, "Three Women in a Bathtub." It could also be called the "wandering statue," as the very next day Congress moved it to the basement. The NWP complained, so the statue was moved to crypt where George Washington's tomb was to have been, but then the Capitol guides complained. The statue was pushed aside once again. It finally returned to the Rotunda in 1997.[51]

Prohibition Begins

From the Civil War until the Great War, Americans overwhelmingly drank lager beer—the gift of millions of German immigrants who set up breweries in every city and town where they settled. Sutlers brought suds to the Union Army camps, where thousands of German soldiers were serving, and the rest of the army acquired a taste for beer. Beer rapidly eclipsed whiskey as the nation's preferred beverage. Alcohol historian William Rorabaugh showed how beer consumption rose stratospherically from 3.5 gallons per capita in 1865 to 15.2 gallons in 1895 to 20.2 gallons in 1915. Most of the brewers in America were born in Germany. And that was a problem, especially once the United States declared war on Germany in 1917.[52]

Set against this backdrop of a beer-sipping nation were the abstaining reformers known as the temperance movement. They had every intention of shutting down the liquor traffic and dumping the beer kegs in the sewer. The century-long social reform movement had been waging its own war on American drinking habits. It used the opportunity of the Great War to foist Prohibition upon the nation in 1920.

The temperance movement became one of the key players in the Progressive Era, a time when activists used the federal government to improve American society. There was a high sense of moral purpose—in fact, the temperance movement has been called the dry crusade. It was a movement of white evangelicals who viewed alcohol as a social evil, who vilified drink by calling it Demon Rum. And their leading lobby, the Anti-Saloon League denounced saloons as the devil's tool. The ASL figured that closing the saloons would lop off the head of the monster. Without a place to sell its goods, the industry would collapse. This was a supply-side solution. Unfortunately for the ASL, it never adequately addressed the demand side. Why did Americans want to drink in the first place?

The ASL achieved its first major national victory with the Webb-Kenyon Act of 1913, which was designed to halt interstate shipments of beer and liquor from wet states to dry states. President William Howard Taft, a wet, vetoed the law, but Congress overrode him. The ASL had arrived as a national political player. The very next year, the organization proposed the Eighteenth Amendment to ban alcohol through the Constitution. It won considerable votes, though it failed to achieve the necessary two-thirds in the House of Representatives. This near-victory emboldened the ASL to push its agenda. Changing the Constitution seemed within reach. And with the Sixteenth Amendment establishing the federal income tax, the federal government had a source of replacement income for alcohol excise taxes.[53]

Although temperance was an evangelical issue, Prohibition did not happen because of the will of God; rather, it happened because Wayne Wheeler made it so. Wheeler steadily advanced in the organization and proved his political prowess. He became the ASL's legislative superintendent. In 1916, Wheeler moved to Washington, D.C., to push through the Prohibition amendment. He was a diminutive man in a flannel suit, with a pince-nez, mustache, and a receding hairline. He looked the part of a bureaucrat or school board member. It was easy to underestimate Wheeler, judging by his appearance, but politicians seldom got the chance to cross him twice. He was in fact one of the savviest political operators in American history. Wheeler invented the term "pressure group," as he knew how to put the fear of God into politicians to vote dry—or else. More than anyone else, it was Wheeler who foisted Prohibition on the country.[54]

The Anti-Saloon League understood that the window to enact Prohibition was closing. The country was rapidly urbanizing, and by the 1920 U.S. census, cities with their multicultural populations—full of Catholic and Jewish immigrants—would tip the balance. The dry cause would lose to an emerging pluralistic society.[55] Wayne Wheeler stated to the ASL's 1917 annual convention: "We have got to win it now, because when 1920 comes and reapportionment is here, forty new wet Congressmen will come from the great wet centers with their rapidly increased population."[56] The ASL took the unconstitutional step of preventing Congressional redistricting after the 1920 census in order to ensure a majority rural vote in Congress.[57]

The ASL realized that the problem in cities was nearly hopeless: urban areas were unapologetically wet and unsupportive of dry activism. Yet the ASL stood up for immigrant rights and the working class to save them from alcoholism or spending their meager wages at the saloon. Industrialists like Henry Ford and John D. Rockefeller Jr. embraced temperance to reduce workplace accidents. Politicians voted dry because of ASL political pressure, even if they were wet in their personal lives.

The temperance movement had a strong nativist sentiment. The Protestants who dominated the country felt they were being eclipsed by the vast waves of Catholic immigrants. Cities gained strength at the expense of rural communities as the population shifted with immigration and industrialization. While the South never really went dry, its Democratic leaders saw political advantage in embracing temperance as a cudgel to break the Republican Party and further control African-Americans.[58]

Prohibitionists chipped away at the ability of brewers and distillers to produce alcoholic beverages in the name of the war effort. Distillers were ordered to halt distilling in September 1917, while brewers saw their access to grain reduced. They could only produce 3 percent beer, and then that was reduced to 2.75 percent beer in January 1918. People thought "war beer," as it became known, was watery and weak, but that was better than no beer at all, which was what the Anti-Saloon League intended. The ASL had higher goals than just reducing people's access to beer: it used the Great War to amend the Constitution to ban alcohol.

With the war declaration against Germany, the Anti-Saloon League realized its moment had arrived to win the war against alcohol. Its greatest obstacle, the beer-drinking German-American, was swept aside. Senator Morris Sheppard introduced the Eighteenth Amendment to the upper chamber in 1917. A Democrat from Texas, he was one of the leading progressives in the Senate and an ASL ally.

The Senate approved the Eighteenth Amendment on August 1, 1917 by a vote of 65 to 20. The House of Representatives passed a modified resolution on December 17 by a vote of 282 to 128, and the next day the Senate approved the revision. The states now had seven years to ratify the amendment, but it took just thirteen months.

Mississippi became the first state to ratify the Prohibition amendment in January 1918, and on January 16, 1919, Nebraska put the amendment over the top, just nine weeks after the Armistice. Only two states—Connecticut and Rhode Island—failed to ratify, as both had significant Catholic populations that opposed dry law. Even New York, the most populous state and the home of the nation's largest city, a melting pot of immigrants, voted for Prohibition. Americans now had exactly one year to stock up on their favorite alcoholic beverages before national Prohibition went into effect. Brewers and distillers had to find a buyer for their property or to repurpose their business. Most could not and simply went out of business. Many hotels that depended on alcohol sales, like the famed Knickerbocker in New York, closed their doors.

President Wilson was no ally to the temperance movement. Being a Presbyterian, he enjoyed an occasional whiskey and kept a wine collection in the White House. He keenly sidestepped the issue of Prohibition. Constitutional amendments do not require a presidential signature: once Congress approves, it goes directly to the states for ratification without passing the president's desk. Wilson had little to gain by stepping into the fight over Prohibition, and much to lose, given that his time was focused on winning the Great War. Part of the Democratic coalition was not only dry white Southerners, but also big-city Irishmen who were Catholic and staunchly in the wet column. Wilson did in fact sign the actual amendment in March 1919, two months after it was ratified; it is a common practice of presidents to sign constitutional amendments either as an endorsement or a matter of public record. [59]

There was a reason why the Eighteenth Amendment was ratified so quickly: Wayne Wheeler was the man behind the curtain who made it happen. But he was not done. He seized the opportunity to humiliate the ASL's biggest opponent—the German-American brewers—and keep the pressure up during the ratification process.

With the war declaration in 1917, drinking beer became unpatriotic. A Wisconsin politician, John Strange, leveled an accusation that brewers were guilty of treason: "We have German enemies across the water," he said. "We have German enemies in this country, too. And the worst of all our German enemies, the most treacherous, the most menacing, are Pabst, Schlitz, Blatz and Miller. They are the worst Germans who ever afflicted themselves on a long-suffering people." Pabst fired back by suing Strange for slander, but the case was dismissed. [60]

Wayne Wheeler insinuated that Germany controlled the brewers. When documentation arose showing that the brewers had funded the National German-American Alliance, Wheeler demanded that the NGAA's charter be revoked for lobbying against Prohibition. He wrote Theodore Roosevelt, "There is no good reason why Congress should give this Alliance a special charter to stab the government in the back in time of war." Wheeler found an ally in Senator William H. King of Utah, who agreed to hold hearings if Wheeler would provide witnesses. Wheeler wrote in a private letter, "We are not willing it be known at present that we started the investigation," as he wanted to avoid the appearance that the hearings were politically motivated, which they clearly were. Wheeler appropriated $50,000 toward the investigation, one of the best investments he ever made—in fact, he would claim that the ASL received more than one million dollars in free advertising as a result of the hearings.[61]

Senator King began the hearings on February 23, 1918. The star witness was Gustavus Ohlinger, an attorney and president of the Toledo, Ohio, chamber of commerce, who claimed that the National German-American Alliance was simply a tool for German propaganda, that it was subordinate to the German high command, and that it worked to stir up the Irish against the war. "If the war had not intervened the conversion of America into a satellite nation of Kaiserdom would have been perfected," Ohlinger said with considerable hyperbole. "The war has been America's salvation." He claimed that Charles Hexamer, the president of the alliance until November 1917, was the Kaiser's "ruler of the German people in the United States." Other witnesses explained how the alliance had raised money from the brewers and the German embassy and openly lobbied against dry law. It made splendid copy for headlines. After more than a month of testimony, the NGAA agreed to disband, rather than wait for Congress to rescind its charter.[62]

Wheeler was not done destroying the brewers' reputation. In May 1918 he mischievously wrote Mitchell Palmer, the custodian of alien property: "It is reported to me that the Annhauser [sic] Busch Company and some of the Milwaukee Companies are largely controlled by alien Germans. . . . Have you made any investigations?" He hinted that he could help. Wheeler must have imagined the possibility of the federal government confiscating and shutting down the nation's largest breweries. It never went that far, but not for lack of trying.[63]

In September, Palmer announced that he had uncovered a scheme from at least a dozen brewers and the United States Brewers Association to secretly buy an American newspaper to spread German propaganda. He hinted that it was a prominent Washington daily—and essentially accused the brewers of treason. "The organized liquor traffic of the country is a vicious interest because it has been unpatriotic; because it has been pro-German in its sympathies and its conduct," Palmer said.[64]

The newspaper in question was the *Washington Times,* and soon the Senate opened an investigation into the brewers' financing for

Arthur Brisbane's purchase of the newspaper in 1917. Brisbane publicly acknowledged that friends, including several brewers, had loaned him $375,000 to buy the *Times*, but the brewers never owned the paper. It was merely a financial transaction. There was no impropriety.[65] Brisbane was a steadfast opponent of Prohibition, which made him a target to the Anti-Saloon League, but he was also a staunch supporter of the war effort, and that undermined Palmer's claim of actual German ownership. It appeared to many—falsely, as it turned out—that the brewers were publishing pro-German propaganda, but it made for good headlines during wartime.[66]

Ten days after the Armistice, the *New York Times* published a misleadingly titled article called "Enemy Propaganda Backed by Brewers." The article in fact showed just the opposite, that the brewers had stood against munitions sales to the Allies in 1915 on the principle that the U.S. ought to remain neutral, but that once war was declared, they encouraged German-Americans to support their adopted country. The *Times* did highlight that the U.S. Brewers Association maintained a list of companies that it refused to do business with—predominantly because these were dry-leaning companies. That was hardly a crime. The brewers had spent no money on "propaganda" once the U.S. entered the war.[67]

The Senate hearings paid off spectacularly for Wheeler and the ASL. The brewers were thrown onto the defensive and distracted from campaigning against the existential threat to their business: the Eighteenth Amendment. The United States Brewers' Association was silenced as a lobbying force as the Anti-Saloon League spun beer drinking into treason. Wheeler could have hardly used this opportunity better. Once the Eighteenth Amendment was ratified in January 1919, the Congressional hearings and investigations conveniently came to an end. They had served their purpose. Wheeler now turned his attention to crafting legislation that would turn the country bone dry.

Prohibition would dry up the country in 1920, but drys wondered how to hasten the process. They came up with the idea of Wartime Prohibition, which would put harsh restrictions on producing alcohol during the war. Senator Morris Sheppard, champion of the dry cause in Congress, cleverly bundled the Wartime Prohibition Act into an emergency agricultural appropriation, a critical source of funding for the war effort. Congress passed the appropriation on November 18, 1918—a full week after the Armistice. It headed to President Wilson's desk. The *New York Times* fumed at the bill, calling it a "dishonest, hypocritical, and superfluous law," and demanded that the president veto it. "For the ostensible purpose of promoting efficiency in war, the country is to be as dry as long as possible in peace," the *Times* wrote, pointing out that the bill was unnecessary, given that the ratification process of the Eighteenth Amendment was well underway. Furthermore, this would cause a $1 billion hit on federal revenue, as alcohol was heavily taxed.[68]

Despite his trepidations, President Wilson signed Wartime Prohibition into law on November 21. The new law superseded his earlier executive order. It banned wine production as of May 1, 1919 and ended the production of beer higher than 2.75 percent alcohol as of July 1. Not only was it illegal to distill liquor, but now it was illegal to sell spirits. Wartime Prohibition would be in effect until the president declared that full war mobilization had ended—and not just that the fighting had stopped.[69]

While Wilson was at the Paris Peace Conference, his private secretary Joe Tumulty kept him apprised of events in the United States. As the July 1, 1919 date approached for Wartime Prohibition to begin, Tumulty cabled the president to raise the embargo on beer and wine, noting that even Congressional Republicans wanted the ban lifted. The Eighteenth Amendment was set to begin in just six months, and lawmakers believed that it was a much stronger basis for law than the wartime measure, especially now that the war was effectively over.[70] But Wilson refused to budge. He took a principled approach that war mobilization had not ended, and thus he could not end Wartime Prohibition.[71] This had little to do with the Prohibition question itself; Wilson was deep in the Paris peace treaty negotiations and felt that if Congress declared an end to the war, it would undermine his ability to negotiate.[72]

While Wartime Prohibition was drying up the country, Congress was fashioning an enabling act to give teeth to the Eighteenth

Amendment. Wayne Wheeler largely penned the legislation, whose main sponsor was Minnesota Representative Andrew Volstead. It became known as the Volstead Act. Whereas the Prohibition amendment had vaguely declared that the manufacture, sale, and transportation of "intoxicating liquors" was illegal, the Volstead Act specified what exactly was meant by intoxicating. The law replaced Wartime Prohibition by drastically abolishing production of any alcohol above 0.5 percent alcohol. This meant that even the light 2.75 percent "war beer" would be illegal, as would be all wine.

Wilson vetoed the Volstead Act on October 27, 1919. But did the president actually write the veto and sign it himself? It is questionable. This was three weeks after his stroke, and he was in almost total seclusion in the White House. His views were well known to his staff, especially to Joe Tumulty. The Volstead Act was "the wrong way of doing the right thing," Tumulty noted Wilson saying. "You cannot regulate the morals and habits of a great cosmopolitan people by placing unreasonable restrictions upon their liberty and freedom."[73] Given the president's precarious health, Tumulty may have penned the veto message. He was cagey about this in his 1921 memoir. He simply wrote, "When the Volstead Act reached the President, he found, upon examining it, that it in no way repealed war-time prohibition, and so he vetoed it." In any case, Wilson was in no condition to lobby on behalf of his interests. Congress was now deeply in the Anti-Saloon League's control and overrode Wilson's veto the very next day.[74]

President Wilson only made one attempt to disarm Wartime Prohibition, and that was one week before national Prohibition commenced in January 1920. He was ready to declare an end to war mobilization, and thus the ban on beer sales could be lifted. It was far too late for such a feeble move. Joe Tumulty warned that the country would go into a final binge before Prohibition began. Wilson sent Tumulty to inquire Supreme Court Justice Louis Brandeis's opinion, who was a close friend of the president's. "The Judge and I discussed the matter at great length," Tumulty cabled. "He was of the opinion, and requested me so to inform the President, that the President had no power to lift the ban." Wartime Prohibition stayed in effect until national Prohibition began. [75]

There was no great, final binge of drinking before Prohibition began. Nor was there a flood of customers seeking to buy last-minute bottles of booze like it was Christmas Eve. The reality was that any last-minute shopper was out of luck, as liquor stores had long since held closeout sales to eliminate inventory. Drinkers had to stock up far in advance—a difficult prospect in many places, given that many states had dry laws on the books, and Wartime Prohibition had put severe restrictions in place for the past six months. Clothing designers predicted that men's hip pockets would grow smaller and possibly be eliminated entirely, as there would be no more reason to carry hip flasks. How wrong that turned out to be. [76]

Prohibition was set to begin as the clock struck midnight on January 16, 1920. That evening, former baseball superstar and now tent revival temperance preacher Billy Sunday held a mock funeral for John Barleycorn in Norfolk, Virginia. Ten thousand people attended the event at Sunday's tabernacle church. He ended the eulogy: "Goodbye John. You were God's worst enemy; you were hell's best friend. I hate you with a perfect hatred; I love to hate you." [77] At the same time, the leading drys in the country met for worship service at First Congregational Church in Washington, D.C. Among them were Anna Gordon of the WCTU, Howard Hyde Russell and Wayne Wheeler of the ASL, Secretary of the Navy Josephus Daniels, Virginia's Methodist bishop James Cannon, and Congressman Andrew Volstead. Shortly before midnight, William Jennings Bryan rose to deliver a forty-five-minute sermon that stirred the crowd. He boasted that American productivity would rise so high that Europe would ban alcohol too just to keep up. He concluded with a biblical reference to King Herod's soldiers, who sought to kill the infant Jesus: "They are dead that sought the child's life. They are dead. They are dead," he thundered to great applause. [78]

Prohibition was born at midnight, but this child turned out to be far more disobedient and fickle than anyone expected. And this newborn sorely wanted a drink.

Most Americans took a wait-and-see attitude toward Prohibition. They were probably surprised at how draconian the terms of the Volstead Act were. Many people supported the closing of the saloons but believed that low-alcohol beverages ought still to be available, especially everyone's favorite: beer. In his March 1920 message to Congress, President Wilson called for modifying the Volstead Act to allow beer and light wine. The Anti-Saloon League would have none of that. It had zero tolerance toward any alcohol consumption.[79]

Cracks began to appear in Prohibition's foundation almost immediately. Historian Frederick Lewis Allen noted how the Progressive Era came crashing down with the disillusionment from the Great War, and this set the stage for Prohibition's failure. "Spartan idealism was collapsing. People were tired of girding up their loins to serve noble causes. They were tired of making the United States a land fit for heroes to live in," Lewis wrote. "They wanted to relax and be themselves. The change of feeling toward prohibition was bewilderingly rapid."[80]

Police forces in cities like Boston, Chicago, and New York were heavily Irish and Catholic. They knew that Prohibition was targeted at their fellow immigrants, and they really wanted nothing to do with it. Many policemen and Bureau of Prohibition agents were happy to take a bribe to tip off a speakeasy owner of an impending raid. Prohibition rolled out the welcome mat to organized crime, which seized the opportunity to make a fortune in untaxed dollars. Prohibition became a pandemic of boozy corruption.

New York City—the city on a still, as wets were fond of calling it—was one of the wettest in the country. The Anti-Saloon League staked much on proving that Prohibition could work there. That meant cracking down on the ethnic and immigrant groups that made up the bulk of the city's population. It meant that working-class groups were harassed, while high society was left alone. During the run-up to Prohibition, New York Democratic state senator (and later mayor) Jimmy Walker blasted his Republican counterparts in Albany. He understood who would bear the brunt of Prohibition enforcement: the working class. "This measure you Republicans are fathering was born in hypocrisy, and there it will live," he denounced from the floor of the Senate. The rich would fill up their cellars and be immune from prying eyes, while the workingman who only wanted a glass of beer would face arrest. He called for "a real search and seizure act that will apply to the rich as well as to the poor."[81]

The rich and the extremely wealthy were less impacted by Prohibition, as they could use their wealth to avoid it. Larz Anderson and his wife Isabel were two of the richest people in the country. They loved to entertain with cocktails and wine, and Larz detested Prohibition. "And, behold! there were many cocktail parties, for this Prohibition, the most vicious and vindictive legislation ever enacted, has made many men drink the more and many drink who never drank before," he noted in his diary in the spring of 1920. Anderson filled the cellar of his mansion with wine bottles before Prohibition began—enough to last at least a decade (in fact, there were still unopened bottles in 1933 when Prohibition ended). Since this wine was purchased before Prohibition began, it was his personal property and could not be confiscated.[82]

The New York Times published an investigative report less than four months after national Prohibition began, and discovered that New Yorkers were imbibing as fervently as before. Drinking was driven underground in the illicit market of bootleggers and speakeasies. Soda fountains hawked liquor from under the counter. Restaurants quietly sold wine to the inquisitive and served cocktails in coffee mugs and teacups. Stores kept a hidden room with a side door for customers to enter discreetly for a drink. Law-abiding citizens carried hip flasks wherever they went, and some even installed stills in their homes. "And it is all done, apparently, in the face of popular approval, in spite of the fact that everybody knows and agrees that it is against the law," the Times observed.[83]

New York police estimated that the city had 35,000 speakeasies, including 2,200 around Wall Street.[84] Washington, D.C., had 267 licensed saloons before Prohibition, but during Prohibition had as many as 3,000 speakeasies, more than ten times the number of formerly legal drinking establishments.[85] Booze seeped through the porous Canadian border. A fleet of motorboats crossed the mile-wide Detroit River from Windsor, Ontario, for Detroit, loaded with liquor and with nothing to stop them. Rumrunners like Bill McCoy anchored ships outside the three-mile coastal limit off the coasts of the Atlantic and the Gulf of Mexico, while speedboats cruised out at night for resupply, then raced for shore. The Coast Guard was small and inadequate to patrol the entire lengthy coastline against thousands of bootleggers.

All Prohibition had effectively done was to deregulate the alcohol market. Now anyone could get in on the game. Americans still wanted to drink, and where there was supply, someone would meet that demand. With Prohibition dawned the age of the bootlegger. The money earned, largely in cash, was not taxed because it was illicit commerce.

Breweries, distilleries, and wineries around the country closed their doors, many forever. Distilleries sat idle, their rickhouses packed full of booze, which could only be removed with a license. Breweries had a bit more flexibility. Some brewers repurposed their businesses to make new products: Anheuser-Busch in St. Louis made malt extract, while Yuengling in Pennsylvania produced ice cream. Many others turned to soft drinks and yeast but with little success. Some produced near-beer, only to discover that the public was less than interested. They wanted the real thing—beer with a kick.

Washington, D.C.'s largest brewer, Christian Heurich, had completed a massive new ice plant in 1912. Selling ice was how he weathered Prohibition without laying off workers. However, his extensive brewhouse sat unused. "The buildings have been idle since 1917 when prohibition began in the District of Columbia," Heurich complained, "but I still have to pay high taxes on them."[86]

The American Medical Association had long understood that alcohol was not medicine, but once Prohibition went into effect it changed its tack, as thousands of doctors could now write prescriptions for "medicinal whiskey." Prescriptions could be filled at drugstores and pharmacies. A patient could be prescribed a pint every ten days, and doctors could write one hundred prescriptions per month. This was easily and widely abused. Drugstores such as Walgreens exploded in numbers during Prohibition as they dispensed medicinal liquor.

The alliance between suffrage and temperance led to the Eighteenth and Nineteenth Amendments going in effect in 1920. That was no historical coincidence. But now women found themselves drinking as the alliance fell apart. The younger generation of women came of age, bobbed their hair, took up smoking cigarettes, and visited speakeasies. They had equal rights now, and given that it was illegal to drink, they could break the law equally with men over cocktails. The pace of life quickened in the 1920s as America jettisoned its rural past and women were freed from time-consuming chores, thanks to household appliances like the dishwasher and washing machine.

As Prohibition approached, H. L. Mencken made preparations in his Baltimore home. He converted the cellar into a vault, then sold his automobile in December 1918 and invested the proceeds in buying liquor and wine. "The vault, in fact, was packed to the ceiling, and by the time I began to notice a shortage the severe drought that followed Prohibition was over, and the bootleggers were offering plenty of replenishments," he wrote. [87] In the first year of Prohibition, he learned that bootlegged hooch was expensive, with a case of fine whiskey going for $125. As bootleggers stepped up their activities to supply the market, the price came down. [88]

Being of German descent, Mencken was particularly fond of beer. He began home brewing in 1919, then shared his knowledge with his fellow Baltimoreans. He reminisced years later in *Heathen Days*, "My seminary was run on a sort of chain-letter plan. That is to say, I took ten pupils, and then each of the ten took ten, and so on *ad infinitum*." Mencken had no intention of obeying the law of the land; far from it—he actively and flagrantly violated dry law and encouraged others to do the same. [89]

Mencken soon learned of another easy way to fill his beer mug: transatlantic ocean liners that docked in New York harbor. He was invited to visit a foreign ship and stay into the early hours of the morning, sipping pilsner and snacking on black bread and leberwurst. "Thereafter, we visited that lovely ship every time it was in port, which was about once every five weeks," Mencken recalled. He built relations with other foreign liners "until in the end we had a whole fleet of them, and had access to Pilsner about three weeks out of four, and not only to Pilsner but also to Münchner, Dortmunder, Würzburger and Kulmbacher," all German-style beers. [90]

In June 1920, Mencken attended the Democratic national convention in San Francisco. He was at the Republican convention in Chicago weeks before, a city made surprisingly, rigidly dry—at least for a few weeks—a situation that Mencken found unforgiveable. But San Francisco was another story. He was delighted that the mayor, James Rolph, had ensured a proper supply of aged bourbon for the delegates and the press. "No matter what a delegate ordered he got Bourbon—but it was Bourbon of the very first chop, Bourbon aged in contented barrels of the finest oak, Bourbon of really ultra and super quality," Mencken crooned. "And there was no bill attached." [91]

Anti-Saloon League legislative director Wayne Wheeler attended both conventions to keep the political parties committed to Prohibition. He admitted a fault line appeared in the 1920 election, as congressmen began feeling the heat from constituents about their Volstead Act vote. Many people thought that beer and wine would still be legal, and constituents began calling for modifications to the law. Wheeler admitted, "In almost 300 Districts out of 435, candidates announced themselves unfriendly to some part of the Volstead Act." He had his hands full keeping congressmen and senators in line until his death in 1927. It was ultimately the uncompromising position of the ASL that led to its downfall. [92]

Even Congress saw no need to obey the dry law. Sure, they voted for the Eighteenth Amendment and appropriated funds to enforce the Volstead Act, but what was the harm in raising a glass on occasion? Congress got much of its business done in smoke-filled backrooms over hands of poker and glasses of whiskey. Soon after Prohibition began, congressmen and senators began looking for ways to quench their own thirst. Congressional demand soon met its supply.

Sometime in 1920, army veteran George Cassiday landed a business opportunity that would turn around his fortunes. Returning from France, Cassiday could not find work. "I tried but failed to pass the physical examination for my old railroad job. I got married, but conditions were no so good right after the war, and I could not find steady work," he wrote. One day a friend in Washington, D.C., introduced him to two Southern congressmen who asked if he could supply them with booze. Why yes, he could. Satisfied with the procured whiskey, they referred additional Congressional customers, and Cassiday soon found that business was booming. He proved so popular that he was provided an office in the Cannon House Office Building, where congressmen could find a decent supply from the "Man in the Green Hat," as Cassiday became known. It was the beginning of Cassiday's ten-year career bootlegging for Congress—a tale that he would spill in the *Washington Post* in October 1930, exposing Congressional hypocrisy. Cassiday would claim that four out of five congressmen and senators drank alcohol.[93]

Prohibition proved a Pyrrhic victory for the temperance movement, which won the political battle to change the Constitution, but ultimately lost the war to dry up the country. Despite the good intentions about creating a sober society, the national consensus was simply not there. Americans still wanted to drink. The wets would get the last laugh after nearly fourteen sort-of but not really dry years when the Twenty-first Amendment repealed Prohibition in 1933.

All that was still in the future. The citizens of 1920 had no idea that Prohibition would come to an ignominious end. In the meantime, they cultivated warm relations with bootleggers and imbibed substandard booze. H. L. Mencken humorously captured the sense of how the drinking public settled for the rotgut equivalent of hot dogs and sandwiches. "Let us, while waiting for the end of the Methodist hellenium, do the best we can," he encouraged. "Let us keep on improving the sandwich, and let us give some attention to the dog."[94]

TEN

Normalcy

After a three-year self-imposed editorial exile because of his pro-German views, H. L. Mencken penned his first article for the *Baltimore Evening Sun* in February 1920. Ever the libertarian, he complained mightily about what the Great War had cost in terms of civil liberties and personal freedom. Mencken had much spleen to vent, especially against President Wilson. "Between Wilson and his brigades of informers, spies, volunteer detectives, perjurers and complaisant judges, and the Prohibitionists and their messianic delusion, the liberty of the citizen has pretty well vanished in America," he wrote in an article called, "A Carnival of Buncombe." But he also saw hope that Americans had grown tired of the wartime impositions and just wanted things to return to normal.[1]

The country's idealism had fallen hard, descending into partisan squabbling and finger-pointing. John Carter complained in the *Atlantic Monthly* in September 1920 that "the older generation had certainly pretty well ruined this world before passing it on to us." It was now the younger generation's turn—and they would run amok with a new moral code (or lack thereof, as older Americans viewed it), visiting speakeasies, kissing before marriage and openly discussing sex, smoking cigarettes, and going on late-night car trips. The young generation grew up quickly during the war and just as quickly shed the Victorian propriety of their parents.[2]

The generation that fought the Great War became known as the "Lost Generation." They came home adrift, disillusioned, and disoriented from the experience after being told that their crusade would lead to world peace. The expression originated with the modernist writer Gertrude Stein, but was first used in print by Ernest Hemingway in *The Sun Also Rises*. The lost generation's chief spokesman was F. Scott Fitzgerald, who published his first critically acclaimed novel, *This Side of Paradise*, in 1920. He also gave the era its name: the Jazz Age. That same year, Sinclair Lewis published his novel *Main Street*, which skewered small-town America. He would repeat the deed two years later with *Babbitt*, this time taking down Midwestern values of conformity and social uplift. Scott Fitzgerald went on to catalog the growing cynicism of the era in *The Great Gatsby*, his 1925 novel modeled on the life of Cincinnati bootlegger George Remus.

A generation of young men and women who had lived through the war wrote about it in fictionalized accounts. Ernest Hemingway published *A Farewell to Arms*; John Dos Passos wrote *Three Soldiers*; while E. E. Cummings published his first book, *The Enormous Room*. All three men had served as ambulance corps drivers. Willa Cather, who witnessed the war from the safety of New York City, won the Pulitzer Prize for her 1922 wartime novel *One of Ours*.

The high cost of living, or HCL, that had paralyzed the economy and resulted in countless strikes, came crashing down. Food prices plummeted, as farmers had overplanted wheat during the war. Four million sailors and soldiers were released from service and struggled to find work, while wartime industrial production was no longer necessary. Factories that had retooled during the war now faced the expensive task of converting back to consumer production. As a result, the American economy dove into recession in 1920, but began recovering the follow year. The decade after that became known as the Roaring Twenties for the booming economy.

Baseball's reputation had been terribly tarnished after the revelations that the 1919 World Series had been fixed. The sport began to recover in 1920, when the Boston Red Sox traded away a promising player, George Herman "Babe" Ruth, to the second-rate New York Yankees. Ruth immediately began hitting home runs and electrifying fans with his dazzling fielding. He hit fifty-four home runs that first season. Ruth helped restore the public's faith in the sport. A year later, the Baby Ruth candy bar was introduced, a clear takeoff on the baseball star's name.

The year 1920 was Woodrow Wilson's last full year in the White House. He was, as Wilson biographer Scott Berg called him, "the lamest duck ever to inhabit the White House." He was still chronically ill after his stroke, and he could accomplish little in terms of legislation. The Republican Party was solidly in control of Congress. Wilson was depressed at the outcome of the Senate's Treaty of Versailles vote in March, and he had no energy for political fights.[3]

The president's health would never recover. He could walk short distances, but his left side was nearly paralyzed, and he spent much of his time in a wheelchair. Wilson took to sitting outdoors under the White House's south portico, where he could look out on the south lawn and the Washington Monument. He thought delusionally that he might run for the presidency again in 1920, but Wilson was in no condition for a campaign.

Wilson called his cabinet to meet on April 14, his first cabinet meeting in more than seven months. Josephus Daniels recorded his impressions in his diary: "He [Wilson] was seated at his desk and did not rise when we entered as was his custom. He looked fuller in the face, lips seemed thicker and face longer, but he was bright and cheerful." Secretary of the Treasury David Houston thought that Wilson "looked old, worn, and haggard." The cabinet heatedly debated Mitchell Palmer's roundup of anarchists and radicals, as well as labor unrest and the high cost of living. After a while, Edith Wilson and Dr. Grayson entered the room. Edith declared, "This is an experiment, you know," and reminded her husband that the meeting should end soon, lest it tax his recovering health.[4]

Six days later, the cabinet met again. Wilson spoke about the bitter defeat of his dream, the League of Nations. "It is dead," he said, "and lies over there. Every morning I put flowers on its grave." Wilson was politically defeated and physically shattered.[5]

William Hawkins interviewed the president in September 1920, a confidential interview only granted on the promise that Hawkins would publish none of its details. The journalist noted how much the president's health had affected his appearance. "The ravages of his long illness were visible in his face. His left arm lay helpless at his side, the fingers of the hand half clenched as if drawn permanently in that position," Hawkins wrote. "Here was the shell of a man literally burned out by the fire of his own ideal. But the mind and the ideal were still there, even if the body had broken down at the time when they most needed it."

Hawkins asked about foreign policy and current events, and Wilson discussed the men who served as secretary of state. William Jennings Bryan "has a very high forehead but he is not a high-brow," Wilson deadpanned.

"What of Lansing?" Hawkins asked.

"Oh, Lansing, he wasn't even true," the president responded regretfully.[6]

Wilson made his first public appearance in more than a year on October 27. He met with fifteen pro-League Republicans. They were stunned at how he looked, and he spoke so low that they could hardly hear him. He read a statement rehashing the lost fight for the country to join the League of Nations.[7]

Likewise, Ray Baker visited the White House in November and was shocked to see the president's decline, as he wrote in his diary: "It was dreadful. I cannot get over it yet. A broken, ruined old man, shuffling along, his left arm inert, the fingers drawn up like a claw, the left side of his face sagging frightfully. His voice is not human: it gurgles in his throat, sounds like that of an automaton. And yet his mind seems as alert as ever." Though Edith and Dr. Grayson chatted amiably, in part to keep a positive environment for the president, their patient was sullen and depressed. "At luncheon, Mrs. W. cared for him as for a baby, pinned his napkin up to his chin," Baker wrote. Yet Wilson displayed a note of humor. "You see," he told Baker, "I have to wear a bib. It does not imply bibulousness."[8]

◆

Two hundred thousand maimed and wounded American men survived the war and had to rebuild their lives. Socialist Oscar Ameringer's son was gassed and terribly wounded in the Argonne Forest. "For this and for the loss of a career as a brilliant musician, he draws a pension of one hundred dollars a month," the columnist wrote.[9] Congress consolidated federal veterans programs under the Veterans Bureau in 1921, and President Herbert Hoover later elevated it to the Veterans Administration in 1930.

Others who had experienced the war moved on with their lives. Captain Harry Truman returned to Kansas City. He was thirty-five years old and married his fiancée Bess in June 1919. He teamed up with a close friend from the army, Eddie Jacobson, to open a men's haberdashery known as Truman & Jacobson. He borrowed heavily against his family farm to buy merchandise to sell at the store. The store fell victim to the postwar economic downturn. By 1922, the business had gone bankrupt. Truman would eventually go into politics.

Conscientious objector Ernest Meyer had evaded a court-martial and was released from the army in December 1918. He noted that some 171,000 men had evaded the draft, and of the millions of men who had reported for military service, 3,989 had declared themselves conscientious objectors. Nearly ninety percent of these were religious pacifists. Some 1,300 were assigned to noncombatant jobs, another 1,200 were given farm furloughs, while 99 were assigned to the American Friends Reconstruction Unit in France. Many of the others, including Meyer, fell through the legal cracks—but 450 were court-martialed and sent to Alcatraz or Fort Leavenworth. In November 1920, the last imprisoned conscientious objectors were released, two years after the war had ended.[10]

In fact, Secretary of Defense Newton Baker recorded that 350,000 men did not register for the draft, double the estimate that Meyer gave. There was a lingering question about what to do with so many scofflaws but given their sizable numbers and the fact that the war had ended, nothing was done. [11]

After his release from the army, Meyer went to Washington, D.C. to work for the American Union Against Militarism. There were some who were calling for a permanent increase in the size of the standing army and for peacetime universal conscription. The AUAM fought against this and largely won, mailing thousands of pamphlets to influence public opinion and Congress. If they had written against the draft during wartime, they would have been declared seditious, but instead their ideas were warmly received. The plan for peacetime conscription was shelved.

Wilson considered offering amnesty and a general pardon to dissenters who were imprisoned for speaking or writing against the war. The day after the Treaty of Versailles was signed, he wrote Joe Tumulty: "It seems to me that this would not be only a generous act but a just act to accompany the signing of the peace." Tumulty relayed the opinion of Attorney General Palmer, who believed such an amnesty should wait until Wilson returned to the states. "He says there have been no convictions of people for mere expression of opinion. Every case has been a conviction for obstructing the war under statute." Palmer seems to have missed the broader point, that amnesty was about reconciliation—and that people had in fact been convicted for speaking out against the war. [12]

After the war, President Wilson pardoned numerous people, including conscientious objectors and people convicted under the Espionage Act, but there was one person he refused to forgive: Eugene Debs, the Socialist Party leader whom he had called a "traitor to his country." This was despite the fact that the chorus for pardon was loud from both the left and the right, and even within his own cabinet. [13] In the meantime Debs's confinement in the Atlanta penitentiary made him a martyr to the cause of free speech. He ran for the presidency from prison in 1920 (he won 3.4 percent of the vote) and railed against

Wilson for betraying his ideals. "It is he, not I, who needs a pardon," Debs said. President Harding partially commuted Debs's sentence on Christmas 1921.[14] Wilson was unrepentant, telling journalist Ida Tarbell, "Debs never should have been released. Debs was one of the worst men in the country."[15]

The League of Nations organized in Geneva, Switzerland, in January 1920 with forty-two founding members. The United States was not one of them. The league was not able to rectify the huge mistakes in the Treaty of Versailles, despite Wilson's insistence that it would prevent future conflicts. Later that year, Wilson received the Nobel Peace Prize for creating the league. It came with a cash prize of $40,000. He was only the second president to be awarded the prize. Theodore Roosevelt received the prize for brokering peace after the Russo-Japanese War. Two other presidents have been awarded the Nobel since: Jimmy Carter and Barack Obama.

The 1920 Election

By 1920, the doughboys had largely come home from Europe and wartime mobilization was over as the economy struggled in recession. The United States looked forward to peace and the presidential elections that fall as the Wilson era ended. The Democrats chose Ohio Governor James Cox with Franklin Delano Roosevelt as his running mate. Party leaders hoped to rope in the fame of the Roosevelt brand.

Larz Anderson, a wealthy, longtime Taft supporter, attended the GOP convention in Chicago. He was still bitter about Theodore Roosevelt splitting the Republican vote in 1912 and putting Wilson in the White House. "Lest we forget—remember that Roosevelt is directly and inexcusably to blame for the past seven years," he wrote in his diary.[16] Theodore Roosevelt should have been the Republican presidential candidate in 1920. With his death in January 1919, however, the GOP had to search for a new man. It ultimately found its candidate on the backbench, a mediocre first term senator from Ohio named Warren Gamaliel Harding. Governor Calvin Coolidge of Massachusetts was his running mate, the man who had broken the Boston Police strike.

Harding was affable and likeable, an anti-intellectual, in many ways the opposite of Woodrow Wilson. He was exactly what the country wanted in 1920. Unfortunately, he was gullible and indecisive, and had no vision for what he wanted to accomplish. And his language skills were full of malapropisms. At a speech in Boston, Harding awkwardly stated, "America's present need is not heroics but healing; not nostrums but normalcy; not revolution but restoration." He was widely derided for saying *normalcy* when he likely meant *normality*, but in fact the word already existed. Harding stumbled into a brilliant word, one that has since been regularly and widely adopted into the English language. [17] Herbert Hoover understood the appeal of normalcy: "It was just what the people wanted to do after all the emotional and other strains of the war. It was a sort of 'leave-me-alone' feeling after a fever." Normalcy was the perfect word for the postwar era. [18]

H. L. Mencken wrote pointedly about Harding's language, which he called "Gamalielese" after the president's unusual middle name: "He writes the worst English that I have ever encountered." It was frankly frustrating to a penman like Mencken, who prided himself on the appropriate use of words like boobery, Comstockery, intolerable, and Puritanism. [19] Mencken held in low esteem the ability of his fellow Americans to choose a good president. "On some great and glorious day the plain folks of the land will reach their heart's desire at last, and the White House will be adorned by a downright moron," he wrote, not prophetically, but in response to the GOP picking Harding. [20]

On June 13, the *New York Times* took the rare step of publishing a front-page editorial denouncing Harding, calling him "a very respectable Ohio politician of the second class." It went on to call him "faint and colorless," a blind follower of Senator Lodge's campaign against the League of Nations. The editorial denounced the Republican Party leadership as having lost its moral compass that guided the party in the time of Lincoln. "And for principles, they have only hatred of Mr. WILSON and a ravening hunger for the offices." [21] The *Times* would not run another such front-page editorial until 2015 on the issue of gun control.[22]

A year after the 1920 election, Joe Tumulty recalled that dubious Democrats had called on him to play the race card against Harding, claiming they had documents that proved Harding was partly black. He acted not only to discredit them, but he recommended to Wilson that they apprise the Harding campaign of this attempted smear. "If we can't win this fight by fair means, we will not attempt to win it by unfair means," Wilson responded.[23]

Edith Wilson remembered the Harding race card quite differently in her 1938 memoir, and she blamed Tumulty. She recalled the secretary racing up to the president one day. "Governor, we've got 'em beat!" Tumulty exclaimed. "Here is a paper which has been searched out and is absolutely true, showing that Harding has negro blood in him. This country will never stand for that!" The president would have none of that. "Even if that is so, it will never be used with my consent. We cannot go into a man's genealogy; we must base our campaign on principles, not on backstairs gossip. That is not only right but good politics. So I insist you kill any such proposal."[24]

Two versions of the same story by two eyewitnesses two decades apart leaves one questioning Edith's bias against Tumulty—and Tumulty's own willingness to play the race card. In any case, the rumor of Harding's African ancestry was disproved, but one rumor hung around his neck like an albatross: he had in fact sired a child out of wedlock, though DNA evidence would not prove this for certain until a century later.[25]

Despite Harding's flawed English, the allegations about his lineage, and his clear lack of leadership, he won the election by a landslide. Harding won sixty percent of the popular vote. Republicans captured supermajorities in Congress, rendering Democrats politically moot. The next decade belonged to the Republican Party, ending only with the onset of the Great Depression. It put to bed the idea of the U.S. joining the League of Nations. The country in fact would never join.

Warren Harding was perhaps the most handsome president ever to grace the Oval Office. He looked like a movie star. Looks can be deceiving of course: he was also one of the most corrupt and ineffective, and his two years and five months in office would be marked by intrigue, scandal, and finally by his own death. He was a tool for his friends' greed, who would use his presidency to loot the U.S. treasury with the Teapot Dome and numerous other scandals. H. L. Mencken called him a "tin-horn politician with the manner of a rural corn doctor and the mien of a ham actor." Historians widely consider him one of the country's worst presidents.[26]

At the final cabinet meeting on March 1, 1921, President Wilson's cabinet asked what he would do next. He rejected the idea of writing a history of his administration, as he had governed openly and believed the citizens knew everything (one might take exception to the period after his stroke). When pressed, however, he remarked, "I am going to try to teach ex-presidents how to behave," which was to stay out of the limelight, unlike the path that Theodore Roosevelt had chosen. "There will be one very difficult thing for me, however, to stand, and that is Mr. Harding's English."[27]

The cabinet members said farewell to Wilson and expressed their appreciation for working for the man. Wilson attempted to respond, but soon his lips trembled and tears welled up in his eyes. It was an unusual display of emotion for a man so self-controlled. "Gentlemen, it is one of the handicaps of my physical condition that I cannot control myself as I have been accustomed to do," he finally said in a broken voice. "God bless you all."[28]

The Cost of American Isolation

Warren Harding was sworn in as president on March 4, 1921. His inauguration speech declared that the United States would retain its isolationism, or as he described it, "the wisdom of the inherited policy of non-involvement in Old World affairs." It was a code word for the League of Nations, but also reinforced the tradition handed down from George Washington that the country should remain free of entangling alliances.[29]

A general sense of disillusionment swept across America after the Great War. Instead of high-minded rhetoric and lofty success that Wilson seemed to promise, the country was jaded from the war experience. Author Willa Cather, who had expressed such hope for world peace at the time of the Armistice, changed her worldview considerably. She wrote a letter in 1922 declaring, "It seems to me that everything has gone wrong since the Armistice. Why they celebrate that day with anything but fasts and sack-cloth and ashes, I don't know."[30] Historian Frederick Lewis Allen noted that Americans "were less concerned with making the world safe for democracy than with making America safe for themselves." The isolationists roared back, intent on keeping the U.S. from messy global politics. The country resumed its time-tested practice of go-it-alone nationalism. In the years after the war, many Americans concluded that getting involved in the Great War was a mistake.[31]

With the Senate's rejection of the Treaty of Versailles, the United States still had to make peace with Germany. The Harding administration negotiated a separate treaty that was not nearly as punitive as the treaty Wilson helped create. Peace between Germany and the U.S. was declared on November 11, 1921—the third anniversary of the Armistice. The German economy was in a tailspin, and by 1922 it was clear that the Germans would default on their reparations payments. The French occupied the industrial Ruhr district in January 1923 and held onto it through 1925. The Germans engaged in passive resistance to the French occupation, and ultimately the French yielded considerably on the reparations terms. The U.S. stepped in with a loan in 1924 so that the Germans could make their reduced reparations payment. Though the Germans had blunted the French, the Ruhr crisis was a blow to German national pride that further contributed to the rise of right-wing nationalists like the Nazis.

The Harding administration hosted the Washington Naval Conference in late 1921, which won an agreement to limit the number of battleships that the three great naval powers—Great Britain, Japan, and the United States—could build. It was designed to head off an arms race as seen between England and Germany in the decade before the Great War. It did not foresee that battleships would soon be obsolete in the face of naval aviation, a point that the acerbic and ambitious commander of the army air corps, General Billy Mitchell, sought to make. In 1921, he used airborne bombers to sink the captured German battleship SMS *Ostfriesland*. This was two decades before the Japanese attack on Pearl Harbor that made Mitchell's conclusion abundantly clear: naval air power was on the ascendancy. He was court-martialed for insubordination in 1925 and resigned from the army. Mitchell died in 1936, not living long enough to see his prophecy fulfilled, nor the creation of the U.S. Air Force as a separate branch in 1947.

Harding's scandal-plagued presidency did not survive long. He died in August 1923 during a trip to the West. Historian Frederick Lewis Allen concluded, "The Harding Administration was responsible in its short two years and five months for more concentrated robbery and rascality than any other in the whole history of the Federal Government." Vice President Calvin Coolidge was sworn in as president. [32]

Racism and xenophobia saw a resurgence in America in the 1920s, marked by a rise of the Ku Klux Klan. The previous decades had witnessed immigration that had shifted the American population toward a more racially diverse culture. Conservatives saw this as a challenge to a white-dominated, Protestant society and slammed the gates shut on new entrants. The Immigration Act of 1924 put tight limits on "undesirables" like Eastern Europeans and Italians, while banning Asian immigrants entirely. A strict quota system was established that heavily favored white western European immigrants. The law was not reformed until 1965.

Many Americans who had served in the Great War expanded their horizons. Older politicians wanted to keep America free from global entanglements, but the generation that fought the war was forever changed. When they came of age to serve in Congress, theirs had a far more expansive worldview than Senator Lodge's generation. Ernest Hemingway had gone to Europe as a naïve eighteen-year-old but returned with a kindled fire and viewed the world's citizens with equality. "There isn't going to be any such thing as 'foreigners' for me after the war now," he wrote his mother. "Just because your pals speak another language shouldn't make any difference." [33]

Meanwhile a new global threat was rising: fascism. It began in Italy, one of the sore winners at the Paris Peace Conference, where Benito Mussolini and his blackshirt *Fascisti* marched on Rome and seized power in October 1922, overthrowing the liberal government. In Germany, former army corporal Adolf Hitler decried the downward spiraling economy and above all the loss to Germany's national prestige from the Treaty of Versailles. He teamed with former General Erich Ludendorff in November 1923 to overthrow the Bavarian government in the so-called Beer Hall Putsch, modeled on Mussolini's takeover. Both Ludendorff and Hitler were arrested when the coup failed.

While in jail Hitler wrote his memoirs, *Mein Kampf*, a book that laid out exactly how he would restore Germany's national honor, conquer Europe, and exterminate the Jews. The German and Italian fascists would find common cause with another sore winner at Paris: Japan. At the core of fascist ideology was victimhood, which demagogues spun into populist resentment. These three countries resented the peace treaty—and they would steer the world into a second global cataclysm even deadlier than the first. The United States would be pulled into that world war as well after two decades of denying its role in stopping global totalitarianism. And at the end, democracy would be restored in the enemy nations as the U.S. embraced Wilsonian diplomacy.

The Retreat to S Street

W oodrow Wilson left the White House in March 1921 with a profound feeling of disappointment. The fight and failure for the Treaty of Versailles ratification had wrecked his health. He would never recover from his stroke—in fact, it would shorten his life. Wilson was unable to defend himself, his record, or what he had accomplished at Paris. By 1923, only three major countries had *not* joined the League of Nations: Germany, the Soviet Union, and the United States. The failure to ratify the Treaty of Versailles meant that the U.S. would never join the league.

As their days in the White House ran down, Edith and Woodrow Wilson made post-presidential plans. They needed to find a new home. Whereas every president had left Washington after completing his term, Wilson would be different. This was in part because of the access to the Library of Congress—Wilson hoped to write a book about government, though he never got past the dedication to Edith—but above all, because he needed access to health care. Dr. Cary Grayson would continue serving as Wilson's physician, despite being on active duty in the navy.

Edith set out looking at houses in Washington. After exploring at a number of properties, she visited a townhouse at 2340 S Street, NW in the Kalorama neighborhood, where America's wealthiest families had built mansions, and where embassies were beginning to be established. She wrote later, "I found an unpretentious, comfortable, dignified house, fitted to the needs of a gentleman's home." It was a relatively new Georgian Revival townhouse, built in 1915. The house was deceptively small from the outside but built into a hillside, and came with every modern appliance from the era, including electricity and a gas-and-coal fired stove.[1]

Trusting in his wife's judgment, Woodrow quietly purchased the house sight unseen for $150,000, then surprised her by presenting the deed. Wilson had no pension or regular source of income, so he used the cash award from the Nobel Peace Prize for the house's down payment. His financial benefactors, including Bernard Baruch, contributed the remainder, providing enough funds to add a garage and to upgrade the service elevator so Wilson could ride in it, as he could not navigate stairs.

One of the reasons the house attracted Edith was because it had a wall sufficiently large to display the Gobelin tapestry that the French had given her during the war. As it was a personal gift, rather than a gift to the White House, Edith kept it. She would hang the tapestry in the drawing room; even there it is too large, and it is rolled up slightly at the bottom.

The day that the Wilsons left the White House on March 4, 1921, they rode with incoming President Harding to the Capitol. (Two months earlier, Secretary of War Newton Baker asked Wilson if he would ride with Harding to the swearing-in ceremony. "I hope you will not go if it is a cold and sleety day," he stated. Wilson responded, "Oh that will not matter. I will wear a gas mask anyhow."[2]) Harding bounded up the steps, leaving the ailing Wilson behind to search for an elevator. He took his place in the Capitol's President's Room as representatives and senators came by the pay their respects. Shortly before noon, Wilson's senatorial foe Henry Cabot Lodge entered the room and announced, "Mr. President, we have come as a committee of the Senate to notify you that the Senate and House are about to adjourn and await your pleasure." Joe Tumulty thought the president might lash out at the man, but instead he gave the wisp of a smile and formally responded, "Senator Lodge, I have no further communication to make. I thank you. Good morning."[3]

Wilson quickly tired and was escorted to his car before the swearing in began. He joked to reporters, "Well, the Senate threw me down before, and I don't want to fall down myself again." Wilson walked slowly with a cane and a limp. The Wilsons drove down Pennsylvania Avenue, past the White House, to their new home. As they turned the corner onto S Street, they were met by a throng of five hundred well-wishers who greeted the Wilsons from both sides of the street. After lunch, Wilson appeared on the balcony to wave to the crowd a dozen times, but he declined to give a speech. A delegation entered the house to deliver flowers, and former cabinet secretaries dropped by to wish him well. It was an exhausting day for the now-former president.[4]

Along with the transport vans carrying the Wilsons' furniture was a truck bearing a special cargo: their wine collection. Prohibition had made the manufacture, sale, and transportation of alcohol illegal, but not its possession. Wilson had no desire to leave behind his collection for President Harding, who was known to throw a good party. The former president could have simply removed the wine and no one would have asked questions; however, being a man of principle, Wilson applied for the appropriate legal permits from the Prohibition Bureau to move the collection. "In the shipment was a whole barrel of fine Scotch whiskey, besides a variety of rare wines and liquors," the *New York Times* reported. Numerous outgoing cabinet members and congressmen likewise shipped their collections home with Bureau permission.[5]

Wilson's wine bottles were taken down the service staircase to the basement, where they were placed on wooden shelves for storage. Edith would continue adding to the collection during Prohibition, many of them fine French vintages, quite possibly from the connections that the Wilsons had with the French embassy. Embassies were considered foreign territory, and therefore they could import alcohol for their own use. The wine cellar still remains, a rare Prohibition-era gem.[6]

Taking care of the former president became a full-time job for a number of people. The Wilsons could no longer rely on White House staff to support them. They were now private citizens and hired two African-American servants to run the house: Isaac and Mary Scott, "the best of the old-time coloured Virginia stock," as Edith described them. The Scotts were efficient and hard-working, facing long days of attending to every detail of an ailing man and his household. Isaac was Wilson's personal manservant, and he was constantly at his side during waking hours. Mary took care of the cooking, the housekeeping, the laundry, and worked as Edith's servant.[7]

Another important staff member was Edith's brother Randolph Bolling, who functioned as the president's secretary. Randolph took the downstairs office and handled the correspondence. To look after the president at night, the Wilsons hired a nurse, who slept in the small room between Woodrow and Edith's bedrooms. Wilson had a replica of the White House's "Lincoln bed" built for his room. It was an unusually large bed to accommodate Abraham Lincoln's large height. Wilson came to appreciate its size during his lengthy illness. In his bedroom was also the brass casing from the first artillery shell that American soldiers fired in the Great War.

Wilson was bitter, depressed, and in bad health. As an invalid, he was emotionally needy and constantly demanded Edith's attention. She arranged her schedule entirely around his and did her best to cheer her husband. The Wilsons filled the house with a large number of state gifts, in particular from Wilson's months at the Paris Peace Conference. At the time, presidents could keep their gifts (today they become property of the American people). The house in essence became a museum to the Wilson presidency.

Wilson took his leather swivel chair from the Oval Office to his new home and placed it behind the desk in his library, where he spent many of his waking hours. He also brought eight thousand books into the house. Edith recalled a visitor asking her husband if he had read every book. "Not every line," he replied, "but I believe I know what is in them all." She frequently read to her husband as his eyesight steadily worsened. [8]

After Wilson woke and ate breakfast, his manservant Isaac Scott helped him shave and dress for the day. Scott accompanied Wilson down the elevator and helped him into the library, where the former president spent much of his day. With his left leg out of commission, Wilson could not wander in the large garden behind the house, but he could bask in the sunlight of the solarium adjacent to his library. Edith called her husband "a wounded eagle chained to a rock."[9] Wilson walked with a cane, which he called his "third leg." After a daily automobile drive, Scott helped Wilson change into a robe and slippers. He almost never used the formal dining room, which, he felt, would require him to dress in finer attire. He ate most of his meals in the library. [10]

Wilson enjoyed the movies, which were still silent until the end of the 1920s. In 1922, Douglas Fairbanks gave him a movie projector, and a pull-down screen was installed in the library. On occasional Saturdays, the Wilsons continued their tradition of seeing live vaudeville shows at Keith's Theatre. Dr. Grayson recalled one night the cast presented him with a huge bouquet of flowers. "We simply want to tell you that we love you dearly," a woman told him. Crowds always gathered when the former president left his home. People retained a deep affection for him. [11]

Wilson briefly went into private legal practice with former secretary of state Bainbridge Colby, but he had to recuse himself from so many cases that they dissolved the partnership. He considered running for the presidency again in 1924, a delusional idea given his precarious health. Although Wilson dreamed of publishing another book, he only wrote a short article of little consequence in the *Atlantic Monthly* called, "The Road Away from Revolution," for which he was paid $300. His essay addressed the question of the Russian Revolution and how a passionate minority managed to seize the levers of power. "The world has been made safe for democracy," he claimed, "But democracy has not yet made the world safe against irrational revolution." His answer was that the world needed more Christian charity to address societal ills and to create a just international community. [12]

After leaving the White House, Wilson only made two public appearances: the unveiling of the Tomb of the Unknown Soldier in 1921, and the funeral of his successor in 1923. Despite the use of dog tags that helped identify wounded and dead soldiers in the Great War, there were many unidentified remains. One of these was chosen for a new memorial in Arlington National Cemetery, dedicated on the third anniversary of Armistice Day. The cruiser USS *Olympia* brought the remains of the unknown soldier back from France. Among the pall-bearers were three Congressional Medal of Honor recipients: Charles Whittlesey, who had led the Lost Battalion in the Argonne Forest, Samuel Woodfill, and Alvin York. Traumatized by the deaths of his men, Whittlesey committed suicide a week later.

President Harding oversaw the tomb's dedication with General John Pershing, but first he was caught in a traffic jam as the procession attempted to cross the Potomac River when a car ran out of gas on the bridge and blocked the roadway. Former President Wilson was invited but was snubbed in the lineup, and it was a difficult, long day for him. Appreciative former soldiers gathered around Wilson's carriage. When the Wilsons finally made it home, they found their street crowded with people who wanted to see the former chief.[13]

The second public event that Wilson attended was President Harding's funeral at the White House on August 8, 1923. Harding was deeply flawed, though Wilson never publicly criticized the man's many faults or scandals. Instead, Wilson "retired into dignified silence," as Dr. Grayson called it. The day of the funeral was very hot, and Marines in their dress uniforms fainted from the heat. Though the former president maintained his dignity and did not seem bothered by the heat, he lost his cool when a colonel approached to ask a question, as Grayson recalled.

"'Could you tell me whether Senator Lodge has arrived or not?'"

"Mr. Wilson replied: 'I can not.' And then asked me what asylum that Colonel had escaped from."[14]

Cabinet members and others close to Wilson began publishing their memoirs. Ray Baker, Wilson's press secretary at Paris, wrote a 1919 apologia called *What Wilson Did at Paris*. Public relations man George Creel published *The War, the World and Wilson* in 1920, an energetic defense of Wilson's leadership that also sought to rebut John Maynard Keynes's *Economic Consequences of the Peace*. (As it turns out, Keynes was largely correct that the Treaty of Versailles was a disaster.) In 1921, Robert Lansing published *The Peace Negotiations: A Personal Narrative*, a book that made clear his divergent views from Wilson's. Baker followed his short 1919 apologia with the three-volume *Woodrow Wilson and World Settlement* in 1923, using Wilson's papers from the Paris Peace Conference. Joe Tumulty published his memoirs of his eleven years working as Wilson's private secretary in 1921, a book called *Woodrow Wilson as I Know Him*. Frank Cobb of *The World* died of cancer in December 1923, and a special collection of his most notable editorials was prepared for publication in a book. Cobb had long been a Wilson supporter, and Wilson was asked to write a short foreword. Wilson put together four sentences for the book, which came out in 1924 as *Cobb of "The World."*[15]

The former president tired quickly. Guests were limited to brief visits, though there was a constant stream of visitors. Edward House dropped by the Wilson home in October 1921, but the Wilsons were out riding, and they did not summon him back. Georges Clemenceau visited the Wilsons in December 1922. The normally grumpy former French premier was charming and pleasant. David Lloyd George likewise visited in October 1923. This came around the time that Wilson's health took a sharp decline. His eyesight worsened in his one good eye until he was nearly blind. He grew more fidgety and hypochondriacal. He grew nervous and slept less. He demanded ever more attention as his suffering increased. But he made one last public communication, this time on the budding technology known as radio.[16]

Radio broadcasting was taking off in the 1920s as the public embraced the new medium. For the fifth anniversary of the Armistice, Bernard Baruch's daughter Belle had an idea. She was a leader in the Nonpartisan League, which lobbied for America's entry into the League of Nations. She and a friend proposed that Wilson address the nation over the radio on the eve of Armistice Day. The president struggled for weeks preparing the speech. On the day of the address, a microphone was installed in the library, and the broadcast equipment was parked in the driveway. Wilson was nervous and suffered a daylong headache, but at 8:31 P.M. he stepped up to the microphone and delivered his four-minute speech. Indeed, Wilson always preferred to stand when he spoke, and this was no different. He denounced the country's retreat into isolation following the war: "We turned our backs upon our associates and refused to bear any responsible part in the administration of peace, or the firm and permanent establishment of the results of the war—won at so terrible a cost of life and treasure—and withdrew into a sullen and selfish isolation."[17]

Wilson's speech was broadcast nationally. Imagine if this radio network had been available just four years earlier when Wilson made his national barnstorming tour for the Treaty of Versailles, and how that may have spared his health. To those who had seen Wilson speak in person, hearing him on the radio must have been shocking. His voice once filled crowded halls and stadiums; now his voice was husky, and he stumbled over the words. Some heard a woman's voice quietly prompting him, possibly Edith's.[18]

The next day, November 11, thousands of people gathered outside the Wilson house, and though Wilson was exhausted, he gave a short speech giving credit to the soldiers and to Pershing for defeating the Germans. After a band played a hymn, Wilson added a triumphant postlude: "I am not one of those that have the least anxiety about the triumph of the principles I have stood for. I have seen fools resist Providence before, and I have seen their destruction, as will come upon these again, utter destruction and contempt. That we shall prevail is as sure as that God reigns." The crowd applauded the president's prophesy that the country would one day rejoin the international community.[19] They would have to wait two decades until the U.S. helped establish the United Nations in 1945 to replace the League of Nations.

The president seemed to rally in the month after the Armistice Day speech. It proved fleeting. For the former president's sixty-seventh birthday on December 28, 1923, Wilson's friends presented him with a Rolls-Royce, painted black with orange trim, the colors of Princeton University. These were the same friends who had helped cover the cost of the house and made it accessible for Wilson.[20]

In his declining months, Wilson seems to have found grace in his political defeat, knowing that he would die with his life's great work uncompleted. "I think it was best after all that the United States did not join the League of Nations," he told his daughter Margaret. When she asked why he felt this way, Wilson responded, "Because our entrance into the League at the time I returned from Europe might have been only a personal victory. Now, when the American people join the League it will be because they are convinced it is the right thing to do, and then will be the *only right* time for them to do it."[21]

In late January 1924, Dr. Grayson was worn out and planned a hunting vacation with Bernard Baruch. The last conversation that Edith recorded of her husband dealt with Grayson's weary departure and Wilson's depression. "I always feel badly now, little girl, and somehow I hate to have Grayson leave," Wilson told her. When Edith said she would run downstairs to stop the doctor from departing, Wilson stopped her. "It won't be very much longer, and I had hoped he would not desert me; but that I should not say, even to you."[22]

Over the next several days, Wilson's health rapidly declined from arteriosclerosis. Edith telegraphed Grayson, who quickly returned to Washington, and soon other doctors arrived as well. For several days the president lingered in a stupor, his body failing. Visitors dropped by to pay their respects, including former secretary Joe Tumulty. Wilson spoke his last words on Friday, February 2. "I am a broken piece of machinery. When the machinery is broken . . ." Wilson said trailing off, then added, "I am ready." Edith stepped out of the bedroom for a moment, and Wilson whispered his last word: "Edith."

The former president drifted in and out of consciousness on Saturday and Sunday as Edith, Dr. Grayson, his daughter Margaret, and brother Joseph maintained a vigil at his bedside while his heartbeat faded. At 11:15 A.M. on Sunday, February 3, Wilson briefly opened his eyes but said nothing and fell back to sleep. Edith held his right hand, while Margaret held his left. Ten minutes later his heart stopped. Wilson died peacefully in his sleep.

A crowd had gathered in front of the Wilson house for the past several days once word got out that Wilson was on his deathbed.

Minutes after Wilson's death, Dr. Grayson stepped outside to make a brief tearful statement to the press. Men removed their hats and many wept. Some knelt in prayer on the sidewalk.[23]

President Calvin Coolidge soon made a visit to the house to pay his respects. He declared an official thirty-day mourning period and for flags to be lowered to half-staff. Congress recessed for two days until after the funeral. "Saddened by the death of Woodrow Wilson, I wore a black tie," penned Carter Bealer, a federal employee, in his diary. "At the office I found that nearly everybody else wore black—the women black dresses and the men black ties. That they should all separately decide to wear black seemed to me a sign of sincere regard for the memory of Woodrow Wilson."[24]

All of the foreign embassies in Washington lowered their flags in honor of the funeral except one: the German embassy. Germany was still angry at Wilson's perceived betrayal at the Paris Peace Conference. The ambassador argued that Wilson was a private citizen. The next morning, however, a small crowd staged a protest at the German embassy. One man climbed the portico above the main entrance and hung an American flag, which the police soon took down. The Germans got the message and agreed to lower their flag to half-staff.[25]

Wilson's funeral was a private ceremony held in the home's drawing room on February 5. Edith made it clear that neither Edward House nor Senator Lodge were welcome. Most of Wilson's cabinet attended the short service, as did President Coolidge. Afterward the former president was interred at the National Cathedral, which was still under construction.

Wilson's extensive library went to the Library of Congress, as did his presidential papers. But the remaining artifacts from his presidency and his life remain in the Woodrow Wilson House. Edith understood that this was a former president's home, and so maintained it in museum-like condition. She remained in the house for another four decades until her death in 1961, then willed the house and all of its contents to the National Trust for Historic Preservation. It is today a presidential museum in Washington, D.C.

Wilson the man died, but his ideas lived on. Wilson's vision was one of grand idealism in the name of humanity and world peace, but his execution was one of overreach. He failed in his life's greatest ambition, creating the League of Nations, and his country refused to accept its global role. Ray Baker wrote in 1923 that the United States "has so far rejected its opportunity of world leadership, has considered its interests, its fears, and its rights, rather than its duties and responsibilities."[26]

Johann von Bernstorff, the former German ambassador to the United States, admired Wilson's commitment to peace but also passed the world's judgment on him. He concluded: "The man who wanted to be *Arbiter Mundi* was shattered by the magnitude of his task. Like Moses on Mount Pisgah, Wilson saw the Promised Land, but he did not reach it. The world applauded his purpose overmuch, and then passed too harsh a judgment on his want of power to carry it out."[27] In August 1939, literally days before the outbreak of World War II, the League of Nations erected the Celestial Sphere Woodrow Wilson Memorial at its Geneva headquarters, dedicated to the man who made the League possible.

The lessons from Wilson's tenure were not forgotten. A Constitutional amendment, the Twenty-fifth, specifically addressed the question of a living president no longer being able to perform the duties of the office, such as had happened after Wilson's stroke. The vice president shall serve as acting president until the president is fit to serve again. The amendment was adopted in 1967.

Faced with the crushing Great Depression, Franklin Delano Roosevelt became president in 1933 and continued Wilson's progressive agenda with the New Deal. He too would go to war, fighting the catastrophic Second World War that Wilson had warned against. Wilson's reputation staged a remarkable recovery: he had provided the model for others to follow in international diplomacy. It was FDR's successor, Harry Truman—the artilleryman who had captained a battery of French 75s—who built the institutions that would win the Cold War against the Soviet Union, largely by embracing Wilsonian diplomacy and promoting democracy abroad. The U.S. led the founding of the United Nations in 1945, the successor to the League of Nations, and this time there was little dissent as to the necessity of joining. It works to this day to mitigate conflict, though no one has yet found a way to prevent war entirely.

One lesson was not learned: in the Great War, some five thousand Germans were interned in camps. These were largely sailors and a few resident aliens who were deemed a security risk. Overall the number of detainees was fairly small, given the size of the German-American population. In World War II, however, the United States categorically detained an entire class of people—120,000 Japanese-Americans, of whom two-thirds were citizens. These people were held in concentration camps for four years, specifically targeted for their race. Although the U.S. was at war with both Germany and Italy in addition to Japan, millions of German and Italian-Americans remained free.

One crucial outcome from World War II was that the United States embraced its role as a global power, in part because the country recognized an existential threat posed by the Soviet Union and global communism. George Washington in his farewell address had warned the country against "permanent alliance," and Woodrow Wilson's framework in the League of Nations hoped to end military coalitions, but the U.S. initiated a number of alliances shortly after the war's end. Chief among them was the North Atlantic Treaty Organization, or NATO, which defended Europe from the communist threat. The U.S. became committed to its global leadership.

Thomas Marshall, the former vice president, raised the question of Wilson's legacy and America's role in the world. It is a question as relevant today as it was in the 1920s: "Some time again a great moral question will confront the people of the United States, and then again we shall have real politics. We shall have men whose convictions are strong enough to submerge their interests."[28]

Acknowledgments

N o book is ever written in a vacuum. Though the work is your own, there are many people who assist you along the way, providing insight, access to sources, and open doors. Writing *The Great War in America* has been more than just a three-year project, but a labor of love of all things history from a consequential period in American history. I am deeply grateful to a number of people for their help with this book.

Bob Enholm, the former director at the Woodrow Wilson House, was a key influence in how I interpreted Wilson's time in office. Bob described the last years of Wilson's presidency as a Greek tragedy and was fond of mentioning that Wilson envisioned the world at peace. Bob literally opened up his office and was more than patient while I ransacked through the *Papers of Woodrow Wilson*.

I have been associated with the Woodrow Wilson House since 2006 when I organized my very first walking tour, the Temperance Tour of Prohibition-related sites in the nation's capital. (If you ever visit, ask to see the house's wine cellar, which is not normally open to the public.) Over the years, since joining the advisory council, I have had the privilege of becoming acquainted with the house museum's tremendous staff: interim directors Carrie Villar and Susan Berning, the program manager Sarah Andrews, the business and operations manager John Pucher, and the many excellent docents who share a love of interpreting history. A firm thank you as well to my fellow advisory council members at the museum.

I have worked with Sarah Andrews for more than a decade, and Woodrow Wilson House is fortunate to have her. She opened many doors for me and spent hours looking through and providing photographs from the house museum's archives. Sarah also clarified the role of numerous objects in the house's 8,000-plus item collection.

Anderson House—home of the Society of the Cincinnati—has a fantastic archive, and librarian Ellen Clark was enormously helpful in helping me locate materials related to Larz and Isabel Anderson. She tells a fascinating story about learning that Larz's personal journals, long considered lost, were in the possession of one of his relatives in North Carolina. She was on the road the next day to visit the family, who very generously loaded up her car with the forty bound volumes as a gift to the Society. She rescued the diaries from oblivion.

Washington, D.C.'s largest brewer, Christian Heurich, left behind a beautiful Victorian mansion that has de facto become the district's brewing museum. Executive director Kim Bender has long been my friend, and she and her staff opened their archives so that I could quote liberally from Christian's memoirs and his wife Amelia's diaries. Not that I'm counting, but that's three books she has assisted with, starting back in 2011 with *Prohibition in Washington, D.C.*

Special thanks go to Dale Archer and David Hamon of the United States World War One Centennial Commission, and Allison Finkelstein of Arlington County's World War I Commemoration Task Force.

For all of my books, I have relied on Kenny Allen to create and design the maps. Kenny is a skilled graphic designer and always leaves me impressed. Thanks again for the collaboration, as a map is a crucial part of interpreting history.

This is my first book I've written with the privilege of having a literary agent. I fortuitously met Tom Miller of the Carol Mann Agency while on the ferry to Provincetown and signed on with him soon after that. He is a friend and a compassionate human being who has pushed me to become an ever-better writer. My thanks for championing this project and my writing career. To many more books together!

Lastly—but certainly not least—to the fine professionals at Pegasus Books, the publisher of the book in your hands. Publisher Claiborne Hancock took a chance on me, and I'll be forever grateful. Special thanks to Maria Fernandez, Jessica Case, Sabrina Plomitallo-González, and copyeditor Drew Wheeler. Charles Brock designed a brilliant, dramatic cover that conveyed both celebration and tragedy, as the Great War was a lost opportunity for peace.

To all of you, I extend my heartfelt thanks for support. And to you, the reader, my gratitude for continuing to read and love books. Keep on reading and supporting your local bookstores and libraries.

Garrett Peck
Arlington, Virginia

Bibliography

BOOKS

Ackerman, Kenneth D. *Young J. Edgar: Hoover, the Red Scare, and the Assault on Civil Liberties*. New York: Carroll & Graf, 2007.

Allen, Frederick Lewis. *Only Yesterday: An Informal History of the 1920's*. New York: Harper & Row, 1931.

Allen, Henry T. *The Rhineland Occupation*. Indianapolis: Bobbs-Merrill, 1927.

Ameringer, Oscar. *If You Don't Weaken: The Autobiography of Oscar Ameringer*. Norman: University of Oklahoma Press, 1983.

Anderson, Isabel. *Zigzagging*. Boston and New York: Houghton Mifflin, 1918.

Annual Report of the Attorney General. Washington, D.C.: U.S. Government Printing Office, 1918.

Annual Report of the Secretary of War. Vol. 1. Washington, D.C.: U.S. Government Printing Office, 1919.

Auchincloss, Louis, ed. *Theodore Roosevelt: Letters and Speeches*. New York: Library of America, 2004.

Axelrod, Alan. *Selling the Great War: The Making of American Propaganda*. New York: Palgrave MacMillan, 2009.

Baker, Newton D. *Why We Went to War*. New York: Harper & Brothers, 1936.

Baker, Ray Stannard. *What Wilson Did at Paris*. Garden City, N.Y.: Doubleday, Page, 1919.

———. *Woodrow Wilson and the World Settlement*. 3 vols. Garden City, N.Y.: Doubleday, Page, 1923.

Barkley, John Lewis. *Scarlet Fields: The Combat Memoir of a World War I Medal of Honor Hero*. Lawrence: University of Kansas Press, 2012.

Barry, John M. *The Great Influenza: The Story of the Deadliest Pandemic in History.* New York: Penguin, 2009.

Berg, A. Scott. *Wilson.* New York: Putnam, 2013.

Bernstorff, Johann Heinrich von. *Memoirs of Count Bernstorff.* New York: Random House, 1936.

————. *My Three Years in America.* New York: Scribner, 1920.

Blum, Howard. *Dark Invasion: 1915: Germany's Secret War and the Hunt for the First Terrorist Cell in America.* New York: HarperCollins, 2014.

Blumenson, Martin, ed. *The Patton Papers 1885–1940.* New York: Da Capo Press, 1998.

Boghardt, Thomas. *The Zimmermann Telegram: Intelligence, Diplomacy, and America's Entry into World War I.* Annapolis, Md.: Naval Institute Press, 2012.

Carroll, Andrew. *My Fellow Soldiers: General John Pershing and the Americans Who Helped Win the Great War.* New York: Penguin, 2017.

Chernow, Ron. *The House of Morgan: An American Banking Dynasty and the Rise of Modern Finance.* New York: Atlantic Monthly Press, 1990.

Coblentz, Edmond D. *William Randolph Hearst: A Portrait in His Own Words.* New York: Simon and Schuster, 1952.

Cooke, Alistair, ed. *The Vintage Mencken.* New York: Vintage Books, 1990.

Cooper, John Milton, Jr. *Woodrow Wilson: A Biography.* New York: Knopf, 2009.

Corder, J. Kevin and Christina Wolbrecht. *Counting Women's Ballots: Female Voters from Suffrage through the New Deal.* Cambridge: Cambridge University Press, 2016.

Craig, Lee A. *Josephus Daniels: His Life & Times.* Chapel Hill: University of North Carolina Press, 2013.

Creel, George. *The War, The World and Wilson.* New York: Harper, 1920.

Cronon, E. David, ed. *The Cabinet Diaries of Josephus Daniels: 1913–1921.* Lincoln: University of Nebraska Press, 1963.

Cummings, E. E. *The Enormous Room.* New York: Liveright Publishing, 1978.

Davenport, Matthew J. *First Over There: The Attack on Cantigny, America's First Battle of World War I.* New York: Thomas Dunne Books, 2015.

Davis, Richard Harding. *With the Allies.* New York: Charles Scribner's Sons, 1919.

Dickson, Paul. *Words from the White House.* New York: Walker, 2013.

Dilliard, Irving, ed. *Mr. Justice Brandeis, Great American.* St. Louis, Mo.: Modern View Press, 1941.

Doenecke, Justus D. *Nothing Less Than War: A New History of America's Entry into World War I.* Lexington: University Press of Kentucky, 2011.

Downing, Michael. *Spring Forward: The Annual Madness of Daylight Saving.* Washington, D.C.: Shoemaker & Hoard, 2005.

Englund, Will. *March 1917: On the Brink of War and Revolution.* New York: W.W. Norton, 2017.

Forgue, Guy J., ed. *Letters of H. L. Mencken.* Boston: Northeastern University Press, 1981.

Garraty, John A. *Henry Cabot Lodge: A Biography.* New York: Knopf, 1968.

Gavin, Lettie. *American Women in World War I: They Also Served.* Boulder: University Press of Colorado, 1997.

Geisst, Charles R. *Wall Street: A History.* New York: Oxford University Press, 2012.

Gibbons, Floyd. *And They Thought We Wouldn't Fight.* New York: George H. Doran, 1918.

Grayson, Cary T. *Woodrow Wilson: An Intimate Memoir.* New York: Holt, Rinehart and Winston, 1960.

Hagedorn, Ann. *Savage Peace: Hope and Fear in America, 1919.* New York: Simon & Schuster, 2007.

Harbord, James G. *Leaves From a War Diary.* New York: Dodd, Mead, 1925.

Harris, Stephen L. *Harlem's Hell Fighters: The African-American 369th Infantry in World War I.* Washington, D.C.: Brassey's, 2003.

Heaton, John, ed. *Cobb of "The World."* New York: Dutton, 1924.

Hemingway, Ernest. *Death in the Afternoon.* New York: Scribner, 1932.

Hodgson, Godfrey. *Woodrow Wilson's Right Hand: The Life of Colonel Edward M. House.* New Haven, Conn.: Yale University Press, 2006.

Hoover, Herbert. *The Memoirs of Herbert Hoover: The Cabinet and the Presidency 1920–1933.* New York: Macmillan, 1952.

———. *The Memoirs of Herbert Hoover: Years of Adventure 1874–1920.* New York: Macmillan, 1951.

Houston, David F. *Eight Years with Wilson's Cabinet: 1913 to 1920,* Vols. I and II. New York: Doubleday, 1926.

Hurley, Edward. *The Bridge to France.* Philadelphia: J. B. Lippincott, 1927.

Jewell, Andrew and Janis Stout, eds. *Selected Letters of Willa Cather.* New York: Knopf, 2013.

Kazin, Michael. *War Against War: The American Fight for Peace 1914–1918.* New York: Simon & Schuster, 2017.

Kerr, K. Austin. *Organized for Prohibition: A New History of the Anti-Saloon League.* New London, Conn.: Yale University Press, 1985.

Keynes, John Maynard. *The Economic Consequences of the Peace.* New York: Macmillan, 1920.

Kiplinger, W. M. *Washington is Like That.* New York: Harper & Brothers, 1942.

Lansing, Robert. *The Peace Negotiations: A Personal Narrative.* Cambridge, Mass.: Riverside, 1921.

———. *War Memoirs of Robert Lansing: Secretary of State.* New York: Bobbs-Merrill, 1935.

Larson, Erik. *Dead Wake: The Last Crossing of the Lusitania.* New York: Crown, 2015.

Lee, Hermione. *Edith Wharton.* New York: Alfred Knopf, 2007.

Lejeune, John Archer. *The Reminiscences of a Marine.* Philadelphia: Dorrance, 1930.

Lerner, Michael A. *Dry Manhattan: Prohibition in New York City.* Cambridge, Mass.: Harvard University Press, 2007.

Lewis, Tom. *Washington: A History of Our National City.* New York: Basic Books, 2015.

Liggett, Hunter. *Commanding An American Army: Recollections of the World War.* Cambridge, Mass.: Riverside Press, 1925.

———. *A.E.F.: Ten Years Ago in France.* New York: Dodd, Mead, 1927.

Link, Arthur S. ed. *The Papers of Woodrow Wilson.* 69 vols. Princeton, N.J.: Princeton University Press, 1966–1994.

Lippmann, Walter. *Liberty and the News.* Princeton, N.J.: Princeton University Press, 2008.

Lord, Alexandra M. *Condom Nation: The U.S. Government's Sex Education Campaign from World War I to the Internet.* Baltimore: The Johns Hopkins University Press, 2010.

Lowenstein, Roger. *America's Bank: The Epic Struggle to Create the Federal Reserve.* New York: Penguin, 2015.

Lubin, David M. *Grand Illusions: American Art & the First World War.* New York: Oxford University Press, 2016.

Ludendorff, Erich. *Ludendorff's Own Story: August 1914–November 1918*, Vol. II. New York: Harper & Brothers, 1919.

Luebke, Frederick C. *Bonds of Loyalty: German-Americans and World War I.* DeKalb: Northern Illinois University Press, 1974.

MacArthur, Douglas. *Reminiscences.* New York: Ishi Press International, 2010.

MacMillan, Margaret. *Paris 1919: Six Months That Changed the World.* New York: Random House, 2003.

Marshall, George C. *Memoirs of My Services in the World War 1917–1918.* Boston: Houghton Mifflin, 1976.

Marshall, Thomas R. *Recollections of Thomas R. Marshall: Vice-President and Hoosier Philosopher: A Hoosier Salad.* Indianapolis: Bobbs-Merrill, 1925.

McAdoo, William G. *Crowded Years: The Reminiscences of William G. McAdoo.* Boston and New York: Houghton Mifflin, 1931.

McCullough, David. *Truman.* New York: Simon & Schuster, 1992.

McWhirter, Cameron. *Red Summer: The Summer of 1919 and the Awakening of Black America.* New York: Henry Holt, 2011.

Mencken, H. L. *Heathen Days 1890–1936.* Baltimore: The Johns Hopkins University Press, 1996.

———. *My Life as Author and Editor.* New York: Alfred A. Knopf, 1993.

———. *Thirty-five Years of Newspaper Work.* Baltimore: Johns Hopkins University Press, 1994.

Meyer, Ernest L. *"Hey! Yellowbacks!" The War Diary of a Conscientious Objector.* New York: John Day, 1930.

Miller, Kristie. *Ellen and Edith: Woodrow Wilson's First Ladies.* Lawrence: University Press of Kansas, 2010.

Mitchell, William. *Memoirs of World War I.* New York: Random House, 1960.

Morris, James McGrath. *The Ambulance Drivers: Hemingway, Dos Passos, and a Friendship Made and Lost in War.* Boston: Da Capo Press, 2017.

Nasaw, David. *The Chief: The Life of William Randolph Hearst.* New York: Houghton Mifflin, 2000.

Neu, Charles E. *Colonel House: A Biography of Woodrow Wilson's Silent Partner.* New York: Oxford University Press, 2015.

Niven, Penelope. *Carl Sandburg: A Biography.* New York: Scribner, 1991.

O'Brien, Francis William, ed. *The Hoover-Wilson Wartime Correspondence: September 24, 1914 to November 11, 1918.* Ames: Iowa State University Press, 1974.

Ogle, Maureen. *Ambitious Brew: The Story of American Beer.* Orlando, Fla.: Harcourt, 2006.

Okrent, Daniel. *Last Call: The Rise and Fall of Prohibition.* New York: Scribner, 2010.

Orlean, Susan. *Rin Tin Tin: The Life and the Legend.* New York: Simon & Schuster, 2011.

Parson, Edwin C. *I Flew with the Lafayette Escadrille.* Indianapolis: E.C. Seale, 1963.

Peck, Garrett. *The Prohibition Hangover: Alcohol in America from Demon Rum to Cult Cabernet.* New Brunswick, N.J.: Rutgers University Press, 2009.

———. *Prohibition in Washington, D.C.: How Dry We Weren't.* Charleston, S.C.: The History Press, 2011.

Pershing, John J. *My Experiences in the World War.* 2 vols. New York: Harper & Row, 1931.

Preston, Diana. *A Higher Form of Killing: Six Weeks in World War I That Forever Changed the Nature of Warfare.* New York: Bloomsbury, 2015.

———. *Lusitania: An Epic Tragedy.* New York: Walker Publishing, 2002.

Proceedings of the 1917 Convention of the Anti-Saloon League of America. Westerville, Ohio: American Issue Publishing, 1917.

Proctor, John Clagett, ed. *Washington Past and Present: A History,* Vol. I. New York: Lewis Historical Publishing, 1930.

Puleo, Stephen. *Dark Tide: The Great Boston Molasses Flood of 1919.* Boston: Beacon Press, 2004.

Reed, John, *Ten Days That Shook the World.* New York: Vintage Books, 1960.

Remarque, Erich Maria. *All Quiet on the Western Front.* New York: Ballantine Books, 1982.

Rickenbacker, Eddie V. *Fighting the Flying Circus.* Garden City, N.Y.: Doubleday, 1965.

Rogers, Will. *Rogers-isms: The Cowboy Philosopher on the Peace Conference.* New York: Harper & Brothers, 1919.

Roosevelt, Eleanor. *This is My Story.* Garden City, N.Y.: Doubleday, 1937.

Roosevelt, Elliott, ed. *F.D.R.: His Personal Letters: 1905–1928.* New York: Duell, Sloan and Pearce, 1948.

Rorabaugh, William J. *The Alcoholic Republic: An American Tradition.* New York: Oxford University Press, 1979.

Rowley, Hazel. *Franklin and Eleanor: An Extraordinary Marriage.* New York: Farrar, Straus and Giroux, 2010.

Russell, Ina, ed. *Jeb and Dash: A Diary of Gay Life 1918–1945.* Boston: Faber and Faber, 1993.

Sandburg, Carl. *The Chicago Race Riots: July, 1919.* New York: Harcourt, Brace and Howe, 1919.

Seymour, Charles, ed. *The Intimate Papers of Colonel House.* 4 vols. Cambridge, Mass.: Riverside Press, 1926–1928.

Spanier, Sandra and Robert W. Trogdon, eds. *The Letters of Ernest Hemingway Vol. 1: 1907–1922.* New York: Cambridge University Press, 2011.

Srodes, James. *On Dupont Circle: Franklin and Eleanor Roosevelt and the Progressives Who Shaped Our World.* Berkeley, Calif.: Counterpoint, 2012.

Sterling, Bryan B. and Frances N. Sterling, eds. *A Will Rogers Treasury.* New York: Crown Publishers, 1982.

Steuart, Justin. *Wayne Wheeler: Dry Boss.* New York and Chicago: Fleming H. Revell Company, 1928.

Tuchman, Barbara W. *The Guns of August: The Outbreak of World War I.* New York: Random House, 2014.

———. *The Zimmermann Telegram: America Enters the War, 1917–1918.* New York: Random House, 2014.

Tumulty, Joseph P. *Woodrow Wilson as I Know Him.* New York: Doubleday, Page, 1921.

Walker, William. *Betrayal at Little Gibraltar: A German Fortress, a Treacherous American General, and the Battle to End World War I.* New York: Scribner, 2016.

Weinstein, James. *The Decline of Socialism in America, 1912–1925.* New Brunswick, N.J.: Rutgers University Press, 1984.

Weisman, Steven R. *The Great Tax Wars.* New York: Simon & Schuster, 2002.

Wilkerson, Isabel. *The Warmth of Other Suns: The Epic Story of America's Great Migration.* New York: Vintage Books, 2010.

Wilson, Edith Bolling. *My Memoir.* New York: Bobbs-Merrill, 1938.

Woodward, David R. *The American Army and the First World War.* Cambridge: Cambridge University Press, 2014.

Yockelson, Mitchell. *Forty-seven Days: How Pershing's Warriors Came of Age to Defeat the German Army in World War I.* New York: NAL Caliber, 2016.

JOURNAL, DIARIES, AND MANUSCRIPTS

Anderson, Larz III. *Journal, 1920.* Society of the Cincinnati Library, Washington, D.C.

Heurich, Amelia. Personal diary, Heurich House Museum, Washington, D.C.

Heurich, Christian. *From My Life: 1842–1934.* Trans. and ed. Eda Offutt, 1985. Washington, D.C.: privately published, 1934.

———. *I Watched America Grow,* as told to W.A.S. Douglas, Washington, D.C., self-published, 1942.

ONLINE SOURCES

Harry Truman World War I correspondence, www.trumanlibrary.org.

Holmes, Oliver Wendell, *Schenck v. United States 249 U.S. 47,* Opinion, March 3, 1919. Legal Information Institute. www.law.cornell.edu.

"Inflation and CPI Consumer Price Index 1913–1919," www.inflationdata.com.

Mencken, H. L. "Ludendorff," *Atlantic Monthly,* June 1917, www.theatlantic.com.

Okrent, Daniel. "Wayne B. Wheeler: The Man Who Turned Off the Taps," *Smithsonian Magazine*, May 2010, www.smithsonianmag.com.

"Robert La Follette's 'Free Speech in Wartime,'" www.nolo.com.

Trickey, Erick. "Fake News and Fervent Nationalism Got a Senator Tarred as a Traitor During WWI," October 19, 2017, www.smithsonian.com.

U.S. census 1910 and 1920, www.census.gov.

PERIODICALS

Carter, John F. "These Wild Young People," *Atlantic Monthly*, September 1920: 301–4.

"Civil Liberty Dead," *The Nation*, September 14, 1918: 382.

Du Bois, W.E.B. "Returning Soldiers," *The Crisis*, May 1919: 13.

Lewis, Reuben A. "How the United States Takes Care of German Prisoners," *Munsey's Magazine*, Vol. 64, June to September, 1918: 137–45.

Olds, Frank Perry. "Disloyalty of the German-American Press," *Atlantic Monthly*, July 1917: 136–40.

Palmer, A. Mitchell. "The Vast Amount of Enemy Property in the United States," *Munsey's Magazine*, Vol. 64, No. 2, July 1918: 233–38.

Pattullo, George. "The Second Elder Gives Battle," *The Saturday Evening Post*, April 26, 1919: 1–4.

Posselt, Erich. "Prisoner of War No. 3598," *American Mercury*, July 1927: 313–23.

Steiner, Edward A. "Wrong Strategy," *Outlook*, January 2, 1918: 14–15.

Wilson, Woodrow. "The Road Away from Revolution," *Atlantic Monthly*, August 1923: 395–98.

NEWSPAPER ARTICLES

"1 Dead, Many Hurt in Cleveland Riot," *New York Times*, May 2, 1919.

"12 Killed When Tank of Molasses Explodes," *New York Times*, January 16, 1919.

"27 Ships Taken Here," *New York Times*, April 7, 1917.

"73 Red Centres Raided Here by Lusk Committee," *New York Times*, November 9, 1919.

"40,000 Applaud Wilson as He Pledges Anew to Uphold Nation's Rights," *Washington Post*, March 6, 1917.

"60,187 Men Taken in Slacker Raids," *New York Times*, September 8, 1918.

"Alice Paul Sentenced," *New York Times*, October 23, 1917.

"All Germans Here Under New Watch," *New York Times*, November 20, 1917.

"Allies Must First Consult," *New York Times*, December 13, 1916.

"America Enrolls Today for the Fight," *New York Times*, June 5, 1917.

"Americans Exhausted After Four Day Siege," *New York Times*, October 10, 1918.

"Americans Rescued from Enemy Trap," *New York Times*, October 9, 1918.

"Army Bill Signed by the President," *New York Times*, June 4, 1916.

"Army Draft Ends by Baker's Order," *New York Times*, November 12, 1918.

"Arrest Four More Pickets," *New York Times*, October 21, 1917.

"Arrest Karl Muck as an Enemy Alien," *New York Times*, March 26, 1918.

"Arrest Rumely; Say Germany Owns the Evening Mail," *New York Times*, July 9, 1918.

"Asked Wilson's Support," *New York Times*, February 11, 1916.

"Asks to End Outrages," *Washington Post*, August 22, 1917.

"Auto Causes Huge Tangle in Traffic," *Evening Star*, November 11, 1921.

Baker, Peter. "DNA Shows Warren Harding Wasn't America's First Black President," *New York Times*, August 18, 2015.

"Battalion Spurned Offer of Safety," *New York Times*, October 11, 1918.

"Big Raid on I.W.W. and Socialists; Haywood Taken," *New York Times*, September 6, 1917.

"Billy Sunday Fires Hot Shot at Kaiser," *New York Times*, February 19, 1918.

"Billy Sunday Speeds Barleycorn to Grave," *New York Times*, January 17, 1920.

"Bomb Exploded in the Capitol," *New York Times*, July 3, 1915.

"Bomb Kills Six, Injures Scores in Defense Parade," *New York Times*, July 23, 1916.

"Boston 'Peace' Parade Mobbed," *New York Times*, July 2, 1917.

"Both Safe, Say Captains," *New York Times*, July 8, 1915.

"Brisbane Tells of Brewers' Help," *Evening Star*, December 6, 1918.

"Bureau to Defend Lovers of Peace," *New York Times*, July 3, 1917.

"Burleson Tells Newspapers What They May Not Say," *New York Times*, October 10, 1917.

"Calls Post Factor in Revolution Plan," *New York Times*, June 2, 1920.

Cassiday, George. "Cassiday, Capitol Bootlegger, Got First Rum Order From Dry," *Washington Post*, October 24, 1930.

"Censorship at an End," *New York Times*, November 15, 1918.

"Change in Time Begins Tomorrow," *New York Times*, March 30, 1918.

"City Goes Wild with Joy," *New York Times*, November 8, 1918.

"Coffins Short in District; Aid Asked from Outside," *Washington Post*, October 10, 1918.

"Col. House Calls, Wilson Not at Home," *New York Times*, October 14, 1921.

"Colonel Denounces Wilson Peace Views," *New York Times*, January 23, 1917.

"Comment of Today's Newspapers on the President," *New York Times*, April 3, 1917.

"Confer in White House," *New York Times*, August 20, 1919.

"Congress United in Support," *New York Times*, February 4, 1917.

"Dead Hero Borne from Capitol to Last Resting Place in Burst of Glory and Patriotic Fever," *Evening Star*, November 11, 1921.

"Debs, Unrepentant, Denounces Wilson," *New York Times*, February 2, 1921.

"Defense and Loyalty Keynotes of the President's Address," *New York Times*, December 8, 1915.

"The Defense of America," *Washington Post*, February 20, 1917.

"Denounce League as War Promoter in Lodge Report," *New York Times*, September 11, 1919.

"Deportation Methods Denounced by Taft," *New York Times*, May 2, 1920.

"Draft Camps Open," *New York Times*, September 9, 1917.

"Draft Raids Here Anger Senators," *New York Times*, September 6, 1918.

"Embassies Lower Flags; Germans Display None," *Washington Post*, February 5, 1924.

"Enemy Propaganda Backed by Brewers," *New York Times*, November 21, 1918.

"Espionage Bill is Signed," *New York Times*, June 16, 1917.

"Family is Gassed in D.C. Home When Tear Bomb Breaks," *Washington Times*, August 4, 1918.

"'Fight,' Says Bryan, 'To Last, If Invaded,'" *New York Times*, February 3, 1917.

"'Flu' Deaths Climb," *Washington Post*, October 19, 1918.

"Flynn Prepares Big Haul of Reds," *New York Times*, June 19, 1919.

"Food Administration Adopts Mrs. F. D. Roosevelt's Plan as Model," *New York Times*, July 17, 1917.

"Ford Hopes Troops Will Start a Strike," *New York Times*, November 30, 1915.

"Former Senator Scott is Affected by Gas," *Evening Star*, August 5, 1918.

Fox, Albert W. "President Holds Gain; Improvement Not Yet Decisive, Grayson Says," *Washington Post*, October 5, 1919.

"Funds to Purchase Times Came from Group of Brewers," *Evening Star*, September 19, 1918.

"Garrison Favors Universal Service," *New York Times*, January 8, 1916.

"Gave Fortune to German Red Cross," *Evening Star*, March 10, 1918.

"German-Americans Urged to Be Loyal," *New York Times*, February 10, 1917.

"German Alliance Branded as Cloak for Propaganda," *New York Times*, February 24, 1918.

"German Brewers Buy Big Newspaper," *New York Times*, September 15, 1918.

"German Embassy Issues Warning," *New York Times*, May 1, 1915.

"German Embassy to Pay Flag Tribute to Wilson," *Washington Post*, February 6, 1924.

"German Ships Meet Our Transport Needs," *New York Times*, April 7, 1917.

"German Ships Seized by the Government," *New York Times*, April 7, 1917.

"Germany Wars Against the World, *New York Times*, February 1, 1917.

"Germany's Last Word," *New York Times*, August 19, 1914.

"Germany's Nightmare," *New York Times*, June 1, 1915.

"Germany's Peace Note," *New York Times*, December 13, 1916.

"Gold Cruiser to Sail Today," *New York Times*, August 6, 1914.

Grasty, Charles H. "House Slipped Quietly Away from Paris," *New York Times*, January 22, 1918.

"The Gun Epidemic," *New York Times*, December 5, 2015.

"Halt Senate Action Upon Slacker Raids," *New York Times*, September 7, 1918.

"Hang Suffrage Banner as Wilson Speaks," *New York Times*, December 6, 1916.

"Harding for World Court," *New York Times*, March 5, 1921.

"Heard Over a Wide Area," *New York Times*, November 11, 1923.

"Heir to Austria's Throne is Slain with His Wife by a Bosnian Youth to Avenge Seizure of His Country," *New York Times*, June 29, 1914.

"Henry Mencken Cables Story of 'Ticklish Moments' in Berlin," *Baltimore Sun*, March 6, 1917.

"Holt is Muenter, Say Associates," *New York Times*, July 5, 1915.

"House for Suffrage, 274 to 136," *New York Times*, January 11, 1918.

"How Germany has Worked in U.S. to Shape Opinion," *New York World*, August 15, 1915.

"How Peace Struck Man in the Street," *New York Times*, November 12, 1918.

"Hughes Condemns Lynching of Negro," *New York Times*, May 6, 1919.

"Hunger Striker is Forcibly Fed," *New York Times*, November 9, 1917.

"Huns Sink Four Barges, Burn Tug at Cape Cod," *Evening Star*, July 22, 1918.

"The Hylan Plot Exposed," *New York Times*, October 31, 1917.

"Immigration Bill Enacted Over Veto," *New York Times*, February 6, 1917.

"Indiana Sergeant Fired First Shot," *New York Times*, October 31, 1917.

"Influenza Stops Flow to the Camps of Drafted Men," *New York Times*, September 27, 1918.

"Inspected by Officials," *New York Times*, July 11, 1916.

"Intruder Has Dynamite," *New York Times*, July 4, 1915.

"Jails are Waiting for Them," *New York Times*, July 4, 1917.

"John Barleycorn Died Peacefully at the Toll of 12," *New York Times*, January 17, 1920.

"Kaiser's Picture Torn Down," *Baltimore Sun*, March 19, 1917.

Kelly, John. "Answer Man Remembers the 'Temporary' Office Buildings That Once Blighted D.C.," *Washington Post*, January 8, 2017.

"La Follette Faces a Threat of Arrest," *New York Times*, September 22, 1917.

"Lansing Admits Shantung Dissent," *New York Times*, August 7, 1919.

"Lansing Quits After Clash," *New York Times*, February 14, 1920.

"Lansing Tells the World of Purpose to Arm Ships and Supply Navy Gunners," *New York Times*, March 13, 1917.

"Last Rites for Wilson to Be Held Wednesday; Funeral to Be Private," *Evening Star*, February 4, 1924.

"Lawyers Denounce Raids on Radicals," *New York Times*, May 28, 1920.

"League to Enforce Peace is Launched," *New York Times*, June 18, 1915.

"Letter Received by the Star Thought to Have Bearing on the Explosion," *Evening Star*, July 3, 1915.

"Lieut. Roosevelt Falls in Fair Fight, Believed Killed," *New York Times*, July 18, 1918.

"Lodge Addresses Senate," *New York Times*, December 22, 1918.

"Lodge Demands a Dictated Peace, Won by Victory," *New York Times*, August 24, 1918.

"Lodge Knocks Down Pacifist Assailant," *New York Times*, April 3, 1917.

"Lodge Outlines Five Reservations to League Plan," *New York Times*, August 13, 1919.

"Lodge Resolution Beaten," *New York Times*, November 20, 1919.

"The Lost Battalion," *New York Times*, October 12, 1918.

"Louis Post Defends Rulings on Aliens," *New York Times*, May 9, 1920.

"Loyalty and Peace Parades Stopped," *Evening Star*, March 30, 1917.

"Lynch Negro Who Confessed Crime," *New York Times*, June 27, 1919.

MacAdam, George. "Ebb of Pacifism in America," *New York Times*, December 23, 1917.

"Making a Joke of Prohibition in New York City," *New York Times*, May 2, 1920.

"Malone Waits Up All Night," *New York Times*, April 6, 1917.

"May Prosecute Ship Lines That Blacklist Goods," *New York Times*, July 20, 1916.

McCann, Erin. "Solving a Mystery Behind the Deadly 'Tsunami of Molasses' of 1919," *New York Times*, November 26, 2016.

"Mencken, at Kirkwall, Sees Searching of Ships," *Baltimore Sun*, February 14, 1917.

Mencken, H. L. "A Carnival of Buncombe," *Baltimore Evening Sun*, February 9, 1920.

———. "A Gang of Pecksniffs," *Baltimore Evening Sun*, May 2, 1922.

———. "Bayard vs. Lionheart," *Baltimore Evening Sun*, July 26, 1920.

———. "'The Diary of a Retreat': Dark Days for Americans," *Baltimore Sun*, March 14, 1917.

———. "'The Diary of a Retreat;' In Sunny Spain at Last," *Baltimore Sun*, March 20, 1917.

———. "Gamalielese," *Baltimore Evening Sun*, March 7, 1921.

———. "Hot Dogs," *Baltimore Evening Sun*, November 4, 1929.

———. "Lodge," *Baltimore Evening Sun*, June 15, 1920.

———. "Negro Spokesman Arises to Voice His Race's Wrongs," *New York Evening Mail*, September 19, 1917.

———. "The Woman of Tomorrow," *New York Evening Mail*, May 2, 1918.

"Militants Freed at Wilson's Word," *New York Times*, July 20, 1917.

"Millions of Persons Heard and Felt Shock," *New York Times*, July 31, 1916.

"Mobilization for Tonight," *Washington Post*, July 20, 1919.

"Mr. Bryan Sounds Knell of Liquor at Midnight Hour," *Evening Star*, January 17, 1920.

"Munition Explosions Cause Loss of $20,000,000," *New York Times*, July 31, 1916.

"Must Exert All Our Power," *New York Times*, April 3, 1917.

"Nation to Operate the Cape Cod Canal," *New York Times*, July 24, 1918.

"Nation-wide Joy Result of Hoax," *Evening Star*, November 8, 1918.

"N.B. Scott, 'Gassed,'" *Washington Post*, August 4, 1918.

"Negroes Attack Girl—White Men Vainly Pursue," *Washington Post*, July 19, 1919.

"Negro Regulars Riot Near Houston, Texas," *New York Times*, August 24, 1917.

"New York Ready for Big Parade," *New York Times*, May 13, 1916.

"Night Attack on Border," *New York Times*, March 10, 1916.

"The Nomination of Harding," *New York Times*, June 13, 1920.

"No Time to Think of Peace," *New York Times*, August 9, 1918.

"Offer T.R. Chance to Fight," *New York Times*, May 16, 1915.

"On Display for All to See," *Washington Post*, June 27, 1997.

"The Order to Shut Down Industries and Save Fuel," *New York Times*, January 18, 1918.

Oulahan, Richard V. "Wilson Cables the Navy," *New York Times*, April 7, 1919.

"Ovation to the President," *New York Times*, July 11, 1919.

"Pabst Charge is Filed," *Milwaukee Journal*, February 13, 1918.

"Pacifist Crusaders Fail to Fill Trains," *New York Times*, April 2, 1917.

"Pacifist Professor Gets Year in Prison," *New York Times*, October 31, 1918.

"Pacifist's Apology Procures Release," *Evening Star*, April 3, 1917.

"Palmer Submits Documents About Times Purchase," *Evening Star*, September 20, 1918.

"Palmer Warns Reds They Cannot Succeed," *New York Times*, June 18, 1919.

"Patriot Legions to Visit Capital," *New York Times*, March 31, 1917.

"Pershing Won Fame in Moro Campaigns," *New York Times*, May 19, 1917.

Philpott, A. J. "Biggest Art Colony in the World in Provincetown," *Boston Globe*, August 27, 1916.

"'Picket' White House," *Washington Post*, January 10, 1917.

"Plans for National Army," *New York Times*, May 19, 1917.

"Pledge Loyalty to U.S.," *Washington Post*, March 29, 1917.

"Police Lower Flag Nailed at Entrance of German Embassy," *Washington Post*, February 7, 1924.

"Police Protect Pickets," *New York Times*, August 17, 1917.

"Possibly Three U-Boats," *New York Times*, October 9, 1916.

"President Approves the Shipping Bill," *New York Times*, September 8, 1916.

"President Demands That Lynchings End," *New York Times*, July 27, 1918.

"The President Goes to France," *New York Times*, November 19, 1918.

"President Leads Red Cross Parade," *New York Times*, May 19, 1918.

"President Marches Up Avenue at Head of 60,000 Paraders," *Evening Star*, June 14, 1916.

"President Vetoes Daylight Repeal," *New York Times*, August 16, 1919.

"President's Aims Widen," *New York Times*, November 20, 1918.

"President's Final Shot is Resented by Congressmen," *Evening Star*, March 5, 1919.

"President's Proclamation of a State of War, and Regulations Governing Enemy Aliens," *New York Times*, April 7, 1917.

"The President's Triumph," *New York Times*, January 11, 1918.

"Pro-Leaguers See Wilson," *New York Times*, October 28, 1920.

"Proclamation by the President," *Evening Star*, November 11, 1918.

"Prohibition to Cause Hip Pockets to Shrink," *Evening Star*, January 10, 1920.

"Race Rioters Fire East St. Louis," *New York Times*, July 3, 1917.

"Renew Compromise Talk," *New York Times*, November 18, 1919.

"Report Six Killed in Sailor-Negro Riot," *New York Times*, May 11, 1919.

"Rhine Must Be Held, Says Marshal Foch," *New York Times*, April 19, 1919.

"Ridder Repudiates Zimmermann Plot," *New York Times*, March 4, 1917.

"Roosevelt Assails President's Speech," *New York Times*, December 4, 1918.

"Roosevelt for Prompt Action," *New York Times*, May 12, 1915.

"Roosevelt Regrets President's Action," *New York Times*, October 14, 1918.

"Roosevelt Renews Attack on Wilson," *New York Times*, January 29, 1917.

Ruane, Michael E. "An American Filmed the German Army in WWI," *Washington Post*, February 7, 2017.

"Rumely Sentenced to Year and a Day," *New York Times*, December 21, 1920.

"Rumor Busy About Wilson," *New York Times*, October 13, 1919.

"Says Dr. Hexamer is Kaiser's Deputy," *New York Times*, February 25, 1918.

"Says Wilson Feared Aim to Replace Him," *New York Times*, February 15, 1920.

"Sea Visitor Unheralded," *New York Times*," October 8, 1916.

"Secretary Lansing's Two Statements Regarding Peace Note to Belligerents," *New York Times*, December 22, 1916.

"Seize 20,000 Here in Slacker Search," *New York Times*, September 4, 1918.

"Senate Calls on Palmer to Reveal Brewers' 'Deal,'" *Evening Star*, September 19, 1918.

"Senate Caucus Votes at Albany for Prohibition," *New York Times*, January 28, 1919.

"Senate Passes Food Control Bill by Vote of 66 to 7," *New York Times*, August 9, 1917.

"Senate Passes Prohibition Bill," *New York Times*, November 19, 1918.

"Senate Questions Absentee Powers," *Evening Star*, December 3, 1918.

"Senators See President," *New York Times*, December 6, 1919.

"Ships' Frames Damaged," *New York Times*, April 7, 1917.

"The Sinking of the Lusitania," *Baltimore Sun*, May 8, 1915.

"Sixty Day Crisis in Food Faces Us, Asserts Hoover," *New York Times*, February 22, 1918.

"Soldiers in Khaki Storm Socialist Meeting in Garden," *New York Times*, November 26, 1918.

"Soldiers Riot at Bolshevist Rally," *New York Times*, November 27, 1918.

"Stamping Out Treason," *Washington Post*, April 12, 1918.

"Stirring Up Anti-German Feeling," *Morning Olympian*, March 9, 1917.

"Suffrage Statue Moved," *Washington Post*, September 24, 1921.

"Suffrage Statue Moves," *New York Times*, February 14, 1922.

"Suffragists Take 60-Day Sentence, Won't Pay Fines," *New York Times*, July 18, 1917.

Sullivan, Patricia. "Prague Honors Woodrow Wilson with Statue," *Washington Post*, October 4, 2011.

"Summoning of President's Ship is Interpreted as Meaning Prompt Action in Case of Deadlock," *New York Times*, April 8, 1919.

"The Suspended Socialists," *New York Times*, January 9, 1920.

"Teuton Propaganda Against U.S.," *Evening Star*, February 24, 1918.

"Text of the Armistice Terms Told Congress by President," *Evening Star*, November 11, 1918.

"Text of the White House Announcement of the Makeup of the Peace Delegation," *New York Times*, November 30, 1918.

"This Nation's Gratitude," *Washington Bee*, July 26, 1919.

"Thousands Engage in Riot," *New York Times*, September 29, 1919.

"Tons of Data Go with Wilson Party," *New York Times*, December 4, 1918.

"Took German Ships to Protect Ports," *New York Times*, February 8, 1917.

"A Tory and the Curse of Meroz," *New York Times*, January 30, 1917.

"Troops Fight Race Rioters in Knoxville," *New York Times*, September 1, 1919.

"Truce Electrifies Congress," *New York Times*, November 12, 1918.

"Unity Plea by Alliance," *New York Times*, April 13, 1918.

"Wall Street Explosion Kills Thirty; Injures 300," *New York Times*, September 17, 1920.

"War President's End Came Peacefully," *New York Times*, February 4, 1924.

"War by Assassination," *New York Times*, May 8, 1915.

"War Problems Shifting," *New York Times*, January 29, 1918.

"'War' Prohibition," *New York Times*, November 20, 1918.

"Washington Crowd Eggs Suffragettes," *New York Times*, July 15, 1917.

"Washington Exposes Plot," *New York Times*, March 1, 1917.

"Washington Hears Often," *New York Times*, December 6, 1918.

"Washington Police Bar Pacifist Parade," *New York Times*, March 30, 1917.

"White Sox Again Defeated by Reds," *New York Times*, October 3, 1919.

"Wilhelmina Cargo Seized by British," *New York Times*, February 12, 1915.

"Will Deport Only Real Communists," *New York Times*, April 10, 1920.

"Will Deport Reds as Alien Plotters," *New York Times*, November 9, 1919.

"Will Not Send Roosevelt," *New York Times*, May 19, 1917.

"Wilson Backs Amendment for Woman Suffrage," *New York Times*, January 10, 1918.

"Wilson Braves Rain, Makes War Speech," *Washington Post*, June 15, 1917.

"Wilson By Radio Calls Our Attitude 'Ignoble, Cowardly,'" *New York Times*, November 11, 1923.

"Wilson Likely to Sign the Resolution This Afternoon, Bringing Conflict Officially with Germany," *Washington Post*, April 6, 1917.

"Wilson Not Welcome to All," *New York Times*, November 27, 1918.

"Wilson Overcome Greeting Pilgrims; Predicts Triumph," *New York Times*, November 12, 1923.

"Wilson Signs Bill to Make Country 'Dry' From July 1 Until Army is Demobilized," *New York Times*, November 22, 1918.

"Wilson Takes Oath; Sworn Again Today," *Washington Post*, March 5, 1917.

"Wilson Vouches for German Plot Note," *Washington Post*, March 2, 1917.

"Wilson's Exit is Tragic," *New York Times*, March 5, 1921.

"Wilson's Stock of Liquor is Moved," *New York Times*, March 5, 1921.

"World Peace Plan Outlined by Taft," *New York Times*, June 17, 1915.

"Would Vacate Wilson's Office," *New York Times*, December 3, 1918.

"Zeal for Peace May Complicate, Says Mr. Lodge," *Evening Star*, February 28, 1919.

"Zimmermann Defends Act," *New York Times*, March 4, 1917.

Endnotes

INTRODUCTION

1   John J. Pershing, *My Experiences in the World War*, Vol. I (New York: Harper & Row, 1931), xvii.

2   Ibid., 168.

ONE: THE GREAT WAR

1   "Heir to Austria's Throne is Slain with His Wife by a Bosnian Youth to Avenge Seizure of His Country," *New York Times*, June 29, 1914.

2   Herbert Hoover, *The Memoirs of Herbert Hoover: Years of Adventure 1874–1920* (New York: Macmillan, 1951), 166.

3   *The Intimate Papers of Colonel House*, Vol. I. Charles Seymour, editor (Cambridge, Mass.: Riverside Press, 1926), 255.

4   Ibid., 249.

5   Ibid., 282.

6   Ibid., 10.

7   George Creel, *The War, The World and Wilson* (New York: Harper, 1920), 32–33.

8   Will Rogers, *Rogers-isms: The Cowboy Philosopher on the Peace Conference* (New York: Harper & Brothers, 1919), 12.

9   *The Intimate Papers of Colonel House*, Vol. I. Charles Seymour, editor (Cambridge, Mass.: Riverside Press, 1926), 114–15.

10   Newton D. Baker, *Why We Went to War* (New York: Harper & Brothers, 1936), 101–2.

11 Elliott Roosevelt, editor, *F.D.R.: His Personal Letters: 1905–1928* (New York: Duell, Sloan and Pearce, 1948), 233.

12 Charles R. Geisst, *Wall Street: A History* (New York: Oxford University Press, 2012), 141.

13 John Heaton, editor, *Cobb of "The World"* (New York: Dutton, 1924), 253–54.

14 "Germany's Last Word," *New York Times*, August 19, 1914.

15 Richard Harding Davis, *With the Allies* (New York: Charles Scribner's Sons, 1919), xiv.

16 Herbert Hoover, *The Memoirs of Herbert Hoover: Years of Adventure 1874–1920* (New York: Macmillan, 1951), 198.

17 Johann Heinrich von Bernstorff, *My Three Years in America* (New York: Scribner, 1920), 54.

18 "Gold Cruiser to Sail Today," *New York Times*, August 6, 1914.

19 Amelia Heurich diary, July 25, 1914.

20 Christian Heurich, *I Watched America Grow*, Book Three, as told to W.A.S. Douglas, Washington, D.C., unpublished manuscript, 1942.

21 Herbert Hoover, *The Memoirs of Herbert Hoover: Years of Adventure 1874–1920* (New York: Macmillan, 1951), 156.

22 Ibid., 170.

23 *The Hoover-Wilson Wartime Correspondence: September 24, 1914 to November 11, 1918*, Francis William O'Brien, editor. (Ames: Iowa State University Press, 1974), 5.

24 Herbert Hoover, *The Memoirs of Herbert Hoover: Years of Adventure 1874–1920* (New York: Macmillan, 1951), 201–2.

25 Garrett Peck, *Prohibition in Washington, D.C.: How Dry We Weren't* (Charleston, S.C.: The History Press, 2011), 122.

26 Hermione Lee, *Edith Wharton* (New York: Alfred Knopf, 2007), 461.

27 Herbert Bruce Brougham, memorandum, December 14, 1914, in Arthur S. Link, editor, *The Papers of Woodrow Wilson*, vol. 31 (Princeton, N.J.: Princeton University Press, 1979), 458–60.

28 Charles R. Geisst, *Wall Street: A History* (New York: Oxford University Press, 2012), 121.

29 Roger Lowenstein, *America's Bank: The Epic Struggle to Create the Federal Reserve* (New York: Penguin, 2015), 262.

30 Steven R. Weisman, *The Great Tax Wars* (New York: Simon & Schuster, 2002), 1.

31 Cary T. Grayson, *Woodrow Wilson: An Intimate Memoir* (New York: Holt, Rinehart and Winston, 1960), 19.

32 Johann Heinrich von Bernstorff, *My Three Years in America* (New York: Scribner, 1920), 27, 28.

33 Joseph P. Tumulty, *Woodrow Wilson as I Know Him* (New York: Doubleday, Page & Co., 1921), xii.

34 Ibid., xiii.

ENDNOTES

35   David F. Houston, *Eight Years with Wilson's Cabinet: 1913 to 1920*, Vol. II (New York: Doubleday, 1926), 174, 183.

36   H. L. Mencken, "Negro Spokesman Arises to Voice His Race's Wrongs," *New York Evening Mail*, September 19, 1917.

37   Justus D. Doenecke, *Nothing Less Than War: A New History of America's Entry into World War I* (Lexington: University Press of Kentucky, 2011), 300.

38   Lee A. Craig, *Josephus Daniels: His Life & Times* (Chapel Hill: University of North Carolina Press, 2013), 216–18.

39   Ibid., 245.

40   Ibid., 89–90.

41   Paul Dickson, *Words from the White House* (New York: Walker, 2013), 95–96.

42   "The Archangel Woodrow," *The Smart Set*, January 1921, in *The Vintage Mencken*, gathered by Alistair Cooke (New York: Vintage Books, 1990), 116.

43   Guy J. Forgue, ed., *Letters of H. L. Mencken* (Boston: Northeastern University Press, 1981), 189.

44   Diana Preston, *A Higher Form of Killing: Six Weeks in World War I That Forever Changed the Nature of Warfare* (New York: Bloomsbury, 2015), 2.

45   Theodore Roosevelt to Cleveland Dodge, May 11, 1918, *Theodore Roosevelt: Letters and Speeches* (New York: Library of America, 2004), 736.

46   An Appeal to the American People, August 18, 1914, in Arthur S. Link, editor, *The Papers of Woodrow Wilson*, vol. 30 (Princeton, N.J.: Princeton University Press, 1979), 393–94.

47   *The Intimate Papers of Colonel House*, Vol. I. Charles Seymour, editor (Cambridge, Mass.: Riverside Press, 1926), 286.

48   Theodore Roosevelt to Arthur Hamilton Lee, August 22, 1914, in *Theodore Roosevelt: Letters and Speeches* (New York: Library of America, 2004), 683–4.

49   Woodrow Wilson speech, April 20, 1915, in Arthur S. Link, editor, *The Papers of Woodrow Wilson*, vol. 33 (Princeton, N.J.: Princeton University Press, 1980), 38–40.

50   Johann Heinrich von Bernstorff, *My Three Years in America* (New York: Scribner, 1920), 30.

51   Thomas R. Marshall, *Recollections of Thomas R. Marshall: Vice-President and Hoosier Philosopher: A Hoosier Salad* (Indianapolis: Bobbs-Merrill, 1925), 263–64.

52   *The Intimate Papers of Colonel House*, Vol. II. Charles Seymour, editor (Cambridge, Mass.: Riverside Press, 1926), 8.

53   Johann Heinrich von Bernstorff, *My Three Years in America* (New York: Scribner, 1920), 8.

54   Ibid., 65.

55   William G. McAdoo, *Crowded Years: The Reminiscences of William G. McAdoo* (Boston and New York: Houghton Mifflin, 1931), 294.

56   Barbara W. Tuchman, *The Guns of August: The Outbreak of World War I* (New York: Random House, 2014), 370.

57   "Wilhelmina Cargo Seized by British," *New York Times*, February 12, 1915.

58   "German Ships Seized by the Government," *New York Times*, April 7, 1917.

59   Diana Preston, *Lusitania: An Epic Tragedy* (New York: Walker Publishing, 2002), 68–70.

60   Joseph P. Tumulty, *Woodrow Wilson as I Know Him* (New York: Doubleday, Page, 1921), 228.

61   Johann Heinrich von Bernstorff, *My Three Years in America* (New York: Scribner, 1920), 132.

62   William Jennings Bryan to James Watson Gerard, February 10, 1915, in Arthur S. Link, editor, *The Papers of Woodrow Wilson*, vol. 32 (Princeton, N.J.: Princeton University Press, 1980), 207–10.

63   "German Embassy Issues Warning," *New York Times*, May 1, 1915.

64   Diana Preston, *Lusitania: An Epic Tragedy* (New York: Walker Publishing, 2002), 303; Erik Larson, *Dead Wake: The Last Crossing of the Lusitania* (New York: Crown, 2015), 236–249, 300.

65   "War by Assassination," *New York Times*, May 8, 1915.

66   "The Sinking of the Lusitania," *Baltimore Sun*, May 8, 1915.

67   Johann Heinrich von Bernstorff, *My Three Years in America* (New York: Scribner, 1920), 141.

68   Joseph P. Tumulty, *Woodrow Wilson as I Know Him* (New York: Doubleday, Page & Co., 1921), 232.

69   *The Intimate Papers of Colonel House*, Vol. I. Charles Seymour, editor (Cambridge, Mass.: Riverside Press, 1926), 434.

70   An Address in Philadelphia to Newly Naturalized Citizens, May 10, 1915, in Arthur S. Link, editor, *The Papers of Woodrow Wilson*, vol. 33 (Princeton, N.J.: Princeton University Press, 1980), 147–49.

71   "Roosevelt for Prompt Action," *New York Times*, May 12, 1915.

72   "Offer T.R. Chance to Fight," *New York Times*, May 16, 1915.

73   "Germany's Nightmare," *New York Times*, June 1, 1915.

74   William G. McAdoo, *Crowded Years: The Reminiscences of William G. McAdoo* (Boston and New York: Houghton Mifflin, 1931), 338, 340.

75   David F. Houston, *Eight Years with Wilson's Cabinet: 1913 to 1920*, Vol. I (New York: Doubleday, 1926), 149.

76   Charles E. Neu, *Colonel House: A Biography of Woodrow Wilson's Silent Partner* (New York: Oxford University Press, 2015), 194.

77   Johann Heinrich von Bernstorff, *My Three Years in America* (New York: Scribner, 1920), 175–76.

78   "World Peace Plan Outlined by Taft," *New York Times*, June 17, 1915; "League to Enforce Peace is Launched," *New York Times*, June 18, 1915.

TWO: PREPAREDNESS

1   *The Intimate Papers of Colonel House*, Vol. II. Charles Seymour, editor (Cambridge, Mass.: Riverside Press, 1926), 19.

2   Robert Lansing, *War Memoirs of Robert Lansing: Secretary of State* (New York: Bobbs-Merrill, 1935), 23.

3   "Ford Hopes Troops Will Start a Strike," *New York Times*, November 30, 1915.

4   *The Intimate Papers of Colonel House*, Vol. II. Charles Seymour, editor (Cambridge, Mass.: Riverside Press, 1926), 96–97.

5   "Defense and Loyalty Keynotes of the President's Address," *New York Times*, December 8, 1915.

6   Michael Kazin, *War Against War: The American Fight for Peace 1914–1918* (New York: Simon & Schuster, 2017), xii.

7   *The Intimate Papers of Colonel House*, Vol. II. Charles Seymour, editor (Cambridge, Mass.: Riverside Press, 1926), 163.

8   A. J. Philpott, "Biggest Art Colony in the World in Provincetown," *Boston Globe*, August 27, 1916.

9   Michael E. Ruane, "An American Filmed the German Army in WWI," *Washington Post*, February 7, 2017.

10   Cary T. Grayson, *Woodrow Wilson: An Intimate Memoir* (New York: Holt, Rinehart and Winston, 1960), 81.

11   Edith Bolling Wilson, *My Memoir* (New York: Bobbs-Merrill, 1938), 56.

12   Ibid., 236, 252.

13   Godfrey Hodgson, *Woodrow Wilson's Right Hand: The Life of Colonel Edward M. House* (New Haven, Conn.: Yale University Press, 2006), 11.

14   David F. Houston, *Eight Years with Wilson's Cabinet: 1913 to 1920*, Vol. I (New York: Doubleday, 1926), 158.

15   "Garrison Favors Universal Service," *New York Times*, January 8, 1916; "Asked Wilson's Support," *New York Times*, February 11, 1916.

16   Guy J. Forgue, ed., *Letters of H. L. Mencken* (Boston: Northeastern University Press, 1981), 79.

17   Justus D. Doenecke, *Nothing Less Than War: A New History of America's Entry into World War I* (Lexington: University Press of Kentucky, 2011), 111.

18   "Army Bill Signed by the President," *New York Times*, June 4, 1916; Justus D. Doenecke, *Nothing Less Than War: A New History of America's Entry into World War I* (Lexington: University Press of Kentucky, 2011), 193.

19   "New York Ready for Big Parade," *New York Times*, May 13, 1916.

20   "President Marches Up Avenue at Head of 60,000 Paraders," *Evening Star*, June 14, 1916.

21   "Bomb Kills Six, Injures Scores in Defense Parade," *New York Times*, July 23, 1916.

22   David F. Houston, *Eight Years with Wilson's Cabinet: 1913 to 1920*, Vol. I (New York: Doubleday, 1926), 161, 181.

23   Steven R. Weisman, *The Great Tax Wars* (New York: Simon & Schuster, 2002), 307–8.

24   "Wilson Could Laugh at a Joke on Himself," *A Will Rogers Treasury*, Bryan B. Sterling and Frances N. Sterling, eds. (New York: Crown Publishers, 1982), 50–54.

25   John J. Pershing, *My Experiences in the World War*, Vol. I (New York: Harper & Row, 1931), 26–27.

26   Robert Lansing, *War Memoirs of Robert Lansing: Secretary of State* (New York: Bobbs-Merrill, 1935), 41, 111.

27   *The Intimate Papers of Colonel House*, Vol. II. Charles Seymour, editor (Cambridge, Mass.: Riverside Press, 1926), 226.

28   Ibid., 200.

29   An Address in Washington to the League to Enforce Peace, May 27, 1916, in Arthur S. Link, editor, *The Papers of Woodrow Wilson*, vol. 37 (Princeton, N.J.: Princeton University Press, 1981), 113–16.

30   "Inspected by Officials," *New York Times*, July 11, 1916.

31   "Sea Visitor Unheralded," *New York Times*," October 8, 1916; "Possibly Three U-Boats," *New York Times*, October 9, 1916.

32   "May Prosecute Ship Lines That Blacklist Goods," *New York Times*, July 20, 1916; "President Approves the Shipping Bill," *New York Times*, September 8, 1916.

33   Ron Chernow, *The House of Morgan: An American Banking Dynasty and the Rise of Modern Finance* (New York: Atlantic Monthly Press, 1990), 186, 189, 200; Charles R. Geisst, *Wall Street: A History* (New York: Oxford University Press, 2012), 139.

34   Isabel Wilkerson, *The Warmth of Other Suns: The Epic Story of America's Great Migration* (New York: Vintage Books, 2010), 9, 42, 161.

35   Howard Blum, *Dark Invasion: 1915: Germany's Secret War and the Hunt for the First Terrorist Cell in America* (New York: HarperCollins, 2014), 39–41, 85–90.

36   Ibid., 183–84.

37   Robert Lansing, *War Memoirs of Robert Lansing: Secretary of State* (New York: Bobbs-Merrill, 1935), 73.

38   *The Intimate Papers of Colonel House*, Vol. II. Charles Seymour, editor (Cambridge, Mass.: Riverside Press, 1926), 103.

39   "Bomb Exploded in the Capitol," *New York Times*, July 3, 1915.

40   "Letter Received by the Star Thought to Have Bearing on the Explosion," *Evening Star*, July 3, 1915.

41   "Intruder Has Dynamite," *New York Times*, July 4, 1915.

42   "Holt is Muenter, Say Associates," *New York Times*, July 5, 1915.

43   "Both Safe, Say Captains," *New York Times*, July 8, 1915.

44   William G. McAdoo, *Crowded Years: The Reminiscences of William G. McAdoo* (Boston and New York: Houghton Mifflin, 1931), 324.

45   "How Germany has Worked in U.S. to Shape Opinion," *New York World*, August 15, 1915.

46   "Millions of Persons Heard and Felt Shock," and "Munition Explosions Cause Loss of $20,000,000," *New York Times*, July 31, 1916.

47   Cary T. Grayson, *Woodrow Wilson: An Intimate Memoir* (New York: Holt, Rinehart and Winston, 1960), 110.

48   Joseph P. Tumulty, *Woodrow Wilson as I Know Him* (New York: Doubleday, Page, 1921), 144–53, and Lee A. Craig, *Josephus Daniels: His Life & Times* (Chapel Hill: University of North Carolina Press, 2013), 267–73.

49   "Night Attack on Border," *New York Times*, March 10, 1916.

50   David F. Houston, *Eight Years with Wilson's Cabinet: 1913 to 1920*, Vol. I (New York: Doubleday, 1926), 180.

51   Theodore Roosevelt to Newton Diehl Baker, July 6, 1916, in *Theodore Roosevelt: Letters and Speeches* (New York: Library of America, 2004), 707–8.

52   Barbara W. Tuchman, *The Zimmermann Telegram: America Enters the War, 1917–1918* (New York: Random House, 2014), 87.

53   Will Englund, *March 1917: On the Brink of War and Revolution* (New York: W.W. Norton, 2017), 176–7.

54   Raymond Lonergan, "A Steadfast Friend of Labor," in Irving Dilliard, ed., *Mr. Justice Brandeis, Great American* (St. Louis, Mo.: Modern View Press, 1941), 42.

55   Thomas R. Marshall, *Recollections of Thomas R. Marshall: Vice-President and Hoosier Philosopher: A Hoosier Salad* (Indianapolis, Ind.: Bobbs-Merrill, 1925), 336.

56   Edith Bolling Wilson, *My Memoir* (New York: Bobbs-Merrill, 1938), 113.

57   Ibid.

58   "Germany's Peace Note"; "Allies Must First Consult," *New York Times*, December 13, 1916.

59   "Secretary Lansing's Two Statements Regarding Peace Note to Belligerents," *New York Times*, December 22, 1916.

60   Robert Lansing, *War Memoirs of Robert Lansing: Secretary of State* (New York: Bobbs-Merrill, 1935), 111–12, 174, 186–87.

61   Johann Heinrich von Bernstorff, *My Three Years in America* (New York: Scribner, 1920), 321.

62   *The Intimate Papers of Colonel House*, Vol. II. Charles Seymour, editor (Cambridge, Mass.: Riverside Press, 1926), 412.

63   Ibid., 416.

64   An Address to the Senate, January 22, 1917, in Arthur S. Link, editor, *The Papers of Woodrow Wilson*, vol. 40 (Princeton, N.J.: Princeton University Press, 1982), 535–39.

65   "Colonel Denounces Wilson Peace Views," *New York Times*, January 23, 1917.

66   "Roosevelt Renews Attack on Wilson," *New York Times*, January 29, 1917.

67   "A Tory and the Curse of Meroz," *New York Times*, January 30, 1917.

THREE: THE DECISION

1   Johann Heinrich von Bernstorff, *My Three Years in America* (New York: Scribner, 1920), 358.

2   Ibid., 376–78; *The Intimate Papers of Colonel House*, Vol. II. Charles Seymour, editor (Cambridge, Mass.: Riverside Press, 1926), 431–33.

3   "Germany Wars Against the World," *New York Times*, February 1, 1917.

4   "'Fight,' Says Bryan, 'To Last, If Invaded,'" *New York Times*, February 3, 1917.

5   *The Intimate Papers of Colonel House*, Vol. II. Charles Seymour, editor (Cambridge, Mass.: Riverside Press, 1926), 439.

6   David F. Houston, *Eight Years with Wilson's Cabinet: 1913 to 1920*, Vol. I (New York: Doubleday, 1926), 229.

7   David F. Houston, *Eight Years with Wilson's Cabinet: 1913 to 1920*, Vol. I (New York: Doubleday, 1926), 230.

8   *The Intimate Papers of Colonel House*, Vol. II. Charles Seymour, editor (Cambridge, Mass.: Riverside Press, 1926), 442; "Congress United in Support," *New York Times*, February 4, 1917.

9   "Took German Ships to Protect Ports," *New York Times*, February 8, 1917.

10   "German–Americans Urged to Be Loyal," *New York Times*, February 10, 1917.

11   "The Defense of America," *Washington Post*, February 20, 1917.

12   Theodore Roosevelt to Henry Cabot Lodge, February 20, 1917, in *Theodore Roosevelt: Letters and Speeches* (New York: Library of America, 2004), 718–9.

13   Justus D. Doenecke, *Nothing Less Than War: A New History of America's Entry into World War I* (Lexington: University Press of Kentucky, 2011), 257.

14   "Immigration Bill Enacted Over Veto," *New York Times*, February 6, 1917.

15   H. L. Mencken, *My Life as Author and Editor* (New York: Alfred A. Knopf, 1993), 173–74; 189.

16   Ibid., 174.

17   H. L. Mencken, *Heathen Days 1890–1936* (Baltimore: The Johns Hopkins University Press, 1996), 158.

18   "Mencken, at Kirkwall, Sees Searching of Ships," *Baltimore Sun*, February 14, 1917.

19   H. L. Mencken, *Thirty-five Years of Newspaper Work* (Baltimore: Johns Hopkins University Press, 1994), 62–63.

20   "Henry Mencken Cables Story of 'Ticklish Moments' in Berlin," *Baltimore Sun*, March 6, 1917.

21   H. L. Mencken, "'The Diary of a Retreat': Dark Days for Americans," *Baltimore Sun*, March 14, 1917.

22   H. L. Mencken, *Thirty-five Years of Newspaper Work* (Baltimore: Johns Hopkins University Press, 1994), 66.

23   H. L. Mencken, "'The Diary of a Retreat;' In Sunny Spain at Last," *Baltimore Sun*, March 20, 1917.

24   H. L. Mencken, *My Life as Author and Editor* (New York: Alfred A. Knopf, 1993), 174.

25   H. L. Mencken, "Ludendorff," *Atlantic Monthly*, June 1917, accessed on www.theatlantic.com.

26   Joseph P. Tumulty, *Woodrow Wilson as I Know Him* (New York: Doubleday, Page, 1921), 160.

27   Thomas Boghardt, *The Zimmermann Telegram: Intelligence, Diplomacy, and America's Entry into World War I* (Annapolis, Md.: Naval Institute Press, 2012), 77–78.

28   Ibid., 93–94; Barbara W. Tuchman, *The Zimmermann Telegram: America Enters the War, 1917–1918* (New York: Random House, 2014), 142–43.

29   Thomas Boghardt, *The Zimmermann Telegram: Intelligence, Diplomacy, and America's Entry into World War I* (Annapolis, Md.: Naval Institute Press, 2012), 100–2.

30   Barbara W. Tuchman, *The Zimmermann Telegram: America Enters the War, 1917–1918* (New York: Random House, 2014), 175.

31   A Memorandum by Robert Lansing, March 4, 1917, in Arthur S. Link, editor, *The Papers of Woodrow Wilson*, vol. 41 (Princeton, N.J.: Princeton University Press, 1983), 321–27; "Washington Exposes Plot," *New York Times*, March 1, 1917; "Wilson Vouches for German Plot Note," *Washington Post*, March 2, 1917; "Zimmermann Defends Act," *New York Times*, March 4, 1917. See also Robert Lansing, *War Memoirs of Robert Lansing: Secretary of State* (New York: Bobbs-Merrill, 1935), 226–31.

32   William G. McAdoo, *Crowded Years: The Reminiscences of William G. McAdoo* (Boston and New York: Houghton Mifflin, 1931), 368.

33   "Wilson Takes Oath; Sworn Again Today," *Washington Post*, March 5, 2017, and "40,000 Applaud Wilson as He Pledges Anew to Uphold Nation's Rights," *Washington Post*, March 6, 1917.

34   The Second Inaugural Address, March 5, 1917, in Arthur S. Link, editor, *The Papers of Woodrow Wilson*, vol. 41 (Princeton, N.J.: Princeton University Press, 1983), 332–35.

35   *The Intimate Papers of Colonel House*, Vol. II. Charles Seymour, editor (Cambridge, Mass.: Riverside Press, 1926), 458.

36   "Lansing Tells the World of Purpose to Arm Ships and Supply Navy Gunners," *New York Times*, March 13, 1917.

37   Frederick C. Luebke, *Bonds of Loyalty: German-Americans and World War I* (DeKalb: Northern Illinois University Press, 1974), 29–30.

38   Johann Heinrich von Bernstorff, *My Three Years in America* (New York: Scribner, 1920), 19–20.

39   Theodore Roosevelt to Mrs. Ralph Sanger, December 22, 1914, in *Theodore Roosevelt: Letters and Speeches* (New York: Library of America, 2004), 694.

40   Frederick C. Luebke, *Bonds of Loyalty: German-Americans and World War I* (DeKalb: Northern Illinois University Press, 1974), 47.

41   Guy J. Forgue, ed., *Letters of H. L. Mencken* (Boston: Northeastern University Press, 1981), 128.

42   "Ridder Repudiates Zimmermann Plot," *New York Times*, March 4, 1917.

43   Josephus Daniels, *The Cabinet Diaries of Josephus Daniels: 1913–1921*. E. David Cronon, editor. (Lincoln: University of Nebraska Press, 1963), 106.

44   Edith Bolling Wilson, *My Memoir* (New York: Bobbs-Merrill, 1938), 97.

45 Frederick C. Luebke, *Bonds of Loyalty: German-Americans and World War I* (DeKalb: Northern Illinois University Press, 1974), 45, 271.

46 Guy J. Forgue, ed., *Letters of H. L. Mencken* (Boston: Northeastern University Press, 1981), 104.

47 "Kaiser's Picture Torn Down," *Baltimore Sun*, March 19, 1917.

48 Christian Heurich, *From My Life: 1842–1934*. Trans. and ed. Eda Offutt, 1985. Washington, D.C.: privately published, 1934, 48.

49 *The Intimate Papers of Colonel House*, Vol. I. Charles Seymour, editor (Cambridge, Mass.: Riverside Press, 1926), 299.

50 Christian Heurich, *From My Life: 1842–1934*. Trans. and ed. Eda Offutt, 1985. Washington, D.C.: privately published, 1934, 48.

51 Amelia Heurich diary, March 23, 1917.

52 Amelia Heurich diary, March 14, 1917.

53 Amelia Heurich diary, March 16, 1917.

54 Amelia Heurich diary, March 19, 1917.

55 Amelia Heurich diary, March 29, 1917.

56 Christian Heurich, *From My Life: 1842–1934*. Trans. and ed. Eda Offutt, 1985. Washington, D.C.: privately published, 1934, 44.

57 Johann Heinrich von Bernstorff, *My Three Years in America* (New York: Scribner, 1920), 22.

58 "Pledge Loyalty to U.S.," *Washington Post*, March 29, 1917.

59 David Nasaw, *The Chief: The Life of William Randolph Hearst* (New York: Houghton Mifflin, 2000), 261.

60 "The Hylan Plot Exposed," *New York Times*, October 31, 1917.

61 Edmond D. Coblentz, *William Randolph Hearst: A Portrait in His Own Words* (New York: Simon and Schuster, 1952), 83.

62 "Stirring Up Anti-German Feeling," *Morning Olympian*, March 9, 1917.

63 Josephus Daniels, *The Cabinet Diaries of Josephus Daniels: 1913–1921*. E. David Cronon, editor. (Lincoln: University of Nebraska Press, 1963), 117–18.

64 Ibid., 118.

65 Robert Lansing, A Memorandum of the Cabinet Meeting, March 20, 1917, in Arthur S. Link, editor, *The Papers of Woodrow Wilson*, vol. 41 (Princeton, N.J.: Princeton University Press, 1983), 436–44.

66 *The Intimate Papers of Colonel House*, Vol. II. Charles Seymour, editor (Cambridge, Mass.: Riverside Press, 1926), 462.

67 Ibid., 464–65.

68 Josephus Daniels, *The Cabinet Diaries of Josephus Daniels: 1913–1921*. E. David Cronon, editor. (Lincoln: University of Nebraska Press, 1963), 125.

69 *The Intimate Papers of Colonel House*, Vol. III. Charles Seymour, editor (Cambridge, Mass.: Riverside Press, 1928), 47.

70 John Heaton, editor, *Cobb of "The World"* (New York: Dutton, 1924), xvi; 267–70.

71 "Loyalty and Peace Parades Stopped," *Evening Star*, March 30, 1917; "Washington Police Bar Pacifist Parade," *New York Times*, March 30, 1917; "Patriot Legions to Visit Capital," *New York Times*, March 31, 1917; "Pacifist Crusaders Fail to Fill Trains," *New York Times*, April 2, 1917.

72 "Pacifist's Apology Procures Release," *Evening Star*, April 3, 1917; "Lodge Knocks Down Pacifist Assailant," *New York Times*, April 3, 1917.

73 An Address to a Joint Session of Congress, April 2, 1917, in Arthur S. Link, editor, *The Papers of Woodrow Wilson*, vol. 41 (Princeton, N.J.: Princeton University Press, 1983), 519–27.

74 "Must Exert All Our Power," *New York Times*, April 3, 1917.

75 Joseph P. Tumulty, *Woodrow Wilson as I Know Him* (New York: Doubleday, Page, 1921), 256.

76 "Comment of Today's Newspapers on the President," *New York Times*, April 3, 1917.

77 "Wilson Likely to Sign the Resolution This Afternoon, Bringing Conflict Officially with Germany," *Washington Post*, April 6, 1917; Michael Kazin, *War Against War: The American Fight for Peace 1914–1918* (New York: Simon & Schuster, 2017), 184.

FOUR: MOBILIZATION

1 Thomas R. Marshall, *Recollections of Thomas R. Marshall: Vice-President and Hoosier Philosopher: A Hoosier Salad* (Indianapolis: Bobbs-Merrill, 1925), 340.

2 Edith Bolling Wilson, *My Memoir* (New York: Bobbs-Merrill, 1938), 162.

3 Charles E. Neu, *Colonel House: A Biography of Woodrow Wilson's Silent Partner* (New York: Oxford University Press, 2015), 295.

4 Josephus Daniels, *The Cabinet Diaries of Josephus Daniels: 1913–1921*. E. David Cronon, editor. (Lincoln: University of Nebraska Press, 1963), 133.

5 Elliott Roosevelt, editor, *F.D.R.: His Personal Letters: 1905–1928* (New York: Duell, Sloan and Pearce, 1948), 367.

6 H. L. Mencken, "Ludendorff," *Atlantic Monthly*, June 1917, accessed on www.theatlantic.com.

7 Guy J. Forgue, ed., *Letters of H. L. Mencken* (Boston: Northeastern University Press, 1981), 105.

8 "Malone Waits Up All Night," *New York Times*, April 6, 1917; "27 Ships Taken Here," *New York Times*, April 7, 1917; "German Ships Seized by the Government," *New York Times*, April 7, 1917; "German Ships Meet Our Transport Needs," *New York Times*, April 7, 1917; "Ships' Frames Damaged," *New York Times*, April 7, 1917.

9 Robert Lansing, *War Memoirs of Robert Lansing: Secretary of State* (New York: Bobbs-Merrill, 1935), 272–80.

10 *The Intimate Papers of Colonel House*, Vol. III. Charles Seymour, editor (Cambridge, Mass.: Riverside Press, 1928), 42–45.

11   Joseph P. Tumulty, *Woodrow Wilson as I Know Him* (New York: Doubleday, Page, 1921), 285–88.

12   "Plans for National Army"; "Will Not Send Roosevelt"; "Pershing Won Fame in Moro Campaigns," *New York Times*, May 19, 1917.

13   Douglas MacArthur, *Reminiscences* (New York: Ishi Press International, 2010), 47.

14   Josephus Daniels, *The Cabinet Diaries of Josephus Daniels: 1913–1921*. E. David Cronon, editor. (Lincoln: University of Nebraska Press, 1963), 307.

15   "America Enrolls Today for the Fight," *New York Times*, June 5, 1917.

16   Theodore Roosevelt to John J. Pershing, May 20, 1917, in *Theodore Roosevelt: Letters and Speeches* (New York: Library of America, 2004), 721.

17   "Draft Camps Open," *New York Times*, September 9, 1917.

18   Josephus Daniels, *The Cabinet Diaries of Josephus Daniels: 1913–1921*. E. David Cronon, editor. (Lincoln: University of Nebraska Press, 1963), 199.

19   Alexandra M. Lord, *Condom Nation: The U.S. Government's Sex Education Campaign from World War I to the Internet* (Baltimore: The Johns Hopkins University Press, 2010), 26.

20   Douglas MacArthur, *Reminiscences* (New York: Ishi Press International, 2010), 46.

21   "Former Senator Scott is Affected by Gas," *Evening Star*, August 5, 1918, "N.B. Scott, 'Gassed,'" *Washington Post*, August 4, 1918, "Family is Gassed in D.C. Home When Tear Bomb Breaks," *Washington Times*, August 4, 1918.

22   William G. McAdoo, *Crowded Years: The Reminiscences of William G. McAdoo* (Boston and New York: Houghton Mifflin, 1931), 432.

23   James McGrath Morris, *The Ambulance Drivers: Hemingway, Dos Passos, and a Friendship Made and Lost in War* (Boston: Da Capo Press, 2017), 6.

24   E. E. Cummings, *The Enormous Room* (New York: Liveright Publishing, 1978), 14.

25   Ernest L. Meyer, *"Hey! Yellowbacks!" The War Diary of a Conscientious Objector* (New York: John Day, 1930), 177.

26   Ibid., 34.

27   Ibid., 55.

28   Ibid., 118.

29   Ibid., 188–90.

30   William G. McAdoo, *Crowded Years: The Reminiscences of William G. McAdoo* (Boston and New York: Houghton Mifflin, 1931), 414, 423.

31   Ibid., 375.

32   Steven R. Weisman, *The Great Tax Wars* (New York: Simon & Schuster, 2002), 290.

33   Ibid., 279–82; 307–8; 327–28; 337.

34   William G. McAdoo, *Crowded Years: The Reminiscences of William G. McAdoo* (Boston and New York: Houghton Mifflin, 1931), 378–79.

35   Ibid., 391.

36   Ibid., 408–10.

37   Charles R. Geisst, *Wall Street: A History* (New York: Oxford University Press, 2012), 144.

38   Willa Cather to Mary Virginia Boak Cather, February 2, 1917, in *Selected Letters of Willa Cather*, Andrew Jewell and Janis Stout, eds. (New York: Knopf, 2013), 236.

39   "Inflation and CPI Consumer Price Index 1913–1919," Inflationdata.com, 2014.

40   "The Order to Shut Down Industries and Save Fuel," *New York Times*, January 18, 1918.

41   William G. McAdoo, *Crowded Years: The Reminiscences of William G. McAdoo* (Boston and New York: Houghton Mifflin, 1931), 464.

42   Ibid., 488–90.

43   Ibid., 482.

44   Josephus Daniels, *The Cabinet Diaries of Josephus Daniels: 1913–1921*. E. David Cronon, editor. (Lincoln: University of Nebraska Press, 1963), 271.

45   "War Problems Shifting," *New York Times*, January 29, 1918.

46   "Dollar-a-Year Men," *A Will Rogers Treasury*, Bryan B. Sterling and Frances N. Sterling, eds. (New York: Crown Publishers, 1982), 54–55.

47   "Change in Time Begins Tomorrow," *New York Times*, March 30, 1918; "President Vetoes Daylight Repeal," *New York Times*, August 16, 1919; Michael Downing, *Spring Forward: The Annual Madness of Daylight Saving* (Washington, D.C.: Shoemaker & Hoard, 2005), 20.

48   W. M. Kiplinger, *Washington is Like That* (New York: Harper & Brothers, 1942), 194.

49   "Race Rioters Fire East St. Louis," *New York Times*, July 3, 1917.

50   Woodrow Wilson to Thomas Watt Gregory, July 7, 1917, in Arthur S. Link, editor, *The Papers of Woodrow Wilson*, vol. 43 (Princeton, N.J.: Princeton University Press, 1983), 116.

51   "Negro Regulars Riot Near Houston, Texas," *New York Times*, August 24, 1917; John Milton Cooper Jr., *Woodrow Wilson: A Biography* (New York: Knopf, 2009), 408–9.

52   "Asks to End Outrages," *Washington Post*, August 22, 1917.

53   U.S. census 1910 and 1920, www.census.gov.

54   John Kelly, "Answer Man Remembers the 'Temporary' Office Buildings That Once Blighted D.C.," *Washington Post*, January 8, 2017.

55   "Senate Passes Food Control Bill by Vote of 66 to 7," *New York Times*, August 9, 1917; Garrett Peck, *Prohibition in Washington, D.C.: How Dry We Weren't* (Charleston, S.C.: The History Press, 2011), 33.

56   Herbert Hoover, *The Memoirs of Herbert Hoover: Years of Adventure 1874–1920* (New York: Macmillan, 1951), 267.

57   Herbert Hoover to Woodrow Wilson, November 15, 1917, *The Hoover-Wilson Wartime Correspondence: September 24, 1914 to November 11, 1918*, Francis William O'Brien, editor. (Ames: Iowa State University Press, 1974), 100.

58   "Food Administration Adopts Mrs. F. D. Roosevelt's Plan as Model," *New York Times*, July 17, 1917.

59   Woodrow Wilson to Herbert Hoover, November 20, 1917, *The Hoover-Wilson Wartime Correspondence: September 24, 1914 to November 11, 1918*, Francis William O'Brien, editor. (Ames: Iowa State University Press, 1974), 104–5.

60   Herbert Hoover to Woodrow Wilson, June 5, 1918, *The Hoover-Wilson Wartime Correspondence: September 24, 1914 to November 11, 1918*, Francis William O'Brien, editor. (Ames: Iowa State University Press, 1974), 202–3.

61   Josephus Daniels, *The Cabinet Diaries of Josephus Daniels: 1913–1921*. E. David Cronon, editor. (Lincoln: University of Nebraska Press, 1963), 287.

62   Woodrow Wilson to Morris Sheppard, May 28, 1918, in Joseph P. Tumulty, *Woodrow Wilson as I Know Him* (New York: Doubleday, Page, 1921), 412–13.

63   *The Hoover-Wilson Wartime Correspondence: September 24, 1914 to November 11, 1918*, Francis William O'Brien, editor. (Ames: Iowa State University Press, 1974), 259–60.

64   "Sixty Day Crisis in Food Faces Us, Asserts Hoover," *New York Times*, February 22, 1918.

65   William G. McAdoo, *Crowded Years: The Reminiscences of William G. McAdoo* (Boston and New York: Houghton Mifflin, 1931), 484–87.

66   Ibid., 523.

67   Herbert Hoover, *The Memoirs of Herbert Hoover: Years of Adventure 1874–1920* (New York: Macmillan, 1951), 262.

68   Edward Hurley, *The Bridge to France* (Philadelphia: J. B. Lippincott, 1927), 18.

69   Ibid., 32.

70   Ibid., 79.

71   Ibid., 147.

72   Ibid., viii.

73   Alan Axelrod, *Selling the Great War: The Making of American Propaganda* (New York: Palgrave MacMillan, 2009), xi.

74   Ibid., 112–3, 124.

75   Frederick C. Luebke, *Bonds of Loyalty: German-Americans and World War I* (DeKalb: Northern Illinois University Press, 1974), 219.

76   "President's Proclamation of a State of War, and Regulations Governing Enemy Aliens," *New York Times*, April 7, 1917.

77   "Wilson Braves Rain, Makes War Speech," *Washington Post*, June 15, 1917.

78   Flag Day Address, June 14, 1917, in Arthur S. Link, editor, *The Papers of Woodrow Wilson*, vol. 42 (Princeton, N.J.: Princeton University Press, 1983), 498–504.

79   "Espionage Bill is Signed," *New York Times*, June 16, 1917.

80   Frank Perry Olds, "Disloyalty of the German-American Press," *Atlantic Monthly*, July 1917, 136–40.

81   Guy J. Forgue, ed., *Letters of H. L. Mencken* (Boston: Northeastern University Press, 1981), 109.

82 *Annual Report of the Secretary of War*, Vol. 1 (Washington, D.C.: U.S. Government Printing Office, 1919), 189–90.

83 "Arrest Karl Muck as an Enemy Alien," *New York Times*, March 26, 1918.

84 Erich Posselt, "Prisoner of War No. 3598," *American Mercury*, July 1927, 313–323; see also Reuben A. Lewis, "How the United States Takes Care of German Prisoners," *Munsey's Magazine*, Vol. 64, June to September, 1918, 137–45.

85 "La Follette Faces a Threat of Arrest," *New York Times*, September 22, 1917.

86 "Robert La Follette's 'Free Speech in Wartime,'" NOLO.com, accessed October 21, 2017; Erick Trickey, "Fake News and Fervent Nationalism Got a Senator Tarred as a Traitor During WWI," *Smithsonian.com*, October 19, 2017.

87 "All Germans Here Under New Watch," *New York Times*, November 20, 1917; Amos A. Fries, "The District of Columbia in the World War," *Washington Past and Present: A History*, Vol. I, John Clagett Proctor, editor (New York: Lewis Historical Publishing, 1930), 399.

88 *Annual Report of the Attorney General* (Washington, D.C.: Government Printing Office, 1918), 26.

89 Maureen Ogle, *Ambitious Brew: The Story of American Beer* (Orlando, Fla.: Harcourt, 2006), 174–78.

90 A. Mitchell Palmer, "The Vast Amount of Enemy Property in the United States," *Munsey's Magazine*, vol. 64, No. 2, July 1918, 233–38.

91 "Arrest Rumely; Say Germany Owns the Evening Mail," *New York Times*, July 9, 1918; "Brisbane Tells of Brewers' Help," *Evening Star*, December 6, 1918; "Rumely Sentenced to Year and a Day," *New York Times*, December 21, 1920.

92 Kenneth D. Ackerman, *Young J. Edgar: Hoover, the Red Scare, and the Assault on Civil Liberties* (New York: Carroll & Graf, 2007), 19.

93 "Burleson Tells Newspapers What They May Not Say," *New York Times*, October 10, 1917; James Weinstein, *The Decline of Socialism in America, 1912–1925* (New Brunswick, N.J.: Rutgers University Press, 1984), 144.

94 Oscar Ameringer, *If You Don't Weaken: The Autobiography of Oscar Ameringer* (Norman: University of Oklahoma Press, 1983), 301; James Weinstein, *The Decline of Socialism in America, 1912–1925* (New Brunswick, N.J.: Rutgers University Press, 1984), 327.

95 Oscar Ameringer, *If You Don't Weaken: The Autobiography of Oscar Ameringer* (Norman: University of Oklahoma Press, 1983), 315–18, 325, 334.

96 Ibid., 340–44.

97 "Big Raid on I.W.W. and Socialists; Haywood Taken," *New York Times*, September 6, 1917.

98 H. L. Mencken, *My Life as Author and Editor* (New York: Alfred A. Knopf, 1993), 188.

99 "Billy Sunday Fires Hot Shot at Kaiser," *New York Times*, February 19, 1918.

100 Edward A. Steiner, "Wrong Strategy," *Outlook*, January 2, 1918, 14–15.

101 Frederick C. Luebke, *Bonds of Loyalty: German-Americans and World War I* (DeKalb: Northern Illinois University Press, 1974), 3–10.

ENDNOTES

102   "Stamping Out Treason," *Washington Post*, April 12, 1918.

103   "President Demands That Lynchings End," *New York Times*, July 27, 1918.

104   Christian Heurich, *I Watched America Grow*, as told to W.A.S. Douglas, Washington, D.C., self-published, 1942, 139.

105   Joseph P. Tumulty, *Woodrow Wilson as I Know Him* (New York: Doubleday, Page & Co., 1921), 505.

106   "Bureau to Defend Lovers of Peace," *New York Times*, July 3, 1917.

107   "Jails are Waiting for Them," *New York Times*, July 4, 1917.

108   "Boston 'Peace' Parade Mobbed," *New York Times*, July 2, 1917.

109   George MacAdam, "Ebb of Pacifism in America," *New York Times*, December 23, 1917.

110   "Soldiers in Khaki Storm Socialist Meeting in Garden," *New York Times*, November 26, 1918; "Soldiers Riot at Bolshevist Rally," *New York Times*, November 27, 1918.

111   Guy J. Forgue, ed., *Letters of H. L. Mencken* (Boston: Northeastern University Press, 1981), 126.

112   "Seize 20,000 Here in Slacker Search," *New York Times*, September 4, 1918; "60,187 Men Taken in Slacker Raids," *New York Times*, September 8, 1918.

113   "Draft Raids Here Anger Senators," *New York Times*, September 6, 1918; "Halt Senate Action Upon Slacker Raids," *New York Times*, September 7, 1918.

114   "Civil Liberty Dead," *The Nation*, September 14, 1918, 382.

115   "Pacifist Professor Gets Year in Prison," *New York Times*, October 31, 1918.

116   Oliver Wendell Holmes, *Schenck v. United States 249 U.S. 47*, Opinion, March 3, 1919. Legal Information Institute.

FIVE: THE YANKS ARE COMING

1   Edward Hurley, *The Bridge to France* (Philadelphia: J.B. Lippincott, 1927), 73; *The Intimate Papers of Colonel House*, Vol. III. Charles Seymour, editor (Cambridge, Mass.: Riverside Press, 1928), 3, 190.

2   Floyd Gibbons, *And They Thought We Wouldn't Fight* (New York: George H. Doran, 1918), 55.

3   James G. Harbord, *Leaves From a War Diary* (New York: Dodd, Mead, 1925), 85.

4   John J. Pershing, *My Experiences in the World War*, Vol. I (New York: Harper & Row, 1931), 18, 30–33.

5   *The Intimate Papers of Colonel House*, Vol. III. Charles Seymour, editor (Cambridge, Mass.: Riverside Press, 1928), 301.

6   John J. Pershing, *My Experiences in the World War*, Vol. I (New York: Harper & Row, 1931), 38–39.

7   Ibid., 271–72.

8   Woodrow Wilson to Herbert Hoover, December 10, 1917, *The Hoover-Wilson Wartime Correspondence: September 24, 1914 to November 11, 1918*, Francis William O'Brien, editor. (Ames: Iowa State University Press, 1974), 121–2.

9   George C. Marshall, *Memoirs of My Services in the World War 1917–1918* (Boston: Houghton Mifflin, 1976), 6.

10 John J. Pershing, *My Experiences in the World War*, Vol. I (New York: Harper & Row, 1931), 92–93.

11 Ibid., 95.

12 *The Intimate Papers of Colonel House*, Vol. III. Charles Seymour, editor (Cambridge, Mass.: Riverside Press, 1928), 304–5.

13 Edward Hurley, *The Bridge to France* (Philadelphia: J.B. Lippincott, 1927), 224.

14 Josephus Daniels, *The Cabinet Diaries of Josephus Daniels: 1913–1921*. E. David Cronon, editor. (Lincoln: University of Nebraska Press, 1963), 309.

15 "Huns Sink Four Barges, Burn Tug at Cape Cod," *Evening Star*, July 22, 1918.

16 "Nation to Operate the Cape Cod Canal," *New York Times*, July 24, 1918.

17 John J. Pershing, *My Experiences in the World War*, Vol. I (New York: Harper & Row, 1931), 81.

18 *The Intimate Papers of Colonel House*, Vol. III. Charles Seymour, editor (Cambridge, Mass.: Riverside Press, 1928), 268.

19 John J. Pershing, *My Experiences in the World War*, Vol. I (New York: Harper & Row, 1931), 189–91.

20 John J. Pershing, *My Experiences in the World War*, Vol. II (New York: Harper & Row, 1931), 189.

21 David R. Woodward, *The American Army and the First World War* (Cambridge: Cambridge University Press, 2014), 378.

22 David McCullough, *Truman* (New York: Simon & Schuster, 1992), 114–17.

23 George C. Marshall, *Memoirs of My Services in the World War 1917–1918* (Boston: Houghton Mifflin, 1976), 66.

24 "Indiana Sergeant Fired First Shot," *New York Times*, October 31, 1917; Floyd Gibbons, *And They Thought We Wouldn't Fight* (New York: George H. Doran, 1918), 156–57.

25 John J. Pershing, *My Experiences in the World War*, Vol. I (New York: Harper & Row, 1931), 277.

26 Floyd Gibbons, *And They Thought We Wouldn't Fight* (New York: George H. Doran, 1918), 191–92.

27 Martin Blumenson, ed., *The Patton Papers 1885–1940* (New York: Da Capo Press, 1998), 404, 433.

28 Ibid., 508–9.

29 Douglas MacArthur, *Reminiscences* (New York: Ishi Press International, 2010), 53, 70.

30 Harry Truman to Bess Wallace, March 25, 1918, www.trumanlibrary.org.

31 David McCullough, *Truman* (New York: Simon & Schuster, 1992), 120–23.

32 Cameron McWhirter, *Red Summer: The Summer of 1919 and the Awakening of Black America* (New York: Henry Holt, 2011), 30.

33 John J. Pershing, *My Experiences in the World War*, Vol. II (New York: Harper & Row, 1931), 45–46.

34 Ibid., 97.

35 Ibid., 117.

36 Ibid., 116–17.

37 Stephen L. Harris, *Harlem's Hell Fighters: The African-American 369th Infantry in World War I* (Washington, D.C.: Brassey's, 2003), 178.

38 Ibid., 197–200.

39 Lettie Gavin, *American Women in World War I: They Also Served* (Boulder: University Press of Colorado, 1997), x.

40 Eleanor Roosevelt, *This is My Story* (Garden City, N.Y.: Doubleday, 1937), 188.

41 Lettie Gavin, *American Women in World War I: They Also Served* (Boulder: University Press of Colorado, 1997), 44, 214–15.

42 Isabel Anderson, *Zigzagging* (Boston and New York: Houghton Mifflin, 1918), viii.

43 Ibid., 174.

44 William Mitchell, *Memoirs of World War I* (New York: Random House, 1960), 143.

45 Ibid., 193–94.

46 Ibid., 191–92; Eddie V. Rickenbacker, *Fighting the Flying Circus* (Garden City, N.Y.: Doubleday, 1965), 21–22.

47 Eddie V. Rickenbacker, *Fighting the Flying Circus* (Garden City: Doubleday, 1965), 32.

48 George Cassiday, "Cassiday, Capitol Bootlegger, Got First Rum Order From Dry," *Washington Post*, October 24, 1930.

49 William Mitchell, *Memoirs of World War I* (New York: Random House, 1960), 62.

50 Harry Truman to Bess Wallace, January 21, 1919, www.trumanlibrary.org.

51 Edwin C. Parsons, *I Flew with the Lafayette Escadrille* (Indianapolis: E.C. Seale, 1963), 101, 215–221.

52 John J. Pershing, *My Experiences in the World War*, Vol. I (New York: Harper & Row, 1931), 281–82.

53 Ibid., 203–4.

54 Martin Blumenson, ed., *The Patton Papers 1885–1940* (New York: Da Capo Press, 1998), 548.

55 George C. Marshall, *Memoirs of My Services in the World War 1917–1918* (Boston: Houghton Mifflin, 1976), 217.

56 John Reed, *Ten Days That Shook the World* (New York: Vintage Books, 1960).

57 James Srodes, *On Dupont Circle: Franklin and Eleanor Roosevelt and the Progressives Who Shaped Our World* (Berkeley, Calif.: Counterpoint, 2012), 79–83.

58 *The Intimate Papers of Colonel House*, Vol. III. Charles Seymour, editor (Cambridge, Mass.: Riverside Press, 1928), 302.

59 Charles H. Grasty, "House Slipped Quietly Away from Paris," *New York Times*, January 22, 1918.

60   The Fourteen Points Address, January 8, 1918, in Arthur S. Link, editor, *The Papers of Woodrow Wilson*, vol. 45 (Princeton, N.J.: Princeton University Press, 1984), 534–39.

61   "The President's Triumph," *New York Times*, January 11, 1918.

62   An Address to a Joint Session of Congress, February 11, 1918, in Arthur S. Link, editor, *The Papers of Woodrow Wilson*, vol. 46 (Princeton, N.J.: Princeton University Press, 1984), 318–24.

63   An Address to a Joint Session of Congress, February 11, 1918, in Arthur S. Link, editor, *The Papers of Woodrow Wilson*, vol. 46 (Princeton, N.J.: Princeton University Press, 1984), 320–21.

64   An Address, April 6, 1918, in Arthur S. Link, editor, *The Papers of Woodrow Wilson*, vol. 47 (Princeton, N.J.: Princeton University Press, 1984), 267–70.

65   *The Intimate Papers of Colonel House*, Vol. III. Charles Seymour, editor (Cambridge, Mass.: Riverside Press, 1928), 420.

66   *The Intimate Papers of Colonel House*, Vol. IV. Charles Seymour, editor (Cambridge, Mass.: Riverside Press, 1928), 14–15.

67   An Address to a Joint Session of Congress, May 27, 1918, in Arthur S. Link, editor, *The Papers of Woodrow Wilson*, vol. 48 (Princeton, N.J.: Princeton University Press, 1985), 162–65.

SIX: INTO THE BREACH

1   Hunter Liggett, *A.E.F.: Ten Years Ago in France* (New York: Dodd, Mead, 1927), 2.

2   John J. Pershing, *My Experiences in the World War*, Vol. I (New York: Harper & Row, 1931), 289.

3   Edward Hurley, *The Bridge to France* (Philadelphia: J.B. Lippincott, 1927), 122.

4   David R. Woodward, *The American Army and the First World War* (Cambridge: Cambridge University Press, 2014), 236.

5   George C. Marshall, *Memoirs of My Services in the World War 1917–1918* (Boston: Houghton Mifflin, 1976), 95.

6   Matthew J. Davenport, *First Over There: The Attack on Cantigny, America's First Battle of World War I* (New York: Thomas Dunne Books, 2015), 12.

7   William Walker, *Betrayal at Little Gibraltar: A German Fortress, a Treacherous American General, and the Battle to End World War I* (New York: Scribner, 2016), 53.

8   George C. Marshall, *Memoirs of My Services in the World War 1917–1918* (Boston: Houghton Mifflin, 1976), 96.

9   Isabel Anderson, *Zigzagging* (Boston and New York: Houghton Mifflin, 1918), 177.

10   Ibid., 184–87.

11   Erich Ludendorff, *Ludendorff's Own Story: August 1914–November 1918*, Vol. II. (New York: Harper & Brothers, 1919), 237.

12   John J. Pershing, *My Experiences in the World War*, Vol. II (New York: Harper & Row, 1931), 61.

13   Floyd Gibbons, *And They Thought We Wouldn't Fight* (New York: George H. Doran, 1918), 304.

14   James G. Harbord, *Leaves From a War Diary* (New York: Dodd, Mead, 1925), 303; John Archer Lejeune, *The Reminiscences of a Marine* (Philadelphia: Dorrance, 1930), 295.

15   Floyd Gibbons, *And They Thought We Wouldn't Fight* (New York: George H. Doran, 1918), 338.

16   "Lieut. Roosevelt Falls in Fair Fight, Believed Killed," *New York Times*, July 18, 1918; Andrew Carroll, *My Fellow Soldiers: General John Pershing and the Americans Who Helped Win the Great War* (New York: Penguin, 2017), 252–55.

17   William Mitchell, *Memoirs of World War I* (New York: Random House, 1960), 242.

18   Ibid., 220–21.

19   John J. Pershing, *My Experiences in the World War*, Vol. II (New York: Harper & Row, 1931), 163–64.

20   Hunter Liggett, *A.E.F.: Ten Years Ago in France* (New York: Dodd, Mead, 1927), 119–20; 123–4.

21   George C. Marshall, *Memoirs of My Services in the World War 1917–1918* (Boston: Houghton Mifflin, 1976), 117.

22   John J. Pershing, *My Experiences in the World War*, Vol. II (New York: Harper & Row, 1931), 162.

23   Ibid., 211.

24   Erich Ludendorff, *Ludendorff's Own Story: August 1914–November 1918*, Vol. II. (New York: Harper & Brothers, 1919), 326, 332.

25   John M. Barry, *The Great Influenza: The Story of the Deadliest Pandemic in History* (New York: Penguin, 2009), 149.

26   Ibid., 171–2.

27   "Influenza Stops Flow to the Camps of Drafted Men," *New York Times*, September 27, 1918.

28   Hazel Rowley, *Franklin and Eleanor: An Extraordinary Marriage* (New York: Farrar, Straus and Giroux, 2010), 81.

29   "Coffins Short in District; Aid Asked from Outside," *Washington Post*, October 10, 1918; "'Flu' Deaths Climb," *Washington Post*, October 19, 1918; Herbert Hoover, *The Memoirs of Herbert Hoover: Years of Adventure 1874–1920* (New York: Macmillan, 1951), 274; Tom Lewis, *Washington: A History of Our National City* (New York: Basic Books, 2015), 286.

30   John M. Barry, *The Great Influenza: The Story of the Deadliest Pandemic in History* (New York: Penguin, 2009), 4, 238.

31   Ernest Hemingway to Hemingway family, May 17–18, 1918, *The Letters of Ernest Hemingway Vol. 1: 1907–1922*, Sandra Spanier and Robert W. Trogdon, eds. (New York: Cambridge University Press, 2011), 100.

32 "President Leads Red Cross Parade," *New York Times*, May 19, 1918.

33 Ernest Hemingway to Dale Wilson, May 19, 1918, *The Letters of Ernest Hemingway Vol. 1: 1907–1922*, Sandra Spanier and Robert W. Trogdon, eds. (New York: Cambridge University Press, 2011), 105.

34 Ernest Hemingway, *Death in the Afternoon* (New York: Scribner, 1932), 136.

35 Theodore B. Brumback to Clarence and Grace Hall Hemingway, July 14, 1918, *The Letters of Ernest Hemingway Vol. 1: 1907–1922*, Sandra Spanier and Robert W. Trogdon, eds. (New York: Cambridge University Press, 2011), 115.

36 Ernest Hemingway to Ruth (Morrison?), late June–early July 1918, *The Letters of Ernest Hemingway Vol. 1: 1907–1922*, Sandra Spanier and Robert W. Trogdon, eds. (New York: Cambridge University Press, 2011), 113.

37 Theodore B. Brumback to Clarence and Grace Hall Hemingway, July 14, 1918, *The Letters of Ernest Hemingway Vol. 1: 1907–1922*, Sandra Spanier and Robert W. Trogdon, eds. (New York: Cambridge University Press, 2011), 115.

38 Ernest Hemingway to Hemingway family, July 21, 1918, *The Letters of Ernest Hemingway Vol. 1: 1907–1922*, Sandra Spanier and Robert W. Trogdon, eds. (New York: Cambridge University Press, 2011), 118.

39 John J. Pershing, *My Experiences in the World War*, Vol. II (New York: Harper & Row, 1931), 235.

40 George C. Marshall, *Memoirs of My Services in the World War 1917–1918* (Boston: Houghton Mifflin, 1976), 139.

41 John J. Pershing, *My Experiences in the World War*, Vol. II (New York: Harper & Row, 1931), 260–61.

42 William Mitchell, *Memoirs of World War I* (New York: Random House, 1960), 239, 243.

43 Martin Blumenson, ed., *The Patton Papers 1885–1940* (New York: Da Capo Press, 1998), 585.

44 John J. Pershing, *My Experiences in the World War*, Vol. II (New York: Harper & Row, 1931), 270.

45 Eddie V. Rickenbacker, *Fighting the Flying Circus* (Garden City, N.Y.: Doubleday, 1965), 184.

46 Susan Orlean, *Rin Tin Tin: The Life and the Legend* (New York: Simon & Schuster, 2011), 28–30.

47 Douglas MacArthur, *Reminiscences* (New York: Ishi Press International, 2010), 64.

48 Hunter Liggett, *A.E.F.: Ten Years Ago in France* (New York: Dodd, Mead, 1927), 258.

49 John J. Pershing, *My Experiences in the World War*, Vol. II (New York: Harper & Row, 1931), 294.

50 David R. Woodward, *The American Army and the First World War* (Cambridge: Cambridge University Press, 2014), 330.

51 Eddie V. Rickenbacker, *Fighting the Flying Circus* (Garden City, N.Y.: Doubleday, 1965), 215.

52 Martin Blumenson, ed., *The Patton Papers 1885–1940* (New York: Da Capo Press, 1998), 617.

53 William Walker, *Betrayal at Little Gibraltar: A German Fortress, a Treacherous American General, and the Battle to End World War I* (New York: Scribner, 2016), 8; Mitchell Yockelson, *Forty-seven Days: How Pershing's Warriors Came of Age to Defeat the German Army in World War I* (New York: NAL Caliber, 2016), 130.

54 "Americans Rescued from Enemy Trap," *New York Times*, October 9, 1918; "Americans Exhausted After Four Day Siege," *New York Times*, October 10, 1918; "Battalion Spurned Offer of Safety," *New York Times*, October 11, 1918; "The Lost Battalion," *New York Times*, October 12, 1918.

55 Hunter Liggett, *Commanding An American Army: Recollections of the World War* (Cambridge, Mass.: Riverside Press, 1925), 86–7.

56 John Lewis Barkley, *Scarlet Fields: The Combat Memoir of a World War I Medal of Honor Hero* (Lawrence, Kan.: University of Kansas Press, 2012), 167–79.

57 George Pattullo, "The Second Elder Gives Battle," *The Saturday Evening Post*, April 26, 1919, 1–4.

58 William Mitchell, *Memoirs of World War I* (New York: Random House, 1960), 265–66.

59 Ibid., 268.

60 George C. Marshall, *Memoirs of My Services in the World War 1917–1918* (Boston: Houghton Mifflin, 1976), 175.

61 John J. Pershing, *My Experiences in the World War*, Vol. II (New York: Harper & Row, 1931), 327.

62 Douglas MacArthur, *Reminiscences* (New York: Ishi Press International, 2010), 66–7.

63 An Address at Mount Vernon, July 4, 1918, in Arthur S. Link, editor, *The Papers of Woodrow Wilson*, vol. 48 (Princeton, N.J.: Princeton University Press, 1985), 514–17.

64 An Address in the Metropolitan Opera House, September 27, 1918, in Arthur S. Link, editor, *The Papers of Woodrow Wilson*, vol. 51 (Princeton, N.J.: Princeton University Press, 1985), 127–33.

65 Erich Ludendorff, *Ludendorff's Own Story: August 1914–November 1918*, Vol. II. (New York: Harper & Brothers, 1919), 386.

66 "No Time to Think of Peace," *New York Times*, August 9, 1918.

67 "Lodge Demands a Dictated Peace, Won by Victory," *New York Times*, August 24, 1918.

68 Theodore Roosevelt to Henry Cabot Lodge, October 24, 1918, *Theodore Roosevelt: Letters and Speeches* (New York: Library of America, 2004), 744.

69 "Roosevelt Regrets President's Action," *New York Times*, October 14, 1918.

70 From the Diary of Henry Fountain Ashurst, October 14, 1918, in Arthur S. Link, editor, *The Papers of Woodrow Wilson*, vol. 51 (Princeton, N.J.: Princeton University Press, 1985), 338–40; see also A Memorandum by Homer Stillé Cummings, *PWW* vol. 51, 389–93.

71   Josephus Daniels, *The Cabinet Diaries of Josephus Daniels: 1913–1921*. E. David Cronon, editor. (Lincoln: University of Nebraska Press, 1963), 343.

72   *The Intimate Papers of Colonel House*, Vol. IV. Charles Seymour, editor (Cambridge, Mass.: Riverside Press, 1928), 88.

73   An Appeal for a Democratic Congress, October 19, 1918, in Arthur S. Link, editor, *The Papers of Woodrow Wilson*, vol. 51 (Princeton, N.J.: Princeton University Press, 1985), 381–82.

74   Josephus Daniels, *The Cabinet Diaries of Josephus Daniels: 1913–1921*. E. David Cronon, editor. (Lincoln: University of Nebraska Press, 1963), 348.

75   *The Intimate Papers of Colonel House*, Vol. IV. Charles Seymour, editor (Cambridge, Mass.: Riverside Press, 1928), 68.

76   Josephus Daniels, *The Cabinet Diaries of Josephus Daniels: 1913–1921*. E. David Cronon, editor. (Lincoln: University of Nebraska Press, 1963), 344.

77   John A. Garraty, *Henry Cabot Lodge: A Biography* (New York: Knopf, 1968), 343.

78   John J. Pershing, *My Experiences in the World War*, Vol. II (New York: Harper & Row, 1931), 350–51.

79   Ibid., 366–67.

80   *The Intimate Papers of Colonel House*, Vol. IV. Charles Seymour, editor (Cambridge, Mass.: Riverside Press, 1928), 94.

81   Hunter Liggett, *Commanding An American Army: Recollections of the World War* (Cambridge, Mass.: Riverside Press, 1925), 124–5.

82   John Archer Lejeune, *The Reminiscences of a Marine* (Philadelphia: Dorrance, 1930), 391–2.

83   Will Rogers, *Rogers-isms: The Cowboy Philosopher on the Peace Conference* (New York: Harper & Brothers, 1919), 5.

84   "City Goes Wild with Joy," *New York Times*, November 8, 1918, "Nation-wide Joy Result of Hoax," *Evening Star*, November 8, 1918.

85   George C. Marshall, *Memoirs of My Services in the World War 1917–1918* (Boston: Houghton Mifflin, 1976), 192.

86   Harry Truman to Bess Wallace, November 11, 1918, www.trumanlibrary.org.

87   George C. Marshall, *Memoirs of My Services in the World War 1917–1918* (Boston: Houghton Mifflin, 1976), 197–99.

88   John Archer Lejeune, *The Reminiscences of a Marine* (Philadelphia: Dorrance, 1930), 402–3; 406.

89   Eddie V. Rickenbacker, *Fighting the Flying Circus* (Garden City, N.Y.: Doubleday, 1965), x.

90   James G. Harbord, *Leaves From a War Diary* (New York: Dodd, Mead, 1925), 399.

91   John J. Pershing, *My Experiences in the World War*, Vol. II (New York: Harper & Row, 1931), 395–96.

92   William Mitchell, *Memoirs of World War I* (New York: Random House, 1960), 292.

93   Ernest Hemingway to the Hemingway family, November 11, 1918, *The Letters of Ernest Hemingway Vol. 1: 1907–1922*, Sandra Spanier and Robert W. Trogdon, eds. (New York: Cambridge University Press, 2011), 150; EH to William B. Smith, December 13, 1918, Ibid., 163.

94   Edith Bolling Wilson, *My Memoir* (New York: Bobbs-Merrill, 1938), 170.

95   Josephus Daniels, *The Cabinet Diaries of Josephus Daniels: 1913–1921*. E. David Cronon, editor. (Lincoln: University of Nebraska Press, 1963), 348.

96   "How Peace Struck Man in the Street," *New York Times*, November 12, 1918.

97   Willa Cather to Frances Smith Cather, November 11, 1918, in *Selected Letters of Willa Cather*, Andrew Jewell and Janis Stout, eds. (New York: Knopf, 2013), 260–61.

98   *The Intimate Papers of Colonel House*, Vol. IV. Charles Seymour, editor (Cambridge, Mass.: Riverside Press, 1928), 143.

99   "Proclamation by the President," *Evening Star*, November 11, 1918.

100   Frederick Lewis Allen, *Only Yesterday: An Informal History of the 1920's* (New York: Harper & Row, 1931), 13.

101   "Text of the Armistice Terms Told Congress by President," *Evening Star*, November 11, 1918; "Truce Electrifies Congress," *New York Times*, November 12, 1918; Ray Stannard Baker, *Woodrow Wilson and the World Settlement*, Vol. I (Garden City, N.Y.: Doubleday, Page, 1923), 177.

102   "Army Draft Ends by Baker's Order," *New York Times*, November 12, 1918.

103   "Censorship at an End," *New York Times*, November 15, 1918.

104   John J. Pershing, *My Experiences in the World War*, Vol. II (New York: Harper & Row, 1931), 388–89.

105   Erich Maria Remarque, *All Quiet on the Western Front* (New York: Ballantine Books, 1982), 294.

106   Hunter Liggett, *Commanding An American Army: Recollections of the World War* (Cambridge, Mass.: Riverside Press, 1925), 138.

107   Henry T. Allen, *The Rhineland Occupation* (Indianapolis: Bobbs-Merrill, 1927), 22.

108   Ibid., 68–72.

109   William Mitchell, *Memoirs of World War I* (New York: Random House, 1960), 307–8.

110   Ibid., 308–10.

111   Henry T. Allen, *The Rhineland Occupation* (Indianapolis: Bobbs-Merrill, 1927), 130, 281.

SEVEN: THE PROPHET OF DEMOCRACY

1   Josephus Daniels, *The Cabinet Diaries of Josephus Daniels: 1913–1921*. E. David Cronon, editor. (Lincoln: University of Nebraska Press, 1963), 342, 381; "The President Goes to France," *New York Times*, November 19, 1918.

2   "The President Goes to France," *New York Times*, November 19, 1918; "President's Aims Widen," *New York Times*, November 20, 1918; "Wilson Not Welcome to All," *New York Times*, November 27, 1918; "Text of the White House Announcement of the Makeup of the Peace Delegation," *New York Times*, November 30, 1918.

3   Will Rogers, *Rogers-isms: The Cowboy Philosopher on the Peace Conference* (New York: Harper & Brothers, 1919), 9.

4   John Milton Cooper Jr., *Woodrow Wilson: A Biography* (New York: Knopf, 2009), 456–57.

5   "Lodge Addresses Senate," *New York Times*, December 22, 1918.

6   Herbert Hoover, *The Memoirs of Herbert Hoover: Years of Adventure 1874–1920* (New York: Macmillan, 1951), 433.

7   Robert Lansing, *The Peace Negotiations: A Personal Narrative* (Cambridge, Mass.: Riverside, 1921), 3.

8   David F. Houston, *Eight Years with Wilson's Cabinet: 1913 to 1920*, Vol. I (New York: Doubleday, 1926), 350.

9   Josephus Daniels, *The Cabinet Diaries of Josephus Daniels: 1913–1921*. E. David Cronon, editor. (Lincoln: University of Nebraska Press, 1963), 342.

10   Robert Lansing, *The Peace Negotiations: A Personal Narrative* (Cambridge, Mass.: Riverside, 1921), 20.

11   *The Intimate Papers of Colonel House*, Vol. IV. Charles Seymour, editor (Cambridge, Mass.: Riverside Press, 1928), 210.

12   Joseph P. Tumulty, *Woodrow Wilson as I Know Him* (New York: Doubleday, Page & Co., 1921), 335.

13   Herbert Hoover, *The Memoirs of Herbert Hoover: Years of Adventure 1874–1920* (New York: Macmillan, 1951), 213.

14   George Creel, *The War, The World and Wilson* (New York: Harper, 1920), 160–61.

15   An Annual Message on the State of the Union, December 2, 1918, in Arthur S. Link, editor, *The Papers of Woodrow Wilson*, vol. 53 (Princeton, N.J.: Princeton University Press, 1986), 274–86.

16   From the Diary of Henry Fountain Ashurst, December 2, 1918, in Arthur S. Link, editor, *The Papers of Woodrow Wilson*, vol. 53 (Princeton, N.J.: Princeton University Press, 1985), 305.

17   Josephus Daniels, *The Cabinet Diaries of Josephus Daniels: 1913–1921*. E. David Cronon, editor. (Lincoln: University of Nebraska Press, 1963), 352.

18   From the Diary of Henry Fountain Ashurst, December 3, 1918, in Arthur S. Link, editor, *The Papers of Woodrow Wilson*, vol. 53 (Princeton, N.J.: Princeton University Press, 1985), 313.

19   "Roosevelt Assails President's Speech," *New York Times*, December 4, 1918.

20   "Lodge Addresses Senate," *New York Times*, December 22, 1918.

21   "Senate Questions Absentee Powers," *Evening Star*, December 3, 1918; "Would Vacate Wilson's Office," *New York Times*, December 3, 1918.

22   "Tons of Data Go with Wilson Party," *New York Times*, December 4, 1918.

23   Will Rogers, *Rogers-isms: The Cowboy Philosopher on the Peace Conference* (New York: Harper & Brothers, 1919), 11.

24   Ray Stannard Baker, *Woodrow Wilson and the World Settlement*, Vol. I (Garden City, N.Y.: Doubleday, Page, 1923), 120.

25   "Washington Hears Often," *New York Times*, December 6, 1918.

26   A Memorandum by Isaiah Bowman, December 10, 1918, in Arthur S. Link, editor, *The Papers of Woodrow Wilson*, vol. 53 (Princeton, N.J.: Princeton University Press, 1986), 353–56.

27   Larz Anderson III, *Journal, 1920*. Society of the Cincinnati Library, Washington, D.C.

28   Penelope Niven, *Carl Sandburg: A Biography* (New York: Scribner, 1991), 323–25.

29   Edith Bolling Wilson, *My Memoir* (New York: Bobbs-Merrill, 1938), 178.

30   *F.D.R.: His Personal Letters, 1905–1928*, Elliott Roosevelt, ed. (New York: Duell, Sloan and Pearce, 1948), 447.

31   "12 Killed When Tank of Molasses Explodes," *New York Times*, January 16, 1919; Stephen Puleo, *Dark Tide: The Great Boston Molasses Flood of 1919* (Boston: Beacon Press, 2004), x; 96; Erin McCann, "Solving a Mystery Behind the Deadly 'Tsunami of Molasses' of 1919," *New York Times*, November 26, 2016.

32   Robert Lansing, *The Peace Negotiations: A Personal Narrative* (Cambridge, Mass.: Riverside, 1921), 106–8, 121.

33   Ray Stannard Baker, *What Wilson Did at Paris* (Garden City, N.Y.: Doubleday, Page, 1919), 3–4.

34   Herbert Hoover, *The Memoirs of Herbert Hoover: The Cabinet and the Presidency 1920–1933* (New York: Macmillan, 1952), 21.

35   Ibid., 22.

36   Herbert Hoover, *The Memoirs of Herbert Hoover: Years of Adventure 1874–1920* (New York: Macmillan, 1951), 430.

37   John Maynard Keynes, *The Economic Consequences of the Peace* (New York: Macmillan, 1920), 256.

38   Ray Stannard Baker, *Woodrow Wilson and the World Settlement*, Vol. I (Garden City, N.Y.: Doubleday, Page, 1923), 269–70.

39   Edith Bolling Wilson, *My Memoir* (New York: Bobbs-Merrill, 1938), 233.

40   Robert Lansing, *The Peace Negotiations: A Personal Narrative* (Cambridge, Mass.: Riverside, 1921), 170.

41   *The Intimate Papers of Colonel House*, Vol. IV. Charles Seymour, editor (Cambridge, Mass.: Riverside Press, 1928), 290–93.

42   Ray Stannard Baker, *Woodrow Wilson and the World Settlement*, Vol. I (Garden City, N.Y.: Doubleday, Page, 1923), 280.

43   Ibid., 239.

44   *The Intimate Papers of Colonel House*, Vol. IV. Charles Seymour, editor (Cambridge, MA: Riverside Press, 1928), 316–17.

45   Ibid., 385.

46   "Zeal for Peace May Complicate, Says Mr. Lodge," *Evening Star*, February 28, 1919.

47   John A. Garraty, *Henry Cabot Lodge: A Biography* (New York: Knopf, 1968), 339.

48   Will Rogers, *Rogers-isms: The Cowboy Philosopher on the Peace Conference* (New York: Harper & Brothers, 1919), 20.

49   "President's Final Shot is Resented by Congressmen," *Evening Star*, March 5, 1919.

50   Ray Stannard Baker, *Woodrow Wilson and the World Settlement*, Vol. I (Garden City, N.Y.: Doubleday, Page, 1923), 307.

51   "President's Final Shot is Resented by Congressmen," *Evening Star*, March 5, 1919.

52   *The Intimate Papers of Colonel House*, Vol. IV. Charles Seymour, editor (Cambridge, Mass.: Riverside Press, 1928), 379.

53   Ray Stannard Baker, *Woodrow Wilson and the World Settlement*, Vol. I (Garden City, N.Y.: Doubleday, Page, 1923), 296.

54   Grayson diary, March 13, 1919, in Arthur S. Link, ed. *The Papers of Woodrow Wilson*, vol. 55 (Princeton, N.J.: Princeton University Press, 1986), 486–88.

55   Edith Bolling Wilson, *My Memoir* (New York: Bobbs-Merrill, 1938), 245–46.

56   Ray Stannard Baker, *Woodrow Wilson and the World Settlement*, Vol. I (Garden City, N.Y.: Doubleday, Page, 1923), 307; Edith Bolling Wilson, *My Memoir* (New York: Bobbs-Merrill, 1938), 245–46.

57   Charles E. Neu, *Colonel House: A Biography of Woodrow Wilson's Silent Partner* (New York: Oxford University Press, 2015), xii.

58   Ibid., 406.

59   Godfrey Hodgson, *Woodrow Wilson's Right Hand: The Life of Colonel Edward M. House* (New Haven, Conn.: Yale University Press, 2006), 216–17.

60   Ray Stannard Baker, *Woodrow Wilson and the World Settlement*, Vol. I (Garden City, N.Y.: Doubleday, Page, 1923), 308.

61   *The Intimate Papers of Colonel House*, Vol. IV. Charles Seymour, editor (Cambridge, Mass.: Riverside Press, 1928), 386.

62   Ray Stannard Baker, *What Wilson Did at Paris* (Garden City, N.Y.: Doubleday, Page, 1919), 41; Ray Stannard Baker, *Woodrow Wilson and the World Settlement*, Vol. I (Garden City, N.Y.: Doubleday, Page, 1923), 311; Joseph P. Tumulty, *Woodrow Wilson as I Know Him* (New York: Doubleday, Page & Co., 1921), 520.

63   Edward Hurley, *The Bridge to France* (Philadelphia: J.B. Lippincott, 1927), 314.

64   Willa Cather to Meta Schaper Cather, December 27, 1918, in *Selected Letters of Willa Cather*, Andrew Jewell and Janis Stout, eds. (New York: Knopf, 2013), 266–67.

65   Martin Blumenson, ed., *The Patton Papers 1885–1940* (New York: Da Capo Press, 1998), 693–4.

66   John Archer Lejeune, *The Reminiscences of a Marine* (Philadelphia: Dorrance, 1930), 445, 455.

67   Douglas MacArthur, *Reminiscences* (New York: Ishi Press International, 2010), 72–3.

68   Erich Posselt, "Prisoner of War No. 3598," *American Mercury*, July 1927, pp. 313–323.

69   Ray Stannard Baker, *Woodrow Wilson and the World Settlement*, Vol. I (Garden City, N.Y.: Doubleday, Page, 1923), 151.

70   Ray Stannard Baker, *Woodrow Wilson and the World Settlement*, Vol. II (Garden City, N.Y.: Doubleday, Page, 1923), 32.

71   Ibid., 34.

72   From the Diary of Colonel House, April 28, 1919, in Arthur S. Link, editor, *The Papers of Woodrow Wilson*, vol. 58 (Princeton, N.J.: Princeton University Press, 1988), 185–86.

73   Cary T. Grayson, *Woodrow Wilson: An Intimate Memoir* (New York: Holt, Rinehart and Winston, 1960), 70–71.

74   Ibid., 77–78.

75   Herbert Hoover, *The Memoirs of Herbert Hoover: Years of Adventure 1874–1920* (New York: Macmillan, 1951), 391.

76   Robert Lansing, *The Peace Negotiations: A Personal Narrative* (Cambridge, Mass.: Riverside, 1921), 209.

77   Josephus Daniels, *The Cabinet Diaries of Josephus Daniels: 1913–1921*. E. David Cronon, editor. (Lincoln: University of Nebraska Press, 1963), 379.

78   From the Diary of Colonel House, April 14, 1919, in Arthur S. Link, editor, *The Papers of Woodrow Wilson*, vol. 57 (Princeton, N.J.: Princeton University Press, 1987), 335.

79   Ray Stannard Baker, *Woodrow Wilson and the World Settlement*, Vol. I (Garden City, N.Y.: Doubleday, Page, 1923), xxix.

80   *The Intimate Papers of Colonel House*, Vol. IV. Charles Seymour, editor (Cambridge, Mass.: Riverside Press, 1928), 401–2.

81   Richard V. Oulahan, "Wilson Cables the Navy," *New York Times*, April 7, 1919; "Summoning of President's Ship is Interpreted as Meaning Prompt Action in Case of Deadlock," *New York Times*, April 8, 1919.

82   Cary T. Grayson, *Woodrow Wilson: An Intimate Memoir* (New York: Holt, Rinehart and Winston, 1960), 61.

83   Ray Stannard Baker, *Woodrow Wilson and the World Settlement*, Vol. II (Garden City, N.Y.: Doubleday, Page, 1923), 380–81.

84   Ray Stannard Baker, *Woodrow Wilson and the World Settlement*, Vol. I (Garden City, N.Y.: Doubleday, Page, 1923), 324.

85   *The Intimate Papers of Colonel House*, Vol. IV. Charles Seymour, editor (Cambridge, Mass.: Riverside Press, 1928), 334–36.

86   "Rhine Must Be Held, Says Marshal Foch," *New York Times*, April 19, 1919.

87   Ray Stannard Baker, *Woodrow Wilson and the World Settlement*, Vol. II (Garden City, N.Y.: Doubleday, Page, 1923), 54.

88   Ibid., 495.

89 Edith Bolling Wilson, *My Memoir* (New York: Bobbs-Merrill, 1938), 260; Godfrey Hodgson, *Woodrow Wilson's Right Hand: The Life of Colonel Edward M. House* (New Haven, Conn.: Yale University Press, 2006), 233–4.

90 *The Intimate Papers of Colonel House*, Vol. IV. Charles Seymour, editor (Cambridge, Mass.: Riverside Press, 1928), 181.

91 Lee A. Craig, *Josephus Daniels: His Life & Times* (Chapel Hill: University of North Carolina Press, 2013), 357–58.

92 Robert Lansing, *The Peace Negotiations: A Personal Narrative* (Cambridge, Mass.: Riverside, 1921), 260.

93 Ray Stannard Baker, *Woodrow Wilson and the World Settlement*, Vol. II (Garden City, N.Y.: Doubleday, Page, 1923), 501–2.

94 Ray Stannard Baker, *Woodrow Wilson and the World Settlement*, Vol. I (Garden City, N.Y.: Doubleday, Page, 1923), 125.

95 *The Intimate Papers of Colonel House*, Vol. IV. Charles Seymour, editor (Cambridge, Mass.: Riverside Press, 1928), 458.

96 Ray Stannard Baker, *Woodrow Wilson and the World Settlement*, Vol. II (Garden City, N.Y.: Doubleday, Page, 1923), 502–5.

97 Ibid., 505.

98 Johann Heinrich von Bernstorff, *My Three Years in America* (New York: Scribner, 1920), 61.

99 *The Intimate Papers of Colonel House*, Vol. IV. Charles Seymour, editor (Cambridge, Mass.: Riverside Press, 1928), 459.

100 Johann Heinrich von Bernstorff, *My Three Years in America* (New York: Scribner, 1920), 369.

101 Ray Stannard Baker, *Woodrow Wilson and the World Settlement*, Vol. II (Garden City, N.Y.: Doubleday, Page, 1923), 513.

102 *The Intimate Papers of Colonel House*, Vol. IV. Charles Seymour, editor (Cambridge, Mass.: Riverside Press, 1928), 474.

103 Douglas MacArthur, *Reminiscences* (New York: Ishi Press International, 2010), 73.

104 Will Rogers, *Rogers-isms: The Cowboy Philosopher on the Peace Conference* (New York: Harper & Brothers, 1919), 30.

105 *The Intimate Papers of Colonel House*, Vol. IV. Charles Seymour, editor (Cambridge, Mass.: Riverside Press, 1928), 466.

106 Remarks at Suresnes Cemetery on Memorial Day, May 30, 1919, in Arthur S. Link, editor, *The Papers of Woodrow Wilson*, vol. 59 (Princeton, N.J.: Princeton University Press, 1988), 606–10.

107 Ann Hagedorn, *Savage Peace: Hope and Fear in America, 1919* (New York: Simon & Schuster, 2007), 207–8.

108 Cary T. Grayson, *Woodrow Wilson: An Intimate Memoir* (New York: Holt, Rinehart and Winston, 1960), 83–84.

109 *The Intimate Papers of Colonel House*, Vol. IV. Charles Seymour, editor (Cambridge, Mass.: Riverside Press, 1928), 487.

110   Patricia Sullivan, "Prague Honors Woodrow Wilson with Statue," *Washington Post*, October 4, 2011.

111   Garrett Peck, *The Prohibition Hangover: Alcohol in America from Demon Rum to Cult Cabernet* (New Brunswick, N.J.: Rutgers University Press, 2009), 116–17.

112   *The Intimate Papers of Colonel House*, Vol. IV. Charles Seymour, editor (Cambridge, Mass.: Riverside Press, 1928), 489.

113   Ibid., 488.

114   Ibid., 498.

115   Robert Lansing, *The Peace Negotiations: A Personal Narrative* (Cambridge, Mass.: Riverside, 1921), 8–9.

116   Willa Cather to Ferris Greenslet, December 21, 1914, in *Selected Letters of Willa Cather*, Andrew Jewell and Janis Stout, eds. (New York: Knopf, 2013), 198.

117   John Milton Cooper Jr., *Woodrow Wilson: A Biography* (New York: Knopf, 2009), 7.

118   Margaret MacMillan, *Paris 1919: Six Months That Changed the World* (New York: Random House, 2003), 481–82.

119   *The Intimate Papers of Colonel House*, Vol. IV. Charles Seymour, editor (Cambridge, Mass.: Riverside Press, 1928), 487.

120   George Creel, *The War, The World and Wilson* (New York: Harper, 1920), 299.

121   John Maynard Keynes, *The Economic Consequences of the Peace* (New York: Macmillan, 1920), 36–40.

122   Ibid., 31–32.

123   Ibid., 123.

124   Will Rogers, *Rogers-isms: The Cowboy Philosopher on the Peace Conference* (New York: Harper & Brothers, 1919), 19.

125   Margaret MacMillan, *Paris 1919: Six Months That Changed the World* (New York: Random House, 2003), 192, 480.

126   John Maynard Keynes, *The Economic Consequences of the Peace* (New York: Macmillan, 1920), 248–49.

EIGHT: CARTHAGINIAN PEACE

1   "Ovation to the President," *New York Times*, July 11, 1919.

2   Cary T. Grayson, *Woodrow Wilson: An Intimate Memoir* (New York: Holt, Rinehart and Winston, 1960), 85.

3   Edward Hurley, *The Bridge to France* (Philadelphia: J.B. Lippincott, 1927), 290.

4   John Heaton, editor, *Cobb of "The World"* (New York: Dutton, 1924), 279.

5   "Lodge," *Baltimore Evening Sun*, June 15, 1920, in *The Vintage Mencken*, gathered by Alistair Cooke (New York: Vintage Books, 1990), 81.

6   "Lansing Admits Shantung [Shandong] Dissent," *New York Times*, August 7, 1919.

7   Ray Stannard Baker, *Woodrow Wilson and the World Settlement*, Vol. I (Garden City, N.Y.: Doubleday, Page, 1923), 33.

8   "Confer in White House," *New York Times*, August 20, 1919.

9   Ray Stannard Baker, *Woodrow Wilson and the World Settlement*, Vol. I (Garden City, N.Y.: Doubleday, Page, 1923), 35–36.

10   *The Intimate Papers of Colonel House*, Vol. III. Charles Seymour, editor (Cambridge, Mass.: Riverside Press, 1928), 61; Ray Stannard Baker, *Woodrow Wilson and the World Settlement*, Vol. I (Garden City, N.Y.: Doubleday, Page, 1923), 34–35.

11   "Confer in White House," *New York Times*, August 20, 1919.

12   John Milton Cooper Jr., *Woodrow Wilson: A Biography* (New York: Knopf, 2009), 514.

13   John A. Garraty, *Henry Cabot Lodge: A Biography* (New York: Knopf, 1968), 369–70.

14   Ibid., 370.

15   Edith Bolling Wilson, *My Memoir* (New York: Bobbs-Merrill, 1938), 274.

16   *The Intimate Papers of Colonel House*, Vol. IV. Charles Seymour, editor (Cambridge, Mass.: Riverside Press, 1928), 515–16.

17   Edward Hurley, *The Bridge to France* (Philadelphia: J.B. Lippincott, 1927), 327–28.

18   *The Intimate Papers of Colonel House*, Vol. IV. Charles Seymour, editor (Cambridge, Mass.: Riverside Press, 1928), 515.

19   Joseph P. Tumulty, *Woodrow Wilson as I Know Him* (New York: Doubleday, Page, 1921), 435.

20   An Address in the San Diego Stadium, September 19, 1919, in Arthur S. Link, editor, *The Papers of Woodrow Wilson*, vol. 63 (Princeton, N.J.: Princeton University Press, 1990), 382.

21   Edith Bolling Wilson, *My Memoir* (New York: Bobbs-Merrill, 1938), 276, 282–83.

22   "Denounce League as War Promoter in Lodge Report," *New York Times*, September 11, 1919.

23   Robert Lansing, *The Peace Negotiations: A Personal Narrative* (Cambridge, Mass.: Riverside, 1921), 269.

24   Joseph P. Tumulty, *Woodrow Wilson as I Know Him* (New York: Doubleday, Page, 1921), 441–43.

25   John Milton Cooper Jr., *Woodrow Wilson: A Biography* (New York: Knopf, 2009), 529.

26   An Address in the City Auditorium in Pueblo, Colorado, September 25, 1919, in Arthur S. Link, editor, *The Papers of Woodrow Wilson*, vol. 63 (Princeton, N.J.: Princeton University Press, 1990), 500–13.

27   Cary T. Grayson, *Woodrow Wilson: An Intimate Memoir* (New York: Holt, Rinehart and Winston, 1960), 97–98.

28   Joseph P. Tumulty, *Woodrow Wilson as I Know Him* (New York: Doubleday, Page, 1921), 447.

29   Cary T. Grayson, *Woodrow Wilson: An Intimate Memoir* (New York: Holt, Rinehart and Winston, 1960), 99–100.

30   Edith Bolling Wilson, *My Memoir* (New York: Bobbs-Merrill, 1938), 287.

31   Ibid., 286, 289.

32   Ibid., 286, 289.

33   Cary T. Grayson, *Woodrow Wilson: An Intimate Memoir* (New York: Holt, Rinehart and Winston, 1960), 53.

34   Kristie Miller, *Ellen and Edith: Woodrow Wilson's First Ladies* (Lawrence: University Press of Kansas, 2010), 218.

35   "White Sox Again Defeated by Reds," *New York Times*, October 3, 1919.

36   Joseph P. Tumulty, *Woodrow Wilson as I Know Him* (New York: Doubleday, Page, 1921), 443–44.

37   Josephus Daniels, *The Cabinet Diaries of Josephus Daniels: 1913–1921*. E. David Cronon, editor. (Lincoln: University of Nebraska Press, 1963), 445; David F. Houston, *Eight Years with Wilson's Cabinet: 1913 to 1920*, Vol. II (New York: Doubleday, 1926), 38–39.

38   Albert W. Fox, "President Holds Gain; Improvement Not Yet Decisive, Grayson Says," *Washington Post*, October 5, 1919; "Rumor Busy About Wilson," *New York Times*, October 13, 1919.

39   "Senators See President," *New York Times*, December 6, 1919.

40   Edith Bolling Wilson, *My Memoir* (New York: Bobbs-Merrill, 1938), 299.

41   David F. Houston, *Eight Years with Wilson's Cabinet: 1913 to 1920*, Vol. II (New York: Doubleday, 1926), 141.

42   John Milton Cooper Jr., *Woodrow Wilson: A Biography* (New York: Knopf, 2009), 7, 535.

43   Thomas R. Marshall, *Recollections of Thomas R. Marshall: Vice-President and Hoosier Philosopher: A Hoosier Salad* (Indianapolis: Bobbs-Merrill, 1925), 364.

44   Kristie Miller, *Ellen and Edith: Woodrow Wilson's First Ladies* (Lawrence: University Press of Kansas, 2010), 186.

45   *The Intimate Papers of Colonel House*, Vol. IV. Charles Seymour, editor (Cambridge, Mass.: Riverside Press, 1928), 509–10.

46   Edith Bolling Wilson, *My Memoir* (New York: Bobbs-Merrill, 1938), 297.

47   "Lodge Outlines Five Reservations to League Plan," *New York Times*, August 13, 1919.

48   Woodrow Wilson to Gilbert Monell Hitchcock, November 18, 1919, in Arthur S. Link, editor, *The Papers of Woodrow Wilson*, vol. 64 (Princeton, N.J.: Princeton University Press, 1991), 58; "Renew Compromise Talk," *New York Times*, November 18, 1919.

49   "Lodge Resolution Beaten," *New York Times*, November 20, 1919; Josephus Daniels, *The Cabinet Diaries of Josephus Daniels: 1913–1921*. E. David Cronon, editor. (Lincoln: University of Nebraska Press, 1963), 462.

50   Josephus Daniels, *The Cabinet Diaries of Josephus Daniels: 1913–1921*. E. David Cronon, editor. (Lincoln: University of Nebraska Press, 1963), 474.

51   Guy J. Forgue, ed., *Letters of H. L. Mencken* (Boston: Northeastern University Press, 1981), 172.

52   From the Diary of Ray Stannard Baker, November 28, 1920, in Arthur S. Link, editor, *The Papers of Woodrow Wilson*, vol. 66 (Princeton, N.J.: Princeton University Press, 1992), 436.

53   Josephus Daniels, *The Cabinet Diaries of Josephus Daniels: 1913–1921*. E. David Cronon, editor. (Lincoln: University of Nebraska Press, 1963), 493, 499.

54   "Lansing Quits After Clash," *New York Times*, February 14, 1920; "Says Wilson Feared Aim to Replace Him," *New York Times*, February 15, 1920.

55   Josephus Daniels, *The Cabinet Diaries of Josephus Daniels: 1913–1921*. E. David Cronon, editor. (Lincoln: University of Nebraska Press, 1963), 500, 502.

56   Woodrow Wilson to Gilbert Monell Hitchcock, March 8, 1920, in Arthur S. Link, editor, *The Papers of Woodrow Wilson*, vol. 65 (Princeton, N.J.: Princeton University Press, 1991), 67–71.

57   George Creel, *The War, The World and Wilson* (New York: Harper, 1920), 5.

58   Herbert Hoover, *The Memoirs of Herbert Hoover: The Cabinet and the Presidency 1920–1933* (New York: Macmillan, 1952), 10–11.

59   Will Rogers, *Rogers-isms: The Cowboy Philosopher on the Peace Conference* (New York: Harper & Brothers, 1919), 23.

NINE: UNINTENDED CONSEQUENCES

1   W.E.B. Du Bois, "Returning Soldiers," *The Crisis*, May 1919, 13.

2   Cameron McWhirter, *Red Summer: The Summer of 1919 and the Awakening of Black America* (New York: Henry Holt, 2011), 13.

3   "Report Six Killed in Sailor-Negro Riot," *New York Times*, May 11, 1919.

4   "Lynch Negro Who Confessed Crime," *New York Times*, June 27, 1919.

5   "Negroes Attack Girl—White Men Vainly Pursue," *Washington Post*, July 19, 1919; "Mobilization for Tonight," *Washington Post*, July 20, 1919.

6   "This Nation's Gratitude," *Washington Bee*, July 26, 1919.

7   Carl Sandburg, *The Chicago Race Riots: July, 1919* (New York: Harcourt, Brace and Howe, 1919), 1.

8   Cameron McWhirter, *Red Summer: The Summer of 1919 and the Awakening of Black America* (New York: Henry Holt, 2011), 146–47.

9   Ibid., 135.

10   Guy J. Forgue, ed., *Letters of H. L. Mencken* (Boston: Northeastern University Press, 1981), 152.

11   "Troops Fight Race Rioters in Knoxville," *New York Times*, September 1, 1919.

12   "Thousands Engage in Riot," *New York Times*, September 29, 1919.

13   "Hughes Condemns Lynching of Negro," *New York Times*, May 6, 1919.

14   An Address in the Marlow Theater in Helena, September 11, 1919, in Arthur S. Link, editor, *The Papers of Woodrow Wilson*, vol. 63 (Princeton, N.J.: Princeton University Press, 1990), 196.

15   Cameron McWhirter, *Red Summer: The Summer of 1919 and the Awakening of Black America* (New York: Henry Holt, 2011), 151–52.

16   Frederick Lewis Allen, *Only Yesterday: An Informal History of the 1920's* (New York: Harper & Row, 1931), 40.

17   Walter Lippmann, *Liberty and the News* (Princeton, N.J.: Princeton University Press, 2008), 17.

18   Kenneth D. Ackerman, *Young J. Edgar: Hoover, the Red Scare, and the Assault on Civil Liberties* (New York: Carroll & Graf, 2007), 24.

19   "1 Dead, Many Hurt in Cleveland Riot," *New York Times*, May 2, 1919.

20   "Palmer Warns Reds They Cannot Succeed," *New York Times*, June 18, 1919; "Flynn Prepares Big Haul of Reds," *New York Times*, June 19, 1919.

21   James Weinstein, *The Decline of Socialism in America, 1912–1925* (New Brunswick, N.J.: Rutgers University Press, 1984), 327.

22   Frederick Lewis Allen, *Only Yesterday: An Informal History of the 1920's* (New York: Harper & Row, 1931), 46.

23   An Address in the Marlow Theater in Helena, September 11, 1919, in Arthur S. Link, editor, *The Papers of Woodrow Wilson*, vol. 63 (Princeton, N.J.: Princeton University Press, 1990), 196.

24   Guy J. Forgue, ed., *Letters of H. L. Mencken* (Boston: Northeastern University Press, 1981), 155.

25   "73 Red Centres Raided Here by Lusk Committee," *New York Times*, November 9, 1919; "Will Deport Reds as Alien Plotters," *New York Times*, November 9, 1919.

26   John Heaton, editor, *Cobb of "The World"* (New York: Dutton, 1924) 345.

27   "The Suspended Socialists," *New York Times*, January 9, 1920.

28   John Heaton, editor, *Cobb of "The World"* (New York: Dutton, 1924) 345.

29   Kenneth D. Ackerman, *Young J. Edgar: Hoover, the Red Scare, and the Assault on Civil Liberties* (New York: Carroll & Graf, 2007), 248.

30   "Will Deport Only Real Communists," *New York Times*, April 10, 1920.

31   "Deportation Methods Denounced by Taft," *New York Times*, May 2, 1920.

32   "Louis Post Defends Rulings on Aliens," *New York Times*, May 9, 1920.

33   "Lawyers Denounce Raids on Radicals," *New York Times*, May 28, 1920.

34   "Calls Post Factor in Revolution Plan," *New York Times*, June 2, 1920.

35   "Wall Street Explosion Kills Thirty; Injures 300," *New York Times*, September 17, 1920.

36   H. L. Mencken, "A Gang of Pecksniffs," *Baltimore Evening Sun*, May 2, 1922.

37   Kenneth D. Ackerman, *Young J. Edgar: Hoover, the Red Scare, and the Assault on Civil Liberties* (New York: Carroll & Graf, 2007), 336.

38   Woodrow Wilson, A Press Release, October 6, 1915, in Arthur S. Link, editor, *The Papers of Woodrow Wilson*, vol. 35 (Princeton, N.J.: Princeton University Press, 1980), 28.

39   "Hang Suffrage Banner as Wilson Speaks," *New York Times*, December 6, 1916.

40   "'Picket' White House," *Washington Post*, January 10, 1917.

41   "Suffragists Take 60-Day Sentence, Won't Pay Fines," *New York Times*, July 18, 1917; "Militants Freed at Wilson's Word," *New York Times*, July 20, 1917.

42 "Washington Crowd Eggs Suffragettes," *New York Times*, July 15, 1917; "Police Protect Pickets," *New York Times*, August 17, 1917.

43 David M. Lubin, *Grand Illusions: American Art & the First World War* (New York: Oxford University Press, 2016), 40.

44 H. L. Mencken, "The Woman of Tomorrow," *New York Evening Mail*, May 2, 1918.

45 "Arrest Four More Pickets," *New York Times*, October 21, 1917; "Alice Paul Sentenced," *New York Times*, October 23, 1917; "Hunger Striker is Forcibly Fed," *New York Times*, November 9, 1917.

46 "Wilson Backs Amendment for Woman Suffrage," *New York Times*, January 10, 1918; "House for Suffrage, 274 to 136," *New York Times*, January 11, 1918.

47 An Address to the Senate, September 30, 1918, in Arthur S. Link, editor, *The Papers of Woodrow Wilson*, vol. 51 (Princeton, N.J.: Princeton University Press, 1985), 158–61.

48 William G. McAdoo, *Crowded Years: The Reminiscences of William G. McAdoo* (Boston and New York: Houghton Mifflin, 1931), 498.

49 Thomas R. Marshall, *Recollections of Thomas R. Marshall: Vice-President and Hoosier Philosopher: A Hoosier Salad* (Indianapolis: Bobbs-Merrill, 1925), 234.

50 J. Kevin Corder and Christina Wolbrecht, *Counting Women's Ballots: Female Voters from Suffrage through the New Deal* (Cambridge: Cambridge University Press, 2016), 6, 30–31.

51 "Suffrage Statue Moved," *Washington Post*, September 24, 1921; "Suffrage Statue Moves," *New York Times*, February 14, 1922; "On Display for All to See," *Washington Post*, June 27, 1997.

52 William J. Rorabaugh, *The Alcoholic Republic: An American Tradition* (New York: Oxford University Press, 1979), 232.

53 K. Austin Kerr, *Organized for Prohibition: A New History of the Anti-Saloon League* (New London, Conn.: Yale University Press, 1985), 137–38.

54 Daniel Okrent, "Wayne B. Wheeler: The Man Who Turned Off the Taps," *Smithsonian Magazine*, May 2010, www.smithsonianmag.com.

55 K. Austin Kerr, *Organized for Prohibition: A New History of the Anti-Saloon League* (New London, Conn.: Yale University Press, 1985), 187–88.

56 *Proceedings of the 1917 Convention of the Anti-Saloon League of America* (Westerville, Ohio: American Issue Publishing, 1917), 75.

57 Daniel Okrent, *Last Call: The Rise and Fall of Prohibition* (New York: Scribner, 2010), 239–41.

58 Ibid., 42.

59 Diary of Ray Stannard Baker, March 13, 1919, in Arthur S. Link, editor, *The Papers of Woodrow Wilson*, vol. 55 (Princeton, N.J.: Princeton University Press, 1986), 489.

60 "Pabst Charge is Filed," *Milwaukee Journal*, February 13, 1918.

61 Justin Steuart, *Wayne Wheeler: Dry Boss* (New York and Chicago: Fleming H. Revell Company, 1928), 119, 120.

62   "German Alliance Branded as Cloak for Propaganda," *New York Times*, February 24, 1918; "Teuton Propaganda Against U.S.," *Evening Star*, February 24, 1918; "Says Dr. Hexamer is Kaiser's Deputy," *New York Times*, February 25, 1918; "Gave Fortune to German Red Cross," *Evening Star*, March 10, 1918; "Unity Plea by Alliance," *New York Times*, April 13, 1918.

63   Justin Steuart, *Wayne Wheeler: Dry Boss* (New York and Chicago: Fleming H. Revell Company, 1928), 121–22.

64   "German Brewers Buy Big Newspaper," *New York Times*, September 15, 1918; "Senate Calls on Palmer to Reveal Brewers' 'Deal,'" *Evening Star*, September 19, 1918.

65   "Funds to Purchase Times Came from Group of Brewers," *Evening Star*, September 19, 1918; "Palmer Submits Documents About Times Purchase," *Evening Star*, September 20, 1918.

66   Justin Steuart, *Wayne Wheeler: Dry Boss* (New York and Chicago: Fleming H. Revell Company, 1928), 123–30.

67   "Enemy Propaganda Backed by Brewers," *New York Times*, November 21, 1918.

68   "'War' Prohibition," *New York Times*, November 20, 1918.

69   "Senate Passes Prohibition Bill," *New York Times*, November 19, 1918; "Wilson Signs Bill to Make Country 'Dry' From July 1 Until Army is Demobilized," *New York Times*, November 22, 1918.

70   Joseph Tumulty to Woodrow Wilson, May 9, 1919, in Arthur S. Link, editor, *The Papers of Woodrow Wilson*, vol. 58 (Princeton, N.J.: Princeton University Press, 1988), 603–4; Joseph Tumulty to Woodrow Wilson, June 25, 1919, in Arthur S. Link, editor, *The Papers of Woodrow Wilson*, vol. 61 (Princeton, N.J.: Princeton University Press, 1989), 183–84; Joseph Tumulty to Woodrow Wilson, June 27, 1919, *PPW*, vol. 61, 294; and Joseph Tumulty to Woodrow Wilson, *PPW*, vol. 61, 351.

71   Woodrow Wilson to Joseph Tumulty, June 27, 1919, in Arthur S. Link, editor, *The Papers of Woodrow Wilson*, vol. 61 (Princeton, N.J.: Princeton University Press, 1989), 291.

72   Woodrow Wilson to Thomas William Lamont, June 27, 1919, in Arthur S. Link, editor, *The Papers of Woodrow Wilson*, vol. 61 (Princeton, N.J.: Princeton University Press, 1989), 290.

73   Woodrow Wilson to House of Representatives, October 27, 1919, in Arthur S. Link, editor, *The Papers of Woodrow Wilson*, vol. 63 (Princeton, N.J.: Princeton University Press, 1990), 601, and Joseph P. Tumulty, *Woodrow Wilson as I Know Him* (New York: Doubleday, Page, 1921), 409–10.

74   Joseph P. Tumulty, *Woodrow Wilson as I Know Him* (New York: Doubleday, Page, 1921), 420.

75   Joseph Tumulty memorandum, January 9, 1920, in Arthur S. Link, editor, *The Papers of Woodrow Wilson*, vol. 64 (Princeton, N.J.: Princeton University Press, 1991), 261–62.

76   "Prohibition to Cause Hip Pockets to Shrink," *Evening Star*, January 10, 1920; "John Barleycorn Died Peacefully at the Toll of 12," *New York Times*, January 17, 1920.

77   "Billy Sunday Speeds Barleycorn to Grave," *New York Times*, January 17, 1920.

78   "Mr. Bryan Sounds Knell of Liquor at Midnight Hour," *Evening Star*, January 17, 1920.

79   Woodrow Wilson to Congress, March 26, 1920, in Arthur S. Link, editor, *The Papers of Woodrow Wilson*, vol. 65 (Princeton, N.J.: Princeton University Press, 1991), 132–34.

80   Frederick Lewis Allen, *Only Yesterday: An Informal History of the 1920's* (New York: Harper & Row, 1931), 216–217.

81   "Senate Caucus Votes at Albany for Prohibition," *New York Times*, January 28, 1919.

82   Larz Anderson III, *Journal, 1920*. Society of the Cincinnati Library, Washington, D.C.

83   "Making a Joke of Prohibition in New York City," *New York Times*, May 2, 1920.

84   Michael A. Lerner, *Dry Manhattan: Prohibition in New York City* (Cambridge, Mass.: Harvard University Press, 2007), 138.

85   Garrett Peck, *Prohibition in Washington, D.C.: How Dry We Weren't* (Charleston, S.C.: The History Press, 2011), 94.

86   Christian Heurich, *From My Life: 1842–1934*. Trans. and ed. Eda Offutt, 1985. Washington, D.C.: privately published, 1934.

87   H. L. Mencken, *My Life as Author and Editor* (New York: Alfred A. Knopf, 1993), 286.

88   H. L. Mencken, *Thirty-five Years of Newspaper Work* (Baltimore: Johns Hopkins University Press, 1994), 105.

89   Ibid., 201.

90   Ibid., 210.

91   Ibid., 179.

92   Justin Steuart, *Wayne Wheeler: Dry Boss* (New York and Chicago: Fleming H. Revell Company, 1928), 164.

93   George Cassiday, "Cassiday, Capitol Bootlegger, Got First Rum Order From Dry," *Washington Post*, October 24, 1930.

94   H. L. Mencken, "Hot Dogs," *Baltimore Evening Sun*, November 4, 1929.

TEN: NORMALCY

1   H. L. Mencken, "A Carnival of Buncombe," *Baltimore Evening Sun*, February 9, 1920.

2   John F. Carter Jr., "These Wild Young People," *Atlantic Monthly*, September 1920, 301–4.

3   A. Scott Berg, *Wilson* (New York: Putnam, 2013), 679.

4   Josephus Daniels, *The Cabinet Diaries of Josephus Daniels: 1913–1921*. E. David
    Cronon, editor. (Lincoln: University of Nebraska Press, 1963), 517–18; David
    F. Houston, *Eight Years with Wilson's Cabinet: 1913 to 1920*, Vol. II (New York:
    Doubleday, 1926), 70.

5   Josephus Daniels, *The Cabinet Diaries of Josephus Daniels: 1913–1921*. E. David
    Cronon, editor. (Lincoln: University of Nebraska Press, 1963), 520.

6   A Report of an Interview by William Waller Hawkins, September 27, 1920, in
    Arthur S. Link, editor, *The Papers of Woodrow Wilson*, vol. 66 (Princeton, N.J.:
    Princeton University Press, 1992), 153–8.

7   "Pro-Leaguers See Wilson," *New York Times*, October 28, 1920.

8   From the Diary of Ray Stannard Baker, November 28, 1920, in Arthur S.
    Link, editor, *The Papers of Woodrow Wilson*, vol. 66 (Princeton, N.J.: Princeton
    University Press, 1992), 435–36.

9   Oscar Ameringer, *If You Don't Weaken: The Autobiography of Oscar Ameringer*
    (Norman: University of Oklahoma Press, 1983), xii.

10 Ernest L. Meyer, *"Hey! Yellowbacks!" The War Diary of a Conscientious Objector*
    (New York: John Day, 1930), 205–6.

11 Josephus Daniels, *The Cabinet Diaries of Josephus Daniels: 1913–1921*. E. David
    Cronon, editor. (Lincoln: University of Nebraska Press, 1963), 359.

12 Woodrow Wilson to Joseph Patrick Tumulty, June 28, 1919, and Joseph Patrick
    Tumulty to Woodrow Wilson, June 28, 1919, in Arthur S. Link, editor, *The
    Papers of Woodrow Wilson*, vol. 61 (Princeton, N.J.: Princeton University Press,
    1989), 351–52.

13 Alexander Mitchell Palmer to Woodrow Wilson, January 29, 1921, in Arthur S.
    Link, editor, *The Papers of Woodrow Wilson*, vol. 67 (Princeton, N.J.: Princeton
    University Press, 1992), 98–102.

14 "Debs, Unrepentant, Denounces Wilson," *New York Times*, February 2, 1921.

15 A Memorandum by Ida Minerva Tarbell, May 5, 1922, in Arthur S. Link,
    editor, *The Papers of Woodrow Wilson*, vol. 68 (Princeton, N.J.: Princeton Uni-
    versity Press, 1993), 48.

16 Larz Anderson III, *Journal, 1920*. Society of the Cincinnati Library, Wash-
    ington, D.C.

17 Paul Dickson, *Words from the White House* (New York: Walker, 2013), 119–20.

18 Herbert Hoover, *The Memoirs of Herbert Hoover: The Cabinet and the Presidency
    1920–1933* (New York: Macmillan, 1952), 35.

19 H. L. Mencken, "Gamalielese," *Baltimore Evening Sun*, March 7, 1921.

20 H. L. Mencken, "Bayard vs. Lionheart," *Baltimore Evening Sun*, July 26,
    1920.

21 "The Nomination of Harding," *New York Times*, June 13, 1920.

22 "The Gun Epidemic," *New York Times*, December 5, 2015.

23 Joseph P. Tumulty, *Woodrow Wilson as I Know Him* (New York: Doubleday,
    Page, 1921), 478–79.

24 Edith Bolling Wilson, *My Memoir* (New York: Bobbs-Merrill, 1938), 305–6.

25 Peter Baker, "DNA Shows Warren Harding Wasn't America's First Black President," *New York Times*, August 18, 2015.

26 H. L. Mencken, "Lodge," *Baltimore Evening Sun*, June 15, 1920.

27 David F. Houston, *Eight Years with Wilson's Cabinet: 1913 to 1920*, Vol. II (New York: Doubleday, 1926), 148.

28 Ibid., 149.

29 "Harding for World Court," *New York Times*, March 5, 1921.

30 Willa Cather to Ellery Sedgwick, November 17, 1922, in *Selected Letters of Willa Cather*, Andrew Jewell and Janis Stout, eds. (New York: Knopf, 2013), 327.

31 Frederick Lewis Allen, *Only Yesterday: An Informal History of the 1920's* (New York: Harper & Row, 1931), 39.

32 Ibid., 133.

33 Ernest Hemingway to Grace Hall Hemingway, August 29, 1918, *The Letters of Ernest Hemingway Vol. 1: 1907–1922*, Sandra Spanier and Robert W. Trogdon, eds. (New York: Cambridge University Press, 2011), 134.

EPILOGUE: THE RETREAT TO S STREET

1 Edith Bolling Wilson, *My Memoir* (New York: Bobbs-Merrill, 1938), 312.

2 Josephus Daniels, *The Cabinet Diaries of Josephus Daniels: 1913–1921*. E. David Cronon, editor. (Lincoln: University of Nebraska Press, 1963), 588.

3 Joseph P. Tumulty, *Woodrow Wilson as I Know Him* (New York: Doubleday, Page, 1921), 509–10.

4 "Wilson's Exit is Tragic," *New York Times*, March 5, 1921.

5 "Wilson's Stock of Liquor is Moved," *New York Times*, March 5, 1921.

6 Garrett Peck, *Prohibition in Washington, D.C.: How Dry We Weren't* (Charleston, S.C.: The History Press, 2011), 42–43.

7 Edith Bolling Wilson, *My Memoir* (New York: Bobbs-Merrill, 1938), 322.

8 Ibid., 323.

9 Ibid., 345.

10 Cary T. Grayson, *Woodrow Wilson: An Intimate Memoir* (New York: Holt, Rinehart and Winston, 1960), 13.

11 Ibid., 25.

12 Woodrow Wilson, "The Road Away from Revolution," *Atlantic Monthly*, August 1923, 395–98.

13 "Dead Hero Borne from Capitol to Last Resting Place in Burst of Glory and Patriotic Fever," *Evening Star*, November 11, 1921; "Auto Causes Huge Tangle in Traffic," *Evening Star*, November 11, 1921.

14 Cary T. Grayson, *Woodrow Wilson: An Intimate Memoir* (New York: Holt, Rinehart and Winston, 1960), 26, 136–37.

15 John Heaton, editor, *Cobb of "The World"* (New York: Dutton, 1924).

16 "Col. House Calls, Wilson Not at Home," *New York Times*, October 14, 1921.

17   A Radio Address, November 10, 1923, in Arthur S. Link, editor, *The Papers of Woodrow Wilson*, vol. 68 (Princeton, N.J.: Princeton University Press, 1993), 466–7.

18   "Wilson By Radio Calls Our Attitude 'Ignoble, Cowardly'," *New York Times*, November 11, 1923; "Heard Over a Wide Area," *New York Times*, November 11, 1923.

19   "Wilson Overcome Greeting Pilgrims; Predicts Triumph," *New York Times*, November 12, 1923.

20   Edith Bolling Wilson, *My Memoir* (New York: Bobbs-Merrill, 1938), 357–58.

21   A. Scott Berg, *Wilson* (New York: Putnam, 2013), 733.

22   Edith Bolling Wilson, *My Memoir* (New York: Bobbs-Merrill, 1938), 359.

23   "Last Rites for Wilson to Be Held Wednesday; Funeral to Be Private," *Evening Star*, February 4, 1924; "War President's End Came Peacefully," *New York Times*, February 4, 1924.

24   Carter Bealer, diary, Monday, February 4, 1924, in Ina Russell, editor, *Jeb and Dash: A Diary of Gay Life 1918–1945*. (Boston: Faber and Faber, 1993), 74.

25   "Embassies Lower Flags; Germans Display None," *Washington Post*, February 5, 1924; "German Embassy to Pay Flag Tribute to Wilson," *Washington Post*, February 6, 1924; "Police Lower Flag Nailed at Entrance of German Embassy," *Washington Post*, February 7, 1924.

26   Ray Stannard Baker, *Woodrow Wilson and the World Settlement*, Vol. II (Garden City, N.Y.: Doubleday, Page, 1923), 522.

27   Johann Heinrich von Bernstorff, *Memoirs of Count Bernstorff* (New York: Random House, 1936), 132.

28   Thomas R. Marshall, *Recollections of Thomas R. Marshall: Vice-President and Hoosier Philosopher: A Hoosier Salad* (Indianapolis: Bobbs-Merrill, 1925), 61.

Index

M

MacArthur, Douglas, 95, 99, 145, 181,
183, 190–191, 199, 206, 234, 247

Machine guns, x, 12, 44, 57, 76, 92,
142–143, 153, 167–170, 173–174, 178,
185–190, 284

MacMillan, Margaret, 255–256

Main Street, 317

Malone, Paul, 172

Marines, 149, 170, 200, 334

Marne, First Battle of the, 8

Marne, Second Battle of the, 171–174

Marshall, George C., 137, 143, 155, 167–
168, 173, 180, 183, 189, 199–200

Marshall, Thomas, 19, 26, 60, 91, 108,
215, 218, 272, 274, 299, 340

Marshall Plan, 259

Martin, Thomas, 18

Marx, Karl, 13, 156, 162

Mary, Queen of England, 218

Maximilian of Baden, 192, 198

Mayflower (yacht), 40, 53, 80

McAdoo, William, 17, 33, 41, 52, 75,
100, 104–108, 115–116, 210, 298

McCarthyism, 294

McCormick, Vance, 108

McCoy, Bill, 312

McKinley, William, 286

McWhirter, Cameron, 281, 285

Mein Kampf, 328

Memorial Day speech, 15, 248–249

Mencken, H. L., 18, 21–22, 42, 69–72,
78, 81, 93–94, 121, 125, 128, 131,
262, 276, 283, 289, 293, 297, 313–316,
323, 325

Mercer, Lucy, 176

Metropolitan Opera House, 191, 229

Meuse-Argonne Offensive, 127, 179–191,
196–197, 204, 234, 268, 320, 334

Mexican-American War, 103

Mexico, 20–21, 43, 53–55, 73–75, 79, 84,
88, 96, 125, 145, 159, 214

Meyer, Ernest, 102–103, 320–321

Mezes, Sidney, 157

Michaelis, Georg, 94

Middle East, ix, 160, 223, 252

Military mobilization, 91–133

Miller, Kelly, 111

Miller, Kristie, 271

Minnehaha, 52

Mitchel, John Purroy, 83

Mitchell, William "Billy," 150–154,
170–172, 180–186, 189, 201–202,
206–207, 327

Molasses Flood, 219

"Monkey Trial," 22

Monroe Doctrine, 54, 68, 228–229, 241,
244, 264, 268

Montfaucon, 185–186

Morgan, J. P. "Jack," 48–49, 51, 104

Morning Olympian, 83

Moses, George, 272

Mott, Lucretia, 300

Muck, Karl, 122, 235

Muenter, Erich, 51–52

Munsey's Magazine, 124

Murmansk, 223

Mussolini, Benito, 328

N

Napoleon III, Emperor, 183

Nation, The, 132

National Alliance for the Advancement
of Colored People (NAACP), 281

National American Woman Suffrage
Association, 295, 297

National Civil Liberties Bureau, 130–
132, 290

National German-American Alliance, 68,
304–305

National Park Service, 14

National Trust for Historic Preservation,
338

National War Labor Board, 109

National Woman's Party, 296–300

Naval Appropriations Bill, 44

Navy, xi, 2, 13, 19–21, 28–29, 37, 42–44,
93, 139–140, 223, 239, 242–243, 250,
258, 330. *See also* Royal Navy

Nearing, Scott, 130

Turkey, 23, 157, 159, 253
Tuscania, 139
Twenty-fifth Amendment, 276, 339

U

U-20, 30
U-53, 47, 68
U-151, 139
U-156, 139
U-boats, 22, 28–33, 45–48, 56, 66, 68, 70, 76, 93, 116, 134, 138–140. *See also* Submarines
Uncle Sam, 118–119, 152
United Nations, xiii, 339
Unknown Soldier, Tomb of, 334
Unrestricted submarine warfare, 22, 28–33, 45, 63–79, 134–140, 159, 192, 247. *See also* Submarines
Untermeyer, Louis, 121

V

Vanzetti, Bartolomeo, 293
Vaterland, 28, 94, 116. *See also Leviathan*
Veracruz, 54
Verdun, Battle of, x, 37, 46, 48, 56–57, 180, 185
Versailles, Treaty of, ix, xiv–xv, 15, 157, 204, 235, 244–260, 263–264, 271, 274–279, 284, 318, 321–322, 326–329, 335–336
Veterans, x, 202, 219, 234–235, 285, 320
Veterans Bureau, 320
Veterans Day, 202
Victoria, Queen of England, 2
Viereck, George Sylvester, 79
Viereck's The American Weekly, 79
Vigilancia, 77
Villa, Francisco "Pancho," 53–55, 73, 96
Virginia Military Institute, 18, 137
Vladivostok, 223, 253
Volstead, Andrew, 308–309
Volstead Act, 308–310, 314
Volunteers, 11, 37–39, 55, 95–101, 113, 149–150, 168–169, 297
Vorse, Mary Heaton, 38

W

Wagner, Richard, 184
Walker, Jimmy, 310
Wall Street, 19, 109, 293, 311
Wallace, Bess, 154, 200, 320
War, address of, xi, xv, 84–90, 95, 296
War, beginning of, 1–2. *See also* Great War
War, end of, 196–206
War, financing, 104–106
War, the World and Wilson, 334
War Address, 86–90, 159
War cabinet, 108, 115
War Gardens, 113
War Labor Board, 108–109
War Prison Barracks, 122, 128, 235
War Trade Board, 108, 116
Warfare, x, 22, 31, 64, 141–151, 170, 173, 184–186, 190–192. *See also* Unrestricted submarine warfare
Warren, Francis, 96
Wartime Prohibition Act, 115, 306–309
Washington, D.C., 9, 60, 81, 83, 99, 112, 123, 150, 176, 282, 301, 309–312, 315, 321, 338
Washington, George, 24, 300, 325, 340
Washington Bee, 283
Washington Post, 68, 129, 282, 315
Washington Times, 100, 125, 305–306
Webb-Kenyon Act, 301
Western Front, 6, 12, 22–23, 31, 42, 57, 134, 141, 163, *165*, 179, 198
Wharton, Edith, 11–12
What Wilson Did at Paris, 334
Wheeler, Wayne, 301–309, 314
White, Edward, 18, 88
Whittlesey, Charles, 187–188, 334
Wilhelm II, Kaiser of Germany, xiii, 2–3, 6, 29–30, 45, 50, 56, 65, 70, 75, 81–83, 121, 129, 193–194, 198, 202, 207, 225, 237, 246, 305
Wilhelmina, 27
Wilkerson, Isabel, 50
Willard Hotel, 46
Williams, William Carlos, 38

Image by Paul Rothstein.

About the Author

Garrett Peck is an author, historian, and tour guide in the nation's capital. *The Great War in America* is his seventh book. Peck is a member of advisory council at the Woodrow Wilson House and has lectured at the Library of Congress, the National Archives, and the Smithsonian Institution, and often speaks at historical societies, literary clubs, and trade associations. A native Californian and graduate of the Virginia Military Institute and the George Washington University, he lives in the Washington, D.C. area.

www.garrettpeck.com